IMAGE AS ARTIFACT:
The Historical Analysis of Film and Television

Material in this book has been developed in conjunction with a larger project of the American Historical Association funded by the National Endowment for the Humanities.

IMAGE AS ARTIFACT

The Historical Analysis of Film and Television

John E. O'Connor,
Editor

American Historical Association

Institutional Services Program

ROBERT E. KRIEGER PUBLISHING COMPANY
Malabar, Florida

1990

Original Edition 1990

Printed and Published by
ROBERT E. KRIEGER PUBLISHING CO., INC.
KRIEGER DRIVE
MALABAR, FLORIDA 32950

Copyright © 1990 by John E. O'Connor

Library of Congress Cataloging-in-Publication Data

Image as artifact: the historical analysis of film and television/
    edited by John E. O'Connor.
        p.   cm. $28.03
    Bibliography: p.
    Includes index.
        ISBN 0–89464–312–6 (alk. paper). ISBN 0–89464–313–4 (pbk.   : alk.
paper)
        1. History—Methodology. 2. Motion pictures in historiography.
    3. Television programs, Documentary. 4. Motion pictures,
Documentary. I. O'Connor, John E.
    D16.18.I45 1989 / 1990
    901′ .8—dc19   88–13854
                                                                CIP

10   9   8   7   6   5   4   3   2

65717

For Warren Susman

John E. O'Connor, the editor and principal author of this volume, is Professor of History at New Jersey Institute of Technology and Editor of the journal Film & History. *His books on early American history and on the historical study of film and television include:* William Paterson: Lawyer and Stateman, 1745–1806 *(1979),* Film and the Humanities *(1977),* American History/American Film: Interpreting the Hollywood Image *(1979),* American History/American Television: Interpreting the Video Past *(1983),* I Am A Fugitive From A Chain Gang (1981), *and* The Hollywood Indian *(1983). O'Connor designed the NEH funded project entitled "The Historian and the Moving Image Media" which he directed for the American Historical Association. This book is an outcome of that larger project, as are his 120 minute* Image As Artifact *video compilation and the pamphlet* Teaching History With Film and Television *(1987), both cross-referenced to this book and both published by the American Historical Association.*

CONTENTS

PREFACE

Historians are becoming increasingly involved with film. This has been the thrust of a score of articles in newspapers and magazines in recent years. Invariably, such articles wind up concentrating on the glamorous business of historians who are "making movies," or are involved in some way in film or television production. In addition to coverage in the popular press, there have been published pieces in professional journals, sessions at major conventions, and at least one entire conference devoted to the experiences and concerns of historian-filmmakers. This is specifically *not* what this book is about. Here we are focusing on the historians' *use* of moving image materials (including films and TV productions made by and with the cooperation of professional historians). It is our starting premise that, important as it may be for interested scholars to be able to influence what gets produced, it is equally important for historians in general to learn to use film and television in critical ways, and to train future generations to view everything they see more critically, in light of traditional humanistic values.

There are many ways in which, with varying degrees of effectiveness, historical scholars make use of the moving image media. It serves: in research, as an archival source to establish or verify historical facts or as an indicator of social/cultural values; in writing, to strike a common chord of experience with the reader or to illustrate a complex point; in teaching, to motivate students and give them the "feeling" for a period or to reinforce lessons learned. Each such type of reference to film or television in historical scholarship might be conducted on several different levels. The present study is meant to focus specifically on that level of application which commences from the close and critical analysis of the film/TV material as historical document or artifact. Although the essays to follow will explore a variety of "frameworks for inquiry" in relation to which such work might take place, attention throughout is directed toward that level of analysis which brings to bear in a coherent way the traditional methodological tools of the historian.

As the field of Cinema Studies or Film and Broadcasting Studies has developed over the past twenty years into an independent academic discipline in its own right, it has drawn upon various other disciplines for certain of its methodological constructs. As communications scholars have sought common and effective criteria for analyzing film and television, and as individuals with training in literature, psychology, sociology, linguistics, and art history, have themselves turned to the study of the moving image, each field has made its own theoretical contribution. Historians have played their part, but the breadth and variety of historical approaches have made it difficult to identify the specific ways in which the historian's tools best apply to the study of moving images.

This study is intended to remedy that lack. In attempting to syn-
thesize a critical methodology for historical analysis of moving image
documents, our primary audience is the historical profession. Here-
after, historians and history teachers who turn to the critical study of
film or television for the first time should find in this volume an
effective guide—a catalog of many of the concerns they should keep
in mind. This book can be assigned in historical methodology courses
so that scholars in training will be able to add "visual literacy" to their
research skills in foreign languages and statistics. In addition, however, it is hoped that our efforts will draw broader attention to the
contributions which traditional historical methodology have to offer
the practice of film and television study in general.

For the purpose of this study, the authors have agreed upon a
prescribed structure. First, they have attempted to lay out a comprehensive survey of the types of methodological issues that must concern
any historian addressing film or television as historical document or
artifact. Second, they have adopted a series of four frameworks for
inquiry designed not to fit the materials per se (newsreel, documentary, feature film, television sit-com, etc.), but rather to address the
different types of investigations in which historians characteristically
use moving image materials and to highlight the varying methodological concerns which each type of argument brings to the fore.

There is another unique aspect to our work. This book is one of
three published resources which are interlinked and cross referenced
so each can be used to its fullest measure. First, there is a two-hour
video compilation of some of the most important moving image materials analyzed in this book. A list of the contents of the compilation
can be found in Appendix 1. Some selections are excerpted; others
appear in thier full length. The compilation is accompanied by a *Study
Guide* of more than 300 pages filled with facsimiles of related archival
documents and study and teaching aides. The individual selections
on the video compilation are most accessible for close analysis if it is
used in the videodisk format, but the program is also available in
videotape. All orders for the compilation should be placed directly
through the American Historical Association, 400 A Street S.E., Washington, D.C. 20003.

Finally, there is a pamphlet entitled *Teaching History With Film and
Television* which draws upon the materials in this book and focuses
especially on applying the historical analysis of film and television in
the classroom. The pamphlet is also heavily referenced to the video
compilation. The pamphlet is automatically included when you order
the video compilation, but it is available separately, also from the
American Historical Association.

ACKNOWLEDGMENTS:

Many people have offered their kind assistance in the preparation of this book by reading and critiquing parts of the manuscript. They include Eugene Asher, Barbara Abrash, Gregory Bush, David Courtright, David Culbert, Daniel Czitrom, Natalie Zemon Davis, Raymond Fielding, Leslie Fishbein, Elizabeth Fox-Genovese, Tom Gunning, Richard Geehr, Douglas Gomery, Sumiko Higashi, William Hughes, Kenneth Hey, Ian Jarvie, Richard Kirkendall, Richard Kozarski, Lawrence Levine, Fred McDonald, Fred Pfister, Richard Raack, Peter Rollins, Robert Rosenstone, Sam Suratt, Kristin Thompson, Wendy Thompson, Robert Toplin, Wilhelm VanKampen, Daniel Walkowitz and James Welsh. Among my colleagues at NJIT who offered a critical eye were Norbert Elliot, Robert Lynch, Michal McMahon, John Opie, and Karl Schweizer. I owe a special debt of gratitude to Rose Scarano who was ever ready to help with every organizational detail. Warren Susman's encouragement and thoughtful criticism were especially important to me in the early stages of this project.

I am particularly grateful to the eleven contributing authors who have helped me to set the tone for this volume and have written essays designed to expand upon my original conception. For any errors in that conception, as for all the sections of this book not credited to one of the contributing authors, I bear sole responsibility.

CHAPTER I
IMAGE AS ARTIFACT:
AN INTRODUCTION

The nineteenth century development of the technology of photography, and later motion pictures, seemed to open great new frontiers for the study and the teaching of history. Not oral or written descriptions, not drawings or paintings, but detailed, verifiable, mirrorlike images [moving images after 1891] of historical personalities, places, and events, could be preserved for the information and instruction of future generations. Yet, only now, as the anniversaries reach one hundred years for movies and fifty years for broadcast television, are historians coming to grasp fully the analytical challenges these materials present to them.

The tidal wave of visual images which began with photography near the middle of the last century has become a major determinant in society and culture. On one level, the mechanical reproducibility of images raised serious questions about the nature of art. On another level it made the visual arts broadly accessible to the general population—now even the poor could hang beautiful pictures on their walls and keep a gallery of family portraits on the mantle.[1] Warren Susman has reminded us of Vachael Lindsay's characterization of America as a "hieroglyphic civilization," one in which "images-turned-icons" allow us to "literally see the fundamental tensions" in the culture.[2]

The focus of this study is on film and television.[3] Such moving images have seldom carried the caste of high art. From the outset they were accessible to practically everyone in society—in Europe and America early film audiences were largely working class. Today the TV is more common in American homes than were the Currier & Ives prints and family photo albums of the last century. The relationship of film images to social and cultural values of the 1930s and 1940s; the centrality of TV watching as a social (or antisocial) activity since the 1950s; the importance of television advertising in the consumer economy and the susceptibility of audiences to judging political figures for their television personalities rather than their substance as public leaders—all are undeniable. In their various publications the contributors to this volume have been arguing for nearly two decades that historians should expand their horizons and begin to do justice to the study of moving images. Now it is time to press that issue further. There are important areas of historical scholarship where the researcher who ignores the close study of moving image evidence has failed to cover the subject; and the number of these areas is sure to increase in the future. Imagine trying to do justice to the historical analysis of the Nazis and their propaganda machine by reading the manuscripts alone; the scholar must listen to the speeches, see the films, and analyze both in terms of their structure and content and the impacts they had on audiences of a half-century ago. It is inconceivable that any scholar could undertake research on the history of any American political campaign since the mid-1960s without detailed consideration of the role of television news and political advertising. In forty years television has created an entirely new electronic realm which encompasses much of what happens in European and American popular culture. The same is true to different degrees in every developed area of the world.

But if film and television demand recognition as forces in twentieth-century society and culture, they must also be recognized as shapers of historical consciousness. Everyone concerned with the ways our society learns from its past should be concerned about the growing frequency of historically oriented television dramas and miniseries. It would be mistaken to presume that the public is developing a deeper historical understanding than it had before. What can be assumed, however, is that whatever many people today do know (or think they know) about history is much less likely to have come from books or from university lectures than from such moving image presentations as "Holocaust," "Roots," "I Claudius," "Shogun," and "The Winds of War." Without having read a book or gone near a classroom, millions of viewers in 1981 thought that they had learned all that was worth knowing about the American Civil War by watching several evenings of an "epic" TV series, "The Blue and The Gray."

The implication of most such popular productions is that history is no more than a straightforward story, to be told like any other narrative. In the stories that make for successful movies or television programs, the motives of major characters must be understood in terms of present-day values and concerns immediately accessible to a general TV audience, and there must always be a satisfying conclusion. The networks' touting of the "meticulous" research that went into the design of sets and costumes encourages the public to understand this production as the most accurate possible portrayal. The "study guides" which many such productions provide for teachers may suggest questions for classroom discussion or sources for additional information. But they never explain how the requirements of producing for popular television have forced the simplification of complex historical characters and intricate patterns of causation to near caricatures; they never point out where dramatic license was taken, nor do they acknowledge that there may be very different but equally defensible interpretations of the issues and events portrayed.

Storytelling narrative stands as one of several accepted strategies for approaching an analysis of the past, but *analysis* is the key word.

Scholars must defend against the notion that history is no more than narration and the historian no more than a "storyteller," stringing together dates and details and arbitrarily moving historical figures around as though they were actors on the set of *Eleanor and Franklin*. History is not alone, to be sure. Neil Postman argues that all forms of serious public discourse are threatened by the influence of the mass media.[4]

One laudable response in recent years has been the contribution of millions of dollars by public and private foundations for the production of better historical films, linking historians and film producers in an effort to ensure intellectual authenticity. Fine work in this area has been done by Robert Brent Toplin, Stephen Nissenbaum, Natalie Zemon Davis, Robert A. Rosenstone, Daniel Walkowitz, and others who will be discussed later in this book. Selections from the work of several of them have been included in the video compilation along with study aids, class assignments, and discussion questions designed to get at the more important historical issues. Historian-filmmakers should be encouraged but they alone are not likely to effect a change in the nation's historical consciousness when flashier and more seductive commercial productions continue to use history to titillate the largest possible viewing public with stories of sex, power, and intrigue which happen to be set in the past. For most commercial producers, the historical facts are no more than the raw materials of drama, as malleable as any other script details to the demands of audience appeal.

Producing films with greater historical integrity is a clear step forward.[5] But given the continuing popularity of commercially produced historical film and docudrama, the premise of this book is that teaching people to be more critical viewers of everything they see on film and television is an even more effective way for historians to influence the public perception of the past. We must teach our students (and indirectly the society at large) the basic skills of visual literacy and engender in them the habit of critical viewing—for example, the ability to identify bias and interpretation in the composition and editing of television news. We must sensitize them to the often complex ways in which, despite claims to objective truth, film and television programs (like books and classroom history lessons) cannot help interpreting in some way the past that they portray. We must teach them to understand the ways in which the techniques and conventions of the media can communicate a subtle (sometimes unintended) point of view, usually without the viewers ever being aware that they are getting a selective view of history. By responding in this manner to one of the less evident ways in which the technology of modern life threatens traditional values—the value of critical thinking in the humanities in general and history in particular—our efforts may assist in rehabilitating the public image of the professional scholar and teacher.

WHAT IS A MOVING IMAGE ARTIFACT AND HOW IS IT DIFFERENT FROM OTHER HISTORICAL ARTIFACTS?

Academic scholars have been pursuing the close study of film and television for decades with tools borrowed from disciplinary perspectives such as linguistics, literary criticism, and psychological and economic theory. There are important insights to be gained from each of these approaches, but it is the purpose of this study to set forth a complementary methodology based upon the traditional tools of historical scholarship. As will be demonstrated over and over in the essays to follow, a sensitivity to historical method can be a crucial determinant in understanding the social and cultural context in which media productions are produced and in which they are received by audiences over time. But this book is informed by a more specific idea—that the analysis of a film or television program *as historical artifact* can contribute to both a fuller understanding of the nature of history and a richer appreciation of the media production. In the history classroom, such analyses teach the skills of historical thinking at the same time as they refine visual literacy.

In this book the term "moving image artifact" (or "moving image document") is used to refer to any form of the motion picture technology first developed in the 1890s: from Edison's earliest experiments to last night's TV news; from classic documentaries to TV sit-coms; from factual footage such as the Zapruder film of the Kennedy assassination to the complete fantasy of some TV docudramas, from relatively "value free" and undeniably accurate images such as the unedited filmed records of scientific experiments to the unbridled propaganda of Leni Riefenstahl and the only slightly more subtle manipulations of everyday television commercials. Calling them "artifacts" may seem strange. The purpose for the term is to start scholars thinking about how to use the traditional tools of the humanist in general and the historian in particular to advance the critical analysis of film and television materials.

That term may seem strange as well. Film and television are not "materials" in the same sense as the manuscripts and documents that historians are more used to working with. Unlike other historical evidence which exists independently as words on a page or as an artifact you can hold in your hand, moving images require a technology—a projector or a VCR—to bring the celluloid or the magnetic patterns on the oxide base to life, and the conditions of viewing can significantly influence the ways in which they communicate. It is important to remember how movies and television work. When the historian or any viewer watches a film, what appears on the screen before them is a rapid succession of still pictures—the moving image exists only inside the mind of the viewer. Moreover, moving images communicate in a different language—visual language—a language which appeals to the viewer's unconscious psychological and/or emotional response as well as to the intellect.

Some obvious practical difficulties in dealing with film and television evidence relate to its relative inaccessibility. While some authors have admitted to doing their film research via late night television, the repeated editing of such films for TV time slots and censorship rules make it most unlikely that such viewers are seeing the entire film as originally produced. In order to avoid editing out sequences while still fitting films into precise TV schedules, some stations have taken to slowing or speeding the projection speed of a film with the aid of an electronic device called a lexicon. By shortening the pauses between sentences and "compressing" the spoken parts, a film can be slowed or speeded by as much as 8 percent without the average viewer even noticing. Equally subtle is the changed aspect ratio between the theater and the TV screen which requires that a large portion of the screen image of many films produced in widescreen formats, such as Cinemascope, be left out in the conversion to the TV screen. The engineers responsible for the conversion often have to "pan and scan" from one speaker to another in a scene where both conversants had originally been on the screen, and the carefully designed visual texture of the wider image is completely lost. (Problems raised by "pan and scan" make the controversy over colorization pale in comparison.)[6] The temptation to rely on video is understandable; videotape releases of hundreds of period films will facilitate study. But the vast majority of fiction films and almost all nonfiction films (newsreels, scientific films, industrials, documentaries, etc.) will remain available only in a few widely dispersed archives with limited access to scarce screening facilities.

Collectively, the archives contain only a small fraction of the many thousands of films actually produced since the invention of the medium. The reasons are technological, economic, and academic. The technological problems relate to the old nitrate chemical base for motion picture film which breaks down over time threatening spontaneous combustion and requiring that archival prints be transferred (at significant expense) to safety stock.[7] Economic concerns have also limited the number of films that survived, because once their commercial value was gone, many old movie prints were destroyed to recover their silver content.[8] Finally, in academic terms, only in recent years have many scholars recognized the value of this kind of evidence.

Scholars must also be aware that just as there are different versions of the same cropped photograph and different editions of the same book, so there are different "releases" of films. Different versions (sometimes shorter and sometimes longer) are often prepared for overseas release or to meet the "standards and practice" requirements for screening on television. The differences can be subtle and elusive, but they can also be significant.

Finally, although it is not unusual for films (like other documents) to be lost over time, moving image documents suffer a second difficulty. Those that have survived may be more difficult to authenticate or to verify for form or completeness than are written or printed sources. The work of scholars such as Kevin Brownlow, in the restoration and reconstruction of films such as Abel Gance's *Napoleon* (1927), and their acknowledgment that the result of their meticulous efforts still does not represent absolute veracity to the original, should give us warning.[9] When factors of age or wear and tear result in pages of a written manuscript being missing, the lacunae is evident to the scholar. Many, if not most, of the films in rental circulation today are missing footage (footage destroyed by hungry projectors or cannibalized by collectors), but unless a splice was made poorly, viewers are likely unaware that anything is missing at all. Not unlike the traditional historians' approach to manuscript sources, specialists in early film history have learned to verify materials and date individual prints by submitting archival films to close physical examination, studying splice marks, sprocket holes, and the spaces between frames. Researchers must check the films they study against other prints, shooting scripts, shot lists, catalog descriptions, early reviews, and any other sources they might find to verify the form and completeness of their documents.

TWO STAGES OF HISTORICAL ANALYSIS

There should be two stages to the analysis of a moving image document. Taken together, they bring a coherent and comprehensive methodology to the study of film and television documents and its integration into the research and teaching of history.

Stage One: Gathering Information on the Content, Production, and Reception of a Moving Image Document

The first stage involves the general analysis of the document in order to glean from it as much information as possible. While certain data will be evident at first viewing, getting at other aspects of it will require: a close study of the content of the film itself—the images which appear on the screen and the sounds on the soundtrack and the ways in which they are brought together to convey meaning; the social, cultural, political, economic, and institutional background of the production and the conditions under which it was made; and the ways in which the film or television program was understood by its original audiences. A detailed explication of this stage of analysis follows in chapter II.

Stage Two: Four Frameworks for Historical Inquiry

In the second stage of historical analysis of moving image documents, the data or information gathered in stage one is endowed with meaning in relation to one or another type of historical inquiry. The many and varied ways in which scholars and teachers have made use of moving image documents can be reduced to four "frameworks for historical inquiry." It might help to think of the first framework as concerned with secondary documents; the next three with primary ones. Although many moving image documents might be studied from multiple perspectives, in each case, different analytical concerns would come to the fore—and different aspects of the data collected in stage one would assume more or less significance. The four frameworks are:

1. The Moving Image as Representation of History

History has provided the subject matter for thousands of documentaries, feature films, and television programs. To a significant extent, these productions have more influence over what the public understands of its history than do history teachers in all our schools and colleges. In recent years historical scholars have themselves become involved in the production of dramatic films and TV docudramas as well as historical documentary films. The close study of these productions can lead to new awareness of historical issues and to a deeper understanding of the potential for historical representation.

2. The Moving Image as Evidence for Social and Cultural History

Films and television provide a rich fund of evidence for the study of social and cultural values, but much that has been written has adopted an overly simple reflective model to explain the connection. Additionally, such analysis must be carried on in the context of knowledge concerning the broader culture. To this type of analysis, historians offer their traditional methodology for working with paper records—by stressing hard evidence as well as sound theoretical foundations.

3. Actuality Footage as Evidence for Historical Fact

There are cases in which film and television provide the best evidence regarding specific historical events—who did what, where, when?. Relying on moving images for this sort of specific data (rather than for the broad cultural information alluded to above) requires a special attention to the language and the editing of images. Film has potential to document the past (or the present for the future) as no other medium can, but there are specific cautions which must be observed, as discussed in section 3 of Chapter III.

4. The History of the Moving Image as Industry and Art Form

Scholars reject most of what passed for "film history" a decade or more ago as a thoughtless pandering to nostalgia. Lately this has given way to the work of a new generation of critical film

historians trained in the discipline of cinema studies. There is
still a chasm, however, between historians who use film and film
historians—a separation that can be traced in part to historians'
resistance to the theoretical apparatus of film studies. The industrial and artistic history of cinema and television deserve historians' attention, but in order to comprehend the most
thoughtful work in these fields we must at least try to understand
the intellectual bases on which today's film historians undertake
their scholarship.

These four categories are not meant to be rigid or limiting in any
way. Neither should they suggest that a complex and dynamic field
can be so neatly divided. In practice, there will *always* be an overlap
among the four; *no one of them can or should be applied without reference
to the others.* The purpose for spelling them out here is to concentrate
attention on the types of analytical issues scholars should be addressing
and to identify particular methodological concerns which relate more
to one of them than to another.

It is also worth reemphasizing that the four frameworks do not
address different types of films, but different types of historical investigation. Any film is open to study under more than one of them.
Consider the July 1932 Universal newsreel story on the rout of the
Bonus Army from the Mall in Washington, D.C., analyzed in Anthony
Aldgate's essay and included in the video compilation. It might invite
study in terms of all four frameworks. It can be studied as historical
interpretation, (framework 1); the narration states that the spectacle
was "unparalleled in the history of the country" and compares the
scene to "actual conditions in France in '17." In a study of the social
and cultural values inherent in the newsreel story (framework 2),
special attention would be devoted to the attitudes suggested in the
editing of the images and in the words and tone of voice chosen for
the narration, in this case a rather bombastic tone referring to "foreign
reds." A scholar more concerned with the details of the event as it
actually took place (framework 3) would hope to transcend the editors'
and the narrator's points of view and use outtakes to try to reconstruct
the raw, unedited footage of the event as it was originally shot. Finally,
a historian of the movie industry (framework 4) might find special
meaning in the types of other stories included in the same newsreel
and in the order and style in which those stories were presented, the
ways in which the newsreel company promoted its product, and in
the cities and neighborhoods in which theaters showed that company's
newsreels rather than another's. The study guide to the video compilation includes the transcript of the narration for this Bonus Army
story. It also includes the descriptive contents sheet published by Universal to accompany the film; the sheet indicates that this story was
last on the bill, immediately following a story on a train wreck in Ohio.

Detailed discussions of these four frameworks constitute the four
sections of chapter III. Each section has an introduction followed by

three essays written by established scholars who, in their own ways, have wrestled with the problems and opportunities of working with the moving image. The first two essays in each section concentrate on research-related concerns with the third focusing on how the particular issues central to that framework for inquiry can be productively addressed in the history classroom.

As a preliminary to those approaches, let us turn to a fuller examination of what is involved in a stage one analysis of a moving image document.

NOTES

1. See for example: Walter Benjamin, "The Work of Art in the Age of Mechanical Reproduction," in Hannah Arendt, editor, *Illuminations* (New York: Harcourt, Brace and World, 1960), pp. 219–253; Neil Harris, "Iconography and Intellectual History: The Half-Tone Effect," in John Higham and Paul K. Conkin, editors, *New Directions in American Intellectual History* (Baltimore: Johns Hopkins University Press, 1979), pp. 196–211. See also: Robert Taft, *Photography and the American Scene* (New York: Macmillan, 1938); Gisele Fruend, *Photography and Society* (Boston: David R. Godine, 1980), and Alan Trachtenberg, editor, *Classic Essays on Photography* (New Haven: Leete's Island Books, 1980).
2. *Culture as History* (New York: Pantheon, 1984), p. xvii.
3. Visual language is not unique to film and television, of course. For observations on the critical and historical analysis of photography see, for example, Jon Berger's *Way of Seeing* (London and New York, 1972) and *Another way of Seeing* (New York, 1982), Susan Sontag's, *On Photography* (New York, 1973), and Alan Trachtenberg, editor, *Classic Essays on Photography.*
4. Neil Postman, *Amusing Ourselves to Death* (New York: Viking, 1985).
5. Among the most effective historian-produced films for teaching are the ones which approach the medium self-consciously and use the opportunity to teach viewers (especially student viewers) something about how the demands of the medium affect the presentation and interpretation of the past. See for example the study guides to *Will Rogers' 1920s: A Cowboy's Guide to the Times* and *Goodbye Billy: America Goes to War, 1917–1918,* both distributed by Churchill Films and discussed in chapter III in the essay by Patricia-Ann Lee.
6. See, for example, "Machine Lets Films Survive Television's Test of Time Slots," *Philadelphia Inquirer,* December 26, 1986, Section C, p. 1; "Tinting Put in a Teapot by Pan and Scan," *Los Angeles Times,* October 22, 1986, Part 6, p. 1; "Creative Furor: High Tech Alteration of Sights and Sounds Divides the Arts World," *Wall Street Journal,* September 2, 1987, p. 1.
7. See John Culhane, "Nitrate Won't Wait," *American Film,* Volume II, no. 5 (March, 1977), pp 54–59; and Lawrence F. Karr, "Film Preservation: Why Nitrate Won't Wait," four page reprint from IATZE *Official Bulletin,* Summer, 1972.
8. The same was true for millions of glass photographic negatives, much of what would have been the basic evidence for the history of photography.
9. See Kevin Brownlow, *Napoleon: Abel Gance's Classic Film* (New York, 1983).

CHAPTER II
HISTORICAL ANALYSIS, STAGE ONE: GATHERING INFORMATION ON THE CONTENT, PRODUCTION, AND RECEPTION OF A MOVING IMAGE DOCUMENT

Historians characteristically ask three basic types of questions of any document or artifact before them, questions about its content, production, and reception. The very same questions can be asked of moving image documents:

a. Questions about its content—what information can be gleaned from the document itself (from a close study of what appears on the screen), either through direct or indirect analysis? How is this information determined by the visual and aural texture of the film? What is the connection between the medium and the message?

b. Questions about its production—what influences were at work in shaping the document and, perhaps, served to limit or bias the information it conveys? Beyond the images themselves, how might the background (personal, political, professional, etc.) of the producer, director, actors, etc., have influenced their performances? How might the institutional conventions and the larger purpose of the sponsoring agency (a Hollywood studio, an industrial organization, or a Washington lobbying group) have colored the message of the production?

c. Questions about its reception—regardless of the nuances of meaning we can derive from an analysis of the document today (comparing it with other contemporaneous materials or judging it in the knowledge of what subsequently took place), what effect if any did the document have on the pace or direction of events at the time it was made? Who saw the film and how might it have influenced them?

By taking this approach to film and television documents, historians can make significant contributions to the evolving methodology of film studies research. At the same time they further sensitize themselves and their students to the skills of visual analysis. It is important that none of these three areas of inquiry be considered in a vacuum. Factors of production often dictate both content and reception, as factors of reception define the content as perceived by the audience. When dealing with the analysis of a specific moving image document, it makes sense to preserve a chronological approach by looking at the production history first. But let us address them here in the order set out above.

QUESTIONS ABOUT CONTENT

Focusing on the content of a moving image document can be more difficult than with a verbal document. In part this is due to the breadth of individual interpretation that the viewer brings to the experience (more on this later in this section and in the section on reception). All critical viewers must bring some elementary information into the screening room. For example, unless an early silent film has been "step printed" to compensate for the change from an 18 to the more modern 24 frame per second standard, we often see such film projected at one and one half times the normal speed. In this and in other more subtle ways the historians use ordinary analytical tools sometimes prove inadequate when applied to moving images.

Early filmmakers realized that film allowed them the ability to play with time and space. Edwin S. Porter, D. W. Griffith, and others pioneered in the use of editing to collapse and to expand time (drawing out a chase for dramatic effect, for example) and to cut from one location to another as an enhancement to dramatic tension (as in intercutting between chaser and chased). In the process they challenged the audiences' expectations and, over time, taught them to understand film (and conceivably other arts and forms of communication) differently.[1] Editing can transform an ordinary series of images into an extraordinary one. An interesting historical example is the famous footage of Hitler's jig after stepping from the railway car in which he had accepted the surrender of France in 1940. It never really happened. With the help of a laboratory device called an optical printer, a team of patriotic British film editors was able to take an otherwise benign image of Hitler raising his leg and turn it into a diabolical little dance. Shown on the newsreel screens of all the allied nations at this psychological low point in the struggle against Nazism, the footage became powerful propaganda, a force for rededicating opposition against the heartless Führer. Filmmakers may not set out to misrepresent, but the creative tools that they use nevertheless reshape and manipulate reality. It should be clear that, to the extent that questions of time, and place, and what really happened, are of concern to historians and history teachers, they must become fluent in the rhetoric of images.

To comprehend more than the surface content of a moving image document, therefore, one must develop at least a basic knowledge of visual language—the elements of a shot (duration, field size, camera angle, camera movement, lighting, color, depth of field, lens characteristics, etc.) and the editing techniques (cuts of various kinds, dissolves, fades, and washes) with which filmmakers communicate their ideas (See chapter V.). It would be foolish indeed to try to study the "Declaration of the Rights of Man and the Citizen" in the original text with students who cannot read French, yet we regularly show them moving image documents without addressing the language of images. This adds complications because unlike the frustrated readers who don't know French, passive viewers unconsciously assume that they have in fact fully comprehended the visual document. (Our cliches are instructive: "Seeing is believing," "Pictures don't lie," "I saw it with my own two eyes.") Untrained viewers may indeed have taken in the message that the filmmaker meant them to (manipulated them to?), but this is never enough. Realizing that surface comprehension represents only the most rudimentary level of meaning, historians would never be completely satisfied with that level of analysis of a written document. We must learn to demand the same depth of analysis in regard to moving images as well. For examples of the importance of close shot-by-shot analysis in the study of newsreel footage see Robert Herzstein's and Anthony Aldgate's essays and the selections from Universal and Movietone newsreels in the video compilation.

The first step is to look closely at the image. For a moving image, close viewing requires repeated viewing, an awareness of the technical tools developed by specialists in cinema studies, and the ability to apply them where appropriate. A moving image document communicates through visual signs and symbols and through the mixing of those visual elements with the dialog and music on the soundtrack. Their meaning may seem self-evident, but it always depends on an interaction or negotiation between the viewer or spectator and the moving image being viewed. The only time that it is correct to think of film as a static object is when it is rolled up in its can on the shelf. Any effort to elucidate meaning from it demands a consideration of the spectator (for the historian this often means a spectator from some past time, but more on this under reception). To a large degree, therefore, studying the content of a film involves the identification of the signs it presents and the consideration of how they work together and with the mind of the audience.

People make meaning from images (or signs) by relating them to a series of codes, among them cultural codes, shared artistic codes, and cinematic codes. Consider, for example, some of the images from *The Plow That Broke the Plains* (1936), which is analyzed as a case study in chapter IV and reproduced in its entirety in the video compilation. There are some images that derive their meaning from cultural experience or tradition, such as the planting of a settler's stake in the virgin soil of the frontier. A European, less sensitive to a historical tradition based on the gradual opening up of the West, might not get the message as quickly. Other images make sense in terms of codes drawn from the other arts. A good example is the body language of the depressed and psychologically defeated farmers pictured in a migrant camp in the closing scenes of the film as they sit dejectedly and whittle while the women do the work of unloading the trucks and trailers. A painter might use the same imagery or an actor might assume the same expressive stance in a stage play to depict victims overwhelmed by their situation and unable to help themselves. Finally, there are cinematic codes, patterns of meaning which derive from the unique elements of film and television in comparison to the other arts. One good example from *The Plow* is the shot which closes the sequence on the establishment of productive farms on the Great Plains with the image of a puffing locomotive which traverses the entire screen from left to right. Besides ending the sequence cinematically by "wiping" the screen clean for the next scene, the train shot suggests the logical end result of the successful farming of grain—the transportation of the product to Eastern markets (screen movement from left to right is usually interpreted as west to east).

By definition, the subject in front of the camera lens must always be something specific, yet filmmakers often intend a shot to lend itself to abstract generalization. The train referred to above was meant to be seen not as a specific train, but as representing the thousands of trains that carried grain to midwestern and coastal cities. Scholars versed in cinema theory might describe the image of the train as a sign (or signifier) and the business in grain it represented as the signified.[2] In his *Signs and Meaning in the Cinema* (Bloomington, Indiana, 1972) Peter Wollen suggests three ways in which cinematic signs can work. They may be (1) *iconic*, referring simply and directly to what they represent; (2) *indexical*, referring to a larger subject of which the specific image is a part or a measure; or (3) *symbolic*, when the only connection between the object and the meaning is an arbitrary intellectual or cultural convention. Early in *The Plow*, the images of huge mule-drawn combines can be understood as iconic—they seem to refer primarily to themselves. Later in the film, when we see rows of tractors breaking the delicate surface of the plains to meet the needs for food in war-torn Europe, the message is more clearly indexical— these specific tractors represent the thousands of others at work on the plains and suggest (especially in comparison with the flanks of tanks intercut with them) a measure of the damage they are doing to the delicate ecology. Other images from *The Plow* that lend themselves to indexical reading include overflowing bags of grain and harvesters working at night, both measures of the great productivity of the soil— at least until the drought came.

Symbolic images are often the most difficult to interpret because the connection between signifier and signified is completely arbitrary. The infant pictured in the film next to an idle plow on an apparently dry and dusty landscape is clearly not meant as an icon (we have no idea of who this specific child is and we have no earlier images of this child or any other children to compare with this one). Neither does the meaning seem to be indexical (there is no reason why we should be led to identify this child with a larger population of children). But there are potential symbolic readings—several of them—based on the basic incongruity of a tiny infant pictured next to a grown man's tool. One might get the message that the farmers of the plains were as powerless as infants in the face of their environment, or the quite different message that the they were as innocent as babes, blameless for the plight that had befallen them.

Other symbols, though just as arbitrary, may be more or less explicit to an audience, depending on the clarity with which they relate to some cultural, shared artistic, or cinematic code. In the montage that closes *The Plow*'s fifth major sequence, shots of belching smokestacks and hoppers overflowing with grain are intercut with images of a stock ticker that goes wild and begins to dance around on its pedestal and other shots of a black jazz drummer. In designing the sequence the filmmaker brought together indexical images of productivity (belching smokestacks and overflowing grain hoppers) with the symbolic images of the musician and the stock ticker to create a visual message about the misplaced optimism of the 1920s. The connection between these things is completely arbitrary. They can only convey their intended meaning to audiences familiar with the cinematic coding device of montage (an intercutting of a series of otherwise unrelated shots, often with a repetition of some of them, in a way that creates new meaning), and with a cultural code that presumes a recognition of the "jazz age" and other indicators of the carefree 1920s—a period which ended, as the sequence does, with the stock ticker "crashing" to the floor. The "crash" seems funny in the film because the symbolic reference to 1929 is so obvious.

Another approach to the study of signs concerns whether they derive their meaning syntagmatically or paradigmatically. *Syntagmatic* meaning is that which is drawn primarily from the relation of the image or sign in question with the other images surrounding it in the film. *Paradigmatic* meaning is less dependent of the context of surrounding images and keyed more to a broader identification of the thing represented with other alternative representations. Thus the shot in the midst of *The Plow*'s sequence on the dust bowl which shows a dog lying on the ground apparently panting for breath, derives some of its meaning paradigmatically (this dog does not look like the dogs we usually see or might expect to see) and some of its meaning syntagmatically (the dog's problems seem to come from having breathed in the blowing dust pictured in the shots immediately preceding and following it). The belching smokestacks mentioned above derive their meaning syntagmatically (the context of the surrounding images of productivity is essential; without them the image might more easily represent pollution than prosperity). The stock ticker which crashes requires little contextualization; its meaning is paradigmatic.

We have said nothing yet about the element of sound in film and television. The dialogue, music, or sound effects that accompany an image can dramatically influence its meaning. Tony Schwartz, well known media consultant and producer of hundreds of award-winning radio and television commercials, argues that sound is more important than sight. He suggests, to prove his point, that people look at almost any television commercial with the sound turned off. One might try this experiment with Tony Schwartz's own famous "daisy spot" from the 1964 Lyndon Johnson presidential campaign, included in the video compilation. Even in such a carefully structured sixty-second production it is usually impossible to get a clear idea of what's going on without the sound component. In contrast, we usually can get the point by listening to the sound without the pictures—much of the power of *The Plow That Broke the Plains* comes from the authoritative voice of the narrator—and the use of music in the film is crucial to its overall impact.[3]

Beyond the close attention to images and sounds, the analytical process should involve the conscious breaking down of the structure of the document (parsing it as one would a sentence) to perceive patterns in it which also communicate meaning, but which might not be apparent at first viewing. The case study of *The Plow That Broke the Plains* contains such a breakdown. Film scholars often turn to models for structural analysis proposed by Russian folklorist Vladimir Propp in his *Morphology of The Folktale* (1928) or by anthropologist Claude Levi-Strauss in his *Structural Anthropology* (1972). It is helpful to outline the basic sequences of a film, dissecting it into its constituent parts, or trying to reconstitute the kinds of "story boards" the film-makers may have used in trying to design and order the images they put into the film in the first place.

Understanding the dramatic structure of Pare Lorentz's second film, *The River*, for example, is crucial to understanding its effectiveness in communicating its points about the need for erosion control and the potential for projects like the then infant Tennesee Valley Authority. The film is in a distinctly nonnarrative style, avoiding chronology for the most part and using the device of narrative and visual repetition to reinforce its arguments. The film takes viewers on two trips down the Mississippi, first as it was when virgin forests covered much of the northern United States, and again after many of the forests had been denuded, industrial cities had been built in the place of small river trading towns, and overintensive agriculture had stripped the fertile soil from much of the South. By the end of the second trip, the unfortunate results of irresponsible environmental policy and unplanned economic development are evident in the terrible flood conditions that Lorentz photographed.[4]

Most films adopt a more tradition narrative structure, but there are always distinctive elements that help to define the film's content and message. From whose point of view is the story being told? If the story unfolds through the eyes of one character, to what extent are viewers restricted to only that person's experience—is the audience privi-ledged with some information while certain other information is kept from them? How might the structure of a scene prejudice an audience to respond in one way or another to a forthcoming event? For ex-ample, consider a sequence from Vincent Minelli's *Lust for Life* (MGM, 1956). This Hollywood biography of Vincent Van Gogh shows him early in life going off as a missionary to a desperately poor mining area of Belgium and winning the respect of a people who regard him at first with disdain. The sequence shows us numerous shots of his interaction with the people there, going down into the mines with them, giving them his food and clothing, even his bedding, and min-istering to their sick. He becomes as poor and as dirty as the people are in order to be accepted by them. Then an inspection team from the Church comes and, appalled at the conditions in which he is living, criticizes him for undermining the image of the clergy. There is no question that the conditions are appalling, but this sequence has been carefully structured so that we tend to side with Vincent against his critics. Had the sequence included earlier shots showing the eccle-siastical administrators worried about ministers in the field getting too close to the people and not living in a properly dignified way, then viewers might read the confrontation with Vincent differently.

Theorists are sometimes faulted for taking their analyses too far. A thoroughgoing semiotician, for example, concentrating on the iden-tification and decoding of every sign, might fail to appreciate the aesthetic qualities of a film. More to the point of this study, too rigorous an attention to such internal analysis of a moving image production might lead scholars to undervalue—or even ignore—his-torical context. The essays in this volume by Robert Sklar and Janet Staiger, both distinguished cinema scholars, demonstrate the value of theory, not as an end in itself, but as a means to historical under-standing. Both of them also stress the integration of theoretical film analysis with the study of more traditional forms of historical evidence. Historians concerned with the moving image cannot afford to simply turn their backs on film theory. The specific structural models put forth by Propp, Levi-Strauss, and others are complex and controver-sial, but there are situations in which individual historians can make use of such preconceived systems for analysis.

It is important to recognize that differences do exist in analyzing the content of images in film and in television. There are characteristic differences in the form and structure of television programs, often driven by institutional and economic pressures and by developing styles in shooting and editing. And the media often influence one another. The standard conventions for the editing of the interview, developed in TV newsrooms in the first decade of television, have become a staple of documentary film producers as well.[5]

To summarize then, although close study of content is the approach a historian would normally take to any document, a moving image document may require resort to different kinds of tools. Historians must consider the nature of visual communication, learning at least some of the technical terminology used to characterize the elements of a motion picture shot and the types of editing devices available to the filmmaker. In addition, we cannot ignore film theory. To the extent that anyone who sits down to study a film has at least an unconscious assumption of what a film is and how it communicates its message, each of us brings some concept of theory to the task of analysis.

QUESTIONS ABOUT PRODUCTION

Whereas the content questions deal with what's on the screen, production questions deal with the background elements: how and why things got on the screen. In studying a letter or a diary entry as a piece of evidence, historians seek to put themselves in the place of the author, trying to understand the conditions under which the document was written and how those conditions may have influenced its content. To some extent, therefore, the analysis of a moving image document requires that we learn something about how it was produced.[6]

Manuscripts or printed documents are often the product of one person, but such individual authorship is rare in moving image documents. Despite the tendency of some critics to credit one *auteur* with the style and creativity of a production, most film and television scholars now recognize that productions are the result of complex collaborative efforts in which scores of people (producers, directors, screenwriters, cinematographers, editors, actors, publicists, etc.) contribute creative ideas at various stages in the process.[7] To some extent our understanding of this collaborative process has been demonstrated most clearly by historians who have concentrated on digging in the recently opened archives of the Hollywood studios in search of a "paper trail" to document the production process.[8] Thomas Cripps's essay in chapter III offers special insights into ways in which the paper records of individuals and studios illuminate the social and political forces which sometimes influence film production.

The production of *The Plow That Broke the Plains* was, more than most films, the work of an individual artist. Pare Lorentz had been a film critic and an outspoken booster of the Roosevelt administration before he won the approval of the Resettlement Administration, one of the myriad new alphabet agencies set up in the early days of the New Deal, to make his first film. The Resettlement Administration wanted a movie that could be used to train its many new employees

and introduce them to the agency's goals, which were to provide rehabilitation loans to farm families and to facilitate the resettlement of
people from depressed areas of the country to places where there
were better opportunities for employment. The Great Plains, a depressed area that was suffering from environmental as well as economic woes, held special interest for Lorentz. In addition, the
Resettlement Administration was impressed by Lorentz's insistence
that such a film could be made with production values advanced
enough to allow commercial release as well. The agency had drawn
sharp criticism from those opposed to Roosevelt's policies, because it
represented the increasing role of government in social planning, and
it saw the film as a much desired opportunity to explain and defend
its programs. Moreover, Lorentz wanted to utilize the dramatic power
of the medium to convince audiences to accept his film's important
social and political messages.

If we took the analysis of the production process this far and no
further we would have access to a much more informed comprehension of the film. Any document means more to a scholar who understands the reasons for which it was written. The production of
commercial entertainment films and television programs must always
be understood as profit driven, but many other types of productions
should be understood in the context of the political or other ideologies
which they were meant to represent and foster. It seems unfair to
compare The Plow to such blatant propaganda as Für Uns (1937), a
Nazi party film analyzed in Robert Herzstein's essay to follow and
reproduced in its entirety in the video compilation.[9] Yet both were
driven by political ideologies and both were intended to influence the
public perception of public issues. The informed scholar should understand in detail what these intentions were, whether or not they
were fulfilled (or even comprehended) by audiences at the time.
Among other types of production related papers, the study guide to
the video compilation includes excerpts from the successful grant applications that led to the production of "Molders of Troy" (1979) and
Women of Summer (1986). How better to begin to judge the success of
a film than to consider it in light of the specific goals set down by the
producers in the planning of the project.

Studying the production background of a film or television program
must include a consideration of the background and experience of
the people involved. As noted above, Lorentz had an abiding identification with both the Great Plains and with the Roosevelt administration; he knew about film as a critic, but he had never made a film
before. The crew he pulled together to work on the project were
extremely talented men who went on to famous and creative careers
as filmmakers and photographers in their own right, but they had
serious differences with Lorentz. This is important information for
anyone who want to understand this film as a historical document.[10]

Thomas Cripps's essay to follow and the study guide to the video
compilation detail the intriguing production history of The Birth of a

Race (1918). Originally conceived as black America's response to *The Birth of a Nation* (1915), much of the money for the project came from a fundraising campaign among black leaders and their liberal white supporters. Before the production was complete, however, the project had changed hands, and the script of the film was transformed to accommodate several new agendas. By the time the movie appeared, neither the originators of the film nor its financial backers could identify the elements of the film they had planned. In the case of this film, as with many others, the full analysis of it as historical document demands a very close study of the production process and a careful consideration of alternative ways that it might have developed. As Cripps demonstrates, the real value of *The Birth of a Race* as a historical document lies as much if not more in an understanding of the forces at work in its production than what viewers can see on the screen.

Besides the intended purposes of a project, the orientation/background of the people involved, and the unexpected experiences faced in the production process, there are always other limitations to be considered. For example, what were the technological limitations of the medium at the time a film or TV program was produced? What went into the decision to make *On The Waterfront* (1954) in black and white even though most other films of the period were in color? Live television drama is usually thought of as one of the special aspects of the golden age of television because the limitations involved forced the actors and directors to innovate, but how may these limitations have also influenced the types of historical dramas attempted and the ways in which they had to be presented?[11] Pare Lorentz's major limitation in making *The Plow* was his very meager budget, but other filmmakers have spent monstrous amounts of money in making films of meager interest.

The social and political influences at work in the production process may be more or less explicit, but they must be taken into account for a complete analysis of the document. Jack Warner's support for FDR and his involvement in the writing of the National Recovery Administration (NRA) code for the motion picture industry clearly influenced the pro-New Deal films made by his studio in the early 1930s. To view these films without such knowledge clearly limits the insights that can be drawn from them. Any attempt at analysis of such a social problem film as Warner Brothers' *Wild Boys of the Road* (1934) without a realization that by that time the form had become a genre in its own right, would surely invite a misreading.

QUESTIONS ABOUT RECEPTION

Questions about reception and spectatorship have been most troublesome for film scholars and historians alike. Many assertions have been made regarding direct impact of film and television upon society. The *Payne Fund Studies* of the 1930s associated movie watching with juvenile delinquency and a perceived general decline of morals in America at the time. More recently, television viewing has been tried as a defense in the courtroom, with a defendant's attorney claiming that, brainwashed by the violence on TV, his client was unable to distinguish right from wrong. Neither of these efforts offered convincing proof. How can one go about evaluating the impact a film or a television program has on its audience? Published reviews are available, but they represent only individual points of view. Studio commercial records (where available) and trade newspapers such as *Variety* provide some data on the financial success of many productions. Yet, no certain way exists to measure the impact of even the most popular film on the people who saw it. Garth Jowett's essay in Section 4 surveys some of the important approaches social scientists have taken to study the impact of the media.

Much of the current work in cinema studies involves what is termed "reception analysis." If a film is seen as communicating through visual symbols which derive their meaning at least partly from the viewer's cultural values or from other films the viewer has seen, then the viewer must be involved in the construction of that meaning. An older "illusionist" position argued that films created the illusion of reality, an illusion which spectators simply absorbed as passive receptacles. Today this is generally replaced by a much more complex understanding of reception in which the viewer is an active agent in the making of meaning from a film. In the *Classical Hollywood Cinema*, David Bordwell borrows from art historian E. M. Gombrich in suggesting that filmmakers build upon traditional formal patterns for the ways of presenting things, "schemata" he calls them, which have been normalized over years of studio production. After looking at scores of films, the viewers have become experienced at interpreting these schemata and have developed a series of "mental sets" through which they processes the images presented to them. The viewing of a film, then, is not a passive experience. Rather the audience member tests each twist in the plot, each cinematic event, against the relevant mental set. If subsequent shots do not obey the schemata, the viewer turns to the next most likely alternative. Piecing together the meaning of a film represents a complex negotiation between producers and viewers.[12]

Another problem relates to the varying experiences and frames of mind that any audience brings to a moving image experience. Different cultural experiences, different racial or class associations, different sexual or political predispositions—all these influence the ways in which people carry on this negotiation. To some extent, therefore, every viewer, or at least every group of viewers distinguished by differences of class, race, or gender, sees a unique version of a film. Feminist film criticism, for example, concentrates on studying the ways in which films make meaning for women. Janet Staiger's essay in chapter III offers several pertinent examples of how differing group concerns influence reception.

Reception characteristics change over time as well. A 1980s audience is very different from a 1930s audience in terms of its experience with interpreting images as well as in the expectations it would apply to social or cultural situations portrayed on the screen. *The Plow That Broke the Plains* was well received by the critics when it was originally released, but viewers responded differently depending on their political orientation and the part of the country they were from. Audiences watching the film today have a very different experience from people who saw it in 1936 with the experience of the depression and the political issues of the period fresh in their minds and, conceivably, with the taste of dust in their mouths. Besides being distanced from the issues, audiences today may be influenced by their wider experience with the media. Familiarity with the fast-paced editing of television may make the pacing of *The Plow* seem too slow.

Certain moving images can be so closely tied to the cultural situation of their times that their point is lost on audiences of a later day. The chief key to the effectiveness of the commercials Tony Schwartz makes is the research he puts into targeting the audience and trying to understanding their state of mind. When students today see the "daisy spot," many of them miss the point entirely. Some even confuse the voice intoning the countdown with President Johnson's and think that the commercial is saying that he will use the bomb. Those viewers who cannot remember the state of mind of America in 1964 can get confused about this commercial because it relies so much on that state of mind to communicate its message. The point of the piece, as Schwartz has explained, was less to give people information than it was to stimulate them to take information (or impressions) that they already had and draw a conclusion based upon them. Although the commercial is clearly meant to focus people's attention on Barry Goldwater's statements regarding the use of the atomic bomb, it does not mention his name. It didn't have to, because everyone who saw it in 1964 understood exactly the point that was being made.

The historian can learn much about our understanding of the past from studying the reception of historical films over time. Consider, for example, Alain Resnais's documentary *Night and Fog*, which combines black and white archival footage of the concentration camps with color images taken at the time of production in 1955. When first released, the film was praised as a comment on the inhumanity of nazism, but perhaps due to the proximity of the war, it was not seen as a "historical film." Since that time, of course, it has become standard fare for many teachers struggling for ways to introduce their students to the plight of the Jews in Nazi dominated Europe and the horrors of the Holocaust. In this context, however, the film has come in for criticism it had not received before. It has recently been argued that the film presents a biased interpretation in that it does not acknowledge the Jewishness of the victims (in fact the narrator mentions the word Jew only once, and the word does not appear at all in the English subtitles). To bring the history of the film full circle, when Resnais was recently asked how he might explain this apparent bias, he explained that it had never been his central purpose to comment on the

Jews and their holocaust in the first place. He reminded the historian asking the question of him that it had been 1955, a time when France was critically embroiled in Algeria, and he explained that his main interest in making the film had been to warn Frenchmen against the dangers of falling into patterns of inhumanity themselves.[13] Resnais's observations allow us to see the film much more clearly as a document of 1955, but the film should also be interesting to us because of the ways that it has influenced (however unintentionally) the historical perception of thousands of history classes since then.

The reception experience with television is very different from that with the big screen. Whatever illusion of reality there may be in the darkened theater is broken in the context of the living room. The viewing experience must be understood in the context of the "flow" of programming (from a news broadcast to a quiz show to a baseball game, for example), all punctuated by commercial interruptions. Watching TV with other people is characterized by very different patterns of personal courtesy; people are much more willing to carry on a conversation over a TV program in their living room (or to put up with one going on around them) than they would be in a movie theater. Although we may not watch the TV screen as attentively as we do the movie screen, we tend to watch it more frequently, and therefore the repetition of TV messages (either the generalized messages of violence in police drama, or the repetition of specific commercial messages) may have more cumulative impact. Finally, the fact that the same electronic box on which so many rely as their prime source for news information also provides so much of everyday entertainment, must necessarily influence the ways in which people "make meaning" about the world around them.

There are cases linking the reception of a moving image document and the progress of historical events. The history of television and of recent American politics offers such interesting examples as the impact of Walter Cronkite's February 1968 special report from Vietnam on Lyndon Johnson's decision not to run for a second complete term and the role of Roger Mudd's special interview with Edward Kennedy in defeating his bid for the 1980 presidential nomination. Edward R. Murrow's March 1954 "See It Now: Report on Senator McCarthy" has often been credited with beginning to turn the public mind against the senator, but there had been many print and at least a few radio journalists who had already taken that stand. Certainly the credibility which Murrow had with the American public must be considered as a factor in the reception of the broadcast, and the tens of thousands letters and telegrams CBS received (90 percent of them agreeing with the program) cannot be discounted. But absolute proof is elusive.[14] The televised Army McCarthy hearings which began only a few weeks later have also been credited with deflating McCarthy, but Daniel Leab has elsewhere pointed out that only a few stations carried those hearings from gavel to gavel. Whenever thoughtful scholars have addressed the problem of audience impact, they have noted the complexity of the connection.[15] Still, imprecise as such connections must be, there is a growing literature on the intersection of media reception and culture. Most impressive is the National Institute of Mental Health's summary of research on the impact of television on American society, *Television and Behavior: Ten Years of Scientific Progress and Implications for the Eighties* (Volume 1, Summary Report, Washington, D.C. 1983), which does make categorical statements (on the relation of TV violence and attitudes among youth, for example).[16]

Popular writers have been quicker to suggest how changes in social values can be credited to popular films—style in the wearing (or not wearing) of men's undershirts, for example, are traced to the bare-chested appearance of Clark Gable in *It Happened One Night* (1932). More important examples center on the changing roles of women and of racial minorities, but they are still impressionistic and substantially undocumented. The patterns of reflection and refraction which form the connection between screen images and social values are wonderfully complex. They will be addressed in some more detail in the essays by Thomas Cripps and Carlos Cortés in chapter III.

Once the content, production background, and reception history of a moving image document have been closely studied, the field is open for a stage two analysis in which one or more of the four frameworks for inquiry are brought into play. In the combination of the two stages of analysis we have a comprehensive adaptation of the traditional tools of historical methodology to the critical study of film and television.

STRATEGIES FOR THE CLASSROOM

With careful planning and preparation, these methodological approaches can be brought to bear fruitfully in the history classroom. They can transform the use of film and television in history and social studies lessons from the simple delivery of information into exciting inquiry-oriented experiences for students. Moreover, rather than reinforcing the passive viewing habits learned by students in front of their home televisions, such lessons provide invaluable training in the development of visual literacy skills.

This point cannot be overstressed. An important aspect of history and social studies education is the teaching of the information and skills needed by people who are to participate actively as citizens in a democratic society. Thirty years ago this meant teaching them to read the newspaper critically, to identify bias there, and to distinguish between factual reporting and editorializing. We must recognize that for the 1990s and beyond, critical viewing skills are an essential element in such citizenship training. Students need to understand the ways in which the construction of the typical TV news interview is an expression of technological limitations and media conventions. They should learn to be sensitive to the ways in which political television commercials may appeal to their unconscious feelings and emotions rather than to their intellectual judgment.

Any society which commits itself, as America does, to preserve the freedom of expression for news agencies and public figures must also assume the responsibility to prepare the public to critically evaluate the messages they receive. There is no more appropriate place for this sort of training, this opening of minds, than the history classroom.

Another goal of history and social studies education is to encourage students to adopt habits of life long learning and to provide them with the analytical skills they will need to learn from their future experiences. Consider the relative importance of teaching students to read and evaluate critically what they read in textbooks or journal articles. Once finished with their high school or college courses, how many are likely to read a history textbook or subscribe to the *American Historical Review*? It seems myopic of us to spend so much class time dealing with the sources important to us as scholars and specialists, without allocating at least a few hours each term to moving image documents. Students then can develop the skills needed to view more critically the historical films and docudramas from which they will probably learn whatever history they do learn in future years. As explained more fully under framework 1, concern here should be less with teaching them to detect factual mistakes and more with alerting them to the characteristic ways in which popular film and television productions often manipulate and trivialize historical issues. More on the positive side, we should help them to understand the ways in which sensitive filmmakers can use the medium to address serious historical questions in unique ways.

These critical skills might be taught in many ways, but the authors of this book argue that it is particularly appropriate for history classes to study moving images as historical documents—reinforcing lessons of historical thinking at the same time that they develop visual literacy. Incorporating one or two such lessons need not take much time. Spending only ten minutes on a detailed analysis of a photograph in a textbook would be a step in the right direction. The treatment of some short documentary film or several sequences of television news might be accomplished in a single class period.

The extent to which a teacher can delve into close historical analysis of a film also depends on the age and intellectual development of the students. A high school or community college teacher would probably be wise to stick to the systematic consideration of a stage one analysis of content, production, and reception. Upper level college classes, and especially methodology classes for undergraduate history majors and graduate students, should consider the second stage as well, noting the ways in which the different types of historical inquiry make it important to ask different questions of the evidence. Certainly no film should be shown in any classroom, especially for its information content, without the students being encouraged to ask who the producers of the film were and what agendas may have been hidden in their minds.

Each of the four sections in Chapter III addresses the analysis of moving image documents in the classroom as well as in historical research. For a fuller discussion of strategies for the classroom, see the American Historical Association pamphlet entitled *Teaching History With Film and Television* and the *Study Guide* to the video compilation available from the American Historical Association.

NOTES

1. For a dramatic example see the excerpt from *The Life of an American Fireman* in the video compilation. It is shown in two versions, one edited the way the film was originally made in 1902 and the other the way it made sense to viewers of a more modern time.
2. These terms and many others in the discussion of the theory of semiology have their roots in the work of linguist Ferdinand de Saussure and have come to film study through the related field of literary theory. For a helpful survey see Terry Eagleton, *Literary Theory: An Introduction* (Minneapolis, 1983).
3. For more on sound in general see chapter V. For more on sound in *The Plow*, see chapter IV.
4. Rollins article from *Journal of Popular Culture* and Bordwell and Thompson, *Film Art: An Introduction*. 2nd edition (New York, 1986) pp. 55–62.
5. See, for example, the selection from *Women of Summer* in the video compilation and study the ways in which the editing is used to weave together various elements of interview and commentary. There is also a selection in the compilation that deconstructs the production of an interview filmed especially for this project. It is a very effective way to demonstrate to students the use of the cutaway in film and video editing.
6. An interesting short survey can be found in the opening chapter of David Bordwell and Kristin Thompson's *Film Art: An Introduction*. For a fuller introduction to some of the important aspects of production in a historical context see: Tino Balio, editor, *The American Film Industry* revised edition (Madison, Wisconsin, 1985), and Douglas Gomery, *The Hollywood Studio System* (New York, 1986). Several of the less technical and more intelligent handbooks for film and video production can also be helpful for the scholar trying to comprehend the production process. See, for example, Jay Kaufman and Laurence Goldstein, *Into Film* (N.Y., 1976), and Brian Winston and Julia Keydel, *Working With Video: A Comprehensive Guide to the World Of Video Production* (London, 1986).
7. See, for example, Donald Chase, ed., *Filmmaking: The Collaborative Art* (Boston, 1975).
8. There are now several edited volumes of production related papers that can be instructive to someone new to the field. Several deal with the making of specific important films such as Robert Carringer's, *The Making of Citizen Kane* (Berkeley, 1986), and John Sayles, *Thinking in Pictures: The Making of Matewan* (Boston, 1987). The more general collections of papers include: Gerald Mast, editor, *The Movies in Our Midst: Documents in the Cultural History of Film in America* (Chicago, 1982); Rudy Behlmer, editor,

Memo From David O. Selznick (New York, 1972); Behlmer, editor, *Inside Warner Brothers, 1935–1951* (New York, 1985); and Richard Taylor & Ian Christie, editors, *The Film Factory: Russian and Soviet Cinema in Documents, 1896–1939* (Cambridge, Mass, 1988).

9. The comparison may seem less unfair when, after reading the case history, the reader realizes that Lorentz was proud to have the film screened on a bill with German and Russian propaganda films, and when one realizes that, as originally released, the film had a quite didactic (propagandistic?) ending which was removed in response to opposition.

10. For more on the production of *The Plow*, see the case study in chapter IV.

11. There has been no comprehensive study of early television historical drama, but some interesting work has been done on the form of televised live drama. See for example, Kenneth Hey, "*Marty*: Aesthetics vs. Medium in Early Television Drama," In John O'Connor, editor, *American History/American Television: Interpreting the Video Past* (New York, 1983), pp. 95–133.

12. David Bordwell, Janet Staiger, and Kristin Thompson, *The Classical Hollywood Cinema: Film Style & Mode of Production to 1960* (New York: Columbia University Press, 1985), pp. 7–9.

13. Charles Krantz, "Alan Resnais *Night and Fog*," *Film & History*. Vol. XV, no. 1 (February, 1985) pp. 2–15.

14. For more on the Murrow broadcast see the O'Connor essay in chapter III and the video compilation.

15. See, for example, Gregory W. Bush, "Edward Kennedy and the Televised Personality in the 1980 Presidential Campaign," in John E. O'Connor, ed. *American History/American Television: Interpreting the Video Past*; David Culbert has written on LBJ and the Cronkite broadcast in his "Johnson and the Media," in Robort A. Divine, editor, *Exploring the Johnson Years* (Austin, Texas, 1981).

16. See also Joshua Meyrowitz, *No Sense of Place: The Impact of Electronic Media on Social Behavior* (New York: Oxford University Press, 1985).

CHAPTER III
HISTORICAL ANALYSIS, STAGE TWO: FOUR FRAMEWORKS FOR HISTORICAL INQUIRY

FRAMEWORK 1:
THE MOVING IMAGE AS
REPRESENTATION OF HISTORY

Unless they are content to speak only with one another, historians must undertake the serious consideration of the moving image as representation or interpretation of history. Until recently, most scholars have been put off by the portrayal of history in film—especially in commercial entertainment film and network docudrama. For a small but growing group of scholars who have participated substantially in the filmmaking process, helping to make more serious films portraying and interpreting the past, the experience has led them to think about their historical subjects in new and challenging ways. In his essay Pierre Sorlin cites the experience of historians who have found the close viewing of certain historical films to be important in refining their knowledge of the past. Daniel Leab's essay focuses more on the cautions which historians must bring to the study of moving image representations of history.

At the outset, a general division should be made between those films constructed of actuality footage (either film shot especially for the production or collected from various archives) and those dramatized films which seek to "recreate" historical events and situations using theatrical sets and costumes and actors reading scripted lines. (Note that we do not mean to discuss here those fiction films which use historical settings merely as a backdrop for comedy or drama). It might seem appropriate to evaluate a dramatized film more as we would a historical novel, reserving for the documentary a standard closer to that of traditional historical scholarship. But the matter is more complex. Once the division is made, the key question becomes: should

historians look differently at a historical documentary than they do
at a dramatization?

Neither the documentary nor the dramatized film is, by its nature,
more historical or more truthful than the other. Both forms offer the
opportunity for thoughtful and sensitive historical interpretation, and
both are susceptible to mindless travesty and intentional misrepre-
sentation. Because they are not limited to those images which happen
to have survived, the dramatic film may be more complete and evocative than the documentary.

The problem of evaluation has less to do with the nature of moving
image media productions themselves than it does with the unreasonable expectations many people have of them. Intelligent viewers of
historical feature films often prefer "unknown" actors and actresses
to star players and look for errors in props and costumes that would
make the movie seem "unrealistic." Fixing their attention on matters
of verisimilitude, they resist the idea that the film is an interpretation
or representation and look instead for a "recreation." Untrained viewers tend to expect a documentary film to present them with an objectively truthful view of reality and are disappointed when they detect
bias. In the words of a recent promotional brochure for a series of
historical film materials, they want to see "the past as it really happened." The advertising campaigns designed to sell Hollywood's historical epics make similar outrageous claims.

The first step in developing a constructive approach to films which
represent history is to dispel these unreasonable expectations and to
recognize that not even the most creditable history book can pretend
to present "wie es eigentlich gewesen" "the past as it really happened."
Van Ranke's goal has proven to be unviable in any medium. While
most scholars would deny having a predefined ideological rationale
for their work, every sincere attempt to evoke the past in print or in
film represents, consciously or unconsciously, an interpretation of
some kind.

Consider a recent documentary on America's experience in Vietnam. Although the producers of the series "Vietnam: A Television
History" (1983) may have sincerely endeavored to make their view as
objective and balanced as possible, almost every sequence has its own,
often subtle, point of view. Consider a less than subtle sequence from
the episode on "The War At Home" dealing with the October 1969
moratorium against the war. Shots of a high school teach-in in Con-
necticut, an impassioned speech by Benjamin Spock, and well-dressed
and articulate protestors in candlelit assembly, are set off against a
rabble of snarling New York construction workers and two men who
parachute into Central Park to express their support for President
Nixon and his policies. The contrast between wisdom and ignorance
needs not be voiced when such visual images make the point so clearly.

"Vietnam: A Television History" was generally well received in the
media, but a flurry of critical comments came from political conserva-
tives who, pointing at passages like the one outlined above, identified

the WGBH series as having a clear liberal bias and complained that the series not only misread the history of our involvement in Southeast Asia but also, by misinforming audiences, wrongfully influenced current opinion regarding America's military support for anticommunists in Latin America. By the summer of 1984, Accuracy in Media, a conservative group of media watchers, had decided to make their own film in direct response to the publically funded WGBH series. The result, "Vietnam: The Real Story," appeared on the same public television network in June 1985.

"Vietnam: The Real Story," like the WGBH series, uses all of the creative power of the filmmakers to sway an audience—in this case, of course, to sway them the other way. Consider the sequence in which the comments of Congressman [now Senator] John McCain, an obviously well-spoken former POW, are heard over a series of still pictures of American prisoners held in "cages" and being otherwise humiliated. This scene is juxtaposed against footage of Jane Fonda visiting a North Vietnamese antiaircraft gunpost where she smilingly takes home movies of the friendly soldiers and tries out the gunner's seat for herself. It ends with images of a rag-tag and dirty bunch of long-haired antiwar protestors. As if the pictures of Ms. Fonda were not damning enough, the filmmaker manipulates them through slow motion and adds an ironic musical background.

The point is not to *complain* about the bias in either film. A production on Vietnam which avoided taking stands on controversial issues would be a dull one indeed. As "creative" as were the editing techniques of both sets of producers, all of the footage used in the two sequences described above was *accurate actuality footage* in that it recorded the images of real people performing actual events (rather than actors recreating them) and it was all from the 1968-1969 period in question. Each production presented a defensible interpretation of the events it reported upon, and each one supported its interpretation through the ordering and juxtaposition of images. Our goal in this book is to sensitize historians—and through them students and the general public—to understand the ways in which a film makes its points, including the implicit visual and sound elements of interpretation (the art of the filmmaker) that might otherwise be taken in only unconsciously.

Every film, even if it's trying to balance alternative positions on a controversial issue, has some point of view. The camera could only record the event from one angle at a time, and someone had to edit the pieces of film together in a way that would make sense to him and the viewer. In any portrayal of a historical event, decisions must be made about where and how to use editing to collapse the passage of time. A production such as *The Wannsee Conference* (1987) an 85 minute dramatized film which recreates *in real time* the hour long 1942 Nazi meeting where the decision was made to pursue "The Final Solution" is a striking exception to the rule. Yet even here there were questions of how quickly to pace the editing, the order in which to present

individual images, whether to use jump cuts or dissolves to get from
one shot to another, and a score of other matters. When interviews
or other types of footage are shot for a film, someone must decide
whether to shoot in black and white or color, what speed film to use,
what lens to put on the camera, how far away to distance the subject,
and whether or not to move the camera while shooting. The answer
to each such question represents a decision about the use of historical
evidence—the same sorts of decisions the print historian must make
every time he writes a sentence. As Rudolf Arnheim has noted,

> Art begins where mechanical reproduction leaves off, where the con-
> ditions of representation serve in some way to mold the object. And the
> spectator shows himself to be lacking in proper understanding when he
> is satisfied to notice merely the content: this is the picture of an engine,
> that a couple of lovers, and this again of a waiter in a temper. He must
> be prepared to turn his attention to the form and to be able to judge
> *how* the engine, the lovers, the waiter, are depicted.[1]

In effect, each choice, combined with all the others, constitutes an
interpretation of the evidence, the construction of a historical point
of view.[2]

In a dramatized film many more choices, more interpretive judgments, have to be made. Whereas the documentary producer constructs his film out of actuality footage—it might be helpful to think
of each such shot as a quotation from the visual evidence—the producer of a dramatized historical film paraphrases the evidence rather
than quoting from it. Choices regarding minute details of props or
costumes can subtly influence the meaning a film imparts. A key
difficulty with the dramatized film is that the filling out of the characterizations and details of plot (the exact words of a private conversation, for example) can seldom be fully supported by direct evidence.
Therefore the producers, writers, and historical consultants (whoever
is involved in making the choices noted above) must seek out indirect
evidence, to present things as they "plausibly may have been." Of
course, once one enters the realm of the plausible, the temptation is
great to change all sorts of things that might make for a more entertaining (more commercially successful?) production. One familiar result is the "modernizing" of characterizations and relationships so that
contemporary audiences will find it easier to identify with the historical
characters.

Every good film—like every good book—is going to involve "the
creative treatment of reality." The scale of judgment should weigh
the extent to which that creative representation of the past can be
supported by the evidence. In a documentary film this should extend
to the way the filmmaker treats the evidence of the film materials
themselves as well as the traditional body of evidence regarding the
subject. If a compilation film on World War II cuts from newsreel

footage to Hollywood representations of battle, the viewer should be informed.[3] In his provocative review of "Vietnam: A Television History," Richard Raack wondered whether the filmmakers were sensitive enough to the bias inherent in footage from different sources. Might viewers have been more circumspect in viewing footage recorded inside North Vietnam (footage which had not been widely seen in America before) if the producers had been more rigorous about indicating on the screen that the footage had been shot by Polish television crews presumably influenced by their politics in the choices of subjects to photograph and the ways to photograph them? Every editing decision will, by definition, involve some manipulation of the actuality material; the question should be whether that manipulation distorts the evidence or helps to clarify its meaning in support of reasoned historical conclusions. In a dramatized film some degree of reading between the lines is necessary to formulate a story and to develop characterizations. A film which does this well is one which "presumes" as little as possible. It does not rely on indirect evidence as a rationale for inventing characters and situations which serve primarily to divert audiences rather than to fill out the historical context.

As historians have opened themselves to new approaches to narration and interpretation, the opportunities offered by the moving image media have become more important to them. The recent work of Hayden White and others stimulated by movements in literary analysis and linguistics has led many historical scholars to think more pointedly about what it means to try to create a verbal model of a past world.[4] In this context, the process of producing a filmic model of the past might not be so different. On certain levels, films may indeed help historians understand aspects of the past which otherwise might not occur to them. Some such ideas might involve information which the historian already knows but which the film helps bring together, providing something of the experience of a past time in a way words on a page cannot. One example cited by Pierre Sorlin in this chapter is Peter Watkins's *Battle of Culloden* which might help scholars (or students) get some clearer approximation of what it must have been like to fight in a face-to-face eighteenth-century battle. Such an experience is not documentary analysis per se, the film can not in any way replace the primary historical sources on the event, but as a secondary source it can inform those primary sources by helping the scholar to study them more meaningfully.

Those who have become involved in the production process experience this more intimately. Historian Natalie Zemon Davis prefers the history of *The Return of Martin Guerre*[5] as told in her book to the portrayal of the same events in the film (for which she served as historical consultant) because the narrative structure of the book allowed her to examine the events from the perspectives of several of the historical characters. In thinking about questions raised in the filmmaking, however, she developed ideas that might not have otherwise occurred to her about the physical setting for the events, the look of the ordinary people of the village, and the background interplay of secondary characters in the drama.[6]

It should immediately occur to viewers of a dramatized feature film that the historical scene had to be interpreted by someone in order to be represented before the cameras. Viewers' naive expectations that actuality-based documentaries are inherently closer to an unvarnished reality may be based partly on the dominant style of documentary filmmaking which seeks to avoid a "voice of God" narration and lets the story "tell itself", for example, through the expressive memories of participants in the past events who are interviewed on the screen. The presence of a narrator's voice, even a nonauthoritarian one, would certainly remind viewers that somebody is telling this story, and telling it in a certain way. When the makers of historical documentaries decide against a narrator, relying more exclusively on archival images and on the comments of interviewees to tell their story, they seriously limit the voice of the historian. Archival images usually don't speak for themselves, especially when the point being made is at all subtle or complex. Images and interviews offer supporting evidence, but if any uniting thread of thoughtful interpretation is intended, a narrator is usually called for. Such a narrator need not be a disembodied voice from heaven. The producers of *Women of Summer* decided to have the narration read by one of the principals. This is a good compromise but not a perfect one; might viewers be confused in distinguishing what this woman observes on her own versus the narration that has been written for her?[7] Of course the least desirable response to the problems associated with narration would be to rely on it too heavily. If the result is no more than an illustrated lecture, the creative potential of the medium has been sacrificed.

Eyewitness testimony raises other issues as well. Especially after years have passed, patterns of individual memory would certainly have led some to forget (or to remember differently) certain aspects of their experience. Eyewitness commentaries are often moving, and they help to involve an audience in the subject. Moreover, the people who are interviewed for compilation documentaries are often ordinary folk who at one point in their lives either witnessed or were caught up in an event that made history. By recording these reminiscences such film projects are collecting historical evidence that might otherwise be lost and exposing the public to a kind of historical evidence that they would not normally see. But historian Jesse Lemisch, one of the founders of the movement to study history from the bottom up, has problems, especially when filmmakers rely exclusively on first-person testimony as a way to avoid a professorial narration and too academic a tone. Lemisch's own work demonstrates the importance of the first-person testimony of ordinary people and points to the way such sources were ignored by the profession until the 1960s, but he equally stresses that such sources are the beginning not the end of historical analysis. "For all the filmmakers 'antiacademism' their characters take on the authority that we associate with the textbook," Lemisch writes. "There is little sense of the complexity of the past and little confrontation between conflicting views. Interviewer's questions are admiring and credulous. The simple repetition of pieties and platitudes by people who were 'there' is not history."[8]

Historian-filmmakers are in a unique position to assist their colleagues in learning about the medium and teaching their students to be critical viewers. Several have published articles or interviews which describe their experiences in production (or as historical consultants) and offer insight into the ways in which the demands of the medium force certain choices (compromises?) in the ways they present their material.[9] Natalie Zemon Davis, for example, has commented on the importance of a production making explicit the claim that it makes to historical truth.

In *The Return of Martin Guerre* this is accomplished at the beginning of the film, when a voice-over narration indicates that the story to be told is a true one. But what does this mean? To whose point of view is it true? In fact, the source for most of the historical information is an account written by Jean Coras, the chief judge at the trial in which the story culminates, but the film does not tell its viewers that the story is true to his recollection rather than someone elses. The filmmakers try to take the viewer back into the sixteenth century, and they do so quite successfully, but in moving an audience to experience the "feel" of an historical period they sacrifice the opportunity to have them "think" historically.

Davis's voice-over commentary in the video compilation and the production-related documents published in the study guide indicate the care that went into the detailed setting of scenes and uses of music and language for this film. In subtle and very effective ways elements of the mise-en-scène contribute to the historical interpretation. For example, the formal negotiation and signing of a marriage contract is intercut with images of a woman kneading bread dough and another plucking a chicken—reinforcing the idea that the legal arrangements of marriage were central to the everyday life of the rural peasant community. The narrative structure chosen for the film, however, ruled out a detailed treatment of some of the historical issues which Davis considered most important in her book—central among them the characterization of Bertrande DeRols.

The central character in the story, Bertrande is abandoned by her husband Martin for eight years, only to have him return (or is it an imposter who looks like him and has learned the details of his life?). In order to appeal to a broader audience, the film was structured as *mystery* rather than *history*, with the audience kept in suspense throughout the film about whether or not the returned Martin was or was not an imposter. An alternative structure might have privileged viewers differently from the outset and had the suspense center on whether imposter and wife would be able to pull off their hoax. Such an approach would have allowed a much fuller dramatic treatment of the life experience of a sixteenth-century peasant woman. Yet another option might have been a *Rashomon* type of structure in which the story was told from several different points of view.[10]

The recent efforts of serious historical filmmakers are noteworthy because until the last ten years or so it was hard to find any commercially produced film which considered accurate portrayals of historical personalities or events as anywhere near as important as audience appeal.[11] Over the previous seven decades of commercial film production it was far more typical for "historical films" to play fast and loose with matters of historical fact and interpretation. As Pierre Sorlin explains below, studying even the distorting ways in which a film interprets events can make for interesting scholarship, but professional historians certainly might have wished for a less cavalier and more accurate recounting of history. It is useful to consider some of these stories of what might be called the Hollywood "history mill" as counterparts to more responsible efforts of today.

In the Hollywood studios (as elsewhere in the world of commercial film production), when filmmakers, even the more responsible ones, conducted what the industry termed "research," they meant something very different from what a scholar does. Often careful attention went into the verification and duplication of sets, costumes, and props. Less often was care given to the nuances of language and expression that the actors would use. At the same time, however, the fabric of issues and events was typically torn to shreds in the interest of the drama or for more pragmatic commercial or political reasons. The interpretation posed in Warner Brothers' *They Died With Their Boots On* (1940), for example, was driven in part by the studio's perception of current events and in part by their desire to keep production costs low. The clearest evidence comes in a studio memo prepared to influence officials in Washington who were being asked to supply assistance to the project such as the use of federal lands and cavalry horses. In the memo screenwriter Aeneas MacKenzie offers a patriotic reason why (although the archival record shows that they had access to convincing scholarship to the contrary) the studio persisted in presenting General George Armstrong Custer as a hero.

> In preparing this scenario on the life of General George Armstrong Custer, all possible consideration was given to the construction of a story which would have the best effect upon public morale in these present days of national crisis.
>
> The theme chosen was the Officer and the Regiment. Through the life of the hero we have endeavored to show the real meaning of these two words: What an officer is, what his standards and obligations are; what a regiment is, and why it is something more than six hundred trained men. I need not mention that this picture will be released at the moment when thousands of youths are being trained for commissions, and when hundreds of new and traditionless units are being formed. If we can inspire these to some appreciation of a great officer and a great

regiment in their own Service, we shall have accomplished our mission. . . . [12]

The memo goes on to explain that in the fulfillment of that mission "certain liberties have been taken with history." The writer explained that, aside from inventing a "dying declaration" for Custer to make on the battlefield, they had always retained "the 'true tone' of history." He concluded that "Every incident in the action is a manipulation of some accurate historical fact or some definite personal characteristic."—language that makes the scholar cringe, but is in fact a rather accurate description of what every filmmaker does.

As with Hollywood movies, there is a variation in historical dramas produced for television from the meretorious to the meretricious. Again, as noted above, the worst of them are those which pander to perceived audience tastes with little if any regard for historical reality. Before the networks would accept a docudrama on the life of George Washington, an additional "love interest" had to be introduced to the story. Sultry "Charley's Angels" veteran Jaclyn Smith was enlisted to play a fabricated love interest to Barry Bostwick's Washington, while a wholesome Patty Duke (as Martha) stood loyally in the background. Interviewed for *TV Guide* at the time the sequel on Washington's presidential years was aired in 1986, Bostwick admitted to having done at least some of the research for his characterization with the help of a psychic who put him in touch with the spirit of George Washington. "The only real note he had for me was that I should work on my anger," Bostwick recalled of his conversation with the first president.[13] When the screenwriter Edward Anhalt was asked about the arbitrary creation of episodes that never happened for his docudrama on "Peter the Great," he replied that it was better to learn history wrong than not at all, and that no reference was made to Peter's epilepsy because "epilepsy is unpleasant." Anhalt summed up the problem as he saw it with the statement that "History is the enemy of art."[14] But need it be so? Horror stories like these notwithstanding, network producers are more aware of the issues than they may have been in the past.[15]

The British origins of televised Docudrama offer an interesting contrast. The English prefer to reverse the order of the terms calling their programs "drama documentaries." Colin MacCabe traces the origins back to the early documentary film movement and the idea of making information on important social issues more accessible to a broader public. British television in the 1950s and early 1960s had some similar programming, but the more recent drama documentary genre can be dated more specifically to the mid-1960s and an effort to develop a form that would allow the "recovery of lost histories" of the lives of ordinary (especially working class) people and "the exposure of social justice, with 'progressive realism.'" The main thing that distinguishes the British *dramadoc* from the American *docudrama* is that the British are first and foremost trying to report a story about the lives of ordinary people. They dramatize the story but retain much of the form and style and most of the journalistic purpose of documentary film. As British producer Leslie Woodhead characterizes it:

> Our priorities, disciplines, sources and basic motivations are journalistic, and where there is a clash with dramatic values, journalism wins. We make bad plays—not a slogan, just a declaration of priorities.[16]

Many commercially produced docudramas in America turn out to be bad plays as well, but along the way they are more likely than the British to have also sacrificed journalistic integrity and historical credibility.[17]

There are important exceptions. While it is now clear that the ABC series "Roots" (1976), based upon Alex Haley's best-selling book, was flawed by that author's errors in research and his edenic scenes of life in Africa, the basic information and the historical representation of slavery were sound. Details of the story and individual characterizations had to be fabricated, but the historical issues were addressed responsibly.[18] Similarly, German historian Wilhelm VanKampen has noted that some viewers were so willing to discount the veracity of the docudrama "Holocaust" when it was screened on German television, because they were seeking any device to help them avoid coming to grips with the reality that the series portrayed. Fictional characters were invented and the time and place of certain events were altered in parts of the series to support the dramatic flow. As VanKampen pointed out in his study guide for the series (Dusseldorf, 1978), however, every event and every form of inhumanity depicted in the film did in fact take place in Nazi-controlled Europe. The value of docudrama series such as "Roots" and "Holocaust" should be unmistakable to historians who may have struggled their entire careers to interest a larger audience than that which sits down in their classrooms. In VanKampen's words the German screening of *Holocaust* became a "media-event," as people all over the country were engaged on a subject which many of them had tried to suppress in their minds for forty years. Interestingly, one of the few changes made in the series as it aired in Germany helped to stir this reassessment. Unlike the version shown to American audiences in which Rudy, the free-thinking young Jewish survivor, is seen leaving to seek his future in Palestine, the German series ended with the principal characters still in Germany trying to sort out their lives in the wake of nazism.[19] If we accept that no representation of history can be perfect, we should also accept that imperfect representations can still help us to understand the past and our perceptions of it.

Over the last decade a handful of professional historians have been intimately involved in the production of a series of historical docudramas for public television in America. The results of these efforts prove that when, rather than merely serving as consultants, historians are able to play a more central role in making production decisions, they can make a real difference. But to be successful they must realize that producing a film or a television show is a vastly different enterprise from writing a book. They must be willing to work with the process and choose carefully where they will compromise and where they will stand firm. Historian-filmmaker Daniel Walkowitz learned this lesson well in the production of his "Molders of Troy," first broadcast over PBS in 1979 and excerpted in the video compilation. Walkowitz explains that, as a scholar, he comes to a film project from a very different angle than the commercial producer. "I am less concerned with the authenticity of the details in a scene—for example, whether the shoes are authentic—than with the pattern of a set of social relationships that exists in a period of time. Historians don't simply describe a moment in time. We usually write because there is a problem in the past that we want to understand and we want to find a strategy for getting people to look at it."[20]

At least some similarity exists, then, in what historical filmmakers and professional historians do. They both try to recreate (in their minds, then on printed pages or on celluloid) a sense of what the past was like. A scholar might want to construct in his mind a believable if partly fictional narrative describing how events might have happened. But in contrast to the commercial producer, the scholar (and the scholar-filmmaker) considers such a narrative description the starting point for analysis, not the finished product. The observations of historian-filmmakers should make us more sensitive to the creative goals of producers—what is it that they would like the viewer to take away from their film?[21]

One additional concern about the production of historical films and docudramas is that their influence is long-lasting. We noted above that no film should be expected to provide the last word on any subject. Unlike a historical monograph, however, a film does tend to have a more permanent presence, at least in the public mind. This longevity is accentuated, of course, when 16mm prints or videocassettes of the film go on the market for classroom use. While a controversial interpretation in print can be easily answered with another article or monograph, once a subject has been treated by a significant film it becomes difficult for a time to justify another movie on the same subject. Meanwhile, the viewing public knows only one point of view. While some historical subjects, such as the Kennedy family, may justify the creative efforts of several filmmakers within the same year or two, others may attract treatment only once in a generation. The cost is simply preemptive.

If some scholars are still reluctant to study films for a clearer understanding of the past they portray, there is near common agreement on the value of such productions for an understanding of a culture's historical mentality. The filmic representation of the past, like most written history, is influenced by contemporary issues and events. Thus *Little Big Man* (1970) was in large part a film about Vietnam and "Roots" was a powerful statement about race relations in the mid-seventies.[22] Historical compilation films such as *The Great Sitdown* (1976) and *With Babies and Banners* (1978), although very different in the ways in which they treated the same events and utilized some of the same images and interview subjects, were both influenced by 1970s concerns about women and labor.[23] One effective technique for studying both historical consciousness and the visual representation of history is to analyze comparatively two films such as those above. Alternatively, a close analysis of the Siege of Leningrad as portrayed in three documentaries (Frank Capra's *Battle of Russia* from the "Why We Fight" series (1944); the British-produced *World at War* series (1973), and the combined Russian/American-produced series *The Unknown War* (1982) offers three distinctly different points of view and a very different usage of some of the very same archival footage. Pierre Sorlin's essay includes an interesting analysis of fascism in Italian films showing the complex associations between screen images and cultural perceptions—and the ways in which each evolved over time.

Patricia-Ann Lee's essay in this chapter concentrates on the classroom analysis of film as interpreter of history, showing how much more fruitful critical viewing can be when it transcends looking for the historical "mistakes."

SUMMARY

In summary, in evaluating a historical film, as in analysing it with students, we should endeavor—to whatever extent possible—to apply the same general standards that we would to either a traditional work of scholarship (for a documentary) or a serious historical novel (for a dramatic film). That judgment should involve the three basic sets of questions raised in the general introduction: questions of content, production, and reception.

Content

Does a close analysis of the content of the film reveal a thoughtful and coherent interpretation of the historical issues and events being portrayed? How does the visual style and narrative structure of the film color its point of view? Can that interpretation be supported by the body of scholarly evidence available? For a dramatized film, to what extent were the script and the characters based upon direct historical evidence and to what extent were they fictionalized? Are the fictionalizations, characterizations, and relationships developed (for either actual or fictional characters) plausible in terms of the historical period, or have they been "modernized" so that contemporary audiences would find it easier to relate to the story? For a documentary film, how does it use its visual evidence? Is the theme of the film presented primarily through the information contained in the images themselves, or do the images serve more often as illustrative backdrop to a dominant voice-over commentary or narration? Are film clips

from other times and places, perhaps even from theatrical films, intercut with actuality footage in a way that the viewer might mistake
them for contemporary actuality? Does the filmmakers' research effort
seem to have been primarily in film sources, or are the producers/
writers well informed about the broader body of evidence and interpretation on the subject? If the on-screen comments of participants
are used, how are they used? Is it made clear that, interesting as it
may be, each memory represents only one perspective, or are memories allowed to stand as the uniting interpretative theme? Does the
film in any explicit way draw attention to the fact that as a whole it
represents one (or at best several) point(s) of view, and that there
might be equally acceptable alternative interpretations?

Production

What can be found out about the circumstances of the film's production and how those circumstances may have influenced production
decisions? For example, was the film funded in whole or in part by
some organization or agency which might have an interest in prof-
fering one or another interpretation? Do the filmmakers bring to the
project a preconceived ideological point of view? If so, is this bias
stated explicitly in the film or is there an effort to hide it or to feign
objectivity? If there were historical consultants involved, what role did
they play? Were they intimately involved throughout the process, or
were they called in at one point or another simply to lend their imprimatur to the product? Were they satisfied with the results? What
were the objectives of the film production? Was it purely a commercial
enterprise in which people might have been less hesitant to sacrifice
historical veracity for audience appeal? Did the filmmaker have any
previous experience in historical filmmaking by which you might begin to gauge his sensitivity or his care for detail? Ultimately one might
ask, how might the goals and purposes of this film compare with the
objectives of traditional scholarship?

Reception

How has the film been received? What type of distribution did it
have, and how did audiences respond to the film? Specifically, how
did specialists in the historical subject area evaluate the films portrayal?[24] A comprehensive analysis of the film as an indicator of the
historical mentality of its intended audience should involve a study
of what the film does not say; that is, the points of information or
interpretation that were so taken for granted by the filmmaker that
they did not have to be fully developed in the narrative or characterizations. Were there different versions of the film produced at different times for different audiences, as with the ending of "Holocaust,"
for example, and how might these changes have altered responses?
If the film is not a recent production, how may have audience reactions

to it changed over time? How might these various responses help us to better understand and appreciate the meaning of the film?

NOTES

1. Rudolf Arnheim, *Film As Art* (Berkeley: University of California Press, 1957).
2. Nearly two decades ago the editors of *Cahiers du Cinema*, the very respected French journal of film criticism, dissected "John Ford's *Young Mr. Lincoln*" in a detailed structural analysis that is still instructive. The piece is reprinted in English in *Screen*, Vol. 13, no. 3 (1972), and in Gerald Mast and Marshall; 1 Cohen, editors, *Film Theory and Criticism: Introductory Readings* (second edition) (New York, 1979).
3. Television documentaries of the 1950s and 1960s such as *The Twisted Cross* and *Nightmare in Red* are notorious examples which are used in history classrooms to this day.
4. For the most accessible introduction to these ideas see Hayden White's "The Burden of History" in his collection of essays entitled *Tropics of Discourse* (Baltimore, 1978), and David Lowentahl's *The Past Is A Foreign Country* (Cambridge and New York, 1985).
5. See selection from *The Return of Martin Guerre* in the video compilation.
6. See Natalie Zemon Davis's book, *The Return of Martin Guerre* (Cambridge, MA, 1983) and her "Interview" in *Film & History*. Vol. XIII, no. 3 (September, 1983) pp. 49–65. (reprinted in the study guide to the video compilation); and Benson, Edward. "The Look of the Past: Le retour de Martin Guerre." *Radical History*. 10th Anniversary Issue (1984). pp. 125–135.
7. For more on the role of narration in historical documentaries see Jeffrey Youdelman, "Narration, Invention & History: A Documentary Dilemma," *Cineaste*, Vol. XII, no. 2 (1982) pp 8–15; and Colin McArthur's chapter on "The Narrator as the Guarantor of Truth," in his *Television and History*, (London, 1978).
8. Jesse Lemisch, "I Dreamed I Saw MTV Last Night," *The Nation*, October 18, 1986, p. 375.
9. See for example, Daniel J. Walkowitz, "Visual Histroy: the Craft of the Historian-Filmmaker," *The Public Historian*, Vol. 7, no. 1 (Winter, 1985), pp. 53–64 (reprinted in study guide to video compilation); Robert Toplin, "The Making of *Denmark Vesey's Rebellion*," *Film & History* Vol. XIII, no. 3 (September, 1982), pp. 49–56.
10. See Natalie Zemon Davis, "Any Resemblance to Persons Living or Dead: Film and the Challenge of Authenticity." *The Yale Review*. Summer, 1987. pp. 457–482.
11. See Robert Rosenstone's observations as historical consultant on the production of *Reds* in, *Organization of American Historians Newsletter*, July, 1981.
12. Interoffice memo, Aeneas MacKenzie to Hal Wallis, May 13, 1941; *They Died With Their Boots On* production files, Warner Brothers Collection, University of Southern California.
13. "George Washington: How Barry Bostwick Fought to Show His Human Side," *TV Guide*, Vol. 34, no. 38 (September 20, 1986), p. 4.
14. Quoted in a review of *Peter the Great*, *Film & History*, Vol. XVI, no. 1 (Feb, 1986) pp. 17–19.

15. See relevant pages from *CBS News Standards* reprinted in the study guide to the video compilation.

16. Quoted in John Caugie, "Progressive Television and Documentary Drama," *Screen*, Vol. 21, no. 3, 1980.

17. For a valuable discussion on these issues centering on the British drama-documentary series "Days of Hope," see Tony Bennett, Susan Boyd-Bowman, Colin Mercer, and Janet Woollacott, editors, *Popular Television and Film* (London, 1981), pp. 285–352.

18. See Leslie Ellen Fishbein, "Roots: Document or Docudrama," in John E. O'Connor, ed. *American History/American Television: Interpreting the Video Past* (New York, Frederick Ungar, 1983).

19. See VanKampen, *Study Guide to Holocaust*

20. Barbara Abrash and Janet Sternberg, eds, *Historians and Filmmakers: Toward Collaboration*, (New York, Institute for Research in History, 1983), p. 13.

21. As an example, the study guide to the video compilation contains an excerpt from the grant proposal Walkowitz wrote to win funding for "Molders of Troy" which outlines the specific objectives the project was aiming to accomplish.

22. Colin McArthur's sixty page monograph, *Television and History*, published in London by the British Film Institute in 1978, is full of interesting observations based on the British experience, but it never successfully gets beyond the notion that dominant bourgeois ideology shapes everything that is broadcast. Pierre Sorlin's *The Film in History: Restaging the Past* (Oxford, 1980) is much broader and based more in a concern for historical issues.

23. See Daniel J. Leab, "Writing History With Film: Two Views of the 1937 Strike Against General Motors by the UAW," *Labor History*, Vol. 21, No. 1, Winter 1979–80.

24. Note that there are now a number of historical journals which regularly publish reviews of films and television programs written by professional historians.

Pierre Sorlin teaches both video and history at the University of Saint-Denis, Paris. He is the author of ten books on the social history of Europe and on the cinema, including: Sociologie du Cineme, Eisenstein's October, *and* The Film in History. *He is a director of documentaries and historical films, the most recent of which deals with the Jews and the French Revolution and has been made for the celebration of the Bicentenary. Sorlin is currently working on a book on the European cinema in the second half of the century.*

HISTORICAL FILMS AS TOOLS FOR HISTORIANS

Pierre Sorlin

Film-specialists have difficulty giving a clear-cut definition of what is a genre but they would immediately discern a western from a musical, a detective-story from a comedy: genres conform to models which make it easy to tell them apart. History films do not constitute a genre. The more dramas or musicals we see, the more we become able to designate similarities between them and to define the lineaments of genre-regularities. Historical movies have nothing in common but their reference to History. The "rules" of genre films are internal; they are simply the patterns whose recurrence prompts the viewers to think: "There is a leading strand throughout these movies, therefore they are a genre." History is external to historical films: it is a concern for the past of human societies which can be traced back up to the origins of writing and which is expressed via the media, including films and TV programs.[1]

Historians have been generally reluctant to look at historical movies.[2] It is often argued that filmmakers, wanting to catch as large an audience as possible, have recourse to the most trite vision of history. This would be absolutely true if we included *The Adventures of Robin Hood* or *Ivanhoe*, films which convey an idea to the Saxon/Norman opposition which is entirely borrowed from Walter Scott and has little to do with the accounts of the actual situation that can be found in the works of English medievalist scholars. But we exclude from this study those pictures which are basically costume comedies or dramas and which only use the past as a colorful background— these pictures that confront us, as Graham Greene says, with "the same complete lack of a period sense and a childlike eye for details".[3] Here, in contrast, the expression "historical film" will be restricted to movies which purposefully aim at depicting, as accurately as possible, a past period. Deciding whether the evocation of another time in a given picture is a mere pretext or one of the objects of the shooting is, more often than not, a question of common sense. However, I think that we can have recourse to more precise tokens; historical films often do provide their viewers with signs (captions, voice over, reproduction of documents, re-enactment of well known scenes) which testify that the pictures are meant to reproduce "what really happened." Who cares for these signs? This raises another aspect of historical movies: their historical value is only warranted for people who share the same concerns and are able to interpret the same clues—in other words for the members of a cultural community. We shall see that important consequences derive from this specificity of historical re-enactments.

Teachers have known for long that audiovisual productions will help them to challenge the influence of the domestic consumption of TV programs; films and videotapes renew a fading interest for the past, make the pupils realize that history is also an insight into the life of other, different men, and trigger discussions. Many experiments have been carried out in this field and we are supplied with a large series of papers telling us to what extent the use of such and such film resulted in a fruitful debate with secondary-school pupils.[4] Summarizing all these texts might be of a real interest for didacticians but would not give us any new basis for a deepening of our reflection on film and history. Therefore I would rather take another way and, in a provocative manner, ask a different question: can research-workers win a better understanding of "their" period by looking at the screen? Is a specialist of modern England bound to see *Winstanley* or *Culloden* and mention these pictures among his sources? Partial answers have already been given to that query and we may cluster them under three headings:

1. Criticism: can historians grasp anything serious from history films?
2. Selective use: what sorts of information dealing with factual aspects of the past, or with mentalities, are to be found on the screen?
3. Indirect use: How can historical pictures tell us more about the context in which they were produced and viewed thus helping us to understand how societies conceive their past, and therefore their present?

I shall begin with a critical examination of these three points. Then, after considering an homogeneous series of history films, I shall try to raise some fresh questions.

1. CRITICISM

"Restaged events inevitably lack ultimate historical verisimilitude"[5] There is a long tradition of skepticism regarding the screening of the

past among historians. Some of them think that the written sources
are more reliable than the pictures;[6] others assume that they have to
ponder over facts, such as those that are recorded in contemporary
documents, not over artifacts[7] and a few specialists delight in detecting
mistakes in the representation of the past.[8] I would not find it exciting
to expand at length either on the uncertainties of many written pieces
of evidence or on the "artificial" character of books and the mistakes
made by serious historians.

It is also said, and this is more relevant, that history films, however
carefully made they are, misinterpret the past.[9] Two case studies will
exemplify this. Given the size of his armor or clothes the specialists
say that king Louis XIV was about five feet, five inches high. Accordingly Rossellini gave the part of the king in his *Rise to Power of
Louis XIV* (France, 1966) to a small actor. But recent research has
proved that the men were not very tall in the Seventeenth Century
and that Louis XIV was not below the standard. Therefore, Rossellini
distorts the events when he shows us his character as a small king
obliged to compel recognition from tall nobles and political advisers.
Reds (U.S.A., 1981) presents us with some moments of John Reed's
life; while participating in the Russian Revolution of 1917, the American journalist foresees the shift from democracy to dictatorship of a
small group of politicians; when he goes to Baku, for the Congress
of Eastern People, he witnesses the first reactions of some Asiatic
nationalists against the Russian hegemony. Now, if we scrutinize
Reed's writings of that period we see no hint that he was aware of
what was to happen during the following decade; we realize also that
Reed paid great attention to class oppositions which are of little importance in the picture.[10] These two movies, while striving for ex-
actness, render imperfectly the sense of events.

Impressive though they look, these critics are not decisive. Historians have scribbled thousands of pages to explain the difficulties of
Louis XIV who, having ascended the throne when he was only five,
had to fight hard to make the French see him as "the Great King".
Rossellini's weakness is not only his, it is characteristic of psychological
history—that sort of history which pretends to interpret "individual
motivations". As for the opinions expressed on the future of the Soviet
Revolution, we all know that historians have been arguing for long
about the "inevitability" of the dictatorship of the Communist Party,
given the problems that the Bolsheviks had to face from 1917 onwards. As soon as they are not satisfied with merely lining up "facts",
historians necessarily "explain" and, by doing so, inevitably lay themselves open to criticism.

A much more interesting discussion upon the documentary value
of historical films has been opened by Rhys Isaac, in his review[11] of
The Return of Martin Guerre (France, 1981). Far from lingering on
details, Isaac raises the question of the nature of history screening.
His attacks are all the more spectacular in that he is himself interested
in movies and in that his reservations are built upon a comparison

between the picture and the book of Natalie Zemon Davis[12] who uses the same sources as the cinematographers and who was even involved in the shooting of the film.

In sixteenth century France, young Martin Guerre marries Bertrande de Rols; both of them live in a small village in the South West and are from well-off families. Martin turns out to be impotent; being constantly mocked by his intimates, he leaves the village; when he comes back after seven years everybody welcomes him and he would lead a quiet life with Bertrande were it not for a financial contest with his step-father. Little by little, the latter convinces the villagers that Martin is an impostor, a veteran who gives himself out to be Bertrandeu's husband. Martin is subjected to a court trial; the return of the real Martin Guerre confounds the impostor who is sentenced to death. This well-known case is fascinating for what it teaches regarding social, familial, economic and religious life and was worth being screened. For obvious reasons—a good cast is always requested to attract a large audience—the parts of Martin and Bertrande were given to famous actors who played according to their already constituted persona rather than according to the state of mind of sixteenth century peasants. "It is in the interpretation of character and motivation" Isaac argues, "that the book moves from complementing the film to offering a challenging alternative . . . The most intense interest focuses on the clear divergence of the film's and the book's interpretation of the wife, Bertrande. It is particularly illuminating to go from the beautiful, sadly smiling but enigmatic lover, as played by Nathalie Baye, to the less romantic but ultimately more fully interpreted village wife as explained by Natalie Davis."

Isaac's objections can be expanded and made more systematic:

1. The film, because it involves living people, presents us more with individual destinies than with generalities on social life. Insofar as we get personally involved in the drama of Martin Guerre we tend to neglect what can be learnt regarding the traditions of early modern France.
2. A film must tell a good story; the film-makers must introduce the characters, cause the spectators to expect something, reach a climax and quickly solve the case. We are lucky enough to have at our disposal good documentation[13] on the preparation and shooting of a Twentieth Century Fox historical film, *Wilson* (U.S.A., 1944). We can see that Zanuck, the producer, and his screenwriter were constantly anxious to find the best possible beginning and end and to introduce the most appropriate scenes. In a letter of October 1943, Zanuck mentions various scenes "eliminated because they were on the narrative and documentary side and lacked effective dramatization . . . We have a documentary story, yet it is told in completely dramatic terms".[14] Historical faithfulness is clearly second to the necessity of the box-office.

3. And there are few chances for a film to be a success without a good cast. Unfortunately famous actors tend to be more themselves than the people they represent. Who is the main character of *Young Mr. Lincoln* (U.S.A., 1939), Abraham Lincoln or Henry Fonda?[15] Zanuck, who wanted to avoid this bias, gave the part of Wilson to a little known stage actor and there is general agreement that the lack of stars contributed to the failure of the film. Consequently there is a big risk of confusing historical figures with modern actors.

Before debating these points we must remind ourselves of two things. First, we are speaking of historians who have previous knowledge of the questions dealt with in the pictures. Second, we are interested in both history and cinema. Not only are we discussing the nature of movies, but the nature of history as well.

Many serious historical books, far from indulging in generalities emphasize particular cases and thereby account better for the variety of social life. In his wonderful *Virginia*[16] Rhys Isaac constantly refers to diaries, letters, memoirs which portray individuals; he himself uses the term, "scenarios" for these short stories which look like flashes on the daily life of Virginians. Historians have to bear in mind that overall statements upon past societies are based upon collections of separate cases. Our forefathers had pleasures and sorrows, suffered from cold, had words, they were living beings and the cinema is consonant with some new trends of historical research when it confronts us with these sides of the past.

The argument regarding narration would be more embarrassing if history itself was not a narration. Interesting things have been recently written in that topic, namely Hayden White's *Metahistory*.[17] White is mainly concerned with a well defined type of historiography the historical work which endeavors at rendering the events "real" by giving them the form of a story; he then puts the emphasis upon the social surroundings which made it possible to organize the historical discourse as a well ordered, and finally moralizing discourse. Even if we do not agree with some of his conclusions we cannot but agree with him that history has to be written; that it is not understandable unless it uses narrative structures and rhetorical devices; that literary processes underlie historical books. A historical study always concentrates upon a period, in other words a moment of time with its beginning, its end. Even if we are given a description of the life and concerns of the contemporaries there is an organization, a setting of the material. The historian narrates and, whenever he deals with an evolution (war, crisis, biography) he is bound to fall upon some sort of climax (turning point of the war, top of the crisis . . .). Instead of opposing their work to narrations historians could get an interesting insight into their own practice if they pondered upon White's main idea that narration, far from being a casual form of writing, is a basic form of contemporary apprehension and description of the outer world.

Eventually, the most relevant argument against the screening of history is the problem of the actors. In his stimulating *Visions of Yesterday*[18] Richards had attempted to answer it in terms which are not necessarily convincing but which deserve consideration. The majority of famous men are faceless; their names have been transmitted throughout the ages but their features remain unknown. Richards takes as an example the builders of the British Empire.[19] We may as well look at the American war for independence, except for the eye of the portrait painter, the actual face of Paul Revere and of the other heroes of Lexington are hidden forever so there is then no harm in clothing them "in the flesh and features" of some players; Paul Revere, as he is figured in Griffith's *America* (1924) is, after all, a possible, credible portrait of an American patriot. The case is of course different with celebrities; we have a great many images of Lincoln. According to Richards it must be said to the credit of films that they endow with life what was previously motionless: "Henry Fonda, looking at times uncannily like portraits of Abraham Lincoln, is superb. He brings Lincoln to life with his loping walk, his shy smile, his social gaucheness and his folksy humor".[20] I confess I find the second part of the argument a bit far-fetched; drawings and photographs document the political period of Lincoln's life and we have little evidence on the previous years. In a few shots, which are mainly intended to link sequences, Fonda conforms to Lincoln's admitted look but, most of the time, especially in important scenes, such as the relationship with the inhabitants of the township or the trial, he plays Henry Fonda. In accordance with Rhys Isaac I believe that the star-system is the sore spot of filmed history. It is not at random that only second rank actors were cast for a part in most of the pictures we are going to examine in the following section.

2. SELECTIVE USE

"The physical *reach* of film—temporal as well as spatial—enables it to reproduce visual information which would otherwise remain inaccessible".[21]

It is generally admitted that one of the major differences between the historical and physical sciences is that the former lack any possibility of experimentation; the events and the conditions in which they happened have vanished for ever, and we are only provided with remains of the past. We must not forget that experiments, in the exact sciences, are often carried out in artificial conditions which have little to do with the actual processes of physical transformations. Would it be possible to artificially recreate the surroundings in which people lived in Ancient Rome or in seventeenth century England? Theoretically it would, at least to a certain extent, but nobody could afford it, except perhaps with the fantastic budgets conceded to filmmakers. American and European archaeologists of the nineteenth century used to build clay models of Babylonian or Greek temples and to paint them in order to recreate a more accurate version of the ancient monuments than the one given by the white, ruined stones of the archaeological sites. The reconstructions made at the same time by cinematographers (*Intolerance* and many others) were not necessarily less faithful than the archaeologists' ones and they were crowded which brought them closer to the "reality" of ancient life.

Nowadays, historians seem less interested in gigantic reconstructions. For their part, filmmakers are more keen on respecting exact locations, clothes, circumstances. When seeing pictures such as *Culloden* (U.K., 1965), *Camisards* (France, 1970), *Winstanley* (U.K., 1975), *Gandhi* (India, 1982), one comes to the idea that historians have something to learn from the cinema.

Historians are aware of the fact that earth has its own history which is slower than man's or societies'. No serious book ignores the description of the natural surroundings in which past communities used to live. Well-informed though they are of the geographical, ecological particularities of the periods that they study, medievalists or specialists of modern Europe have difficulty in making a coherent whole with the details they have collected. In this respect, *Winstanley* or *Camisards* are likely to give them a precise notion of pre-industrial landscapes— a notion which does not contradict but which complements the vision inferred from written texts.

The first picture tells us the story of a former old-clothes man, Gerard Winstanley who, in April 1619, set up, with a small crew of ex-servicemen, a community of self-sufficient, non-violent and egalitarian peasants in a remote district of Surrey. The second deals with the countrymen and tradesmen of Cevennes who, being converted to Calvinism, were considered outlaws in early eighteenth century France, had to hide themselves in caves and were sometimes obliged to fight against the royal army. There is of course a story in both movies, mainly in the former, to engage and sustain the attention of the spectators throughout the projection; Winstanley and his "diggers" are prosecuted by the priest and inhabitants of the nearest township, and are finally obliged to give up. The Camisards try to obtain help from the peasants who are secretly Protestant and also to identify those who are ready to betray them. There is, towards the end, a battle between the soldiers and the outlaws; shortly after the latter are forced to disperse. The plots are based upon a close examination of contemporary documents but, however reliable they are, they are not the most interesting aspects of the films.

What most strikes the historian is the reconstruction of the landscape. Men are dominated by nature. The signs of human control over the surroundings are reduced to very little: small houses, narrow fields, mean cattle, a barren, hard soil, huge forests, no roads, a closed, limited horizon. The pictures, especially *Winstanley*, succeed in giving a fresh, unexpected view of the hardness of the life. The cinematographers have carefully chosen isolated, restricted areas, and have filmed them from diverse angles to create an illusive setting. But one of the specificities of the film is that it is uniquely equipped to play with space and to give an impression of immensity only by combining pictures on the limited surface of the screen. The characters in our movies are often taken in long shot which make them look very weak, defenseless in front of a hostile geography. While watching these films, the historian has to remind himself that the "biotype" of the seventeenth century man was different from ours; he is enabled to observe, nearly to experience another feeling of space: the characters constantly move, they have to go and fetch somewhere else everything they need, but they travel in a very narrow circle, they daily cross the same woods, go up the same lanes.

The specialist can also learn a lot about the endeavor of preindustrial men to conquer the land; elementary materials, wood and stones are used to build shelters, plates and even drinking vessels are made in wood. Many sources, particularly drawings, document the tools or implements of ancient times and portray the way peasants used to plough and harvest. These pictures are unfortunately motionless, they give more a synthesis, an abstract of the workers' attitudes than a clear feeling of the duration and difficulty of agricultural labor. Thanks to the films, we grasp a notion of the physical hardness of that backbreaking toil. Again, we are faced with abstractions. We do not see the real work, we look at players acting in front of movie-cameras. However, we are introduced to another, fundamental aspect of preindustrial life, with a different sense of time. After having watched the harvest scene in *Camisards* or the slow, endless motion of the countryman whetting his sickle in *Winstanley*, one would like to contrive a new way of writing, which would give the reader an understanding of the rhythm of days specific to the pre-industrial people. It might be argued as well that only cinema is able to evoke an experience of time so alien to ours.

War is still war but contemporary wars do not resemble ancient wars. *Culloden*, a reliable picture of the end of the 1745 rebellion and of Prince Charles' failure, will not teach much to the specialist on a purely factual level but the portrayal of a pre-artillery battle adds to the understanding of the situation. Moreover, the film helps the reconsideration of the importance of the event. The result of the encounter between the strictly disciplined English army and the poorly armed, discouraged, undisciplined Scots is easily predictable; therefore the battle appears to be less an event than the final corroboration of a previously achieved transformation.[22]

More importantly, films draw their viewers into the stream of past times' fears, hopes and passions; they enable them to experience a sense of life close to reality. Emotion and sensitivity, which are central to social relationships cannot but briefly and inadequately be expressed on paper, whereas films, by mixing sounds and pictures, by creating a highly emotional rhythm of editing, merge the spectators inside what is happening and get them to participate in the (supposed) feelings of the screened people. *Gandhi* has been rightly criticized for

its over-evaluation of Gandhi's political activities; still, the film is capable of introducing us to the charismatic dimension of the Mahatma
as this might have been experienced by Indians. Brian Shoesmith
comments cleverly upon the scene in which Gandhi goes over the
streets of Calcutta to bring an end to the riots. The episode takes
place during the night, people run in various directions, Gandhi is
nearly crushed by the crowd, we see too many things at the same time,
flashes of light, motion, faces, all shot in half-lit darkness, we are
overwhelmed by cries and shoutings, but we are simultaneously aware
of the fact that Gandhi is the center of the action, that something is
occurring between the Indians and their prophet which is more on
the side of mystical communion than of policy.[23]

While preparing this section of my paper, I was surprised to find
so few works devoted to the historical relevance of historical pictures.
Historians are wary of movies because Robin Hood and his fellows
have disappointed them. They do not realize that films and filmmakers have changed since the 1960s. The cinematographers pay
more and more attention to the adequacy of the documents which
they rely upon. Techniques also have evolved; the pictorial world of
Robin Hood is overlit-and consequently totally artificial—since, in the
1940s, shooting required bright lighting. High-speed film does not
necessitate any specific illumination. *Winstanley* was shot in ambient
light, its images may look a bit dim but they are as reliable as contemporary drawings, with the additional advantage of motion. Film can
open our minds to another, more vivid and human, less literary understanding of the past.[24] However, research workers have almost
unanimously concentrated upon the third approach to filmed history.

3. INDIRECT USE

"Movies offer insight into the psychic state of the time and place in
which they are created".[25]

Many researchers would countersign that sentence and admit that
pictures have much to tell us about mentalities.[26] Arthur Marwick's
Class: Image and Reality[27] argues that films (like novels or other com-
modities of popular culture) generally stick very closely to realities
since they show images that the spectators would never accept if they
were totally at variance with their own experience. Paid for by capitalist companies, made by middle-class people, films are ideologically
orientated and they cannot go too far in distortion if film-makers want
to reach a large audience. "No film-maker can go beyond certain
assumptions accepted within his own country." A fiction has to be
situated in a location, at a given time; the description of characters,
places, circumstances involved in the plot "bring with it indelible cultural imprints from the society" in which the movie was made.[28] There
exists, in any country, a basic knowledge of national history, conveyed
by schools, papers, political programs and speeches, novels, family
talks, which is an important part of the experience common to all the

members of the nation. History functions as folk-lore (or common-lore) which means that when a name, a location, a date are mentioned in a given country, they ring a bell. One could hardly conceive of *Culloden* being made by a Russian crew or *Camisards* being shot in Britain; Bonnie Prince Charlies' last attempt or the war against the Huguenots have been endlessly told to Englishmen or Frenchmen and, when screened, easily win a response from national audiences, whereas foreign spectators would need preliminary explanations which would make the films positively boring.[29]

Historians who study historical cinema care less for facts than for interpretations. They are less likely to dwell on distortions as weaknesses. Rather they see the manner in which movies betray the accepted version of the past as a clue to the beliefs and preconceptions of the time at which they were made. Siegfried Kracauer was a forerunner in this field in the 1940s.[30] His task was to use films to enlighten hidden aspects of German psychology in the 1920s and 30s which might help to explain the final submission to Hitler, and therefore he was not particularly concerned with films about history. Although there have been many critics of his work, Kracauer was the first to attempt a sociological analysis of the cinema, and he did help draw the lines along which historical scholars would argue when they first turned to close analysis of film in the early 1970s. Among the points he seemed to settle was the now commonly accepted idea that history is more often than not a pretext for the screening of contemporary problems. The first question to be asked in the examination of an historical movie is not: "Can we trust it?" but "Why did people choose to conceal their actual preoccupations behind the evocation of that particular period?" A second conclusion to be drawn from Kracauer's work is that history films have often to do with propaganda. Past events are often chosen to contrast with the present situation, they are modified, even travestied, to suggest that solutions to contemporary problems can be found in other times.

Although it may seem unusual to link them in this way, I think that Jeffrey Richards and Colin McArthur can both be considered in their own way as heirs to Kracauer's ideas.[31] I know this sounds odd: Richards was another forerunner in 1973 whereas McArthur arrived at a time when people were used to reading books on history and movies. Richards is resolutely empirical and sticks to the films, whereas McArthur is fiercely theoretical and looks more at the capitalist environment than at the TV screen. Still, both of them are interested in audiovisual products which repeatedly go back to periods of supposed calm and glory. Starting from different premises they find in historical movies a conservative, nostalgic vision of a peaceful society. McArthur speaks of a class structured society in which the cultural institutions (including the film and TV industry) play their part in the reproduction/diffusion of ideology that is to say of the way of life and of the understanding of the relationship between people and their world. The return to the Victorian period is not interpreted by him

as a trite device intended to deceive the viewers but as a way of suggesting a social model that the spectators will then apply to their own
condition of existence. Richards is less sophisticated, he conceives of
the movies he studies as projections of middle-class unfulfillment. The
former considers that "a society going through a period of historical
transition will tend to recreate images of more settled times"[32] while
the latter detects, in the conservative movements which inspired the
films he deals with, "a definite commitment to turning back the clock
to the world of the day before yesterday" and a "need for reassurance
on the part of the middle-classes" which "helped to dictate the format
of the film: the mythic backdrops of unchanging, idealized societies
and the absolute standards of right and wrong, good and bad, us and
them that they reflected".[33]

   McArthur finds the best of his examples in British history programs
shown on British TV sets; two thirds of Richards's book is devoted to
the British Empire. By concentrating upon this case, the two authors
have marked on limitation of Kracauer's theory. History is, basically,
the study of men and societies throughout time, that is to say the study
of changes. British films, even when their plot takes place in a remote
period, can hardly be considered purely or simply historical. In the
exciting overview of British cinema he has written with Anthony Aldgate, Richards refers to only one history film, which is not surprising.[34]
It is of course extremely revealing to observe that some movies tend
to nothing but a depiction of a motionless, ill defined, fundamentally
stable past, but, once the salient features of that imaginary epoch have
been described, that is an end to the matter. Unless research-workers
focus on the visual means used "to produce a vision of *history* as a
country where only feelings reside, not conflicts".[35] By first describing
the conditions of production (studios, screenwriting, cast, technical
crews) and then carefully scrutinizing decors and costume design, Sue
Harper has proved that fantastic differences exist between contemporary history films which tell more or less the same stories and are
situated in the same periods. The plots and the ideas presented in
the screen-play are far less important than the way of representing
the past.[36] In Britain, the Ealing studios, which aimed at creating
quality historical films met a cold response. On the contrary, the pictures made at Gainsbourgh were extremely popular because the visualization of the past was inconsistent with the script and provided the
viewers with a rich variety of feelings; cleverly chosen objects and
settings evoked a remote period but were disposed to catch the viewers' attention, not merely to signify a precise moment of history. The
past was displayed as a sumptuous set of pleasant details, from which
the spectators could freely select; there was then an interesting discrepancy between the moral conclusions which were to be inferred
from the story and the unlimited pleasures which could be derived
from the images; "the contradictions between the verbal level of the
scripts and the nonverbal discourses of decor and costume . . .

provided a space where audience fears and desires could be pleasurably rehearsed".[37]

Kracauer's vision of films, which aims at illuminating the psychical processes at work in a society, relies too much on spoken words or story lines and it is necessary to contrast it with Sue Harper's more elaborate analysis. Yet we enter, with the study of the British studios productions, the world of melodrama, a world which ignores evolution. The long discussion on Kracauer and his heirs has then helped us to better define the nature of history films. The spectators of a costume melodrama recognize objects (that dress, that chair) that designate "the past" but they are content with identifying and enjoying signs. Historical pictures require a more developed participation. Paul Revere has a small part in Griffith's *America* but his interference is of great significance for the picture. The viewers will miss the point and misunderstand a large portion of the story if they are unable to supplement the discontinuous, allusive elements they are shown with their previous knowledge of history; as Richards rightly points it out, *Young Mr. Lincoln* deals with Lincoln's life in the 1830s but presupposes that the audience foresees the future of the president to be.[38]

Another noticeable inference to be drawn from the debate on Kracauer is that screened history is linked with social transformations. Richards pays a tribute to changes of time in the section of his book devoted to the American populist films;[39] his chapters cross-cut the important paper previously published by Garth Jowett.[40] Both insist upon the function of historical pictures in transmitting traditional values and encouraging conformity of attitudes. In the 1950s, American films avoid the themes which could be of any discomfort for the audience but America has evolved since the war and problems strictly banned from the screen one decade earlier, like Indian resistance and its justifications are frequently filmed. These studies, allusive though they are, depart from Kracauer's inheritance and, as early as the beginning of the 1979s, opened a new field of research on history film.

HISTORY AND SOCIAL CONSCIOUSNESS

Historians' concerns with regard to historical cinema have evolved, since the early 1980s, for at least three reasons. First, lots of them tend to question their own practice and to conceive of history not as a reflection of the past but as a social activity closely related to the self-definition and interests of social groups. Long, conflicting debates have tended to prove that some communities or classes lack historical references and have to dig out (or to contrive) their past to provide themselves with an identity. History does not predate books, novels or films, it is built up and constantly reshaped by the media. Second, film analysis has been greatly modified by the work of semioticians; a few specialists have gone too far in their quest for a totalizing theory of cinema but I dare say I do not understand those historians who mock the so-called narrowness and obscurantism of film theoreticians. Semioticians want to know how separate signs, almost meaningless by themselves, produce a significance when they are put together. Historians may be more interested in the final result and its social impact; however, they are coming to realize that any film must be understood in the context of its production, and the way the elements are assembled (the editing process) must be taken into account.[41] Last, film history has become a respectable field of research, movie historians no longer collect anecdotes on stars and directors but look far beyond the studios and use the same sort of documents, the same methodological rules as their social/economic/political counterparts.[42]

It is no wonder that Australians have been particularly anxious to investigate history films as tools for what Anne Hutton calls "the production of Popular Memory".[43] The media are often credited with creating messages which simultaneously reflect the variety of collective representations and order them so as to lay the foundations of social consent. By studying *their* films and TV programs—a very restricted, recent cluster of audiovisual products—the Australians are likely to illuminate aspects of the selective construction of national imagery. When they shot (1981) *Gallipoli* (a minor Turkish port where Australian troops were disembarked in 1915, the expedition resulted in nothing and a great many soldiers were killed) the Australian cinematographers delimited an event in an otherwise nearly blank past; they illustrated, thanks to the characters they had chosen, "Australian behavior and standards" (as opposed to British ones) and gave a critical version of the relationship with the Crown (Australians were unwillingly sent to the disaster by London).

Cinema and TV provide their spectators with historical facts where they did not exist beforehand. Yet, it would not be sufficient to make an inventory of those items. Basing her work on the Australian past, Ina Bertrand has underlined other aspects of the media's functions.[44] The audiovisual products, the building of a past and the knowledge of history, far from being separated, constantly overlap: "a film's specific location in time and space provides validation of already existing popular national stereotypes, and the conformably familiar icons and symbols in a film provide validation of the form in which the historical events have been depicted." History is seen like a net, with its knots (the events already known to everybody) and its gaps, that the media tend to fill up little by little (the reconstruction of Gallipoli). Ina Bertrand has tried to build up a model which, questionable though it is, is extremely stimulating; she distinguishes the paradigmatic elements (recurring stereotypes, well-established patterns) from the syntagmatic flow (the historical development related to specific places and times). Although she does not test her model, she drops the hint that it might help to evaluate the historical accuracy of movies. I am afraid there is an inadequacy in the words. According to semiologists, a syntagm is a co-ordinated set of signs: "Australians were sent to Gallipoli." A paradigm is a series of signs which could occupy *one deter-*

mined position in the syntagm: "(Australians / poor people / soldiers / victims: etc . . .) were sent to (Gallipoli / death / disaster / slaughter / etc . . .)." A syntagm may be built on a completely routine, hackneyed pattern (challenge / climax / ending) and a paradigm may include new, original terms. Now, if we take the words in their original meaning, we see that Bertrand's model is likely to work very well. Does a film assess its historical value by exhausting the paradigms (extending descriptions of people, groups, locations; insistence upon symptomatic objects) or by concentrating upon syntagms (narration of successive events)? Systematically applied to TV historical series (and there are plenty of them in Australia) the model could turn out to be highly valuable. The Australians have not yet completed their inquiry. It is worth noticing that, far from beginning with all empirical description based on ill-defined notions (national characters, national films) they have clearly delineated their methodological framework.

Despite the differences which exist between them most historians share a common conception of their task and duties; they often diverge upon conclusions but there is a general agreement upon methodology and rules of work. The public does not participate in these interests; although more and more people buy history books, attend historical films, watch historical series on their TV sets, there is an obvious gap between those who try to give history a scientific dignity and those who consume the past. However, can we assume that there is no overlapping between the expectations of the readers / viewers and the inquiries of the specialists? Historians, after all, are not time-proof and one cannot imagine that the different activities which cross-cut history (teaching, book writing, film making, film consumption-not to mention the politicians who constantly refer to the past) have their own independent evolution. How is it possible to test their interaction? All isolated film is not convenient evidence since it can have been made by chance. A set of contemporary films is better, for the simultaneous release of several pictures tends to suggest that some sort of questioning is in the air and a long series, spread over several decades is even more relevant.

The trouble is that film series of that sort are extremely rare. The most important one deals with the Russian Revolution but I would be reluctant to study it; if filmmakers were granted a real independence in the years which followed October 1917, the governmental control upon the interpretation of the Great Revolution strengthened to such an extent from 1930 onwards that all the movies had to conform to the official truth. This Russian cinema has much to tell us about the successive conceptions of the causes and developments of the Bolshevik Revolution but can hardly inform us upon an "average" version of the events that people are not allowed to screen, stage or write.

The historical tradition is equally strong in the Italian cinema: *The Fall of Rome* (1905) the first full-length film made in the peninsula (800 feet!), is devoted to the completion of Italian unity in 1870. One of the salient features of the Italian cinema is the fact that, since the end of the War, it has always pictured immediate history. Fascism, resistance, terrorism, the Mafia remain topics for current production. A long series of Italian films have concentrated on Fascism since the first film was made in 1948 and the screening of the Mussolini era has never been interrupted for more than a few years; we are faced with forty years of cinematic production which is something unique; the films included in this set restage a period which is over but is also very recent and still vivid for the Italians.

The cinema is one of many indicators; thousands of novels, essays, historical books and articles have been written on Fascism and no week passes by without the Mussolini period being mentioned in papers or public speeches. Fascism is still a dividing factor in Italian political life, not in the general, vague meaning of the word, but with a clear, exclusive reference to Mussolini. In other words, the *Ventennio Nero*-the Twenty Black Years-is an urgent problem in the peninsula, as much as it is an epoch of recent Italian history. Given this situation the movies are central to an estimation of the function of Fascism in the making of the Italian political mentality. Italian historians have already done good work on the subject but it is very difficult for them to be uninfluenced by the debate on this question. Comparing the screening of Fascism with the publications of historians and with the popular vision of Mussolini's era raises new questions about the nature of history and about the significance of historical representation.

How can we decide that a film deals with Fascism? The location in time is not sufficient; some stories take place in the past but the period, however clearly indicated, has nothing to do with the plot. This rule, common to many historical pictures, does not apply to Fascism. Only a few comedies or war stories, although related to Mussolini's epoch, leave out politics. The Fascist period is never taken as an equivalent to "the good old days of the Twenties and Thirties"; it is a well defined moment of history which runs from 1920 (the struggle for power) to July 1943 (when Mussolini was dismissed by the Fascist party and the king). The two last years of Mussolini's life (July 1943-April 1945) are a different matter; the Duce was then in complete submission to Germany and there is general agreement, even among his admirers, to disregard his "Italian Social Republic." The films related to that period illustrate resistance to Nazism, not Fascism.

Some fifty pictures correspond to the above definition of the Fascist period; most are fictions but a good many (eight) are compilations combining archive footage and interviews.[45] The titles of compilations refer to Mussolini, Fascism or dictatorship and give the cinemagoers sufficient information about the content of the movies. The titles of the fiction films are less precise,[46] the spectators having to detect signs likely to inform them about the period. There are few of these informative clues; the most frequent is Mussolini-not the man himself but his name, his easily apprehensible silhouette, his portraits, his speeches. Other indicators are people wearing black shirts, people raising their arms to salute, and huge popular meetings. This rather narrow series concentrates upon three aspects of the system: the leader, the militarization of Italian society and mass organization—three themes which are particularly well illustrated in Fellini's *Amarcord* (1973).

This film takes place in a small town in central Italy, another characteristic which extends to nearly all of our movies: Fascism is rarely depicted in Rome or in any other large city. We witness it in villages, small town, remote suburbs. The plots are built upon a restricted set of fictional possibilities: 1)a few ambitious, unscrupulous people; 2)the use of violence; 3)a small group of opponents; 4)an amorphous mob. When opponents are strong enough the ambitious are held up to ridicule but, most of the time, the resisters are beaten, killed or banished. Films provide their viewers with a sad, pessimistic vision; under Mussolini force prevailed and crooks turned it to their account. We are never given an insight into the political system, its (missed or successful) attempts to organize Italy, its domestic and foreign policy. This leads us to raise a question: why are Italians fascinated by a period that they depict as gloomy and shameful?

History films are challenging when they compel historians to dig out and question such contradictions. These cannot be resolved only by looking at movies but at least films supply us with another clue: the stories they tell take place in extremely precise periods, which can be defined thanks to the insertion of documents (newspapers, newsreels, radio talks, political events). The films tend to focus the attention on two moments, the beginning and the end; the rise of Fascism till Mussolini's take over of power and its failure from the time of the intervention in the Spanish civil war to July 1943. Far from being casual this division is consonant with Italian political thought and historiograghy.

Mussolini eliminated all the political parties which had been created since the birth of the new kingdom and, from the time of his access to power political leaders dwelled on the same questions: "Why is there Fascism?" The bibliography of "the origins" is enormous and, during the two decades which followed the war, politicians never stopped reminding their supporters: "It happened because . . . ".[47] As for the end, it must be noted first that the opponents of Fascism did not unite their forces until the Spanish civil war had clearly delineated totalitarianism from democracy and second that the war was interpreted as the great punishment (if Mussolini had not gone to war his regime would have lasted for a long time but—his opponents argue—he was doomed to war by the nature of his system).

Italian films have been sticking, for four decades, to a chronological partition of Fascism which prevailed, for political reasons, before cinematographers took an interest in Mussolini. We shall see that, since the end of the 1960s, Italian historians have changed their approach to the "black years." However, the image created by the politicians, and conveyed by pictures and other means of communication are so deeply rooted in the tradition that they will survive for many years. Yet the cinema, which seems so closely linked to the political/historical inheritance is not congruent with it on a very important point. Those who asked "why" attempted to answer the query. For half a century, from 1920 onwards, two main theories were defended. The liberal one saw Fascism as the result of the lack of political maturity in the peninsula; the bankruptcy of the parliamentary system and the inability of Italians to restore it led to dictatorship. According to the Marxist view, which is still sustained by respectable academics, a newly built, weak industry could not sell its products in a predominantly rural peninsula and was threatened by a well organized working class; the bourgeoisie called upon Fascism to put down the revolutionaries and to protect the domestic market against foreign competition. Neither of these theses is illustrated in our films, except in Bertolucci's *1900* (1976) which has as its background a class-conflict between a land-owner and one of his farmers in northern Italy;[48] it must be added that the Marxist interpretation, which is hinted at, is almost entirely veiled by a personal conflict/friendship between the two main characters who, being born the same day, conceive of each other as brother/enemy. Even in this case, the general theory of Fascism is of little importance. In the other pictures, the characters do not seem to know what part they play in the transformation of their country. *Amarcord* is another excellent example. There is no class-conflict in the story; the anti-Fascist is a well-off man who has hated Fascism for years, mainly for ethical reasons; as for the Fascists, they do not defend anything but themselves and their right to be arrogant.

Up to now we have studied the movies as if there had been no significant change for forty years. This is correct as far as the plots, locations and dates are concerned but films cannot be reduced to their story and setting. If we take the chronological order of production into account, we realize that noticeable variations occurred in our series which can be divided into different epochs.

Before 1960 we find less than one film every year. During that period the Christian Democrat, hegemonic party in Parliament, was constantly attacked by a strong Communist party and aimed at getting as much support as possible on its right; given that the left concentrated its criticism upon neo-Fascism, the Christian Democrats were lenient towards the survivors of the past system. A very funny example is to be found in the case of *The Great Dictator*. When Chaplin's film was offered to Italian companies after the war, the distributors decided that they had better cut out all the shots where Jack Oakie plays the part of a fat Mediterranean dictator; it would have been hard to suppress them without spoiling the whole sequence of the visit and the distributors were content with cutting out the shots showing the dictator's wife. Knowing that the producers reluctantly accepted scripts where Fascism was taken as a background filmmakers avoided the Mussolini era. It should be also stated that, in these years, the debate on Fascism and Resistance was central to Italian political life; people were overwhelmed by propaganda (recurring elections, either at national or at local level, constant parliamentary crises) and wanted to enjoy some rest in movie theatres.

The early 1960s witnessed a complete transformation: ten films were shot in five years, one half of which are compilations. Two factors account for this outburst of interest in screened Fascism. The Christian Democrats, having lost their hegemony, could no longer form a one-party government; some of their leaders agreed, in 1960, to include the neo-Fascists on their side[49] but others were not ready to help give Fascism a decent appearance. The left claimed that democracy was endangered in the peninsula and got a large, active response; meetings, street demonstrations, protest rallies and strikes put an end to neo-Fascist participation and cleared the way for what was called the "opening to the left" (inclusion of the left, non-communist parties into the governmental coalition). Compilations played an important part in the anti-Fascist campaign; they did not depart either from the consecrated division in periods or from the chronological depiction of the facts but they contributed to informing those people born after the war who heard daily of Fascism but had little (if any) positive knowledge of the Fascist era.

When looking at bibliographies on Mussolini's Italy one becomes very quickly aware that something changed round the middle of the 1960s: interpretative essays gave place to minute case studies based on primary sources. An extensive list of books pertaining to that "new wave" is unnecessary here but I find it essential to mention Renzo de Felice who acted, to a large extent, as spokesman for his generation. His colossal biography of Mussolini, entirely grounded on archive material or direct testimonies is a good example of history free of interpretation.[50] Compilation films did not give rise to this renewal of historical research but they made the specialists understand that the time had come to investigate archives and, by focusing the attention of cinemagoers upon Fascism, they induced them to buy and read books on the same topic. The case was different with fiction. Italians who were extremely fond of movies after the war became less and less enthusiastic once they were enabled to get cheap TV sets. It was thus necessary to replace the "Roman" comedies, based on puns and verbal jokes, by new, more exciting stories. Oddly enough, Fascism provided themes for half-serious, half-hilarious pictures with stupid Fascists as the baddies and others (generally not politicized people) as the goodies. A strange mixture of severely-beaten opponents and laughable Fascists gave these pictures an ironic, unrealistic tone which can still be found in *Roma* (1972) and *Amarcord*. But, apart from Fellini, very few filmmakers prolonged the comedies after the middle of the 1960s and it is extremely hard to evaluate the influence of these pictures upon the rebuilding of the image of Fascism.

All that has just been said tends to corroborate the previously mentioned hypothesis regarding the connection between historical pictures and the political problems of the period in which they were made. By comparing movies and context we have gained a better understanding of some films but the relationship is so obvious that the conclusions to be inferred from the parallel are slightly disappointing. Moreover, we can wonder whether the link was not all the more strong when the political crisis was strong and the film set well delineated, as this was the case at the beginning of the 1960s.

After a few years of apparent disinterest Fascism has been continuously screened since 1970, to such an extent that half of the pictures which we are concerned with have been made since then. Connections can be found between this series and contemporary events but they are superficial and only concern secondary aspects of the movies.[51] Obviously there has been something new from 1970 onwards since so many films have been devoted to the Mussolini era. Plots, settings and even actors are more or less the same as in the previous decades. What has changed then?

Production first. Finding money for a film has always been hard in Italy but, since 1970, the national television company, the RAI, has become more and more involved in filmmaking. Low budget films as well as spectaculars have been financed by the television and cinematographers have been obliged to adapt to the requirements of the televisual screen. One very good picture sponsored by the RAI is *In the Out of the Way Town of Sarzana* (1980). In 1921 the police were entrusted with preventing "black shirts" from over-running the small town of Sarzana which was at the time administered by the socialists. For the first and only time the policemen shot at the Fascists who could not take the town. The movie describes that unique case of resistance. We are offered few long shots since landscapes are not adequately conveyed by a TV set; there are few motions either for camera panning seems awkward on television. The director, who was perfectly aware of the limitations of the medium concentrated upon motion inside the frame. He also concentrated on faces and details; by lingering upon opposed groups, by exploring clothes, attitudes, seemingly insignificant gestures, the camera induces the spectators to care more about the motivations of people and their state of mind than about the events themselves. *Sarzana* then, offers another, more human vision of the struggle between Fascists and anti-Fascists. The same story might have been screened in the 1960s but the result would have been totally different.

Is this to say that the medium is the message? That would be very simplistic. Although Bertolucci's *The Conformist* (1970) was produced by an independent company[52] we could comment on it as we have done on *Sarzana*; the first shots, with their long pause on Marcello, the main character, and their slow, motionless flashback fit perfectly well on a TV screen. It is partly because, around 1970, the most clever directors began to adopt TV standards; it is also because a new cinematic style prevailed during the 1960s. In other words, images of Fascism changed, centering more on the experience of individuals, in so far as film forms evolved under the dual pressure of new filmic rules and televisual constraints.

We must also take into account the influence of compilations and here, again, 1970 turns out to be a dividing line. Before that year images were subservient to the text in compilation films; small bits of film, borrowed from various archives, were edited together to illustrate a previously written commentary. In the 1970s, the cinematographers let the documents speak for themselves; entire issues of newsreels, full sequences of documentaries were edited with practically no additional words. Historians were the first, in 1960, to dig pieces of evidence out of the archives and to publish them. Ten years after, it dawned on filmmakers that they had their own archive, the Istuto Luce, with its fantastic collection of weekly newsreels going back to 1927. From 1972 onwards a selection of newsreels was projected in various Italian towns and acted as an (ambiguous) eye-opener.[53] On the one hand Fascism appeared, all of a sudden, outdated and people jumped to the conclusion that references to Mussolini were now irrelevant.[54] On the other hand newsreels made by Fascists presented an attractive vision of Fascism with enthusiastic crowds cheering *their* Duce and participating in huge celebrations. *Amarcord* was shot at the time of these newsreel shows. Whether or not Fellini saw the documents, his depiction of a crowd involved in Fascist ceremonial is consonant with the version given by the Luce archives.

Newsreels disclosed one aspect of the discourse of Fascism. Another aspect of this discourse could be obtained by interrogating survivors. De Felice and his colleagues were of course the first to collect interviews but the filmmakers followed them quickly. However, a picture made with direct witnesses is fairly different from a film made with stock-shots; the witness has a look and his attractiveness (or lack of it) is nearly as important as what he says. Interview-based films deal more with people and their feelings than with general assumptions. The longest film ever shot on Fascism, a six-hour TV serial was called *All the Duce's men* (1983) obviously to gain advantage from the success of the antecedent American film but also to inform viewers that the movie-camera focused on men, Mussolini, his fellows and relatives, some of them being still alive and appearing on the screen.

We are now in a position to evaluate the complex reciprocal relationship between historians and filmmakers. During the 1970s, historians understood that, thanks to television, spectators had been introduced to a less formal, more vivid conception of history. If we compare the first volume of de Felice's *Mussolini* to the (provisionally) last one we note that the introduction of direct witnesses had modified the nature of his documentation as well as his style and conception of biography (witnesses emphasize less data than atmosphere and personal motivations). When he wanted to offer his readers a general sketch of Fascism de Felice did not write an essay but preferred the more familiar form of an *Interview on Fascism*.[55] By answering queries he broke off from the canonical sequence of historical accounts (ordering and interpretation of facts according to their chronological succession) and organized the matter under comprehensive, sometimes provocative headings. The *Interview* was so fit for audiovisual media that it gave birth to endless talks, debates, discussions on TV. Filmmakers backed up a historian who had learned to make good use of the media.[56]

Conversely cinematographers learned that they had something to take from historians. De Felice was paid as adviser for *All the Duce's Men*. In this case, the specialist backed up the filmmakers who used his name and knowledge of the period to attest the historical relevance of their picture. More generally, historians' reflections on the document and its ambiguous nature had an effect upon cinematographers. Throughout the 1970s, directors were concerned with the problematic significance of speech as historical evidence. This is particularly well illustrated by Bertolucci's *Spider's Stratagem* (1970); young Athos, who inquires into the death of his father, killed by Fascists, is finally caught in the net of contradictory, inconsistent testimonies as in a spider's web.[57]

The investigation of the function of speech is more sophisticated in *Christ Stopped at Eboli* (1978). Exiled for political reasons in a far township of southern Italy Dr. Carlo Levy discovers a nearly underdeveloped part of his country and we are shown the successive stages of his exploration. What about Fascism then? It is at the same time outside and inside the daily life of the inhabitants. Outside because they are not interested in Mussolini and because there are not apparent signs of Fascism in the township. Apart from a few "black shirts" who appear late in the film the system is reduced to Mussolini's voice transmitted through loudspeakers. Cinematic devices emphasize the extraneity of the Fascist discourse. For instance, while one of the Mussolini's speeches is heard, the camera moves down a hill; the tracking-shot is taken from a point of view which cannot be that of either Levy or any of the inhabitants; Mussolini's voice fills a space which is not referred to any of the characters and thus looks empty. But Fascism interferes also with people's lives, be it only because the Duce's speeches are transmitted at any time of the day or because the leading citizens, insidiously, use Mussolini's slogans in their most trifling talks. Aspects of Fascism are intercut in the plot but the shooting warns us against the temptation of confusing the history of Fascism with the history of the Italians.

In the films made during the 1970s the constant intervention of individual memory, the face to face encounter with witnesses, the quotations from the Fascist discourse, the uncertainty which fringes events are consonant with the approach of specialists. Let us remember that among the classical interpretations of Fascism the first is not concerned with classes and the second knows two classes only. When people began to look at entire issues of newsreels (and not at small, disarranged bits of films) they were surprised to see Fascism presented as a big celebration, a theatrical show involving the Duce and the crowd. Without obliterating the crimes of the initial period or the final disaster, newsreels provided spectators with an unexpected version of the longest, generally forgotten years of Mussolini's era. At the same time de Felice and others were arguing that the "black years" were characterized by a political self-assessment by the middle-class. Here, we have to take into account the specific Italian conception of modern society. Italians use the notion of class but limit it to the ruling class and the working class; in between they conceive of an ill-defined, ill-delimited cluster, the *ceto medio* which might be best translated by middle stratum if stratum were not an awkward, purely technical term.

We are not concerned here with deciding whether "the middle strata remained always the corner-stone of Fascism."[58] We are mainly interested in an amazing convergence: during the same period that Italy underwent the social/economic transformation common to western societies—when everybody in the peninsula was enabled to buy a TV set—audiovisual documents (newsreels, interviews) revealed a new face of Fascism, historians made use of new sources and defended a more balanced interpretation of the Mussolini's era, feature films depicted differently the "black years." Which of these factors came first? none. There was no causation here, only an overlapping.

Our problem is to determine the particular function of movies in the circumstances. One of our queries was: why have Italians continuously screened a period which was, according to the stories which are told, very gloomy? It seems that, by now, we can answer. The tradition was created during the decades which followed the war, by people who were born under Mussolini and had been told for a long time the classical, pessimistic versions of Fascism. Once they have been established, patterns cannot easily be uprooted; filmmakers tended to repeat, with different shapes, the stories already screened by their predecessors and cinemagoers stuck to the model they were used to. Although the fictions were identical, the movies made after 1970 had little in common with those of the postwar era since social/intellectual changes had created new forms for describing the same moments of history and the same facts.

Thanks to movies—and other media—Italians share a common knowledge of their recent past which provides them with a basis for ideological debates and, more simply, for daily talks. A parallel could be drawn with regard to various epochs of Italian history. The Risorgimento—the national revival of the nineteenth century—was the main reference of Italians till the middle of our century. It was then replaced by Fascism. Films played an important part in this transfer as well as in the shaping of a new reference but their function cannot be evaluated separately. Media converge to build an acceptable version of the past and must adapt themselves to the constant shifting of that vision.[59]

I have been working on Italy for years and I think I know most of the documents pertaining to the Sarzana case. Yet, when I saw *In the*

Out of the Way Town of Sarzana I was highly impressed. I had never realized that the men involved in the case knew each other very well, were mates, neighbors, sometimes relatives and that deciding for or against the Fascists was less a political problem than a question of choosing one side of the township against the other. The film brings us back to a time when the die was not yet cast. I wondered, at the beginning of this paper, whether history pictures could be of any use for specialists; I can answer yes. Historians of contemporary Italy have to see *Sarzana*, they will learn something from it and they may mention it in their bibliographies. This is largely due to the fact that filmmaking has considerably changed, in a common interaction between cinema, television and historical work. The transformation is so marked that the old standards of film analysis must be modified. When people irregularly attended movie theatres and had little influence upon programs it was acceptable to consider the pictures as reflections of mentalities and to draw conclusions about the hopes, fears and aims of a society from the cinematic description of history. Now that TV shows are part of events, make events known to everybody at the moment they happen, now that managers anticipate the reactions of viewers to the screening of news[60] filmed history cannot be studied but in its reciprocal relationship to written history and to other social/cultural activities. The end of historical research? Or its opening to new fields of investigation? Why is it, for instance, that Britain and France make few historical films? Why do Americans focus on the Vietnam war and Germans on WWII or on the immediate postwar period? Why do Australians make so many films or serials on the colonial period? Are serials produced in different countries and presented on TV throughout the world likely to develop a less nationalist image of history? Historical pictures trigger an unprecedented curiosity for the past among people who would not read history books. Historians can take advantage of it but they must admit that they are no longer alone in defining the nature and grounds of historical research.

NOTES

1. The studies on genre-films do not mention the historical pictures; see: Stuart Kaminsky, *American Film Genres*, Dayton, 1974 and Robert C. Toll, *The Entertainment Machine*: American Show Business in the 20th Century, Oxford Un. Press, 1982. The *Readers on Film Studies* published by the British Film Institute, which collect the most important writings on various genres do not include any volume on historical movies. The only reader in this field is: Gianfranco Gori ed., *Passato Ridotto*, Florence, 1982.
2. The 21st of January 1911 the *Moving Picture World* started a special survey devoted to the didactic possibilities of films, "The Educational Field" (later to be "The Moving Picture Education") in which many references can be found to the use of movies in history teaching.
3. *The Pleasure Dome*, Ox. Un. Press, 1980, p. 16.
4. Bryan Haworth, "Film in the classroom" in Paul Smith ed., *The Historian and Film*, Cambridge Un. Press, 1976, p. 157. Extensive bibliography in

the same volume, p. 194; add: Daniel A. Kent, "Film and History Teaching in Secondary School" in Karsten Fledelius ed., *History and the Ausiovisual Media*, Copenhagen, 1979, p. 86.

5. R. C. Raack, "Clio's Dark Mirror: the documentary Film in History" *The History Teacher*, VI, 1972, p. 114.

6. "There is an impartiality about the written record which film cannot begin to capture," Penelope Houston, "The Nature of Evidence," *Sight and Sound*, XXXV, 2, 1967, p. 90.

7. "Only unedited newsreels can be regarded as safe insofar as the facts are left to speak for themselves", Judith H. Gane, "History and Film: some reflections on the authenticity question" in Fledelius ed, p. 187.

8. A good example of overcriticism is to be found in C. Highet, "History on the Silver Screen" in *Talents and Geniuses*, Ox. Un. Press 1957. A clever answer to that blind conception of history in John Solomon, *The Ancient World in the Cinema*, South Brunswick, 1950; as Solomon points it out when films "lean too much toward historical authenticity . . . the result is inevitably boredom" (p. 21).

9. Robert C. Allen, "Historiography and the Teaching of History," *Film and History*, X, 2, 1980, p. 25; see also E. Breitbart, "From the Panorama to the Docudrama: Notes on the Visualization of History" *Radical History Review*, 25, 1981; Nicholas Pronay, "The 'Moving Picture' and historical research," *Journal of Contemporary History*, XVIII, 3, July 1983, p. 365; R. C. Raack, "Historiography as cinema: a prolegomenon to film work for historians," id., p. 411; Richard Grenier, "History and Movies: state of the art," id., XIX, Jan 1984, p. 1.

10. Jonathan Rosenbaum, "The Way We Were," *American Film*, April 1982, p. 71; David Culbert, "*Reds*. Propaganda, Docudrama and Hollywood," *Labor History*, 24, 1983, p. 125.

11. "Pictures of Peasantry," *The Age*, May 1984, p. 16.

12. *The Return of Martin Guerre*, Harvard Un. Press, 1983. Isaac Notes: "The book was written as an extension of the work she contributed as historical consultant to the film. Indeed it reveals itself as a subtle counter-statement."

13. Thomas J. Knock, "History with Lightening: the Forgotten Film *Wilson*, *American Quarterly*, 28, 1976, p. 523; Leonard J. Leff & Jerold Simmons, "*Wilson*: Hollywood Propaganda for World Peace," *Historical Journal of Film, Radio and Television*, III, 1, 1983, p. 3; David Culbert, "A Documentary Note on *Wilson*: Hollywood Propaganda for World Peace,'" id., III, 2, 1983, p. 193.

14. Letter to de Rochemont, 3-X-1943, in Culbert, "A Documentary Note . . ." p. 194.

15. Robert C. Roman, "Lincoln on the Screen," *Film in Review*, XII, 1961, p. 87; "John Ford's *Young Mr. Lincoln*" *Screen*, XIII, 3, Autumn 1972, p. 8.

16. *The Transformation of Virginia, 1740–1790*, Un. of North Carolina Press, 1982.

17. *Metahistory*. The Historical Imagination in Nineteenth Century Europe, Baltimore, 1973. See also L.O. Mink, "History and Fiction as Modes of Comprehension," *New Literary History*, I, 3, 1970, p. 544; Frederic Jameson, "Figural Relativism or the Poetics of Historiography" *Diacritics*, VI, 1, Spring 1976, p. 2; Hayden White, "The Value of Narrativity in the Representation of Reality," *Critical Inquiry*, Autumn 1980.

18. London, 1973.

19. Op. cit., p. 3.
20. Id., p. 275.
21. B. Chibnall, C. Rodrigues, J. Collings, "The Use of Film in University Teaching," Brighton, 1974, p. 3. See also Ian C. Jarvie, "Seeing through Movies," *Philosophy of the Social Sciences*, VIII, 4 Dec. 1978, p. 374.
22. On Culloden, Jack W. Duckworth, "*Filmic* versus *Real*. Reality in the History Film" in Fledelius ed., p. 171; for a broader view of the question, Clara I. Grandy, "Audio-visual Aids for English History since 1750: a Critical Review" *History Teacher*, X, Nov. 1976, p. 21.
23. Brian Shoesmith, "*Gandhi*: Producing the East" in Wayne Levy ed., *The Second Australian History and Film Conference Papers*, North Ryde, 1984, p. 175.
24. While sharply criticizing costume films Graham Greene admits that they are sometimes able to render "a quite horrifying sense of reality" Op. cit. p. 17. Interesting remarks on the question in Seymour Chatman, "What Novels can do that Films can't (and Vice Versa)" in W.J.T. Mitchell ed., *On Narrative*, Un. of Chicago Press, 1980.
25. Paul Monaco, "Movies and National Consciousness; Germany and France in the 1920s" in Ken Short ed., *Feature Film as History*, Un. of Tennessee Press, 1981, p. 65.
26. Without paying enough attention to their conceptual formulations: notions like "mentalities," "representations," "psychic state" repose more upon a presupposed evidence than on a concretely tested definition.
27. *Class: Image and Reality in Britain, France and the U.S.A. since 1930*. London and New York, 1980.
28. I have no place or time to enlarge upon that important question. For a discussion, see William Hughes, "The Evaluation of Film as Evidence" in Smith ed., p. 49; Paul Monaco, "Film as Myth and National Folklore" in V. Carabino ed., *Myth in Literature and Film*, Florida Un. Press, 1980, p. 35; Karsten Fledelius, "Fields and Strategies of historical Film Analysis" in K.R.M. Short & Karsten Fledelius ed., *Film and History*. Methodology, Research and Education, Copenhagen, 1980; Eugene C. McCreary, "Film Criticism and the Historians," *Film and History*, XI, 1, Feb 1981; Wolfgang Ernst, "History: Cinema and Historical Discourse" *Journal of Contemporary History*, XVIII, 3, July 1983, p. 397.
29. It must be added that some periods or events seem to be known all throughout the world and are likely to captivate international audiences. This is the case with the French Revolution which was screened in various countries namely in Germany and the U.S.A. Most of these films were shot after WWI and, by picturing the French revolutionaries as ferocious politicians, were intended at prejudicing the spectators against the Bolshevik Revolution; the political bias is generally so obvious that a close examination of films would not provide us with any new insight into German or American political history. Information on the German films is to be found in George Huaco *The Sociology of Film Art*, New York and London, 1965; Paul Monaco, *Cinema and Society: France and Germany during the Twenties*, New York, Oxford Amsterdam, 1976 and in Kracauer's book quoted in note 30.
30. *From Caligari to Hitler: a Psychological History of the German Film*, Princeton, 1947, rep. 1973.
31. *Television and History*, B.F.I. television Monograph 18, London, 1980.
32. McArthur, p. 40.

33. Richards, p. 358.
34. *Best of British: Cinema and Society, 1930–1970*, Oxford, 1983.
35. Sue Harper, "Art Direction and Costume Design" in Sue Aspinall & Robert Murphy ed., *Gainsborough Melodrama*, B.F.I. Dossier 18, 1983, p. 40.
36. "History in Film: two British Studios, 1942–1948" forthcoming in the proceedings of the 10th International IAMHIST Congress; see also from the same author "History with Frills", *Red Letters*, XIV, Winter 1982–83, p. 14 and "The Boundaries of Hegemony" in F. Barker ed., *The Politics of Theory*, Un. of Essex Press, 1983, p. 167.
37. "Art Direction . . . " p. 43.
38. *Visions of Yesterday*, p. 278; see also p. 135.
39. Another short section deals with German cinema but does not say much more than Kracauer's book.
40. "The Concept of History in American Produced Films", *Journal of Popular Culture*, III, 1970, p. 799.
41. Gerald Mast & Marshall Cohen ed., *Film Theory and Criticism*, New York, 1970.
42. Roy Armes, *Problems of Film History*, London, 1981; Douglas Gomery, "History of the (Film) World, Part II," *American Film* VIII, 2, Nov. 1982, p. 53; id, "Film Culture and Industry: Recent Formulation in Economic History," *Iris*, II, 2, Autumn 1984, p. 17; id. "Film and Business History: the development of an American Mass Entertainment Industry," *Journal of Contemporary History*, XIX, Jan. 1984, p. 89.
43. Title of her paper in Anne Hutton ed., *The First Australian History and Film Conference Papers*, North Ryde, 1982, ed., p. 206.
44. "National Identity / National History / National Film: the Australian Experience," *Historical Journal of Film, Radio and Television*, IV, 2, 1984, p. 179.
45. Most of these films are not available outside Italy; therefore I do not find it necessary to list them in my paper. Lists will be found in Guido Fink, "Il Fascismo: il Visibile" i *Momenti di Storia Italiana nel Cinema*, Siena, 1979 and Pierre Sorlin, "Fascisme en Images, Fascisme Imaginaire", *Risorgimento*, 1982, 2, p. 225. For a general view of the recent Italian films, R.T. Witcombe, *The New Italian Cinema*, London, 1982.
46. We are faced with a basic difficulty of film analysis: foreigners often lack the cultural background necessary to share the native understanding of pictures; a good half of the films on Fascism are adapted from novels and Italians know that these books speak of Fascism.
47. Extensive bibliography in Renzo de Felice, *Le Interpretazioni del Fascismo*, Bari, rep. 1971.
48. Andrew Horton, "History as Myth and Myth as History in Bertolucci's *1900*, *Film and History*, X, 1, Feb 1981.
49. The Italian Social Movement (M.S.I.): a neo-Fascist party, created in 1946, expanded rapidly at the beginning of the cold war; in 1958, it won twenty-five seats in Parliament.
50. Turin, from 1965 onwards; five volumes have already been published.
51. Terrorism has been the plague of Italy since 1969. Small groups of neo-Fascist or extreme-Leftists have been, alternatively or simultaneously, making attempts in big cities and kidnapping or killing politicians. Several pictures describe the total inadequacy of legal, verbal opposition to Fascism-an indirect way of prompting the government to stop talking and to put an end to terrorism. In 1973 the Communist party took advantage

of terrorism to try and join the parliamentary coalition; some films focus on communists during the fascist period to prove that they were not faithful fellows at the time.

52. The flash-back leads us to the RAI studios as to tell us that power resides in radio, not in governmental offices. To be precise it must be added that, the same year, the RAI produced Bertolucci's other film, *The Spider's Stratagem*.

53. Pietro Pintus, "Storia e film" in *Trent'anni di Cinema Italiano*, Rome, 1980, p. 157.

54. Pasolini, the well known poet and filmmaker provides us with a good example. Born in 1922 he was not either Fascist or anti-Fascist before the end of the war; taking little interest in politics he accepted the traditional image of Fascism until he was shown the newsreels; his opinion changed all of a sudden: "Today it is impossible to conceive of a leader of that sort not only because what he says is worthless and irrational but also because there is no space, no hope of credibility for him in our present world. Presented on television he would vanish, he would be politically destroyed."

55. Bari, 1975.

56. Nicola Tranfaglia, "Fascismo e Mass-media", *Passata e Presente*, 3, 1983, p. 135.

57. One among many possible interpretations of a difficult film. Pierre Sorlin, "Cinema and Unconscious: a New Field for Historical Research," *Working Paper* 112, Universita di Urbino, 1982.

58. De Felice, *Interpretazioni*, p. 269.

59. Tony Bennet, "Text and History" in P. Windowson ed., *Re-Reading English*, London-New York, 1982, p. 227.

60. Michael Mandelbaum, "Vietnam: the Television War," *Daedalus*, CXI, 4, Fall 1982, p. 157.

Daniel J. Leab is Professor of History at Seton Hall University and Editor of Labor History. *He has been a Senior Fulbright Lecturer at Cologne University and an Adjunct Professor at the University of Pennsylvania. He received his Ph.D. from Columbia University where he taught for nearly a decade. His books include a history of the formation of the American Newspaper Guild, the changing image of blacks in American film, and a bibliography of American working class history.*

THE MOVING IMAGE AS INTERPRETER OF HISTORY— TELLING THE DANCER FROM THE DANCE

Daniel Leab

"History is but a pack of tricks we play on the dead"—with these words the French *philosophe* Voltaire passed an extremely harsh judgment on the eighteenth-century practioners of the discipline. The judgment of this "timeless eminence" (to use a characterization penned, oddly enough, by Jack Valenti while head of the Motion Picture Association of America) remains trenchant for those critics of the discipline concerned with its failure to recognize the impact of the media for the practice of history. The use of the moving image in the interpretation of events remains a difficult task, for as the Irish writer William Butler Yeats pointed out (in a somewhat different context) appearances and reality are deceptive: "How can we know the dancer from the dance." Yet as historians we must make such judgments. The impact of the media leaves no other choice. Historians must avail themselves of the moving image and its interpretation of the past, present, and possible future. Historians must do so for otherwise they well may be reduced to what the French poet Paul Valéry unkindly has described as "fortune tellers of the past."[1]

The past has never been absent from American movies or television. The past, especially the American past, has always been a staple for those in charge of the media, and like some golconda they have ceaselessly mined it. The mother lode has yet to run out. A 1984 book details over 220 productions made for television and motion picture features "based on events from our nation's past." The author touches on several hundred additional efforts but still admits to "leaving out others." The book does not quite run the gamut from A to Z but the entries do range from *Abe Lincoln in Illinois* (a static commercially unsuccessful 1939 rendering of Robert Sherwood's critically acclaimed play) to *The Younger Brothers* (another fast-paced fanciful Technicolor whitewash, released in 1949, of a family of outlaws active in the post-Civil War West). The book's listings also include such network TV fare as *Bridger*, a failed pilot and obviously exaggerated rehash of frontiersman Jim Bridger's activities in the 1830s West, and *Tail Gunner Joe*, a stirring, but biased recapitulation of Senator Joseph McCarthy's checkered political career in the 1940s and 1950s. Almost all the many efforts touched on by this book, as well as the many others unmentioned by it, may have been grounded in the past, but few (certainly not the four mentioned here) can be termed proper history. Two *New York Times* correspondents recognized this failing years ago. In 1938, discussing Hollywood's feature films, they charged that the American people were "being libelled." These newsmen claimed then (and the charge holds true today not only for the movies but also for TV) that the portrait that the "movies are painting . . . for posterity . . . won't be too accurate." Even if what the movies and TV have presented is not a pack of tricks, the newsmen's judgment remains valid.[2]

The moving image differs from an ordinary documentary source, but the historians using it must do so with all the time-problem skills and insights that mark the handling of traditional documents. As the historian William Hughes intelligently argued over a decade ago, "if . . . we ignore some important problems of evidence . . . we limit unnecessarily the range of our information we might extract from film sources." The sources are not all alike. The moving image, like its written counterpart, encompasses different kinds of records. A novel, a newspaper story, a magazine report, eyewitness testimony— all of these may document an event such as a violent confrontation during a strike. Each record needs to be analyzed by the historian using it because of the particular characteristics that mark it. For example, a newspaper story is edited but at its best tries to be objective; a novel may well scorn objectivity and take dramatic license. Just as there are substantial differences between the various kinds of print media, so too are there significant distinctions among the various forms which make up the moving image. The road to the understanding of how film and television interpret history is dotted with many warning signals raised by specific examples of how the media function and relate. We must recognize that the moving image is a portmanteau term and not just a single "thing." For our purposes we can divide the moving images which portray history into three types: non-fiction, docudrama, and entertainment, and I would like to concentrate on the first two.[3]

Nonfiction as a category can be defined as those examples of the moving image that "document life" (to use film scholar Richard Meran Barsam's definition). With them as Bill Moyers has pointed out "we now possess a resource of images that will be as valuable to the future historians' study of our times as diaries and old letters have been to historians exploring centuries gone by." These moving images all record what is happening; some do so with artistry, creativity, and a pronounced point of view. Over the years they have included such disparate manifestations as film records of government agencies and armed services, movie and TV presentation of the news, and reel upon reel of home movies and videos. Historians who wish to make use of any or all of these examples of the moving image must be extremely careful because nonfiction may only approximate truth or reality. As one maker of documentaries stated: "real life depiction is not the same as real life itself." Often the distortion of reality is not deliberate but is occasioned by the shortcomings of a medium: as Arthur Asa Berger puts it, "the camera may report what it sees but it does not see everything."[4]

The compilation genre has a long but occasionally checkered history. Compilations sometimes include newly shot footage, but are generally composed of images put together in the editing room out of existing archive materials. These range from actuality film to TV entertainment programming and can include such diverse elements as news footage and excerpts from cartoons. Because of the needs and desires of those who make them, compilations often manipulate— wittingly or unwittingly—their archival source materials. These films must be used with great care by historians, for as the noted film scholar Jay Leyda warns: "this manipulation, no matter what its motive—art, propaganda, instruction, advertisement—usually tries to hide itself so that the spectator sees only . . . the especially arranged reality that suits the . . . maker's purpose."[5] There are many examples of this kind of manipulation in which archive footage is used to make points totally unintended by its original producers.

The highly regarded film series *Why We Fight*, the core of the US army orientation course for new recruits during World War II, used Nazi propaganda footage to underline the filmmaker's anti-Nazi message. The final product, moreover, was an odd melange which combined authentic combat footage with snippets from feature films. Media historian Erik Barnouw notes, that in the segment *War Comes to America*, "the very real war had a historic background depicted via moments from Griffith's *America*, Twentieth Century Fox's *Drums Along the Mohawk* . . . , Metro-Goldwyn-Mayer's *The Big Parade*, and Warner's *Confessions of a Nazi Spy*."[6]

The prestigious, award-winning NBC television series Project XX, during its 16-year existence focussed on many topics, but in its early years delved mostly into the past. One such effort, *Nightmare in Red*, tracing Russian history from the last days of the Tsar, has been characterized by historian J. Fred MacDonald as "a most direct attack upon Communism" whose "victory was unforgivable." However, among the TV program's celluloid sources were such paeans of praise to the Soviet Revolution as *October*—Eisenstein's celebration of that victory. In reviewing another Project XX effort, *The Great War* (1956), Jay Leyda found that "in some sequences . . . there is about one part real to nine parts unreal," and that in reconstructing the German torpedoeing in 1915 of the passenger liner *Lusitania* the makers of this compilation went overboard " . . . making a hodge podge of various fictions" including submarine scenes from the 1933 German film *Morgenrot.*[7]

Emil de Antonio's 97-minute film *Point of Order* (1963) was drawn from 188 hours of CBS kineoscopes of the Senate hearings arising out of the bitter recriminations between the Pentagon and Senator Joseph McCarthy. The erstwhile TV executive and perceptive media critic Fred Friendly, a stickler for journalistic accuracy, accepts the need for condensation of such an overwhelming amount of material but is outraged at de Antonio's rearranging of the facts. What's shown in several sequences of the film is not what happened but what de Antonio wanted viewers to see. As Friendly unhappily points out, de Antonio imposed his own truth. De Antonio, in his own words, "totally manipulated his source material," and "that's the reason that the last sequence is made out of many days [i.e., constructed out of carefully chosen clips from many days of testimony without informing the viewer] and in addition has that immediate cut to the silent, absolutely empty room" (this image with which *Point of Order* ends is, according to de Antonio, "an artificial ending which I imposed").[8]

For de Antonio, self-characterized as "a Marxist among capitalists," politics played a role in his distillation of reality. For others creativity and visual impact can be the governing factor in obscuring reality. In 1970 the film *Hiroshima-Nagasaki, August 1945* premiered. Except for one short sequence this sixteen-minute film is based on nearly three hours of footage shot in 1945 recording the devastation wreaked on these two cities by the atomic bomb. The first rough cut ran much longer than sixteen minutes but producer Erik Barnouw remembers that in "more than a year of experimentation . . . we kept reducing it in quest of sharper impact."[9]

Prior to World War II, notwithstanding the influence and activities of filmmakers like Robert Flaherty who emphasized and celebrated an idealized, almost idyllic view of their subjects, the dominant mode in Anglo-American documentary film production was summed up by Grierson's phrase "the creative treatment of actuality." Most of the Anglo-American documentarists, politically progressive in outlook, took a propagandistic approach. They wanted to use their films to change society and filmed accordingly. The result was a creative, artistic, and didactic reshaping of reality. Already in the 1930s (and this was their heyday) the documentarists recognized what they were doing in pursuit of their goals. As the iconoclastic Paul Rotha remarked in 1939: "even a plain statement of fact in documentary demands dramatic interpretation in order that it may be 'brought alive' on screen . . . the very act of dramatising causes a film statement to be false to actuality . . . most documentary is only truthful in that it represents an attitude of mind." In this context, did it matter that *Power and the Land*, a 1940 film, made under U.S. government auspices to document the impact of the Rural Electrification Administration on a typical American farm family that gets electricity for the first time was shot on a farm which had been "already outfitted with electricity"?[10]

The March of Time had great influence on documentary filmmakers especially in the 1930s. A unique brand of "pictorial journalism" (a term coined by its creators), this venture sponsored by Time Inc. began in 1935 as a newsreel of sorts and by 1938 had evolved into a series of fifteen- to twenty-minute films, issued monthly until 1951, each dealing with a different subject such as atomic energy, public relations, and Yugoslavia under Tito. It did not eschew controversy and was provocative as well as exciting—many issues are still fun to view (swinging along with what Paul Rotha has described as "a pendulum beat"). But as Henry Luce, head of Time Inc., proclaimed, *The March of Time* was "fakery in allegiance to truth." The various issues used actuality footage but also recreated events, staged scenes, and adapted existing film to suit the producer's purposes. A 1937 release, "War in China," includes authentic and exciting shots of the Japanese bombing China as well as shots of Japanese pilots looking over their handiwork, filmed at an airport in New Jersey. Not long after *The March of Time* began, the writer George Dangerfield pointed out that "one has to realize that *The March of Time* is selling history at a profit, and this can't be done without a trick or two."[11]

The indignant, propagandistic documentary style of the 1930s had a shining but brief moment of glory during the war when talents were mobilized by governments desperate for film to use in training and as propaganda. But peace left the documentarists stranded. The filmmaker Willard Van Dyke looking back on the 1940s from the perspective of the 1960s lamented that "this kind of film disappeared to a large extent." What rescued the documentary, in any form, was television. There is no gainsaying TV producer Burton Benjamin's bold 1962 assertion that "in its relatively short life span, television has done more for documentary than the motion picture industry did in six decades." True, the concept has now been broadened to such an extent that almost everything which is ostensibly nonfiction programming, whether it be a compilation or cinéma vérité, is loosely dubbed documentary. There is even the so-called "minidocumentary"—really a feature story, a report of one kind or another, or varying length dropped into regular local news programs.[12] As one NBC producer made clear, however, network TV producers had to be "more circumspect" than the makers of earlier documentaries. For NBC this meant that a 1961 report on Portugal's suppression of an uprising in its then colony Angola (put together with herculean effort by Robert Young) did not air evidence that the Portuguese were using American-made napalm bombs—network executives excised the material, as Young was told, because the Russians would "use it against us."[13]

Dissatisfaction with this kind of circumspection (which to many differed little from censorship) as well as discontent with the networks' emphasis on objectivity (documentary producer Arthur Barron once complained that "if I were to make a film with Anne Frank, presumably Hitler would have to have equal time") contributed to the production in the 1970s and 1980s of a new wave of documentaries parallel to those produced by the networks. These new documentaries, according to one recent commentator, are "rapidly becoming in the twentieth century what the popular low-priced pamphlet was in the seventeenth century—an important and influential vehicle by which 'special pleaders'. . . bring their case before the public."[14] The creators of this special pleading—on issues such as women's rights, environmentalism, and various political causes—are committed, intelligent, passionate, skilled; their vision is neither the "innocent eye" of a Flaherty nor the "poetic propaganda" of a Grierson. They have (to use Edward R. Murrow's metaphor) a fire in their belly (an outstanding example of a historical film of this kind is *With Babies and Banners*, about which more later).[14]

Their use of documentary as a means of pleading, as a weapon, has been aided immeasurably by dramatic changes in technology, funding, and distribution. The introduction of lightweight equipment, innovations in sound recording, the increased use of videotape—these and other technological developments have made the production of documentaries (indeed of all types of moving images) cheaper and easier: a shooting crew, for example, need now only be two or three people instead of nine or ten or more. Thus it has become possible to escape the cumbersome technology of an earlier day that Fred Friendly characterized as a "ten-ton pencil." Moreover in the United States new sources of funding opened up, including foundations which once had scorned the production of the moving image, the national endowments, and to a limited extent the public broadcasting complex. Still, finance remains a problem for the independent documentarist, as does distribution. The traditional distinctions between television and the movies have become blurred (in 1980 an ABC-TV documentary was nominated for an Oscar, the first network production so honored), but the independent documentary producers have had to press hard to succeed in getting their work seen. The networks, with rare exceptions, continue to refuse airtime to any documentary production not originated by them, but as Erik Barnouw points out, "they are slowly being pushed aside." The creators of the new documentaries have made good use of such traditional channels as nontheatrical distribution as well as intelligently pursuing new ones such as airings over cable TV and public broadcasting stations, and the rental and sale of videocassettes.[15]

For the historian this rash of productions has meant some greater involvement in the creative process. Many funding agencies now require the participation of scholars such as historians. Moreover, sensitive to pointed criticism, the independents (and the networks) want to "get it right." Historians are asked to consult and to advise, but all too often they only serve as a kind of academic window dressing. As the organizers of a 1982 conference on the interaction between historians and filmnakers point out, "some scholars feel that they have been limited to providing an imprimatur to the 'history' represented in a film in which they are identified as consultant or adviser." There is nothing inherently wrong with films that preach a point of view. Many of these new documentaries, for example, are made with a Leftist slant by creators who like their 1930s predecessors have an axe to grind. I have no argument with their ideology, but I am concerned, and fervently hope that others share that concern, about forms of manipulation and visual persuasion which in my opinion distort history.[16]

The Wobblies (1979) is a superior, powerful, attractive documentary—a skillful blend of newly shot film and archival footage—highly partisan to the I.W.W. The production's historical advisers included such eminent and knowledgeable scholars as Joseph Conlin, Philip Foner, and Joyce Kornbluh, all of whom have published extensively about the I.W.W. The Wobblies premiered at the Seventeenth New York Film Festival (despite the film's partisanship or perhaps because of it), achieved fairly widespread distribution (including some runs in theatres), and received respectable notices (some were very good— the reviewer for the British Film Institute's Monthly Film Bulletin considered The Wobblies "inspirational" and "an eloquent celebration"). The film also had its critics whose comments echoed the ongoing historical debate about the I.W.W.'s role in history. They faulted The Wobblies for being "left-wing nostalgia," for failing to provide "a clear sense of how the organization evolved and grew," and for overemphasizing the effect that government repression had in the decline of the I.W.W. In addition, there was the criticism, much more inimical to the film, which charged (to use the words of one reviewer) that the creators of The Wobblies through their presentation "undercut the integrity of the historical 'truths' they claim to present." I believe they did so in filmic ways difficult for the historical advisers (or naive viewers) to deal with. The archival footage, for example, is misused and tricked up: a mid-1920s anti-labor cartoon dealing metaphorically with a hen strike at Alice's Egg Factory spurred on by an outside agitator (Little Red Henski) is implied to have been released a decade earlier, and film is speeded up or slowed down for emotional effect, even both speeded up and slowed down in individual sequences (in one a police charge at demonstrators is presented much faster than their subsequent beating up of people, which occurs in Peckinpahesque slow motion).[17]

Such manipulation of the moving image can also occur when historians are more directly involved with production. Lynn Goldfarb, a social historian, was a producer of With Babies and Banners (1978) and a vital force in the creation of this well-crafted, dynamic, stirring film. It deals primarily with the Women's Emergency Brigade (an outgrowth of the United Auto Workers Women's Auxiliary) during the 1937 sitdown strike of the union against GM, but deals movingly as well with the more general role of women in our society. With Babies

and Banners deserves every one of the many accolades it has received
(including an Academy Award nomination) as a film, as a consciousness-raising documentary, as an exciting look at the past from a feminist perspective. But for me it is bad history, because it doesn't just
sift and intensify; rather, this film distorts and manipulates. Goldfarb
has remarked that during the making of the film "there was always
a tension between what was historically accurate and what was visually
best."[18]

In satisfying this tension, decisions were made which undoubtedly
contributed to the film's powerful, emotional appeal, but these decisions also raise serious questions about the historical validity of *With
Babies and Banners*. At its beginning, nine women are seen reminiscing
about the strike and the times in which it occurred. One of the nine
is a black woman . . . Lillian Hatcher, a veteran UAW activist and
official. But at the time of the strike her husband worked at Chrysler,
she was no part of the Brigade, and there was only one black sit-
downer. Given the comments of Mrs. Hatcher in the film as well as
the archival footage, which visually attests to the Brigade as being
lilywhite, her inclusion leads to a skewing of history that undercuts
the premises of *With Babies and Banners*. Consider also its treatment
of "The Battle of Bulls Run" in which the strikers and their supporters
routed the Flint, Michigan, police who were attempting to evict the
sitdowners. This battle took place during a very chilly January winter
night and early morning. The film illustrates this conflict with footage
obviously shot during the day, probably during the summer, and not
even directly representative of the reminiscence that make up the
sound track. One can appreciate a filmmaker's desire to use archival
footage to represent such a dramatic event, but that this kind of manipulation is unnecessary is clearly illustrated by the treatment of the
same incident in a marvelous TV documentary, *The Great Sitdown*,
from the BBC series "Yesterday's Witness" produced just a few
months earlier and also utilizing reminiscences. *The Great Sitdown* used
contemporary news photographs to illustrate the confrontation on
that cold winter night. The images were still, but they were accurate.[19]

Even without the kind of tension Goldfarb referred to, even when
the makers of a historical documentary hew as closely as possible to
what has been described as "time and place accuracy of all footage in
the films" utilized, there will still be problems of interpretation with
which historians must come to grips. "The World at War," a twenty-
six-part Thames Television series about World War II, has justifiably
received critical accolades, numerous prestigieous awards, and con-
tinual popular success for its intelligent, well-researched innovative
handling of the complex, multifaceted history of World War II. The
creators of the series, as has been acknowledged many times, were as
scrupulous as possible in their handling of the archive footage utilized.
Associate producer Jerry Kuehl, an erstwhile historian, has asserted
that "when you're making a series like this . . . you want to get it right
all of the time." He also remembers that because of the pressures of

time and money "you don't get it right as often as you can." With
"dubious shots," the decision often was not to take them out, but to
be less specific. Kuehl warned the staff "don't say in your commentary
'9:47 a.m., December 13th, 1942, the Hungarians attack' . . . because
it's painfully obvious the film shows Romanian troops . . . " What you
can do in such a situation, Kuehl advised, is "to say 'the kind of war
fought in Transylvania was bloody and bitter,' which avoids positively
identifying . . . or misidentifying the material, which you know is
something other than you would like it to be." Arthur Marwick, a
trenchant and respected historian who has been much involved with
the use of the moving image in the teaching and writing of history,
salutes "The World at War" as "a magnificent achievement," but also
raises some disturbing questions about its conveyance of reality, and
these questions have to do with what accompanies the moving image.
For Professor Marwick, "whatever illusion the viewer had that he was
actually *seeing* the unfolding of events," the series depended heavily
on the commentary ("*spoken* by Britain's leading *actor*, Laurence Olivier") and on numerous eyewitness interviews ("that great cliche of
all television presentations . . . no one ever questioned whether the
impressions of an American sailor at Pearl Harbor, or those of an
English woman immured in wartime Germany, thirty years after, were
reliable.").[20]

A much harsher verdict has been passed on the 1983 thirteen-part
"telehistory" of America's war in Vietnam. Five years in the making,
with a multimillion-dollar budget and an expressed concern on the
part of its creators for "objectivity," "Vietnam: A Television History"
did receive not undeserved plaudits. Typical of this praise was the
response of the shrewd and estimable cold-war historian, Martin Sherwin, who expressed some doubts about the intellectual rigor of the
series' producers and their historical analysis, but concluded that
"Vietnam: A Television History" is "simply the best and most thorough
product of historical TV journalism that has ever been produced."
R. C. Raack, a historian whose scholarly activities include the making
of historical films, responded quite differently and his caveats raised
serious questions about the whole enterprise and its validity. In general,
his criticisms serve as a striking commentary on the failure of certain
kinds of media projects to deal with history. Raack's concern lies with
the way that the creators of this telehistory use the footage available
to them. He charges that they "appear not to have respected the
integrity of the historical film document" (possibly an "innocent error"
arising from a lack of awareness of the historical context of the evidence). Other manipulation he finds less innocent. The integrity of
the film and sound editing is dubious—film is "carefully cut to make
a point, not necessarily to reflect the document's information." Raack
questions the use of "ambient sound (turning pages, typing . . .
motors, footsteps and so on) to enhance the 'realism' of silent footage
or perhaps even the footage where the sound has been judged insufficient." He is understandably disturbed by these "audiovisual

editorials"; often the picture is used "to justify the text, though it may show scenes far removed . . . " Raack is also very concerned about the "omniscient narrator" who may comment emotionally in a "value-padded way."[21]

Compilations and documentaries, no matter what their editorial stance, are designed to be viewed as transcriptions of reality. The expectation of the untrained viewer is that they are observing the actual in distinction to something else which is made up and imaginary. This expectation is not a false assumption. Notwithstanding the visual interpretations, distortions, the manipulations, and the tricks, actuality does remain the operative basis of these genres.

The same cannot be said about docudrama. As the critic Michael Arlen recognizes, docudrama is a "hybrid form . . . too various to be described by exact definition," but in effect as he indicates "a story whose energy and focus have shifted from fiction to what is supposed to have actually happened." Media journalist Bill Davidson argues that even though docudramas are "presented to the public as essentially true stories," they are "tainted with romantic fiction." "Where," as the critic commented, "does the 'docu' end and the 'drama' begin?" The audience is never told. The term itself, point out the intelligent and successful television producers Richard Levinson and William Link, is "troublesome . . . , clearly . . . the product of a semantic shotgun wedding . . . blending two seemingly antithetical forms . . . " In any event this blending makes significant use of various dubious practices such as invented dialogue, plot fabrication, and rearrangement of fact as well as other instances of literary license—all characteristics which can make for cavalier treatment of history.[22]

Docudramas of one sort or another have been broadcast on television almost since regular programming began. A carryover from radio was the CBS program "You Are There." These were dramatic re-creations in which network correspondents using contemporary interviewing and reporting techniques would cover a story such as the trial of Socrates, the death of Joan of Arc, the Boston Massacre, or the last performance of Sarah Bernhardt. The anchorman, who for most of the 1950s programs was Walter Cronkite, would in an opening teaser give the viewer brief background information on the event to be covered, and conclude this introduction with the statement: "All things are as they were then, except You Are There." The shows were interesting, informative, and effective but the producers for all their high standards found it necessary to telescope time and to invent situations, and all too often the characters (no matter what the time frame) spoke a 1950s idiom. Typical of other 1950s docudrama programming was the technically remarkable but skewed and limited 1956 adaptation of Walter Lord's book about the sinking of the *Titanic* and a 1953 Philco Television Playhouse live presentation of David Shaw's treatment of the death of Floyd Collins (the Kentucky spelunker who died in a 1925 cave-in despite strenuous and much-ballyhooed efforts to rescue him). Shaw's work began "this is the true story . . . " but on the cast list "ficticious characters" outnumbered "actual characters" three to one.[23]

A new wave of docudramas began in the mid-1970s; the flow of production continues, albeit in somewhat reduced numbers. Many of these dramas deal with contemporary history—in large part because they are therefore more likely to do well in the ratings. As ABC-TV executive Brandon Stoddard explains, "a docudrama is more likely to attract viewers, if there are actual names and events that are familiar to people to begin with." There have been many series such as "Roots" (1977), "Ike" (1979), and "Robert Kennedy and His Times" (1984) and "one-shots" such as "Fear on Trial" (1975), "A Man Called Intrepid" (1979), "Kent State" (1980), and the "Atlanta Child Murders" (1985).[24]

It is all too easy to take potshots at the American network docudramas. "A Man Called Intrepid" dealt with the intelligence-gathering activities and other operations of a Canadian acting "on Churchill's orders" in the United States both before and after it entered World War II. The historian Hugh Trevor-Roper dismissed this docudrama as "not merely a travesty of fact; it is also a wanton insult to living memory . . . " Time's reviewer scored "Ike" as "a trashy romp through famous events, laced with unprovable innuendoes and raucous caricatures of public figures . . . , as history Ike is a waste of time . . . " "Fear on Trial" was a TV version of one time CBS radio-TV personality John Henry Faulk's blacklisting during the 1950s and his lengthy legal battle for vindication. Faulk, according to one account, "loved" the docudrama which was aired over CBS, but serious questions have been raised about its treatment of his actual personal life (which included a messy divorce) and of the real role of key CBS executives (who were involved in the network's blacklisting activities). The student protest at Kent State University against the American invasion of Cambodia in April-May 1970, as well as the killing of four persons by the National Guard during the course of these demonstrations, was the subject of "Kent State." An eyewitness to the events, including the killings, has maintained that "there is only one important scene without serious error . . . all the others have factual errors that seriously challenge the validity of the film." As for the Kennedy miniseries one critic echoed the beliefs of many when he charged that "the political purpose of the . . . series was barely disguised." And in the process, fact was distorted: Robert Kennedy, as attorney-general, is shown resisting the request of FBI head J. Edgar Hoover to place wiretaps on the Reverend Martin Luther King, Jr., but with no mention that Kennedy did actually authorize such taps.[25]

The makers of docudramas, understandably, have felt concern, dissatisfaction, and anger over the criticisms they have received about their handling of history. Abby Mann, the distinguished veteran writer and co-producer of "The Atlanta Child Murders," was outraged at the critical response his docudrama engendered. He set out to establish the innocence of Wayne Williams, the young black man convicted of two of the murders. CBS prefaced its broadcast of the two-part series with the ambiguous disclaimer that it was "not a documentary but a drama based on certain facts." An angry Mann defended it as "very accurate." The columnist Murray Kempton used such words and phrases as "fictive," "insufficiently scrupulous," and "relatively disgraceful" in reviewing Mann's effort. Mann angrily responded that Kempton "blew the review," and declared that "you have always sacrificed truth for what you think is a 'slant' that might make people think you are a 'clever' writer. You have struck again."[26]

The general response of the docudrama creators, whatever their private feelings, has been more measured. David Rintals, a brave and intelligent writer who has courted blacklisting in support of his ideals and who has scripted various docudramas including *Fear on Trial*, argues that "most writers who dramatize real people and events have a moral code" and that among its strictures were the following: "make no change that is not absolutely necessary to tell the story better, more understandably . . . , never change the essence of the story or the event or the character . . . , never invent unless it is necessary to fill a gap, or for reasons of completeness or clarity." Another writer, Ernest Kinoy, numbers among the docudramas he scripted one dealing with the chain of events leading up to President Truman's firing of General MacArthur in April 1951. A big scene in *Collision Course* (1976) as in real life was a 1950 meeting on Wake Island in a quonset hut at which only the president and the general were present. Kinoy recalled that he "made up that intrinsic big scene, based on what I knew happened afterwards . . . " TV producer-writers Levinson and Link wonder why "historians are not appeased by this." David Wolper, whose various TV creative activities include the production of many docudramas, among them *Roots* and *Collision Course*, in an echo of Grierson has declared "that the docudrama is a creative interpretation of reality." TV producer Allan Landeburg, who was "terribly frustrated by . . . not being allowed in the Oval Office" at the White House to find out what happened said at a seminar "Thank God docudrama came along . . . " And why? Because it allowed him "to guess what was happening in the Oval Office . . . And now I can tell the truth. I can tell what's really going on in the Oval Office." It seems to me that these defenders of the docudrama, whose statements are not atypical, have only made even more clear its shortcomings. There is something of the Orwellian Newspeak in their justification of the docudrama, for while expressing regard for accuracy, truth, and reality their efforts are enhancing or revising what's happened. As newsman Robert MacNeil angrily declared " . . . to a greater or lesser extent—the facts are something to be played with, manipulated, shaded, improved, distorted, colored, exaggerated, even ignored if they are inconvenient to make a better docudrama . . . " A concerned Erik Barnouw warned: "People who rely . . . on television for their knowledge of the past are dealing with . . . a situation where history is constantly being rewritten by the dominant medium to serve the purposes of the present."[27]

David Wolper, reports Robert Sklar, had with a "certain disdain" challenged "professors to tell the story . . . their way to a popular audience . . . and see if anyone would watch." Some historians have attempted to write history in film and video. The results have been mixed, for them and for the viewers of their efforts. Robert Brent Toplin has been involved with the making of a series of docudramas about American slavery. He initially approached the National Endowment for the Humanities for funding and as project director "identified the subject, conducted the research, formed an Advisory Board of scholars, and developed a treatment that shaped the main outlines . . . " As the project developed, he recalls, "we involved [media] professionals at every level," so that, in the end, "producers and directors with screen and TV credits coordinated the production plans, and a screenwriter drafted the shooting script." Toplin's first docudrama, *Denmark Vesey's Rebellion* (which dealt with a failed slave revolt in 1820s South Carolina) was aired over PBS in 1982. The most recent, *Solomon Northrup's Odyssey* (about the twelve year struggle of a free black man sold into slavery to regain his freedom) premiered in 1985. Toplin understands full well that matters of visual authority and minute detail require attention, but he feels strongly that historians' efforts should center on the script—they must play "a central role in the creation of the script" because it is primarily through the script "that a docudrama interprets history." In the case of *Denmark Vesey's Rebellion*, where the historical record is unclear about almost all aspects of what did or did not take place, it was necessary to harry the writer through "twenty-one major script revisions." This was done so that the dialogue would convey "several possible viewpoints through the voices of the characters" and so that viewers would be "challenged to wrestle" with various questions just as historians must do in "evaluating . . . conflicting information that appears in . . . primary documents." Historians must also realize, however, that "compromise" is essential for a successful production. They may "have to make some leaps" and "play with history" where the documented record as with Vesey is insufficient.[28]

Toplin, although he admits to occasional frustration, is satisfied with the outcome of his efforts. Daniel Walkowitz is less so. He initiated a project which resulted in a docudrama, "Molders of Troy" (1979), based on his fine monograph about iron and cotton workers in mid-nineteenth-century upstate New York. It has been aired over PBS and is available on videocassette. Walkowitz expended enormous energy on this docudrama, for which he served as project director, but was left ultimately "with a nagging sense of dissatisfaction." He remains "pleased," however, with many aspects of the finished docudrama, including the representation of work. His problems included difficulty in implementing his historical perspective and interpretation, a problem arising out of the complex production structure occasioned by National Endowment for the Humanities funding. Walkowitz was especially distressed by the portrayal of the leading woman, and the

situation of how to depict a mid-nineteenth-century worker's wife was
not entirely solved by editing. There were also problems with the
distributor who at one point, without Walkowitz's knowledge or consent, cut down the original ninety-minute version to an hour and
distributed that until Walkowitz put a stop to it.[29]

The intellectual leitmotif which informed the efforts of Toplin and
Walkowitz was the "new social history" emphasized in the ordinary
people who served as the protagonists of these historians' films. The
new social history also serves as the basis for the operations of the
American Working Class History Project, which was established at
the beginning of the 1980s to create "a multi-media curriculum on
the history of working people in America." Production of the Project's
first film was completed in late 1984. In the context of post-Civil War
America the film *1877: The Grand Army of Starvation* deals with the
shattering nationwide railroad strike of 1877, a social upheaval that
was a watershed in the history of the United States. Thirty minutes
long and designed to serve as "the pilot for a multi-episode television
series on the history of ordinary Americans", this film is neither docudrama nor compilation: it is a moving, informative committed melange of narrative, actors on camera in costume speaking the words
of contemporary participants, and animation drawn from contemporary cartoons, graphic illustrations, and photographs. In many instances these cartoons have been tinted, retouched, or otherwise
aftered. No attempt has been made to hide these alterations—the
film's credits draw attention to them. Stephen Brier—a historian and
the man responsible for the film—has maintained that the alterations
enhance the validity of the film. For example, by showing the workers
as portrayed by contemporary artists (that is, bestial, armed) and then
through the magic of animation showing these same workers as they
really were according to "reliable" nineteenth-century accounts, the
audience is better able "to understand the role that graphics have
played in creating particular images." For Brier, each image has a
point of view, "a picture is no more representative of 19th-century
'reality' than a person's words are. There is . . . a perspective."[30]

A particular reality has also marked the movie counterpart of the
TV docudrama. Such movies have been with us since the earliest days
of the film industry in the United States (and elsewhere). Long, long
ago, before the word docudrama was even a glint in the eyes of those
who coined the term, there were films which dramatized current
events—and past ones. Among the earliest of the silent American
feature films was Universal's 1913 six-reeler *Traffic in Souls*, a potboiler
and commercial smash hit about "white slavery"—a female plight
which between 1905 and 1915 "anguished and excited . . . American
public opinion." The producers of this overwrought but well-crafted
melodrama (which included good cops, bad politicians, innocents
lured into prostitution, and a virtuous daughter) advertised the film
as "the sensational motion picture dramatization . . . based on actual
reports of the Rockefeller Investigating Committee and the report of

the District Attorney of New York City for the suppression of White Slavery." Since 1913, hundreds of American feature films have dealt with actual events past and present, mixing real people with invented ones as "history is slightly reinforced with imagination" (to use the 1936 judgment of an interested *New York Times* correspondent). The camera's eye has focussed on the efforts of Louis Pasteur and of Karen Silkwood, on the private lives of the astronauts and of Justice Oliver Wendell Holmes, on the activities of various American presidents, on the filament in Edison's incandescent lamp and on the payload in Werner von Braun's rockets, on the pages of famous documents ranging from the Declaration of Independence to Zola's *J'Accuse*, on the achievements of baseball star Lou Gehrig, golfer Ben Hogan, all-round athlete Jim Thorpe, and the racehorse Seabiscuit.[31]

Hollywood in such movies is not committed to a policy of historical inaccuracy but the result is a historian's nightmare, no matter what time epoch is involved, no matter when the film was produced. In *Noah's Ark* (1928) the floods described by the Bible are arranged to save the female lead from the clutches of the villain. D. W. Griffith's *Intolerance* (1916) managed to depict the sixteenth-century St. Bartholomew's Day massacre of the Huguenots without going into its religious significance. The Dick Turpin portrayed by Tom Mix in 1925 was less an unsavory eighteenth-century highwayman than a combination Robin Hood and Good Samaritan. The Charge of Light Brigade of 1854 is presented in Hollywood's 1936 version as due not to misinterpretation or incompetence on the part of the studios' much adored British aristocracy but as occasioned by revenge for actions which supposedly had taken place a few years earlier in India. No genre or subject is immune to such rearrangement or embellishment. Hollywood consistently has tried, with rare exceptions, to avoid what the historian E. P. Thompson has called "the collisions of evidence and the awkward confrontations of experience."[32]

It may be true, as I. C. Jarvie states, that Hollywood lacks "historical sense," but the film industry's rearrangement of the past and the present is also grounded in other elements of feature-film production. Producer Irving Thalberg, a film industry wunderkind of the 1920s and 1930s, once noted that "if, in telling a story, we find it impossible to adhere to historical accuracy in order to get the necessary dramatic effect, we do change it and we do feel it is the right thing to do." Truth, accuracy, and a proper respect for history, then, have been routinely subordinated to the need for dramatic effect and even the whims of the filmmakers. MGM executive Bernie Hyman once produced a film about Johann Strauss. Having heard an aria by Mozart that greatly pleased him, Hyman determined to put it in the film. When told that this was "impractical" as the aria was by Mozart and the film was about Strauss and his music, an angry Hyman growled "who the hell is going to stop me?" The industry, moreover, has invariably focussed "on the individual who stands at the crux of historical currents" (to use one newspaperman's words). In the main Hollywood has focussed on the Great Man, with only an occasional bow to women such as Joan of Arc, Madame Curie, and Amelia Earhart. Underlying the production of these films on the Great Man is an assumption, best expressed long before there were movies, by Thomas Carlyle in *On Heroes*: "In all epochs . . . we shall find the great man to have been the indispensable savior of his epoch—the lightning without which the fuel would never have burnt." These Great Men stride through the films dealing with events. In these movies and in the TV docudramas which ape them, "the rest of time," as one observer has pointed out, "is an unpopulated void between the great moments."[33]

These great moments may change as our perceptions of the past are changed by the beliefs and needs of the present, for the moving image, like the written word, responds to changing interpretations of history. During World War II when the United States and the U.S.S.R. were allies, the American film industry put its traditional anti-Russian attitude into storage, but with the outbreak of the cold war in the mid-1940s, once again a more hostile view of the Russians was adopted. Similarly, films made about World War I, as Bruce Crowther notes, "vary enormously in their approach according to when they were made." What has been dubbed the "Hollywood Faction" of course had its counterpart in other national film industries. The 1937 Soviet film *Lenin in October*, a celebration of the Bolshevik seizure of power in 1917, grants Stalin considerable prominence; the prints currently in distribution, however, have at considerable effort eliminated Stalin entirely. Film scholar Alexander Sesonske, who discovered this rearrangement of history, has asserted that "as a depiction of the events of October, 1917, the new prints of *Lenin in October* are probably more accurate than the 1937 film . . . this time it is the history of cinema which has been rewritten and falsified."[34]

Czarist Russia in its last days was also the on-screen locus for a contretemps that should have taught the studios more respect for history but which only caused them to be a bit more circumspect in their claims. MGM's 1932 extravaganza *Rasputin and the Empress* dealt with the enormous influence wielded by Rasputin on the Russian royal family in the years prior to his murder in 1916 by Prince Felix Youssoupoff (given a different name in the film). For "shock progression," as one history puts it, MGM executive Bernie Hyman ordered a scene included that left no doubt that the film Rasputin raped the assassin's fiancee, a Russian princess who on screen had served as his sponsor at court. Hyman later added an opening title which announced that the movie "concerns the destruction of an empire, brought about by the mad ambition of one man. A few of the characters are still alive. The rest met death by violence." However Hyman's interpretation of the end of Czarist Russia is seen, Prince Felix and his wife (the Czar's niece) took exception to such things as the rape scene. Charging libel, they won a legal victory in Great Britain (being awarded over £100,000 and costs) and a very handsome out-of-court settlement in the United States (estimated to be over $ 1,000,000). Since then, no matter what a film company may claim in its advertising, each movie in one form or another includes a disclaimer to the effect that "the events and characters in this film are fictional and any reference to persons living or dead is purely co-incidental." Similar disclaimers are to be found even on such movies as the 1952 Columbia release *Walk East on Beacon*, which is "suggested" by the writings of then-FBI director J. Edgar Hoover and which begins with a narrator omniciently informing the audience that "this is a drama of real life" about the FBI's fight against foreign espionage and domestic subversion.[35]

The participation of a historian in the production of a Hollywood movie guarantees nothing. Robert Rosenstone, a historian whose biography of John Reed was well-received, served as a "historical consultant" on the film *Reds*. This 1982 film dealt with Reed, Louise Bryant, and the radical bohemian Left in the First World War era. Although Rosenstone was consulted years before shooting began, he regards his contribution as limited. He talked with the producer, "with others involved in the production . . . read the screenplay and offered criticisms and suggestions, both historical and dramatic." Rosenstone also was "occasionally asked specific questions about such things as the number of delegates to the Socialist Party convention in 1919, or the contents of Bryant's and Reed's letters when they were separated." He was, to use his words, "a resource." Rosenstone seems ambivalent in his feelings about *Reds*. Despite its "omissions, errors, and shortcomings," he has argued in one journal that the film "contains far more serious historical data than almost any other such Hollywood effort," and presents "more radical history than has ever been shown in an American film." But elsewhere he points out that *Reds* "takes the biting edge out of radicalism" and asserts that "we must never mistake its domestic drama for history." Rosenstone's ambivalence is not the result of inconsistency. He is caught in a dilemma—no matter how attractive or engaging the real thing may be, the perceptions that rule the creators of the moving image are determined by their supposed answers to the questions "what will make a profit at the box office, what will attract viewers?"[36]

Content analysis has quite properly been judged as extremely important by those like Rosenstone who are concerned with how the moving image interprets history, but as is increasingly being recognized, content analysis should be complemented by a searching analysis of the images themselves. Historian David Culbert points out that "the key to reading a visual image is composition (form) and what psychological meaning it may contain." He recognizes, as should we all, that there is a language to the moving image and that this language plays a great role in how we really see what we view. This language has many different elements, ranging from tempo ("as a rule the longer the scene is held, . . . the more relaxed the tempo; the shorter the scene, the more exciting") to perspective lines ("important in controlling the viewer's gaze").[37]

There is a visual context in the treatment of history by the moving image which must be grasped before we can begin to interpret that treatment. No matter how much effort has been expended on authenticity, on checking costume and decor, on getting right the codes of speech and behaviour, there is an offsetting factor. In the interest of getting the greatest audience possible, always—as English critic Stephan Neale insists—there is "some degree of compromise between 'historical accuracy' and current fashion." That compromise has been an important and continuing influence on the interpretations offered us—as for example the docudrama. Not only is the story line manipulated; so, too, is the visual image.[38]

A different distortion of reality has resulted from certain technical and economic limitations such as those governing the use of color. Most nonfiction filmmakers prior to the 1960s had neither the technical capacity nor the economic wherewithal to shoot in color. Thus until the mid-1950s color was used for what might be called frivolous films such as musicals or escapist fare such as swashbucklers. Reality was assumed to be what was presented in black and white. No longer does color by itself attract attention, for during the 1960s American cinema and television (as well as that of most of the rest of the world) converted to full use of color. Good news or bad, entertainment programming or docudrama, the moving image was in color (except when older black and white films were shown). No longer does reality come in black and white; it comes in all the colors of the rainbow. For those wishing to interpret reality, this conversion presents different problems with regard to authenticity: there are differences between the colors recorded by a lens and our eyes. The creators of the moving image thus "manipulate . . . effects through filters, lighting, choice of . . . stock, . . . even by applying cosmetic correction to the surface photographed." Color may also present another problem. Its very attractiveness may result in the presentation of misleading images: as the documentarist Joris Ivens found while shooting (in black and white) a film about poor miners in early 1930s Belgium, there is "danger in beauty" because the visual attractiveness captured by the footage may run counter to the rationale for undertaking the venture (he scrapped much of what he shot).[39]

Whether in color or black and white, the moving image and our interpretation of it are affected importantly by the differences between a work created for showing on a television screen and one produced for theatrical distribution (though even the production of the latter has been influenced by the fact that ultimately it will be broadcast on TV). There are distinctions in narrative, in presentation, in production—the framework is the same but the idiom is not. Space, for example, is treated differently. As Richard Maltby points out, "the shallow television image revises the [more traditional] visual rhetoric." The solution to this problem is either an expensive use of closeups, thus doing away with the mise-en-scène, or the use of a zoom or telephoto lens, which further flattens the perspective, creating an even shallower depth of field. It is clear that when videotape is used rather than a single film camera, TV's solution to the problem—the use of three cameras—leads to other distortions. The areas to be covered by the three cameras are strictly demarcated, the use of wide-angle shots is inhibited, the use of telephoto lenses is encouraged—the result is an overconcentration on single objects, often shown in spatial isolation. Thus the texture of the image made for television stresses performance over narrative and tends to simplify the complex.[40]

The attribute "complexity" certainly does not characterize much of the entertainment programming that television offers American viewers or the fare generally presented to American moviegoers past and present. Yet such shows and films, such products of Hollywood, which George Orwell has characterized as "synthetic pleasures," are as important to the historian as are the aspects of the moving image already mentioned. There is a great deal to be learnt from entertainment programming and film fare. To paraphrase the French film scholar Phillipe Esnault, every example of the moving image is a document concerning the people who have made it and the people who have seen it. Or to put it differently—as the journalist Max Lerner once said: "movies tell me about the culture of which I am a part."[41]

I have emphasized (and I believe necessarily) the problems of dealing with those manifestations of the moving image which attempt to interpret history. I have also stressed the difficulties faced by historians and others who wish to make use of the raw material provided by the moving image which like so much of the other evidence utilized in the writing of history is dotted with distortion, fabrication, and manipulation.

Notwithstanding the tricks played by the moving image as well as those played on it, all aspects of the moving image can be useful to historians as they put together their interpretations of the past. British historian J. A. S. Grenville, is absolutely correct when he maintains that such evidence "will not enable the historian to present the past as it really was." Will *any* kind of evidence allow historians to present an interpretation that does so? I think not. The writing of history is, to some extent, always a compromise, even when "warts and all" are included. As Richard Hofstadter has noted "what the historian does . . . is to slice out of an endless web of events and themes a limited number that he feels should be developed." History all too often is what those who write it wish the past to be. The American Harvey Klehr and the Russians N. K. Sivćhev and E. Yazkov in discussing the American Communist Party during the 1930s each forcefully present the same facts with very different interpretations. How then in the final analysis do we learn from the moving image in our attempts to interpret history? In what ways, as Grenville asks, do the various aspects of the moving image "offer the historian significant evidence peculiar to itself and not already available in literary form?"[42]

Answers to these questions depend in large part on how historians deal with the moving image's interpretation of history. In recent years there has been a spate of comment about film and television capturing what has been described as "the surfaces of reality" and of providing "unwitting testimony" that otherwise might be lost about everything under the sun. I do not mean to overstate the case, but I feel strongly that such comment is valid no matter what the tricks and dangers inherent in all aspects of the moving image—for "the untruths as well as the fact may help shape historical analysis"[43]

It is impossible to grasp fully how film and television interpret history unless one understands how historians and others have dealt with the interpretations set forth by each aspect of the moving image. The ability to deal with those interpretations depends on an individual's intellectual rigor, powers of analysis, detailed knowledge, level of sophistication, and willingness to slog on. A visual source can be and often is very important. Yet if its use is not, as Arthur Marwick remarks, "to . . . degenerate into the soft option of smart cocktail chat or high-flown waffle unrelated to any hard analysis," then that use must be complemented by proper documentation. It is necessary to ask of any visual source as one would of any other source how did it come into being, who created it and why, what was or is its impact. As Marwick argues, "visual sources . . . should be critically analyzed in the same way as more conventional sources." Failure to do so can result in badly skewed effort.[44]

Consider, for example, the 1950 RKO film *The Woman on Pier 13*, an absolutely dreadful piece of cold war anti-Red claptrap that began life as "I Married a Communist." Its very awfulness makes it distinctive: one writer has headed a chapter on the anti-Communist movies of that era "I Married a Communist and Other Disasters of the Blacklist." The film is a touchstone, not least because various writers have indicated that it served as a "loyalty test." I think it's fair to say that this charge can be traced to the blacklisted director Joseph Losey, who gladly turned down a chance in 1948 to handle this film. Losey, whom the critic Joan Mellen has described as a man "clearly unemancipated from his own Stalinist past" years later claimed "you offered 'I Married a Communist' to anybody you thought was a Communist, and if they turned it down, they were." Howard Hughes, who controlled RKO at this time, indulged in some vicious Red-baiting, but he did not in fact use "I Married a Communist" as a litmus test for political purity. The use of RKO's production files conclusively proves that, but even a perusal of the public record would demonstrate it. Among the men RKO's press department publicly announced as directors of this film were John Cromwell and Nicholas Ray. Both ultimately withdrew from what they considered a demeaning project, and Losey's contention notwithstanding, both within months directed other films for Hughes. *The Woman on Pier 13*, because of its interpretation of the present and the past, can be a very useful visual document for anyone dealing with the cold war, but only if proper attention is paid to the circumstances surrounding its production.[45]

Sensitivity to the broadest possible historical context requires attention to the media environment as well. Pierre Sorlin has noted that "historians who tried to list the historical inaccuracies in *The Birth of a Nation* would be ignoring the fact that their job should not involve bestowing marks for accuracy but describing how men living at a certain time understood their own history." The historian (or anyone else writing about films), however, must place that effort in an even broader context. Sorlin's analysis of *The Birth of a Nation* for all its virtues would benefit from being placed more clearly in the context of American film history. Sorlin pays close and intelligent attention to the film's treatment of blacks and their role in American society (and there is no gainsaying his argument that while the film is set at the time of the Civil War, it is commenting on the United States in 1915). But he overlooks the black stereotypes which dotted the movies between the 1890s and 1915 and which Griffith drew on—stereotypes which were racial libels, a "composite of qualities that were the opposite of the values treasured by white American society."[46]

Today, unlike a generation ago, many historians are concerned with film and TV and its use in the interpretation of history. This change has taken place in a very short time, really since the beginning of the 1970s in the United States (although the interest manifested itself first overseas in West Germany and also in England, where in 1967 the historian A. J. P. Taylor delivered a smashing series of lectures at London University on how film has interpreted history, and how historians should interpret films). Almost a half-century ago the German philosopher Walter Benjamin asserted that a camera "transformed our way of seeing by redefining the meaning of the picture. The camera can 'make' a picture from a perspective that cannot exist for any human spectator." Historians are now trying to explain and interpret that phenomenon for the human spectator and to conquer the fragmentation resulting from technology. The moving image is a new tool for historians, and as with any new tool, the carpenter is tempted for a while to overuse it, neglecting the other tools in his highly professional toolbox. Gradually the new tool assumes its proper place in the box, in the order of things, in the professional life of the carpenter or the historian. The record for the past few years would indicate that historians are able to make use of the image as a tool that can work for them and their audience despite the tricks inherent in it and played on it. To use another metaphor, historians are not stage managing the moving image; rather, they are using it to interpret history.[47]

NOTES

John O'Connor, the editor of this collection and the organizer of the project, assigned me the task of dealing with how the moving image in its various forms has perceived American history—a kind of truth, or "reality" as some would term it, and how that truth or reality has been presented, is interpreted, and may be utilized. I share this task with Pierre Sorlin, an innovative and important pioneer in such endeavors, especially as regards the feature film.

At the behest of John O'Connor, although these divisions are not meant to be mutually exclusive, Sorlin will deal mainly with Europe and I with America. This essay has benefitted enormously from comments on earlier drafts by Raye Farr, Fred Friendly, Jay Leyda, Arthur Marwick, and Robert Toplin.

1. Voltaire quoted in Arthur Marwick, *The Nature of History,* London: Macmillan, 1970, p. 244; Jack Valenti, "Voltaire's Timeless Eminence, *Saturday Review,* March 11, 1967, p. 27. See also J. H. Brumfitt, *Voltaire, Historian,* London: Faber and Faber, 1958. The Yeats quote comes from "Among School Children," Helen Gardner, ed., *The New Oxford Book of English Verse,* New York and Oxford: Oxford University Press, 1972, p. 827,

    > O chestnut-tree, great-rooted blossomer,
    > Are you the leaf, the blooms or the bole?
    > O body swayed to music, O brightening glance,
    > How can we know the dancer from the dance.

    I am indebted to A. R. A. Hobson for the Paul Valéry quote.

2. Michael Pitts, *Hollywood and American Reality: A Filmography of Over 250 Motion Pictures Depicting U.S. History,* Jefferson, NC: McFarland, 1984; Frank Nugent and Douglas Churchill, "Graustark", in Hanson Baldwin and Shepard Stone, eds., *We Saw It Happen: The News Behind the News That's Fit to Print,* New York: Simon and Schuster, 1938, p. 102. An iconoclastic view of the industry's writing of history is George MacDonald Fraser, *The Hollywood History of the World,* London: Michael Joseph, 1988.
3. William Hughes, "The Evaluation of Film as Evidence," in Smith, p. 50. Also please see Daniel J. Leab, "Images, Milages, & the Media: History & the Cinema," *Encounter.* January, 1989, pp. 70–75.
4. Richard Meran Barsam, ed., *Nonfiction Film Theory and Criticism,* New York: E. P. Dutton, Co., 1976, p. 13; "Keynote Address by Bill Moyers," National Jewish Archive of Broadcasting: Opening Ceremonies March 27, 1984; Craig Gilbert, "Reflections on 'An American Family' ", *Studies in Visual Communication,* Winter, 1983, p. 24; Arthur Asa Berger, *Television as an Instrument of Terror,* New Brunswick, NJ: Transaction Books, 1980, p. 90.
5. Jay Leyda, *Films Beget Films,* New York: Hill and Wang, 1968, p. 10.
6. Erik Barnouw: *Documentary: A History of the Non-Fiction Film,* New York: Oxford University Press, 1974, p. 160.
7. J. Fred MacDonald, *Television and the Red Menace: The Video Road to Vietnam,* New York: Praeger, 1985, p. 82; Leyda, p. 99; there is an intelligent detailed analysis of Project XX by Peter Rollins in John O'Connor, ed., *American History/American Television: Interpreting the Video Past,* New York: Ungar, 1983, pp. 134–158.
8. Telephone interview with Fred Friendly, March 28, 1985; de Antonio quoted in Alan Rosenthal, *The Documentary Conscience: A Casebook in Filmmaking,* Berkeley and Los Angeles: University of California Press, 1980, pp. 207, 211.
9. Gary Crowdus and Dan Georgkas, "History Is the Name of All My Films: An Interview with Emile de Antonio," *Cineaste,* No. 2, 1982, p. 23; Daniel Talbot, "On Historic Hearings from TV to Screen," *The New York Times Encyclopedia of Film,* New York: Times Books, 1985, January 12, 1964:

Erik Barnouw, "The Case of the A-Bomb Footage," *Studies in Visual Communication*, Winter, 1982, p. 9. Raye Farr, a superb film researcher who has been involved in the making of a number of compilations and documentaries, feels that the framework of time imposed by broadcast TV forces the kind of compression which means that "the possibilities for sublety" are lost along with the chance "to get it exactly right" (telephone interview with Raye Farr, April 2, 1985).

10. Hardy, *Grierson on Documentary*, p. 13; Paul Rotha, *Documentary Film*, London: Faber and Faber, 1939, 2nd ed. revised and enlarged, p. 134; Richard Dyer MacCann, *The People's Films: A Political History of U.S. Government Motion Pictures*, New York: Hastings House, 1973, p. 103.

11. Louis de Rochmont and Roy Larson quoted in Ray Fielding, *The March of Time*, New York: Oxford University Press, p. 75; Paul Rotha, "Films of Past and Future," *Theater Arts*, March 1938, p. 187; Luce quoted in Barnouw, *Documentary*, p. 121; Dangerfield quoted in Leyda, p. 98.

12. Van Dyke quoted in A. William Bluem, *Documentary in American Television*, New York: Hastings House, 1965, p. 256; Burton Benjamin, "The Documentary Heritage," in Lewis Jacobs, *The Documentary Tradition*, New York: W. W. Norton, 1979, 2nd ed., p. 301: Stanley Field, *The Mini-Documentary*, Blue Ridge Summit, PA: TAB Books, 1975, *passim*

13. Albert Wasserman quoted in Bluem, p. 257; Barnouw, *Documentary*, p. 227 (interestingly enough, since 1963 when Wasserman made this statement he has been involved with a variety of efforts that have taken strong stands on social issues but he has continued to assert that a "television documentary must seem to be much more dispassionate" than an independent documentarist who "can . . . try to persuade the audience of the correctness of his or her point of view." Quoted in Rosenthal, p. 99).

14. Arthur Barron, "Towards New Goals in Documentary," in Jacobs, pp. 495–496; Laurence S. Moss, "Film and the Transmission of Economic Knowledge: A Report," *Journal of Economic Literature*, September, 1979, p. 1005.

15. Friendly quoted in *The Invention of the Television Documentary: NBC News, 1950–1975*, New York: NBC News, 1975, p. 2; Murrow quoted in Leab, "See It Now: A Legend Reassessed," in O'Connor, p. 26; "Erik Barnouw: Reflections on the Past, Present, and Future of TV," *Emmy Magazine*, January/February, 1983, p. 18.

16. Barbara Abrash and Janet Sternburg, eds., *Historians and Filmmakers: Towards Collaboration*, New York: Institute for Research in History, 1983.

17. Paul Taylor, "The Wobblies," *Monthly Film Bulletin*, August, 1980, p. 162; James Hoberman quoted in Dan Georgkas, "The Wobblies: The Making of a Historical Documentary—an interview with Steward Bird and Deborah Shaffer," *Cineaeste*, Spring, 1980, p. 17; Melvin Dubofsky, "Film as History, History as Drama . . . ," *Labor History*, Winter, 1981, p. 138; Joseph Gomez, "History, Documentary, and Audience Manipulation: A View of the Wobblies," *Ibid.*, p. 142.

18. Goldfarb quoted in Susan Reverby, "With Babies and Banners: A Review," *Radical America*, September/October, 1979, p. 66.

19. For an extensive discussion of *With Babies and Banners* see Leab, "Writing History With Film: Two Views of the 1937 Strike against General Motors by the UAW," *Labor History*, Winter, 1979/80, pp. 102–112.

20. Rosenthal, pp. 37. 42; Arthur Marwick, "Print, Pictures, and Sound," *Daedalus*, Fall, 1982, p. 154.

21. Martin J. Sherwin, "Vietnam, A Television History," *OAH Newsletter*, Au-

gust, 1983, p. 20; R.C. Raack, "Caveat Spectator," *Ibid.*, February, 1984, pp. 25–28.

22. Michael Arlen, *The Camera Eye: Essays on Television*, New York: Farrar, Straus, and Giroux, 1981, p. 277; Bill Davidson, "Fact or fiction—Television Docudrama," in Jay S. Harris, ed., *TV Guide: The First 25 Years*, New York: Simon and Schsuter, 1978, p. 240; Stephan Lagerfeld, "History As Soap Opera?" Wilson *Quarterly*, Autumn 1985, p. 156; Richard Levinson and William Link, *Stay Tuned: An Inside Look at the Making of Prime Time Television*, New York: St. Martin's Press, 1981, p. 138.

23. Robert Horowitz, "History Comes to Life and *You Are There*," in O'Connor, pp. 79–94 is a fine overview although much more exciting is Larry Ceplair, "Great Shows: You Are There," *Emmy Magazine*, January/February, 1984, pp. 43–47, which points out that many of the writers had been blacklisted including Abe Polansky, Walter Bernstein, and Arnold Manoff (p. 46); George Roy Hill and John Whedon, "A Night to Remember," in *The Prize Plays of Television and Radio, 1956*, New York: Random House, 1957; William Kaufman, ed., *The Best Television Plays*, New York: The Merlin Press, 1954, pp. 295, 297.

24. Stoddard quoted in Davidson, p. 142. Although I am dealing here with American docudramas, it is important to realize that this form—however it may be termed, and in the U.K. it has been called drama documentary—also has its counterparts elsewhere in the world: indeed such productions are a staple of British TV. A prime mover of drama documentary in British television has been Leslie Woodhead, who has dealt mainly with Eastern European topics such as the Soviet dissident general Grigorenko ("The Man Who Wouldn't Keep Quiet," 1970) and the 1968 Soviet invasion of Czechoslovakia ("Invasion," 1978). For Woodhead "the priority is journalistic: the object is to bring to the screen certain important areas which can't be covered any other way." He has expressed uneasiness about the form, which he has characterized as "an unruly beast," and he has asserted that "if it could be done any other way I'd rather do it that way" (see Robert Brown, "On Television, Under Drama Documentary," *Monthly Film Bulletin*, June, 1983, p. 154; Leslie Woodhead, "Drama Documentary," *Granada, The First Twenty Five Years*, London: British Film Institute, 1981, p. 110; a fine rundown to the drama documentary is BFI Dossier #19, *Drama Documentary*, London: British Film Institute, 1983).

25. Hugh Trevor-Roper quoted in *Halliwell's Television Companion*, London: Granada, 1982, p. 381; Frank Rich, "Love at War With Ike and Kay," *Time*, May 7, 1979, p. 67; John O'Sullivan, "Damned Lies and Docu-Dramas," *The Times*, April 6, 1985, p. 8; Faulk cited in Davidson, p. 242; Jerry M. Lewis, "Kent State, The Movie," *Journal of Popular Film and Television*, Spring, 1981, p. 16.

26. CBS and Mann quoted in O'Sullivan; Murray Kempton, "Misjudgment at Atlanta," *The New York Review of Books*, March 14, 1985. p. 31; Abby Mann, "The Atlanta Child Murders," *Ibid.*, April 11, 1985, p. 44. Kempton's rejoinder to Mann's response was almost as long as his original review, and expressed no repentence: he charged Mann with "a disciplined determination to overlook anything unsuitable to the convenience of his argument" and asserted that he "had never met any [journalists] who would twist an event quite as cavaliery and, I suspect, as erroneously, as Mann has this one" (*Ibid.*, p. 45).

27. Rintels quoted in Levinson andd Link, p. 141; Kinoy quoted in Davidson,

p. 242; Levinson and Link, p. 139; Wolper quoted in *Ibid.*, p. 142; Landsburg quoted by Richard Reeves in *Ibid.*, pp. 142–143; phone interview with Friendly, March 28, 1985; Robert MacNeil, "Why Do They Hate Us?" *Columbia*, June, 1985, p. 17; David Keller, "Eric Barnouw: Reflections . . . ," p. 13.

28. Robert Sklar, *Prime Time America: Life On and Behind the Television Screen*, New York: Oxford University Press, 1980, pp. 169–170; Robert Brent Toplin, "The Making of *Denmark Vesey's Rebellion*," *Film and History*, September, 1982, pp. 50, 52; phone interview with Toplin, March 30, 1985.

29. Daniel Walkowitz, *Worker City, Company Town: Iron and Cotton Worker Protest in Troy and Cohoes, New York, 1955–1884*, Urbana: University of Illinois Press, 1978; phone interview with Walkowitz, March 30, 1985.

30. *American Working Class History Project News*, # 1, December 11. 1981, # 6, December 15, 1984; phone interview with Stephen Brier, March 27, 1985; further explication of Brier's videos are to be found in "A History Film Without Much History," *Radical History Review*, April, 1988, pp. 120–128 (which is part of an interesting issue devoted to "Film and History"); Abrash and Sternburg, p. 26.

31. Daniel J. Leab, "Woman and the Mann Act," *American Studies/Amerika Studien*, # 1, 1976, p. 55: advertisements reproduced in I. G. Edmunds, *Big U: Universal in the Silent Days*, South Brunswick and New York: A.S. Barnes Co., 1977, p. 34 and quoted in Terry Ramsaye, *A Million and One Nights: A History of the Motion Picture*, New York: Simon and Schuster, 1964 (a reprint of the 1926 edition), p. 617; "Charged to the Light Brigade," *New York Times Encyclopedia of Film*, October 25, 1936 A.

32. Thompson quoted in Michael Tracey, "The Poisoned Chalice: International Television and the Idea of Dominance," *Daedalus*, Fall, 1985, p. 51.

33. I. C. Jarvie, *Movies and Society*, New York: Basic Books, 1970, p. 125; Thalberg quoted in Michael Isenberg, *War on Film: The American Cinema and World War I, 1911 1941*, London and Toronto: Associated University Presses, 1981, p. 32; Hyman quoted in S. N. Behrman, "You Can't Release Dante's Inferno in the Summertime," *New York Times Encyclopedia of Film*, July 17, 1966 A; Douglas Churchill, "Hollywood Goes Historical," *Ibid.*, August 4, 1940 A; Carlyle quoted in *Ibid.*; Todd Gitlin, *Inside Prime Time*, New York: Pantheon Books, 1983, p. 162.

34. Bruce Crowther, *Hollywood Faction: Reality and Myth in the Movies*, London: Columbus Books, 1984, p. 9; Alexander Sesonske, "Re-Editing History," *Sight and Sound*, Winter, 1984/1985, p. 58.

35. James Kotsilibas-Davis, *The Barrymores: The Royal Family in Hollywood*, New York: Crown Publishers, 1981, p. 141; Ted Berkman, *The Lady and the Law: The Memorable Life of Fanny Holtzmann*, Boston: Little Brown, Co., 1976, pp. 137, 142; Bosley Crowther, *The Lion's Share*, New York: E. P. Dutton & Co., 1957, p. 227.

36. Robert A. Rosenstone, " 'Reds' Distorts American Radicalism," *OAH Newsletter*, May 1982, pp. 13–14; "*Reds* as History," *Reviews in American History*, September, 1982, pp. 297, 308.

37. David Culbert, "Historians and the Visual Analysis of the News," in William Adams and Fay Schreibman, eds., *Television National News: Issues in Content Research*, Washington, D.C.: Television and Politics Study Program, School of Public and International Affairs, George Washington University, 1978, p. 141; Roy Paul Madsen, *The Impact of Film*, New York: Macmillan Company, 1973, pp. 47, 62.

38. Stephen Neale, "Genre and Cinema," in Tony Bennett, et al., eds., *Popular Television and Cinema*, London: BFl Publishing/Open University, 1981, p. 20. A fascinating West German point of view is to be found in Jan Schulbach, "Vier Anmerkungen zu Schwierigkeiten, die uns die Erstellung historischer Filme bereitet," *ARD Fernsehspiel*, no place of production: ARD, 1977, pp. 16–21.
39. John Fell, *Film: An Introduction*, New York: Praeger, 1975, pp. 99, 102.
40. Richard Maltby, *Harmless Entertainment: Hollywood and the Ideology of Consensus*, Metuchen, NJ: The Scarecrow Press, 1983, p. 333.
41. W. J. West, ed., *Orwell: The War Broadcasts*, London: Duckworth/British Broadcasting Corporation, 1985, p. 73; Esnault quoted in Eugene C. McCreary, "Film and History: Some Thoughts on Their Interrelationship," in E. Bradford Burns, ed., *Latin American Cinema: Film and History*, Los Angeles: UCLA Latin American Center, 1975, p. 50; Max Lerner, *Public Journal*, New York: The Viking Press, 1945, p. 27.
42. Joseph Welch with Richard Hofstadter, et al., *The Constitution*, Boston: Houghton Mifflin & Co., 1956, p. xii; Harvey Klehr, *The Heyday of American Communism: The Depression Decade*, New York: Basis Books, 1983; N. Sevachev and E. Yazkov, *History of the U.S.A. Since World War I*, Moscow: Progress Publishers, 1979; J. A. S. Grenville, *Film in History: The Nature of Film Evidence . . .* , Birmingham,UK: University of Birmingham, 1971, pp. 21, 22.
43. Hughes, p. 65; Marwick quoted in Anthony Aldgate, *Cinema and History: British Newsreels and the Spanish Civil War*, London: Scolar Press, 1979, p. 12; Isenberg, p. 216.
44. Arthur Marwick, "Film in University Teaching," in Smith, p. 151; Marwick, "History on Television: The Open University Series, Britain and America as Visual Evidence," *Journal of Educational Technology*, forthcoming, p. 3 in manuscript.
45. Andrew Dowdy, *The Films of the Fifties: The American State of Mind*, New York: William Morrow and Company, Inc., 1973, Chapt. 2. Among the works which describe *The Woman on Pier 13* as a "loyalty test" are Robert Ottoson, *A Reference Guide to the American Film Noir*, Metuchen, NJ: The Scarecrow Press. 1981, p. 193; Nora Sayre, *Running Time: Films of the Cold War*, New York: The Dial Press, 1982, p. 80: Colin Shindler, *Hollywood Goes to War: Film and American Society, 1939–1952*, London: Routledge and Kegan Paul, 1979, p. 80; Harry Wasserman, "Ideological Gunfight at the RKO Corral: Notes on Howard Hughes' I Married a Communist," *The Velvet Light Trap*, Winter 1974, p. 8; Joan Mellen, "Film and Style: The Fictional Documentary", in Burns, p. 89; Tom Milne, *Losey on Losey*, Garden City, NY: Doubleday, 1968, p. 76. The final screenplay has been published in the "RKO Classic Screenplays" series: *The Woman on Pier 13*, New York: Ungar, 1985. See also Daniel J. Leab, "How Red was my Valley: Hollywood, the Cold War, and *I Married a Communist*," *Journal of Contemporary History*, January, 1984, pp. 59–88, and "*The Iron Curtain* (1948): Hollywood's First Cold War Movie," *Historical Journal of Felm, Radio, and Television*, 8 (No 2, 1988), 153–188.
46. Sorlin, pp. 83, ix, 112; Daniel J. Leab, *From Sambo to Superspade: The Black Motion Picture Experience*, Boston: Houghton Mifflin, 1975, p. 20. For a thorough overview please see Chapter II, "Afro-Americans," in Allen L. Woll and Randall M. Miller, *Ethnic and Racial Images in American Film and Television*, New York: Garland, 1987, pp. 39–178.

47. Among the books which have been published in recent years which involve historians interpreting American film and its interpretation of history are John O'Connor and Martin Jackson, eds., *American History/ American Film, Interpreting the Hollywood Image*, New York: Ungar, 1988, 2nd ed. Randall Miller, ed., *The Kaleidoscopic Lens: How Hollywood Views Ethnic Groups*, Englewood, NJ: Jerome Ozer, publisher, 1980; Peter Rollins, ed., *Hollywood as Historian: American Film in Cultural Context*, Lexington, KY: University Press of Kentucky, 1983.

Patricia-Ann Lee, Professor of History at Skidmore College, studies Elizabethan and early Stuart England. Her recent publications in that field include: "Reflections of Power: Margaret of Anjou and the Dark Side of Queenship" in Renaissance Quarterly *(Summer, 1987), and "A Bodye Politique to Governe: Knox, Aylmer and the Elizabethan Debate on Queenship,"* PLA Report *Vol X, 1988. She has developed new approaches and course materials relating the moving image to the study of history, some of which were discussed in "The Frozen Moment: History and the Uses of Film,"* Film & History, *Vol. XII, no. 2 (May, 1982) pp. 35–43.*

TEACHING FILM AND TELEVISION AS INTERPRETERS OF HISTORY

Patricia-Ann Lee

A source of information to many people, the purveyor of historical "knowledge" to multitudes of television viewers, a reflector of popular opinion and perhaps a maker of it, the moving image document is an increasingly important part of all our lives. The question therefore is not whether film is going to appear in the classroom: it may do so directly; it will certainly do so indirectly through the experience and attitudes as well as the intellectual baggage students bring with them. Given these facts we have an obligation to help students learn to deal with this omnipresent and omnicompetent entity, and to encourage them to apply the same critical and discriminating judgment to the study of film that we expect them to use in evaluating more traditional sources. They must become visually aware and visually literate. Speaking about television and the learning process Umberto Eco compared it to the use of books. "You can use books to teach," he pointed out, "but first you must teach people about books."[1]

The first fact which faces the teacher-historian is that film is radically different from other and more familiar tools. The most obvious differences are probably those associated with the presence in the classroom of complicated machinery, the difficulties of finding, ordering, budgeting for, and showing films, and perhaps the challenge of fitting film into a familiar curriculum. Far more significant, however, is the nature of film itself which is experiential and communal. It requires teachers to think in new ways about *how* to teach and perhaps also about the kinds of things they wish to teach, since process not only interpenetrates subject matter but may itself become subject matter. In the end, film cannot provide us with new answers in history, only the potentiality for asking new questions.

Creating or even defining methodologies is a chancy and dangerous business since it suggests that there are absolutes in a process which must always retain the greatest possible flexibility. In teaching, the task is particularly delicate since methods which the teacher sees as facilitating enquiry and recognizes as practical and provisional, when they are "learned" by a student, can bar other approaches to a problem and other ways of perceiving it. Yet to say such devices can be dangerous is not to say they cannot also be useful and are not necessary. In the case of film where the body of material to be studied is so diverse and so different from what students conventionally think of as historical, the need—and the danger—are all the greater.

Before turning to methodological concerns as they apply specifically to film as interpreter of history in the classroom, it is necessary to address a continuing problem all teacher-historians face, whether they are using film or more traditional sources. That difficulty is the confusion in the minds of many and perhaps most students about what history actually is. Too often students regard history as the past and consider a film to be historical because it seems to recapture a particular aspect of the past in factual detail. That history is not the past but a means by which material of the past can be submitted to informed inquiry and critical discourse, that it is a process and a series of mental constructs, that to write or film history is necessarily to interpret, are things that must be learned anew by every generation of students. Only when they have been learned can the focus of the classroom change—from getting the right answers to asking meaningful questions, from learning history to learning to *do* history which is to say, learning to think like a historian. Teaching history of any kind demands this understanding, but teaching with and from film may make such understanding easier to achieve. The field is still new and so are the means of looking at its materials. It requires that we use different as well as familiar scholarly devices for approaching and interpreting the past. In short it makes us rethink our assumptions about how and what history can tell us.

Having said this, a bare recital of the areas within which an investigation of filmic material can be organized may seem surprisingly conventional. The first is content, the interior history of the document: for whom was it intended (its audience), what is its thesis (texts and subtexts), and so on. This is also the area in which questions of authenticity and factuality will naturally arise. The film document is not born in a vacuum and, like the written document, has to be considered in terms of its provenance or, more accurately, its production. Film is a creature of art but also of commerce. If it has an artistic history which has to be taken into to account, it also has a technical and business one. Marketing concerns, formal and informal agents of censorship including political considerations, and of course cost also shape historical interpretation. To this second area, which combines both interior and exterior considerations, must be added a third that is wholly exterior. It is the reception of the film, its historiography if you will. Just as a document like Magna Carta may change its meaning over time, so a film may alter in terms of its perceived meanings and significance. Content, production, reception: how analysis will proceed within each of them will depend upon the filmic document being studied and the information available as well as the aims of a particular class or course.

Teachers often use historical films for illustration, motivation, or inspiration, a means of arousing curiosity about the past which can then be directed into disciplined inquiry. Highly experienced teachers who approach film in a variety of other ways still find dramatized reenactment useful. Whether a feature film like Olivier's *Henry V*, or a popular TV miniseries such as "Roots," such material can start the historical juices flowing in a class by encouraging sympathetic interest in people and events of another period, by stimulating creative curiosity, and by doing so in a setting which encourages direct interactive and immediate discourse on the film document. Deeper analysis can involve students in examining a film or group of films not so much in terms of their historical information content, but as documents which embody the historical assumptions and express the interpretive concerns of a particular social and cultural moment. Questions of interpretation can then be examined both in filmic terms and through the exploration of other documentary and textual sources. The most difficult and demanding kind of film study, this is also the fullest, most complex, and in the end probably the most rewarding since it makes possible a direct scholarly use of the film document.

Learning how films convey their messages and becoming aware of the ways in which technical process necessarily shapes visual language are important. Recognizing that scholarship may affect those messages less than money considerations, politics, and sheer ignorance is depressing but necessary. The ability not only to vigorously analyze content but to understand process helps to arm the student viewer against too easy acceptance of film as provider of fact and as authoritative interpreter of historical ideas. If the novel is a "machine for generating interpretations" so too is the film and it may well be in that role that it is most useful in the history classroom.[2]

* * * *

Henry V, a work rooted in a powerful literary tradition, shows how rich and how flexible a teaching tool film can be in examining problems of historical interpretation. Based upon Shakespeare's play which itself is based upon Holinshed and other chroniclers, it is in its most obvious reading, a late Tudor study of ideal kingship personified by a fifteenth-century hero king. In 1944 this material, reworked by Lawrence Olivier and his colleagues and trimmed to half its length, was translated into the language of film to rouse and inspire an England then engaged in fighting the Second World War. At one level it is therefore a traditional historical reenactment, referring to real historical events and persons to which factually its interpretation may be (not too usefully) compared. At the same time it is also a mid-twentieth century film about a Tudor play, about a late medieval English king. Or is it? In fact it brings us face to face with the most elemental and challenging problems of historical interpretation and forces a student to examine not a single past but multiple and sometimes conflicting perceptions of several different ones. Thus, although the film can be used to stimulate interest in Shakespeare's period or in Henry's and to encourage further investigation, it also offers possibilities for more complex and significant historical learning.

If the film is not about the "real" Henry Plantagenet (and the most cursory examination will suggest that it is not), what then is its subject matter? One answer has to be that it is about Shakespeare's play. This is explicit in Olivier's work which begins backstage in the "real" Globe Theatre and then moves out front to watch the performance, to which location it returns again at the very end of the film. Certainly any study of the film raises questions about the play and the way it interprets a historical subject in terms of Shakespeare's own concerns, *his* preoccupation with order in society, and *his* interest in the problems of kingship. It must also take into consideration the way he knew and used the historical sources upon which he based his work. Additionally, it should give more than a passing thought to political events and structures of his day as they would have shaped his ideas and the expectations of his audience.

If *Henry V* is about Shakespeare's theatre it may also be about theatre and film in a more general sense. To look at the way in which the "wooden O" informed the language and helped set the shape of the Elizabethan play invites comparison (implicit in the structure of Olivier's work) with the very different possibilities of film. The scenes in the Globe deliberately open out into a world of mingled fantasy and reality which would not have been available in any other medium. What indeed is the relationship of Olivier's play to its Shakespearean progenitor, of a filmed document to a literary one, of a visual medium to a verbal source? *Henry V* is in this sense an interpretive essay on the history of theater.

These and many other questions spring naturally from a careful examination of the content of the film document and of ancillary materials such as play and film scripts, chronicles, and other conventional materials of history. Yet taken alone they can give only a partial and incomplete sense of its interpretive possibilities. For a film, *as film*, has a life and history of its own which students need to examine in its own terms and be able to discuss in its own language. Just as they might analyze passages in the play or script, they need to learn to look at individual film sequences. In learning to identify editing devices (slow dissolves, pans, tracking shots, and so on) and in discovering the ways in which techniques like montage can make out of the associative values of image a language of vision, they will develop their ability to read this or any film. Even a simple trick such as turning off the sound for a particular sequence can emphasize how music and other aural effects serve to create a mood, emphasize a point, or comment on an action. Indeed it is the arrowflight at Agincourt, with its mingling of sight and sound, which is one of the high points of the battle.

To see and hear in the language of film is to begin to understand how it can speak its images of a particular past. From questions properly asked and imaginatively answered, other insights can be developed. It is obvious, for example, that *Henry V* embodies the ideas of Olivier the director and that these ideas are expressed in everything from the script to the camera angles. But what, it might be asked, was the role of Olivier the star, whose style and persona impressed themselves upon the portrayal of the king? What too was the contribution of those joined with him in the production, Filippo Del Giudice (the producer), Reginald Beck (his technical advisor and editor), or Robert Krasker (his cameraman)? Olivier himself has often stressed the degree to which this particular film was the result of a successful team effort. Of course, politics also played a role and *Henry V* cannot be understood apart from the social and political context of the Second World War. Made with official encouragement and assistance at a time of national emergency, it must also be examined as propaganda which aimed to influence and form public opinion. In this sense, whatever else it is about, *Henry V* concerns a modern war whose events explain and are themselves part of its meaning. The process by which the austere, ruthless autocrat of Shakespeare's play became the inspiring and warmly human king of Olivier's film may tell the student little about Tudor England. However, it offers interesting evidence for what was considered a proper style of leadership in the middle of the twentieth century and considerable insight into the ways in which contemporary concerns can influence historical interpretation (or reinterpretation).

The reception of the film suggests yet another range of questions. If the play gained and lost by its translation into film, the film itself has not remained static in meaning. Although the words and celluloid images are substantially the same, their interpretation has altered with changing views of war, of heroes, of the nature of politics, and about the proper relationship of men and women. To approach the film with a class via a feminist critique, or a Marxist one, is to open it up to meanings and perceptions of yet another period, our own.

As these speculations may have suggested (and they have by no means exhausted the subject), a dozen or more courses might easily draw from, make use of, or even be centered upon this single film. I myself have used it in an examination of illusion and reality in the depiction of war. For a colleague it will be part of a series of films dealing with the heroic icon, and in another context it has been joined with *Alexander Nevsky* and *Triumph of the Will* in a study of the film as propaganda. Its popularity in the classroom owes much to its rich literary associations and to the visual splendor and complexity of the work, but also to the availability of supporting materials. These include printed versions of both play and script, many literary critiques, a

wealth of traditional historical material in all its periods, and an excellent film guide in the series published by the University of Indiana.[3]
Its history and historiography can also be traced in newspapers and
in trade and professional journals which are available on microform.
Using these sources the teacher can construct supporting readings,
prepare pre-viewing and post-viewing problems and study questions,
and where appropriate, direct students in further group or individual
research.

Of course, feature film is not the only form of historical reenactment. Indeed it may no longer be the most significant if what is measured is its impact upon large numbers of people. As docudrama
grows in popularity and miniseries proliferate, it becomes ever more
necessary for students to exercise hard critical judgment in examining
the ideas and challenging the assumptions inherent in these productions. From the point of view of the historian, docudrama has always
been a cause of concern. Even the title misleads, since what is presented is usually drama for which "history" merely provides a colorful
background. Rarely do such programs offer any significant insight
into the periods or events they claim to represent. Although reputable
historians may have been consulted in their preparation, the historical
concepts these presentations embody tend to be not only simplistic
but so narrowly defined that they close off other possible interpretations.

There are exceptions, of course. "Roots" for example, was not only
an enormous popular success but encouraged its audience to rethink
at least some of the things it imagined it knew about slavery. Although
trading in the usual dramatic currency of heroes and villains (many
of the latter mere caricatures), it was lengthy enough to allow a lei-
surely look at its subject matter and proved to be a useful corrective
to older historical stereotypes. As a social document, which may or
may not have affected attitudes of blacks and whites, it also merits
attention. In a critical essay, Leslie Fishbein has sketched its history
as well as giving a sense of production problems, executive decisions,
and problems of censorship ("no bared female breast could be larger
than a size 32 or shown within 18 feet of the camera").[4] This essay
helps to put the film's popular triumph in better perspective, makes
its compromises more understandable, and would be a fine starting
point for classroom discussion and analysis. Beyond whatever it has
to say about slavery "Roots" also offers material for an examination
of historical myths, how they are debunked and perhaps also how
they are made. In this context the fact that Haley's book was "laden
with inaccuracies" in the depiction of slavery may be less significant
than its "symbolic truth" although the two need to be clearly distinguished from one another.[5]

Nevertheless, the question of historical accuracy, accuracy in detail
as well as fidelity to the spirit of events, cannot be avoided in material
which claims to be based on fact. Executive producer David Wolper's
assertion that details (in "Roots") were irrelevant because "a film is

not for reference, but for emotional impact to let you know how it was to live at a certain moment in time" can be balanced against others by Natalie Zemon Davis (about *Martin Guerre*).[6] Acknowledging that the past may have significant resonances in the present, she points out that it nevertheless remains the past and "the first thing you do is let the past be the past insofar as you can know it."[7] Taking such statements as a starting point the problem of reality and of historical truth, which has always haunted historians, could here become the focus of class examination. So too could questions of historical perspective. The problem is not just "What was Alex Haley's view?" nor "What was the view of the producer of 'Roots'?" but "What are other possible interpretations?" As Natalie Davis said of her own work, "I wanted to shake people up, because I feel that is what history is about. It is not about confirming what you already know, but about stretching it and turning it upside down and then reaffirming some values, or putting some into question."[8] This is an excellent statement of what the historian does and a well-defined perspective from which any teacher and class might begin their work.

While commercial television reaches greater numbers of people, PBS has witnessed a far more interesting development of the docudrama genre. This is the emergence of a group of films created by filmmakers who are historians or by historians and filmmakers working together. By combining their professional areas of expertise and with the assistance of funding grants, they have created films which embody the best qualities of historical investigation and presentation. Robert Brent Toplin's *Denmark Vesey's Rebellion* (1981) and Daniel Walkowitz's "Molders of Troy" (1979) have helped to set a standard for such work. Shown in the classroom (perhaps in conjunction with commercial productions on the same general subjects) they help students see how scholars think about historical problems.

"Molders of Troy" shares with "Roots" the perspective which has been described as looking at history from the bottom up, that is of looking at it not from the perspective of kings, presidents, and generals, but of ordinary people. It also faced some of the same problems since ordinary lives are rarely recorded in any detail and are therefore difficult to depict. Walkowitz's solution was to create the people and images which would express his views, but to do so within a carefully reconstructed historical framework. In his view " 'fictionalized history,' is the recognition that history is not a setting . . . or a group of discrete facts, but a *process* of changing social relationships."[9] Using his knowledge of the era and the subject the historian creates a " 'real' synthesis in a fictional place. Rather than " 'facts,' authenticity—the conception of the process under study—must be retained."[10] In "Molders of Troy" he uses the story of a working-class family of iron molders in Troy, New York, to examine aspects of the industrial revolution and the labor movement between 1859 and 1876. A class working with Walkowitz's film might well begin by reading the article from which these quotations are taken in order to understand the goals which the historian-filmmaker has set for himself, before examining his work. It would also be useful to look at the book, *Worker City, Company Town*, which covers much of the same ground and on which he was at work during the making of the film. From this kind of comparison they can begin to see how the historian may express his ideas in different mediums and how, when he does, this affects the mode of interpretation.[11]

"Molders of Troy" received funding from the National Endowment for the Humanities as did *Denmark Vesey's Rebellion*. Robert Brent Toplin, the filmmaker, has also written about his experience in making this story of an attempted slave revolt in 1822. As a classroom teaching device, it too is a useful corrective to the simplistic and restricted view of the average commercial reenactment. Rather than presenting one single interpretation of the events, Toplin and his advisory board tried to incorporate a degree of ambiguity and to convey the sense that there were many different ways of looking at what happened. Even the reality of the rebellion was open to question since it was possible that its ramifications existed chiefly in the minds of panicky Charleston whites. Rather than presenting a solution, Toplin's script left the question deliberately open and "allowed the dialogue to convey several possible viewpoints" so that viewers were "challenged to wrestle with the question just as the historian must do in evaluating the conflicting information that appears in the primary document."[12] The way in which "narrativity" can restrict interpretive choice and therefore limit the possibility of understanding the real complexity of historical connections is something of which most students are not aware and about which they need to think.[13] Properly used, films such as *Denmark Vesey's Rebellion*, can help to make the point.

Perhaps the films which have been most consistently used in history teaching are documentary/compilation portrayals of issues and events. The idea of seeing at least some of the events and personalities of the past "as they really were" is seductive. Furthermore, there is a continuing supply of the product since commercial television offers a profitable market for programs which present the background of current problems, or depict dramatic moments in recent history, or which provide information about historical personalities in a way which seems to combine educational values with entertainment.

R. C. Raack has pointed out that rental catalogues are filled with retreads from commercial TV and with old educational films which he describes, (with considerable justification) as "quaint antiques, outdated pedagogically and technically."[14] The former are at best journalistic; the latter, pedantic. Both tend to concentrate on transmitting information "predigested and summarized, as if the great issues of history might be purveyed with finality in neat packages fitting an allotted time slot."[15] Such films do not meet the classroom need for historically accurate material which is challenging and open ended and which invites interpretation rather than attempting to present answers. It is also true that, in the absence of anything better, they will continue to be used, forcing teachers and students to cope as best they can with flawed material. Fortunately, in some cases, even defects can become positive resources for teaching. Implicit as well as explicit messages, and information on attitudes, values, and assumptions (those of the filmmaker as well as of the audience) are imbedded in the film document. In this sense every film is a significant interpreter of its time and thus a valuable source for the study of social and cultural history—and can be examined by students in that light.

Some films are, of course, better than others and present greater possibilities for effective classroom use. *The Life and Times of Rosie the Riveter*, for example, can be used not only to examine attitudes toward women and work in World War II but the perspectives of the present-day filmmaker. Taking the film as a point of departure, students could move outward from it to investigate the general history of the period, problems of racism and sexism, and changing perceptions of women in the work force. If as Dan Walkowitz suggests, the filmmaker has "confused memory with history," that problem can itself become a subject of discussion and bring a class to the heart of one of the classic problems facing the historian.[16] Alice Kessler-Harris, whose review essay would be excellent preparation for a class discussion, also expresses reservations about the filmmaker's approach to her subject. She ends by asking the kinds of questions that the historian must ask about such material and which filmmakers should consider more often:

> Can we . . . applaud [producer-director] Connie Field's heroines for their legitimate accomplishments without raising their experiences to the level of a new gospel? Can we acknowledge their truth . . . without arguing that it is a historical truth? Can we look these five women in the eye, thank them for calling our attention to a forgotten past, and then go on to use the information they gave us to reconstruct a picture of the whole?[17]

The unsatisfactory nature of so many commercially produced historical films can be explained by realizing that their creators lack both historical knowledge and perspective. When historians are consulted it is usually on matters of information rather than structure and ideas. Concentrating on explication and on the dramatic value of his material, the filmmaker is not interested in variant interpretations, let alone ambiguous, unpopular, or conflicting ones. Twenty years ago, writing about the popular BBC-TV series, "The Great War," Christopher Roads ascribed its shortcomings to the fact that its makers were, in his words, sacrificing on the altars of "convention, continuity and, above all, drama."[18] Most producers and directors are doing so still. Yet the situation is not altogether dark and dismal. In fact, there has been a development of great promise for the history classroom.

Documentary/compilation films are being made by historians or by historians and filmmakers working in full partnership with each other.

Exemplifying this process is the work of the Cadre Film Group, which since the early 1970s has produced a series of films specifically for classroom use. Beginning with *Goodbye Billy: America Goes to War, 1917–18*, through *Will Rogers' 1920's: A Cowboy's Guide to the Times*, to *Storm of Fire: World War II and the Destruction of Dresden*, they have shown how the language of film can be used to open significant interpretive problems of history to classroom examination.

While not following a uniform pattern of presentation, all are compilation films using "stills, cartoons, popular songs, and slogans of the period . . . juxtaposed in a non-didactic manner. Carefully selected images, constantly changing editing pace, meaningful transitions and deliberate juxtapositions of sound challenge even the most sophisticated viewer."[19] *Goodbye Billy* eschews narration altogether and through an allusive and ironic use of montage, shakes the viewer out of any easy generalizations about the war experience. As with other films produced by this group, the sound track is an integral part of the film's interpretive apparatus. As Patrick Griffin has written, chronology provides the connecting linkages in the film and it emerges from a joining of visual and aural elements. In this case "authentically placed footage does not attempt to 'tell' history but present though the film an aural and visual document made out of a rich multiplicity of historical experience."[20]

The structure of the film in *Will Rogers' 1920's* is defined in more formal fashion, since it concentrates on Rogers as the evocation and interpreter of his era. Nevertheless, the work retains the open-endedness of a good teaching film and by presenting a carefully constructed collage of material, invites analysis and variant interpretation. This richness of possibility is emphasized and extended in the excellent workbook prepared in conjunction with the film.[21] In *Storm of Fire* as in other Cadre films, the technique of montage is used to make students think not in the customary literary terms, but in the language of sound and vision. This film too is rich in irony and invites, even demands, analysis of various kinds at many different levels. At the level of content and technical presentation these films are designed to be "disassembled" into their constituent parts for critical and analytical consideration. Each has a clear and specific point of view, but this is presented in a way which invites participation by the viewer in making judgments about the film's thesis and about the historical problem it presents. As one of the filmmakers has written, "Cadre demands that the viewer actively participate in the film experience."[22] Such films require and facilitate critical reading of the film document and help students develop analytical abilities which are applicable not only to the study of film but also to the general study of history.

No single kind of compilation film is *the* ideal teaching device. Many such films, some for the power of their images, some for the clarity with which they embody problems of process, others for the rarity of the material on which they are based or for their constructive ambiguity, can stimulate vigorous and creative thinking in student audiences. Commercial theatre film, docudrama, and other types of production each have their own advantages and drawbacks. Furthermore, even films that would be unsatisfactory if uncritically viewed can become a powerful teaching tool in the hands of a thoughtful instructor. With the problem of how to handle film documents in the history classroom there can never be a "last word" except to acknowledge that here as elsewhere the ultimate responsibility for stimulating creative learning remains with the teacher.

NOTES

1. Umberto Eco, "Can Television Teach?" *Screen Education* 31 (Summer 1979): 15. From a talk delivered to a conference sponsored by Thames Television (in association with the independent Broadcasting Authority and the London University Institute of Education) on Schools Television, London, 1 and 2 June, 1978.
2. Ibid., 2.
3. Harry M. Geduld, *Filmguide to Henry V* (Bloomington and London: Indiana University Press, 1973).
4. Leslie Fishbein, "*Roots*: Docudrama and the Interpretation of History," in *American History, American Television: interpreting the video past*, John E. O'Connor, ed., foreword by Eric Barnouw (New York: Frederick Ungar Publishing Co., 1983). p.287.
5. Ibid., 293, 294.
6. Ibid., 297.
7. Barbara Abrash and Janet Sternburg, co-editors, *Historians and Filmmakers: Toward Collaboration*, a roundtable held at the New York Institute for the Humanities, New York University, October 30, 1982 (The Institute for Research in History, 1982), p. 12.
8. Ibid., 12.
9. Daniel J. Walkowitz, "Visual History: The Craft of the Historian Filmmaker," *The Public Historian*, 7 (Winter, 1985): 58.
10. Ibid., 58.
11. Daniel J. Walkowitz, *Worker City, Company Town: Iron and Cotton Worker Protest in Troy and Cohoes, New York: 1855–1884* (Champaign, Illinois: University of Illinois Press, 1981).
12. Robert Brent Toplin, "The Making of *Denmark Vesey's Rebellion*" *Film and History* 12 (September, 1982), 52.
13. Hayden White, "The Value of Narrativity in the Representation of Reality," *Critical Inquiry* (Autumn, 1980), 5–27.
14. R. C. Raack, "Clio's Dark Mirror: The Documentary Film in History," *The History Teacher*, 6 (1972): 110.
15. Ibid.
16. Walkowitz, "Visual History," p. 58.
17. Alice Kessler-Harris, "*Rosie the Riveter*: Who Was She?" *Labor History*, 24 (Spring, 1983): 253.
18. Christopher H. Roads, "Film as Historical Evidence," *Journal of the Society of Archivists*, 3 (1966), 183–191.
19. Peter C. Rollins, "*Storm of Fire* (1978): Reflections on Cadre Films and the Historian as Filmmaker," *The History Teacher*, 12 (1979).
20. Patrick Griffin, "The Making of *Goodbye Billy*," *Film and History*, 2 (1972).
21. Resource materials by Arthur Peterson, editors: Peter C. Rollins, R. C.

Raack, Marilyn L. Raack, *Will Rogers' 1920's: A Cowboy's Guide to the Times*, Film Resources Materials, Study Guide (Audio Visual Center, Oklahoma State University, Stillwater, Oklahoma). There is a similar guide to *Goodbye Billy*.
22. Rollins, op. cit., 540.

FRAMEWORK 2:
THE MOVING IMAGE AS EVIDENCE FOR SOCIAL AND CULTURAL HISTORY

Like any product of a culture, every film and television production is open to analysis as a historical artifact of the culture in which it was created. Films about history and Newsfilms and other types of actuality footage may also be relevant in this framework, but here the history and news stories they tell are less important in themselves than the social and cultural values lurking beneath the surface. For insight into questions on society and culture, what may be equally valuable are the artifacts of popular culture: the entertainment films, television comedies and drama series, the soap operas, and the commercials which punctuate them all. In this type of analysis we are less concerned with capturing the surface factual information communicated by the image than we are with decoding the socially and culturally driven judgments involved in the production and reception process.

In this type of investigation the historian's concerns are the same as those faced in any other enterprise in social and cultural history. One question common to students of all forms of cultural artifacts, for example, is whether one should concentrate on products which might be termed "high" rather than "popular" culture,[1] or only on commercially successful productions. Great novels, fine public buildings, and serious musical compositions reveal much of what literature, architecture, and music have to tell us about a culture, but pulp novels, vernacular architecture, and jukebox favorites also tell us things worth knowing. That a film was not a box-office success need not render it void of interest, but it should influence the questions we pose about it. Although much of the serious work by historians in the cultural analysis of film has tended to concentrate on productions which have been more or less successful at the box office, some of the most recent film scholarship has sought, as a corrective, to study a cross section of films chosen more or less at random. The analysis of film and television also relates well to important trends in recent social and cultural history, such as the study of the inarticulate. The challenge is to recognize the ways in which the methodologies of social and cultural historians can be most appropriately applied to the study of the moving image.

Films are particularly evocative cultural artifacts. There is no more lively expression of the culture of the 1920s and 1930s than its films; no more effective way to recreate some of the ambiance of the period than to project its moving images in a darkened room. The challenge is to get beyond the viewing and enjoyment of those images to an understanding of how they can help us learn about the culture which produced them and the audience which originally enjoyed them. One can accomplish this on various levels. In what one might term an "Analysis of Correspondence," one might view a film closely to consider the plot and the interplay of its characters as expressions of the values and concerns of the period as they *correspond* to other social and cultural factors. In the process one might apply the standards of a Marxist critique or a feminist analysis viewing the films as supportive of a dominant ideology. Alternatively one might suggest ways in which the narrative structure of the film relates to common modes of story-telling in the culture as part of what David Thorburn has called an "aesthetic anthropology." Thorburn also proposes the idea that each culture may have its own "consensus narrative," the articulation of "the culture's mythologies in a widely accessible language, an inheritance of shared stories, plots, character types, cultural symbols and narrative conventions," all of which would lend itself to traditional forms of literary analysis.[2] There may be room for psychoanalytic analysis or sociological content analysis as well.[3] Robert Sklar's essay to follow is an important contribution to the discussion of the role of theory in film and culture studies.

As satisfactory as an analysis of correspondence or some other theoretical approach might be, the tools of the historian—supported by relevant cultural theory—offer much more potential for the study of film and television as social and cultural artifact. For example, much that has been written about the moving picture portrayal of Native Americans has sought to explain, in a rather simple reflection model, that the image on the screen was an expression of widespread racial prejudice. As effective as such films may be as *illustrations* of prejudice, however, prejudice in itself is an insufficient *explanation* for how and why such images were put on the screen. For this kind of information historians naturally look for hard evidence—evidence that has been gradually becoming available over the past decade in the papers of the studio archives and the personal papers of directors and producers. A survey of the production records on films portraying Native Americans does not dispel the atmosphere of prejudice, but it does provide a fuller historical understanding of the ways in which dramatic considerations, political considerations, and commercial considerations—central to so complex an institution as a Hollywood studio—often dictated the ways in which those prejudices were expressed.[4]

If we are unused to thinking of this seeking out of a "paper trail" to document the background of a film or television production, it may be more a function of personal and professional prejudice than anything else. Serious scholars have long recognized the importance of knowing about Van Gogh's psychic state for an understanding of his paintings or a knowledge of the personal notebooks of Henry James[5] for a full appreciation his fiction. Although complicated by the collaborative nature of most filmmaking, applying these traditional methods of inquiry to film and television can give significant new meaning to the popular moving images which we study, as the essay by Thomas Cripps discusses.

The cultural analysis of film demands that attention be given to the ways in which the artifact was understood by historical spectators at the time of its production and release. Lawrence W. Levine has described in his work in the cultural history of America in the 1920s and 1930s how the historian faces a " 'culture gap' which must be bridged by painstaking historical reconstruction and by a series of imaginative leaps that allow him to perform the central act of empathy—figuratively, to crawl into the skins of his subjects."[6] The problem is the same in analyzing any product of culture—what, for example, did the Eiffel Tower mean to Frenchmen in the 1880s? Whether the object of study is a novel, a poem, a concerto, a bridge, or a ride on a train, the goal of the historian is to use the popular understanding of the object to get a fuller comprehension of the ways in which people thought and assigned value to things and ideas.

As Sklar points out in his essay, people in the 1930s who watched a crime film such as *Bullets or Ballots* were sure to have had a different perception of it than a historian or group of students today. The 1930s audiences' response to the film would necessarily have been shaped by all sorts of influences such as their knowledge of contemporary news events of the prohibition era, the popularity of the actors and the stories about them in contemporary fan magazines and other media, and their familiarity with other films of the crime genre seen over the past months or years. For a more visual example, consider the characterization of the prostitute in John Ford's *Stagecoach*. Her profession is never referred to explicitly, but is inferred from her dress, her mode of speech, the way she glances at the other characters, and the way that they treat her. Viewers unfamiliar with the conventions of such a characterization during that period might wonder why this nice lady was being run out of town. It may be impossible completely to re-create the viewing experience of audiences of the past because so much of the meaning depended upon the background knowledge and the perceptions that the viewer brought to it. The closer scholars can be to getting "inside the skin" of that viewer from the 1930s, the more they will learn from their artifact.

In the previous section, on the subject of films as historical interpretation, Pierre Sorlin noted that every nation has its own common historical lore, every national audience its own assumptions that it brings to the viewing of historical films. Similarly, an American audience watching Japanese or Indian comedy or drama is sure to respond differently to the cultural cues or reference points in it. What is it that sustained the popularity of Jerry Lewis among French moviegoers decades after the American audience grew tired of his comedy style?[7] Such a matter of popular taste clearly has something to do with the both the French and the American sensibilities and their idea of what's funny, but defining this more exactly is a complex matter which—like any problem in social or cultural history—requires the adoption (or construction) of some theoretical framework. Some questions arise naturally: What constitutes culture and what determines its nature and the directions in which it might develop or change? What is a film or television program, and what gives an individual moving image production the character and personality that it has? Finally, what is the connection between film and culture?; how do they relate and interact with one another?

The first of these, far too broad to be addressed here, has been the concern of cultural historians for a century or more. Many scholars today answer it at least partially by identifying how close or how far their own ideas may be from those of Karl Marx. Many expressions of Marxist cultural critique, however, paint with too broad a brush, comprehending everything in terms of hegemonic capitalism. Culture is too complex to ever be monolithic. Even at times when national crisis pulls a nation together in response to an overarching crisis, the commitment of various groups to the cause is invariably based on different motives and they are likely to see progress differently. Nor is culture static. It is always in a state of flux, social groups shifting in different ways and at different paces, ideas and values changing. Finally, culture is more than art and literature, film and television; it is imbedded in every aspect of social life.[8]

The second of these questions might seem to be obvious; a film is a film. But several generations of cinema scholars and historians have found different ways to explain the creative character of films and how they came into being. As Janet Staiger argues in her essay in the section on framework 4, all historians of film have such models whether or not they are aware of it. For example, she explains, the earliest students of cinema developed simple cause-and-effect models: films were the products of an industry run by heroic entrepreneurs who could divine what it was that the public wanted; or they were works of art produced by gifted artists; or they were experiments in a newly devised language of visual communications. Whether the film was an industrial product, an artwork, or a message, in each case it was thought to be the creation of an inspired individual. The next generation of what might be called "contextualists," recognized that filmmakers were not simple and unidimensional, but had themselves been shaped by economic, social, political, and cultural factors which should be studied and understood. Following them, in the 1960s, came the first generation of academic film historians who characterized two clearly distinguished approaches: a concentration on avant garde films as works of art and "auteurism" as an approach to more popular films. Each of these theoretical approaches had its own explanatory model of what a film represented, its own sense of the forces at work in the creation of films, and therefore its own idea of how films should be studied.

Sklar's essay directly addresses the third set of theoretical questions regarding the connections between film and culture. He identifies three paradigms, three theoretical models which in successive periods over the last forty years have more or less dominated ideas on how films were related to culture. First was the psychological paradigm, then the esthetic paradigm, and most recently a Marxist paradigm. But Sklar sees each of these sets of theoretical underpinnings being influenced today by a new kind of practical research being opened for historians in the traditional paper archives of the individuals, studios, and other agencies involved in film production. Future theoretical constructs will be adjusted and refined according to the hard evidence historians can bring into the arena of interpretation. Cripps's essay offers wonderful examples of the ways in which tracing the "paper trail" of a film production must lead to a reassessment of the theoretical assumptions, at least for the films he has studied, such as *The Birth of a Race* and *It Happened in Springfield*.

One must remain ever conscious of the variety and complexity of cultures. In any given time and place a film is sure to have meant different things to different people according to age, race, sex, class, and previous viewing experience. Films will naturally have different meanings when viewed by people in different cultures. Third world viewers are likely to miss the dramatic nuances in genre westerns, for example, as they absorb the experience of violence on the frontier— perhaps to the extent of imagining American life as still being punctuated by gunfights and Indian raids. Moreover, cultures change over the course of time, as can be seen in values transformations such as the 1970s sexual revolution in America. Cultures also have undergone changes in the very habits of perception. Building upon Michel Foucault's description of the ways in which people's unconscious epistemic rules or presuppositions have changed from one period to another since the Middle Ages, David Lowe in his *History of Bourgeois Perception* explains the transformation of bourgeois perception "from linearity to multiperspectivity." As it happened, the invention of the cinema and its growth as a medium of entertainment came in a period in the late nineteenth and early twentieth centuries when basic changes were taking place in how people understood and gave value to the two elements which film manipulates most creatively—time and space. In the same milieu in which D. W. Griffith and Edwin S. Porter were experimenting with new narrative structures for moving picture dramas,[9] innovators in painting, literature, philosophy, science, and technology were each in their own way challenging traditional perceptions of time and space. In the type of cultural history represented in Stephen Kern's intriguing *Culture of Time and Space: 1880—1918*, film culture is only one element of a complex multidimensional cultural transformation.[10]

The visual style of a film and its formal structure can also be considered as matters of cultural substance. Will Wright uses a structural analysis of a film genre to approach what he sees as enduring elements in American culture. In his *Sixguns and Society: A Structural Study of the Western*, Wright proposes a classical plot outline and several variations on that standard to help him explain the relevance of the mythology of the West in American society.[11] Other scholars suggest that detailed analysis may show even more intimate associations between the political or social ethos of a specific period and the form and style of films produced at that time. Thomas R. Gunning argues, for example, that in addition to the subject matter, the narrative structure of films that D. W. Griffith made during his years at the Biograph studio were related to the populist politics of the day, to the then current styles of muckraking journalism, and to the socially conscious literature of the period. Specifically, Griffith's *A Corner in Wheat* (1909), a film radically different in its structural organization from other films being produced at Biograph at the time, seems to have been directly based on Frank Norris's books, *The Jungle* and *The Pit* (by then seven and eight years old but still models for the current style of journalism and writing).[12]

Gunning compares the film (included in the video compilation) with Griffith's earlier works: "the cutting patterns become more radical and the relations between the shots more abstract. . . . [as] a series of disparate scenes of American life [are] unified only by their economic relation." There are three distinct narrative threads in the short film: The Farmers (shots 1, 2, 11, 23), The Bakery (shots 7, 9, 12, 18), and The Story of the Wheat King (shots 3–6, 8, 10, 13–17, 19–22). As Gunning explains: "there is no communication between the characters in the three threads. The farmers do not show up at the bakery, nor does the Wheat King go out to inspect the farmer's crop. The only connection between the threads is the economic one of producer, consumer, and speculator."[13] Those economic connections are dramatized as much by the intercutting of shot after shot as they are by the characterizations and mis-en-scène in each individual thread. It is the structure and the visual style of the film which document the social and cultural concerns of the day, to the last shot (drawn directly from Norris's novel) in which the Wheat King is buried alive in his own grain elevator after receiving the news that he has just cornered the world market. Gunning's work should caution historians about setting up too simple a reflective model in looking for social and cultural indicators in popular films.

The very vitality of film as an evocation of past culture may tend to mislead students. Because films seem more immediately accessible than the literature or architecture of a period, students may perceive the films of the 1920s and 1930s (or 50s and 60s for that matter) as the most vital cultural elements of that period. It is easy to believe that the same was true for people living at the time. The naive comment of one student suggests this unspoken assumption: "films had more impact on society in the 1920s than they do in the 1980s because there was so much less going on then than there is today." Analysis is sure to go awry if the focus is on film—and film alone—as cultural indicator. The emphasis should be on relationships between ideas and values as communicated through all types of cultural products.

Many communications scholars have taken a social science approach to the measurement and analysis of what they term "cultural indicators" in the media. Since 1967 a group working under George Gerbner at the Annenberg School of Communications at the University of Pennsylvania has been monitoring the media in a scientific and comprehensive way and proposing ways in which television shapes society. As the literature on Gerbner's program indicates, the range of social and cultural issues they address is comprehensive. In addition to issuing annual reports on violence on television since 1972, they are engaged in studies to:

> relate prime-time and weekend-daytime television to conceptions of aging; women and minorities; sex-role stereotypes; occupations; political interest, knowledge and activity; death and dying; school achievement and aspirations; health-related issues such as safety, nutritions, and medicine; science and scientists; family life; religion; criminal trials and other issues. . . . Public conceptions of and response to issues, policies, people, products, and institutions can no longer be understood without relating them to their most central, common, and pervasive source. Television is that source.[14]

While these social scientists admit that television does not operate in a vacuum, such statements do suggest too limited a focus on one indicator of the culture. A vast body of this social science literature is surveyed by Garth Jowett's essay in the section discussing framework 4.

This is also the "framework for analysis" in which we should include the study of propaganda. The Russians (Eisenstein, Kuhlesov, Pudovkin, et al.), the British (Grierson, Elton, Wright), and the Germans (Reifenstahl) were the first to recognize the potential of the moving image as a propaganda device, but others, including the Americans, were not far behind. It makes sense to be precise about what we mean by propaganda. We have already noted that every film represents a point of view, every treatment of history an interpretation. Although they may be more or less persuasive, every production (film or book) uses language (verbal or visual) to make its point of view more compelling. Some would argue that this makes every film and every historical analysis an instance of propaganda. But such broad use of the term seriously diminishes its value as an analytical concept. Garth Jowett and Victoria O'Donnell offer a good working definition of propaganda in their recent book *Propaganda and Persuasion*: "Propaganda is the deliberate and systematic attempt to shape perceptions, manipulate cognitions, and direct behavior to achieve a response that furthers the desired intent of the propogandist."[15] The preconceived purpose, the intent to *control* response and the effort to contain information in a specific area are essential. Still, the above definition of propaganda is broad enough to allow for the inclusion of the interpretive Russian features of the 1920s (*Battleship Potemkin*, *Ten Days That Shook The World*, *Mother*, *Earth*, etc.) as well as the propagandistic British social documentaries of the 1930s (*Industrial Britain*, *Housing Problems*, etc.) and the racist and political propaganda of the Nazis (*Olympia*, *Triumph of the Will*, etc.). A classroom project to identify the propaganda elements (visual and otherwise) in films such as these would involve students directly in some of the most pertinent issues of both social/political history and visual communication.

Finally, television commercials quite clearly fit all of the criteria in the above definition of propaganda. In addition to manipulating audiences in characteristically distorting ways to buy certain products, advertising has an overwhelming impact on social and cultural values. The history of advertising and its influence in culture is another growing interest among traditionally trained historians in which they can benefit from the work of communications scholars and the methods of film studies.[16] In some ways the most interesting commercials, and the ones most important for study and teaching, are those for political candidates. At least since the early 1960s,[17] such outright propaganda statements have taken a front seat in American politics. Scholars working on election campaigns and political trends cannot avoid studying them.[18] Students unable to view them critically will surely be the unwitting victims of "propagandists" of the future.

Carlos Cortes's essay concentrates on the use of film as social and cultural history in the classroom. He reports on an informal survey which indicates that this is the most common approach assumed in specialized film and history courses in American universities, but which also suggests that many of those courses should be more demanding in terms of critical visual analysis.

SUMMARY

In summary, then, the analysis of a film or video production as historical artifact for the study of social and cultural history should give special attention to the following:

Content

In content analysis, more concern should be given to the values represented and the style assumed in establishing the composition and mise-en-scène than to the accuracy or authenticity of the images. Do the social and cultural concepts represented relate to other known aspects of the society and culture of the period? Does the film or television production lead or trail behind other media in representing those ideas? Are there interpretive biases not necessarily explicit in structure, narration, dialogue, or the surface message of the production, but hidden in its visual language? Look especially for aspects of culture not easily perceived in other types of artifacts, such as patterns of movement, gesture, facial expression, and body language.

Production

As far as the production background is concerned, special attention should be given to the purpose of the production. If the film is strictly a work of commercial entertainment, it can be assumed that the producers were trying to strike existing chords in the society and culture of the time as they recognized them. This sort of assumption may suffice for an "analysis of correspondence," but research scholars will want to at least try to confirm such judgments by studying any production records that might be available. The commercial purpose of an entertainment production might be moderated by a particular point of view—a producer's desire to encourage improved race relations, for example—but, as noted above, a big-budget-studio-produced entertainment film involves the input of many collaborators. One cannot simply presume that *They Died With Their Boots On* represents the considered wisdom of Raoul Walsh. The concept of the *auteur* may have its place, but such an analysis is particularly vulnerable with regard to large-scale commercial productions. Of course there are productions which are dominated by a single point of view, as in an independently produced art film or a television commercial or political campaign film. In each case, access to production records is sure to improve the insights that can be drawn. Where production records are not available, and this will be the case more often than not, it may be necessary to hypothesize upon the motives and rationale of the filmmaker—but students must remember that a hypothesis is different from a conclusion based upon a close analysis of the documented evidence.

Reception

With regard to the reception of the film, perhaps the most important area in defining the social and cultural relevance of a production, film reviews are a good place to start. One must remember, of course, that the reviewer for *The New York Times* does not necessarily get the same message from a film as the reviewer from Richmond or Kansas City, and that none of those reviewers are necessarily in intimate touch with the desires of the nation's moviegoers. There are other types of paper evidence, such as preview response cards, advertising press books, and letters to the editor, but in making this kind of analysis the gaps are almost always going to be greater than the documented spaces. Several theoretical approaches to "reception analysis" can help to bridge these gaps (see more in Janet Staiger's and Garth Jowett's essays in the section on framework 4), but such approaches are always bolstered by incorporating as much solid evidence as possible. Whether theorizing or working from written responses, the researcher must remember that there were many individual or group responses to any film. Different racial, ethnic, gender, or political groups may have perceived the production differently or seen different meanings implicit within it. A review of the newspapers, magazines, and other vehicles of popular culture during the weeks and months that the film was in release helps to establish the context in which viewers saw the production. In whatever ways possible the researcher must try, in Lawrence Levine's terms, to "get inside the skin" of the viewers. Finally, a film need not have been a smashing success or a television show in the top ten of the weekly Neilson ratings to be of value as a document. A production which angers or bores an audience has much relevance as a very popular one when the focus of the inquiry is social and cultural history.

NOTES

1. For a valuable analysis of the history of such categories see Lawrence W. Levine's *Highbrow/Lowbrow: The Emergence of Cultural Hierarchy in America* (Cambridge, MA., 1988).
2. See David Thorburn, "Television as an Aesthetic Medium," *Critical Studies in Mass Communication*, Vol. 4 (1987), p. 169.
3. For a short and accessible survey see Arthur Asa Berger, *Media Analysis Techniques* (Beverly Hills, 1982).
4. See John O'Connor, *Hollywood Indian: Sterotypes of Native Americans in Films* (Trenton, New Jersey, 1984).
5. F. O. Mattiessen and Kenneth Murdock, eds. *The Notebooks of Henry James* (New York: Oxford University Press, 1949).
6. "The Historian and the Culture Gap," in L. P. Curtis, Jr., editor, *The Historians Workshop: Original Essays by Sixteen Historians* (New York, 1970), p. 309.
7. It should be noted that the taste of film scholars does not necessarily reflect the public's and it would not be unusual to find papers on Jerry Lewis films offered at the meetings of the Society for Cinema Studies or the University Film and Television Association.
8. The best single introduction to the breadth of thinking on the concept of culture is still Clifford Gertz, *The Interpretation of Cultures* (New York, 1973).
9. Excerpts from Porter's *Life of an American Fireman*, long cited as a particularly important instance of this innovation, are included in the video compilation.
10. See Michel Foucault, *The Order of Things: An Archaeology of the Human Sciences*, (New York, 1979); David Lowe, *History of Bourgeois Perception* (Chicago, 1982); and Stephen Kern, *The Culture of Time and Space* (Cambridge, Massachusetts, 1983).
11. (Berkekely; University of California Press, 1975).
12. Thomas R. Gunning, "D. W. Griffith and the *Narrator System*: Narrative Structure and Industry Organization in Biograph Films, 1908–1909," Unpublished Ph.D. Dissertation, New York University, 1986. The entire film *A Corner in Wheat* is included in the video compilation.
13. *Ibid.*, pp. 654, 655, and 648–661 passim.
14. George Gerbner, Larry Gross, Michael Morgan, and Nancy Signorielli,

"Cultural Indicators," unpublished paper, The Annenberg School of Communications, p. 1. The paper describes "A research project in television content and viewer conceptions of social reality."

15. (Beverly Hills, 1986) p. 16.

16. Note for example the flurry of studies in the past decade such as Stewart Ewen's *Captains of Consciousness: Advertising and the Roots of the Consumer Culture* (New York, 1976) and Stewart and Elizabeth Ewen's *Channels of Desire: Mass Images and the Shaping of American Consciousness* (New York, 1982). See also T. Jackson Lears "From Salvation to Self-Realization: Advertising and the Therapeutic Roots of Consumer Culture, 1880–1930," in T. Jackson Lears and Richard Wightman Fox, eds., *The Culture of Consumption: Critical Essays in American History* (New York, 1983).

17. The famous "Daisy Spot" from the 1964 Johnson for President Campaign is included in the video compilation.

18. See, for example, Edwin Diamond and Stephen Bates, *The Spot: The Rise of Political Advertising on Television* (Cambridge; MIT Press, 1984) and Lynda Lee Kaid, Dan Nimmo, and Keith R. Sanders, eds., *New Perspectives on Political Advertising* (Carbondale; Southern Illinois University Press, 1986).

Robert Sklar, Professor of Cinema Studies at New York University, is a cultural historian whose writing have centered on the relation of moving image media to American culture and society. His books include Movie-Made America: A Cultural History of American Movies *and* Prime-Time America: Life on and Behind the Television Screen. *He holds a Ph.D. in History of American Civilization from Harvard University and has also written on culture in the 1920s, literature, and theater.*

MOVING IMAGE MEDIA IN CULTURE AND SOCIETY: PARADIGMS FOR HISTORICAL INTERPRETATION

Robert Sklar

In the past quarter century, with the emergence of new concepts and methods in social and cultural history, the moving image media of motion pictures and television have attracted increasing interest as historical evidence—as documents or "traces"—useful for the understanding of past and present societies and cultures. The vast majority of moving image products, in all societies, are created to be seen and used by large numbers of people; therefore they seem particularly suitable documents for scholars who seek to expand the notion of culture to include the mental life of a people, or to understand society as a totality. Such documents, it is reasoned, could not achieve their mass appeal without in some way expressing or reflecting values and attitudes shared by their mass audiences. Thus one can look into or through the moving image screen and see there the minds and feelings of a people.

The foregoing paragraph describes what might be called a "common sense" notion of movies and television as artifacts for the study of social and cultural history. Our everyday experience seems to provide frequent examples: as social and economic roles change for women, so too does their depiction in moving image media; periods when conspiracy is a political issue produce movies about political conspiracy. The moving image media would not have attained their enormous presence and influence in modern societies unless they spoke directly to society's needs and wants and changed in tune with other facets of their culture.

It is ideas such as these that have led scholars increasingly to the moving image media as documents for social and cultural history. But scholarship, of course, is nothing unless it is also a challenge to such ideas—a means of subjecting them to systematic inquiry, a method for testing such hypotheses, for turning them into more rigorous modes of explanation. What we think we know and what knowledge we achieve through the scholarly method of framing and examining our hypotheses are often two disconcertingly different things.

Of the thousands of moving image media products released each year, for example, what criteria do we use to select those that merit our attention? Some scholars, borrowing from the social sciences, have suggested sampling as a technique to reduce the number to manageable proportions.[1] This method, however, implies that the field of inquiry is more or less homogenous; can it account for all the different variables that might make one product different from another, such as production personnel and circumstances, budget, genre, or popular acceptance?

Other scholars have chosen to use the latter variable as the means for organizing the subject field.[2] They make the assumption that popular acceptance is a valid criterion for selecting the individual works of most social and cultural significance. Works that have found greatest popularity are deemed to be most in consonance with the audience's social and cultural concerns, and therefore most deserving of study for social and cultural meanings. But how is popular acceptance judged? Accurate box office records for movies are rarely available; Nielsen data on television viewing is also open to question on methodological grounds.[3] Raw data on box office receipts, attendance, or viewing cannot tell us whether spectators accepted, agreed with, or even paid attention to what the media works communicated. Finally, such raw data does not take into account all the variables that contribute to popular acceptance, such as promotion and marketing of films or program positioning on television.

As these examples make clear, what seems commonsensical and straightforward, based on our intuitions and perceptions, becomes problematical when subjected to scholarly inquiry. In delineating our field of study we must not only construct a method, but also articulate the theories that are the bases of a method. We may choose to call such theories historical paradigms; in order to place the moving image media within society and culture, these theories or paradigms must of necessity be concerned with society and culture.

Three principal paradigms have played a major role in the historiography of moving image media as artifacts of social and cultural history since World War II. Each has within it, of course, its own branches, variations, and conflicts. In order of their dominance they are the psychological paradigm, the aesthetic paradigm, and the ideological/cultural paradigm. Taking them in order, we may have a concise historiography of moving images as social and cultural artifacts over nearly forty years.

THE PSYCHOLOGICAL PARADIGM

The psychological paradigm emerged after World War II in the United States primarily under the aegis of the German refugee scholar Siegfried Kracauer. It also incorporated aspects of contemporary anthropological and sociological concepts of culture. Kracauer's classic statement of the approach was his *From Caligari to Hitler: A Psychological Study of the German Film* (1947). Other important texts were Martha Wolfenstein and Nathan Leites, *Movies: A Psychological Study* (1950) and Barbara Deming's *Running Away from Myself: A Dream Portrait of America Drawn from the Films of the 40's*, completed in 1950, partly published as articles in the early 1950s, but not published in book form until 1969.

Kracauer argued that "the films of a nation reflect its mentality in a more direct way than other artistic media" on the basis of two assumptions: first, that films were products not of individuals but of group endeavor, and "teamwork in this field tends to exclude arbitrary handling of screen material, suppressing individual peculiarities in favor of traits common to many people"; second, that films "address themselves, and appeal to, the anonymous multitude," and "can therefore be supposed to satisfy existing mass desires."[4] Kracauer went on from this assertion to posit not that films reflected what in anthropological, cultural, or social terms we might call popular beliefs, values, or behavior, but rather "psychological dispositions—those deep layers of collective mentality which extend below the dimension of consciousness."[5]

From this ground Kracauer wrote a chronological narrative history of German films from 1918 to 1933 in which he found reflection of a psychological transformation of the German people, a "retrogression," leading the way to the rise and coming to power of fascism.[6] This path-breaking book continues to hold influence over both general historians and film historians.[7] There are a number of ways, however, by which it is open to criticism. Kracauer does not establish the criteria for his selection of films to discuss—many of his films were artistic works which may not have been the most popular—nor does he indicate in every case that he has seen all the films he writes about. Kracauer also makes occasional references to class and/or social divisions within the nation, which gives rise to the question whether all groups in a society share equally in its "collective mentality," or whether differences such as wealth or education fragment the mental unities which his method presupposes.[8] Ultimately, however, these issues are beyond scholarly scrutiny: the psychological method of studying a collective mentality on more than one occasion defines its field of inquiry as the "German soul"—we are told how the screen representation of "strong sadism and an appetite for destruction . . . once more testifies to their prominence in the German collective soul."[9]

One way to test the explanatory power of Kracauer's approach is to see if the method can be applied to the films of other national cultures. Could one study, for example, the Italian films made prior to the March on Rome to learn whether they, too, prefigured the rise of fascism? Could one discover the "American collective soul" by studying Hollywood films? However influenced they were by his approach, Kracauer's followers in the post-World War II period were careful to avoid his metaphysical language and his claims to the "retrodictive" power of film analysis.[10]

Both Wolfenstein/Leites and Deming deal with films within the terminology of dreaming (the "American Dream" may be an equivalence to the "German soul" in the lexicon of collective mentalities). Wolfenstein and Leites speak of "the common day-dreams of a culture" both as sources for and products of film representations. "Where these productions gain the sympathetic response of a wide audience, it is likely," they suggest, "that their producers have tapped within themselves the reservoir of common day-dreams"—a notion of shared collective mentality that is less ambiguous than Kracauer's references to teamwork.[11] They are also more rigorous about their field of inquiry: they state that they have studied all American A films on contemporary urban themes made in a specified period, as well as a number of French and British productions for comparative purposes. Their interest is in "recurrent patterns" in the "treatment of certain major relationships."[12] In a 1970 preface, the authors more specifically clarify the roots of their approach in psychoanalysis and cultural anthropology, which inform their effort to gain general insights into patterns of behavior and feeling in a culture through their expression in narrative forms.[13]

Deming discusses about one hundred film texts made in the 1940s, selected from a "substantial" corpus—she explains that as a film analyst at the Library of Congress from 1942 to 1944, she saw one-quarter of the American feature films produced in those years. She, too, reads films in the framework of dream, in contrast to mirror—as expressions of fears and confusions that beset members of a society, offering a kind of escape through wish fulfillment. Deming credits Kracauer as the originator of the method that underlies her book, but in fact there are significant differences between her and Kracauer. She makes clear that, in her view, movie dreams do not cover the full range of the mental life of a society: "Fortunately, there are dreams that are dreamed outside the confines of our movie houses."[14] This perspective raises the question of how one part of dream experience is represented in movies, and another not. Deming implies that filmmakers have a choice in what they put on the screen and that their choice is to indulge the public, because that is what pays. (She also suggests a "political instinct" at work to avoid stirring up trouble.) At the same time, however, she asserts that filmmakers know little more than the public about the dream content of their work. "One may be shrewd at spotting a subject of general appeal," she writes, "and at the same time quite ignorant of the true nature of that appeal." It takes an artist to be truly aware of one's actual subject, Deming suggests, and whatever else Hollywood filmmakers were, in her view they were not artists.[15]

For the very reason that films were not art, Deming posited the necessity of studying them not individually but collectively. Like Wolfenstein and Leites, she argued that only through observing a large body of films could one discern the "obsessive patterns" that revealed the general circumstance. This was a research standard that few others could attain to in midcentury. Film archives were virtually nonexistent in the United States; even the Library of Congress, the closest equivalent to a national archive of films, retained only a small proportion of films submitted to it for copyright purposes. But there were reasons other than lack of access to materials that brought about the demise of the psychological paradigm in the early postwar years.

Both in psychoanalysis and in cultural anthropology, the fields that had informed the efforts of Wolfenstein and Leites, there was a retreat from models of "collective mentalities" that had reached their zenith, often for reasons of military need, during World War II. In both fields, the focus shifted away from general theoretical forays toward an emphasis on scientific, or social-scientific, method; notions of "soul" and "dream" that had animated the psychological study of film were particularly vulnerable to methodological critique. Moreover, questions of methodology in the study of moving image media became subsumed within a more general debate over "mass culture" and "popular culture." Within the intellectual world of the 1950s, these phenomena were generally seen as antithetical to the values of art and serious culture, if not as fundamental threats. In this framework, the representations of moving image media were hardly of interest at all, while their cultural or social impact could best be studied through quantitative social science survey research techniques.[16]

THE AESTHETIC PARADIGM

It was in this context that the aesthetic paradigm for studying films as artifacts of cultural or social history emerged in the 1950s and 1960s. As interest in studying the social and cultural meanings of moving image representation faded in the social sciences, it began to gather strength in the humanities, particularly in literature and the fine arts. This shift was accompanied—perhaps also partly shaped— by changes in the sociology of film spectatorship in the United States in the 1950s. As television supplanted film as the dominant mass moving image medium, spectatorship began even before scholarship to envision the possibility that film was not only mass culture but also art. So-called "art cinema" theaters and film societies sprang up in university towns, showing European films by Bergman and Fellini. As with the psychological paradigm, in the work of Kracauer and Deming, the ground was laid outside academic discourse for the development of the aesthetic paradigm.

The main impetus came from France, with the "politique des auteurs" advocated by the critics of the new film monthly *Cahiers du
Cinema*, founded in 1951. This doctrine, which valorized a core group
of contemporary film directors as artistic geniuses, was in part a critical
tactic devised by aspiring filmmakers to carve a place for themselves
within the French film industry; among the *Cahiers* critics were Jean-
Luc Godard, Francois Truffaut, Eric Rohmer, Jacques Rivette, and
Claude Chabrol.[17]

The "politique des auteurs" was championed in the United States
by Andrew Sarris, film critic for the *Village Voice*, who popularized
the concept by re-naming it the "auteur theory." Sarris edited a short-
lived monthly *Cahiers du Cinema in English*, of which twelve issues
appeared in 1966–67, carrying some of the first translations of the
"politique des auteurs" polemics. His major contribution, however,
was his 1968 book *The American Cinema: Directors and Directions, 1929–
1968*. Though the volume was largely a compilation of his film director rankings, Sarris devoted a few pages to polemics of his own.
His introduction, "Toward a Theory of Film History," positions himself against the "sociological" perspective of the prior paradigm and
in favor of an approach to film emphasizing its artistry and artists. In
his system of oppositions, he argued for the particular over the general, the "trees" over the "forest," for presentist re-appraisal rather
than historical contextualization of films.[18]

The French "politique des auteurs" and Sarris's "auteur theory"
formed one of the foundations of the aesthetic paradigm that emerged
in the 1950s and 1960s; the other came from the dominant movements
within American literary studies of the period. In literature as in the
social sciences there was a retreat from an earlier interest in the relationship between narratives and social collectivities. The reigning
method was the New Criticism, which emphasized the text as sole
datum of analysis, irrespective of historical or biographical context.
Critics with an interest in larger cultural questions approached them
through study of "great" writers, who were regarded as the most
perceptive interpreters of their cultural surroundings. New critical
methods and cultural analysis were merged in a mode of literary
analysis combining studies of the lives and the texts of "great" writers,
who expressed cultural meanings through the formal properties of
their art.

With the "politique des auteurs" and "auteur theory" providing a
rationale and a canon, and dominant literary critical practices the
method, academic studies of film reemerged in the 1960s based on
the aesthetic paradigm—an approach to film through the works of
the medium's great artist-auteurs. These individual film directors
could not only be studied in the same way one looked at novelists or
poets; they also provided a means of organizing, and locating oneself
within, the vast and inchoate historical data of a "mass" medium
through the framework of a limited number of artist-auteurs' lives
and works. Academic discourse was devoted to establishing and con-

firming the *Cahiers'* canon, the list and line of "greats." Scholarship primarily followed the pattern of literary criticism in the close reading of film texts—importantly insisting upon formal and stylistic elements as central to any comprehension of "meaning"—and using the careers of artist-authors as the wider, organizing unit of study.

The meaning of films as artifacts of social and cultural history, in this paradigm, thus was to be found in the individual film texts themselves, and in the connective styles and themes that cumulatively made up the total career of their artist-auteur. These meanings were to be read as statements to, or interpretations of, a culture, and it was not necessary to connect them to the collective mentality of their spectators or the economic circumstances of their production or reception. What you saw was what you needed, unless, as a mark of special erudition, one could link the principal artist-author to subsidiary artist-authors (writer, cameraman, editor, art director, etc.) or individual films to other individual films within generic typologies.

The aesthetic paradigm was practical as well. It could provide the groundwork for coherent policies to remedy the lack of sources that Deming had lamented. Film archives, 16mm film distribution catalogues, and film society schedules could be constructed based on the canon. The films of Howard Hawks, say, were a difficult but not impractical goal of collection, distribution, exhibition, and scholarship as compared, for example, to all the A films of 1948.

The aesthetic paradigm reached an apex with the publication of Sarris's book in 1968. Its strength in a sense was its weakness. It gave impetus to film studies by narrowing the object of study, but as the field began to develop the limitations of the aesthetic paradigm became more apparent. It was more difficult in film than in literary studies to put aside questions of industry and economics or of genre or code. As early as 1969 Peter Wollen's *Signs and Meanings in the Cinema* suggested the need to expand the purview of the "auteur theory," and began to develop a semiological approach to cinema.[19] In the early 1970s a more theoretically grounded version of the "auteur theory," influenced by Claude Levi-Strauss and called "auteur-structuralism," briefly flourished in Britain.[20] But the major changes that marked cultural life and scholarship at the end of the 1960s made too fundamental an impact on ideas about moving image media for a theoretical revision of the aesthetic paradigm to suffice. Its dominance, like that of the psychological paradigm before it, was coming to an end.

THE IDEOLOGICAL/CULTURAL PARADIGM

The events of May 1968 in France are frequently invoked as a turning point in the intellectual orientation of the past generation. They are an accurate and handy symbol, but of course by no means the whole of it. Events in the United States—the struggle against racism, the movement against the Vietnam War, the rise of the New

Left, the emergence of women's, gay, and other liberation movements within and against the New Left—as well as the campaign for nuclear disarmament in Great Britain, and struggles elsewhere, all contributed to and set the stage for reorientations in theoretical approaches to culture and society. The conflicts of May 1968 in France, however, may have been decisive in casting the theoretical debate over new paradigms largely in Marxian terms.

The experience of May 1968 in France seemed to many to demonstrate the power of the state and its institutions to repel the most severe and widespread challenges. Elsewhere, what also seemed to be decisive transformations in cultural values and behavior, espoused as overt challenges to the status quo, proved in like manner to be rather easily "co-opted" by dominant institutions of communication and commerce. Today's protest seemed to become tomorrow's product. Power seemed impervious to challenge, despite what appeared to be fundamental reorientations of belief and behavior, as in the various rights-asserting and consciousness-raising groups noted above. Among many intellectuals and scholars involved in these activities, there was a general turn (in some cases, a return) to Marxism as a theory more likely than others to provide a framework for the difficulties of the times.

Marxism, in simple terms, proposed that culture and society derived from the mode of production in any particular era, that culture and society were "superstructure" and rested on production, the "base." This concept had, of course, been known for a century of Marxist thought and had produced various efforts at cultural criticism which the postwar generation of scholars had not found persuasive (for example, the notion propounded by some members of the Frankfurt school that mass media manipulated their audiences). In the aftermath of May 1968, Marxist social and cultural criticism received new emphasis. Now an ideological/cultural paradigm based on Marxian concepts is central to the study of moving image media as social and cultural artifacts over the past decade and a half.

The first of these emphases was propounded by the French philosopher Louis Althusser and goes under the general rubric of Structuralist Marxism (there are of course other structuralisms in current theoretical debate). In a 1969 essay, "Ideology and Ideological State Apparatuses," Althusser argued that the central issue for social formations is the reproduction of the conditions of production and that this is accomplished in the superstructural realm through the functioning of ideology. For Althusser, "ideology has the function of 'constituting' concrete individuals as subjects."[21] This function is carried out in "Ideological State Apparatuses" (ISAs), such as churches, schools, and the media, which transform individuals into subjects by reproducing in their consciousness the prevailing conditions of production. Ideology, Althusser asserts, "represents the imaginary relationship of individuals to their real conditions of existence."[22]

While Althusser notes that class struggles do occur within ISAs, his overwhelming emphasis, it seems clear, falls on the inexorability and inevitability of individuals being turned into subjects by the functioning of ideology. This is certainly the aspect of Marxian Structuralism that has been taken up within film and television studies, though it has often been linked with concepts drawn from the psychoanalytic theories of Jacques Lacan, as well as with analyses of representation in the moving image media from feminist, third world, and other perspectives. Simply put, it sets the movie and television industries functioning as ideological state apparatuses to transform spectators into subjects of the dominant ideology. This approach has had little interest in the history of the moving image media as such, following Althusser's own dismissal of historical practice as being one more example of the functioning of ideology. Certain classic texts of so-called Cinestructuralism, including the collective analysis by the editors of *Cahiers du Cinema* of *Young Mr. Lincoln*, have made generalized efforts to link the production of a particular text to a particular historical aspect of the social formation, but their primary emphases have tended to be synchronic rather than diachronic—in other words, to treat cinema or television as ideological apparatuses within the general social formation of capitalism, operating within so broad a historical frame as to make the kinds of questions historians like to ask about conflict and change seem of a secondary order.

Nearly every American historian is familiar with the broad-scale attack leveled against Althusserian Structuralism by the British historian E. P. Thompson, even if one is not acquainted with Althusser's works themselves. In "The Poverty of Theory," Thompson devoted over two hundred pages to a defense of historical practice from a position within the Marxian tradition.[23] Thompson's stance against Structuralism in the ensuing debates within Marxism was given the rubric Culturalism, though Thompson sometimes sought to distinguish his perspective from that of other Culturalists such as Raymond Williams. It is in William's work, however, rather than "The Poverty of Theory" or other writings by Thompson, that the Culturalist alternative to Althusser can most clearly be found.

In general, the Culturalist opposition to Structuralism has centered on the latter's implication that ideology and its state apparatuses sweep all before their path, turning individuals into subjects of the dominating powers. The Culturalist critics and historians have been drawn to research subjects centering on resistance to domination and the ability of groups to carve out oppositional cultural environments. Williams gave that predilection a theoretical foundation in his 1973 essay, "Base and Superstructure in Marxist Cultural Theory," and in many subsequent works. Drawing on the Italian Marxist theorist Gramsci, Williams adopted the concept of hegemony as the basis of his theory of culture in which the dominant forces "select from and consequently exclude the full range of actual and possible human practice."[24] While the dominant groups in a society are constantly practicing "incorporation" of individuals and groups within the cultural framework of their domination, the force of this social process does not have the same overwhelming, all-encompassing power that ideology has in the Althusserian formulation. For Williams, there are always cultural practices that stand somewhat outside the domain of the hegemonic— some of these he calls residual, pertaining to older practices; others he calls emergent, pertaining to innovative practices. It requires a historical analysis to understand the sources of these various practices and to specify the constantly shifting relations among dominant, residual, and emergent aspects of the cultural process.

Having made this important theoretical intervention in the Marxist debate, however, Williams's own examples of how he would study culture, and what aspects of cultural practice are of particular interest, oddly seem to place him closer to the "auteur theory" critics than any other group within moving image studies. One of his central concepts is "structures of feeling," by which he appears to be focusing on alternative practices of a given group of artists in a particular period. While this is of course embedded in a much more elaborated theory of culture than that of the critics of the artist-author persuasion, it does not appear to produce a radically different critical practice.

It has remained for other writers in the Marxian debate to attempt a synthesis between Structuralism and Culturalism, recognizing the problematic aspects of each and stressing how their strengths can be amalgamated. The most dynamic of these synthesizers is Stuart Hall, the most thorough, perhaps, the historian Richard Johnson. Johnson argues, in essence, for linking the most persuasive claims of the two strands in Marxism—on the one hand, that there are powerful ideological forces at work within the institutions of any social formation to inculcate the dominant viewpoint; on the other, that individuals and groups are capable of resistance and struggle and the formulation of alternative conceptions of the world. Methodologically, he argues for the study of ideology in representations and for the study of cultural experience to determine the relation between reality as represented in ideology and reality as lived. From the viewpoint of historical method, however, there can be no simple assumption that reality as represented is the same as reality as lived.[25]

And this returns us, as is so often the case, back to where we started, with the question of how we can understand the moving images of motion pictures and television as artifacts for the study of social and cultural history. Not exactly where we started, however, for if the questions have yielded no simple answers in this tour through nearly forty years of theory, scholarship, and criticism, the questions at least have been considerably complicated and refined. There are no simple answers, but then again, the questions are not quite as simple either.

TRANSFORMATION OF THE FIELD OF INQUIRY

In the meanwhile, as these debates have proceeded in the worlds of theory and scholarship, transformations in the field of documentation have had an equally significant influence on the formulation of our field of inquiry. It should be stressed that the emergence of a body of scholarship, and the expression of its needs, has played a not inconsiderable role in the expansion of the resources for research. The constraints on research of which Barbara Deming spoke in 1950, which had hardly been lessened some twenty-five years later, have in the past decade been rendered almost entirely obsolete.

In the first place, the availability of films and of the technology for the study of films has increased enormously during the past ten years. Efforts by the Library of Congress, the American Film Institute, the Museum of Modern Art, the UCLA Film and Television Archive, the State Historical Society of Wisconsin, the Museum of Broadcasting, and many other institutions, in the preservation of both motion pictures and television, have made available thousands of films and television programs for researchers that were not accessible in earlier years. Although hundreds of films and television programs remain missing or permanently lost, it is now possible to screen a considerable portion of cinema and television history. Flatbed film viewers or video cassette machines make possible stop-frame, slow motion, frame-by-frame movement, and other forms of careful study of the image that simple projection does not afford. One could now probably recapitulate the Wolfenstein and Leites or the Deming research projects— all the A pictures from a particular 1940s season of Hollywood films, or a quarter of the feature films made during World War II—in ways not possible since the days of their contemporaneous release. In short, despite the difficulties involved in travel and time, historians can expand the field of inquiry and see films as they read documents, as E. P. Thompson says, "in bunches and in series."[26] This obviates the tendency to select on the basis of limited availablity, problematic methods such as sampling or using box office figures, or canons based on aesthetic, auteurist, or other critical grounds.

In addition, the same recent period has also brought a concomitant increase in the availability of original documents for the study of film and television history. The aforementioned archives, and others, have been developing their collections of personal and corporate papers. Motion picture and television companies themselves, to a not insignificant extent, have established internal archives which are made open to scholars, when the documents themselves have not been given over to the care of university archives. While access or ease of use is sometimes restricted, this availablity has once again fundamentally transformed historical procedures in moving image studies. No longer is it necessary, and therefore adequate, to collect historical "data" from memoirs, interviews, or press releases, which had once been (or appeared to be) the "primary" sources for historical research. Moving image historians, of course, are not the only ones who have had to contend with "data" designed for making legends or promoting careers, but they have not previously had access to the kind of institutional documentation and records against which such "first-person" accounts can be checked. Evaluating such documentation requires a separate set of procedures, certainly, but its availability raises the standards in the field for thoroughness, accuracy, and for the testing of hypotheses—such as those propounded by the psychological and the aesthetic paradigms discussed above—by more rigorous criteria of evidence and explanation.

A third aspect of the transformation of the field of inquiry in moving image studies should be noted. The expansion of documentation, of films and of archival collections, as well as the growth of a body of scholarship, reconceptualizes the questions historians ask and thereby contributes to the recognition of new sources and avenues of inquiry. In other words, materials which had not seemed relevant or explicable can, within a reformulation of the field, suddenly become sources. Daily newspaper advertisements or even the movie schedule can be seen, within a new frame of understanding of motion picture marketing, as sources for information about the moving image culture of a particular city: how many theaters were operating; which were first run, which sub-run; which connected to major studios, which independent; what aspects of films were advertised and with what emphases—all information that can lead to further understanding of patterns and variations in marketing practices and of the experience of the historical spectator.

RE-HISTORICIZING MOVING IMAGE STUDIES

What does this expansion of the field of inquiry in moving image studies mean to the consideration of movies and television as artifacts of social and cultural history? It means principally what may be called a fundamental re-historicization of the field—an incorporation of moving image studies within some of the general procedures of the historian's discipline. I would suggest that the adoption of past paradigms for the social and cultural study of moving images derived in some degree from a prior conception that the subject was impossibly vast and the data scarce. Thus the psychological and the aesthetic paradigms, and the Structuralist approach as well, served to bring order and possibility to this problematic circumstance by delimiting the field of inquiry, by whatever rationale, to a certain number of film "texts" which could be read for social and cultural meaning through their images. While aspects of each paradigm continue to be important, indeed necessary, to historical methodology in the field, I would argue that there was an element of expediency in their past prominence, a circumstance which the expansion of the field of inquiry now makes obsolete.

Through these multifaceted changes—in the body of material available for research, in the scholar's attitude toward the quantity and variety of available data, in the paradigms which form and govern historical interpretation—it is now possible to investigate the moving image media as *subjects* for social and cultural history (let us discard the term *artifacts* at this point as reflecting some of the prior limitations discussed above), using Raymond Williams's language, within a framework of the processes and practices of cultural production.

Speaking of communications in general, Williams writes,

> In few fields of contemporary social reality is there such a lack of solid historical understanding. The popularity of shallowly-rooted and ideological applications of other histories and other analytic methods and terms is a direct and damaging consequence of this lack. The necessary work, so immense in scope and variety, will be collaborative and relatively long-term.[27]

What this perspective suggests is that studies of the moving image media as subjects for social and cultural history will rest on a foundation of knowledge and interpretation of the media as communications *practices*. In this approach, the screen image is but one of several practices to be studied. Obviously it is not to be ignored, as sometimes seems to happen in new emphases on industrial history; but it also cannot be said to reveal its own cultural and social meanings by virtue of psychological, aesthetic, or ideological interpretation alone. The screen image may now be seen as part of a nexus—as the element of representation within the process of production-representation-reception whereby images acquire and communicate meaning.

Returning to the "common sense" notion of the moving image media impact on culture and society with which we began, it is now perhaps possible to recognize that as consumers and spectators of the media we do not respond to screen images alone. Production and reception are as much a part of our consciousness of the media as is representation through screen images. Indeed, it may be argued that at the present time a considerable part of the populace gains its experience of movies as much through their representation in other media as through direct exposure to the screen image. We perceive and respond to representation in the context of what we have heard about production in all its manifestations (in the case of individual films and also as a system) and also of the environment of reception, which includes the setting in which we see a work, and the climate of publicity and criticism that surrounds it. This is the "common sense" experience of the media that we need to inscribe in our historical practice.

THE "EXPANDED TEXT" OF MOVING IMAGE MEDIA

This recognition of the "expanded text" of moving image media solves a persistent problem for historians while at the same time presenting new opportunities for what historians have traditionally been most accustomed to research. In past eras of historical studies of aesthetic practices, historians have often been troubled by dichotomies of "text" and "context." Historians have been hesitant to enter the realm of formal stylistics, leading to a division of labor between those who study "texts"—theorists and critics—and those who provide the "context," which has almost by definition been seen as a secondary task, of dubious methodological and theoretical import. The notion of an "expanded text" ends this dichotomy and brings to the forefront what historical methods can accomplish in investigating such fundamental questions in moving image studies as authorship and the experience of spectatorship, questions which until the recent past have been formulated almost exclusively in an ahistorical manner.

There have indeed been efforts by historians to create studies on the "expanded text" of the moving image. The first such interventions by historians began, in fact, some years ago with the publication in 1979 of *American History/American Film*, fourteen essays by historians on individual films, edited by John E. O'Connor and Martin A. Jackson. A special issue of *American Quarterly*, the journal of the American Studies Association, also published in 1979, contained a number of articles on individual films. Around the same time, the Wisconsin/ Warner Bros. Screenplay Series was launched, which published twenty volumes, each containing a scholarly introduction utilizing archival materials on the development of individual Warner Bros. screenplays in the collection of the State Historical Society of Wisconsin.[28] Nearly all of the essays, articles, and introductions in the above sources demonstrate the historian's ability to provide contextual evidence to accompany a film "text". A few, however, taking advantage of archival resources which were more difficult of access a decade ago than now, made preliminary efforts to describe or locate an "expanded text" within the framework of data on production and reception which also informed the meanings of representation of the film images themselves.

It is important to note, however, that in every case among these projects, these were studies of *individual* films. No doubt the limitations of a short essay make it advantageous to work with a single title; nevertheless, it should be made clear that the study of individual works in this manner can only be a provisional model for the historian of moving images. In the first place, it tends to retain the obsolescent text/context dichotomy between critic and historian. More significantly, the study of individual films, even as case studies, may ignore or fail to come to grips with what may be the fundamental insight of the study of moving image media as a *practice*, that the "expanded text" is in fact a plurality of texts, for which the word "intertextuality" is a primary methodological starting point.

For the historian, "intertextuality" may be the most important interpretative concept to be drawn from recent structuralist theory and criticism. A basic definition of intertextuality, given by Jonathan Culler, is

the relation of a particular text to other texts. Julia Kristeva writes that 'every text takes shape as a mosaic of citations, every text is the absorption

and transformation of other texts. . . . ' A work can only be read in connection with or against other texts, which provide a grid through which
it is read and structured by establishing expectations which enable one
to pick out salient features and give them a structure.[29]

The insights provided by the concept of intertextuality are necessary
to the historian of moving image media because the practice of production of moving image texts, certainly in American motion pictures
and television, if not in other national practices, is fundamentally
intertextual. Texts are conceived within genres, series, cycles; texts
are remakes of other texts; texts are adaptations of texts from other
media; texts cite and refer to other texts; representational elements,
such as stars, become intertextual elements in the expanded text of
production decisions and spectatorial expectations. Once again, the
issue is the expanded field of inquiry, and the historian's capacity to
organize moving image subject matter "in bunches and in series."

The expanded text and intertextuality are methodological tools
which break open the older notion of the moving image "text" and
move it simultaneously toward two related notions: the links among
representation, production, and reception in a broad-based concept
of moving image media as practices; and the interrelatedness of individual texts in a field of self- and cross-referentiality. It is fair to say
that historical scholarship on moving image media has not yet fully
absorbed the requirements and opportunities laid out by the conjunction of these approaches. One of the requirements, certainly, is
for historians of moving image media to locate their subjects in the
wider realm of society and culture. An expanded text implies expansion into areas beyond the production studio, the image, or the viewing space. Many of the recent theoretical debates in film history—for
example, on narrative forms in relation to concepts of "bourgeois
representation"—can only be carried forward fruitfully by recourse
to social and cultural analysis well outside the limits of film history
itself.

Two tentative conclusions can be drawn. The first focuses on how
historians research, the second on how they interpret, although research and interpretation are, in the historian's practice, inseparable.

First, the developments in moving image studies over the past decade have made clear how central the historian's vocation is to the
most basic understandings of moving image media, not only in the
aspect of social and cultural history, but in all aspects. Historians have
tended to take second place to theorists and critics who seemed, to
many historians, to have superior understanding of the formal and
aesthetic elements of the text. It is now possible to argue that what
historians have been trained to do—to study institutions, groups, the
interrelation of concepts and behaviors; to take large bodies of data
and find patterns and meanings through their juxtaposition—is a
primary element in the study of texts and of the moving image media
generally. This is, I think, an opportunity for historians to move more

boldly to intervene in the construction of knowledge about moving image media through historical research techniques.

Second, and perhaps conversely, however, it is time for historians to relinquish what has been, for some, an overly grandiose view of the social and cultural significance of moving image media. This exaggerated emphasis has sometimes produced a wish for magical solutions to theoretical and methodological concerns—for the illuminating flash of insight that reveals conclusively why, because of the reach or "essence" of moving image media, they are superior signifiers of social and cultural meaning. The more prominent a role we as historians play in studying the media, however, the more we are likely to learn about the ways they are related to, and embedded among, a wide variety of other social and cultural practices. If there does turn out to be a special character to moving image media, our chances of discovering it are enhanced by studying the media as practices, and by *specifying* how their meanings are produced, formed as representations, and received.

NOTES

1. For example, Lary May, *Screening Out the Past: The Birth of Mass Culture and the Motion Picture Industry* (New York: Oxford University Press, 1980). A more extensive sampling method was employed in David Bordwell, Janet Staiger, and Kristin Thompson, *The Classical Hollywood Cinema: Film Style and Mode of Production to 1960* (New York: Columbia University Press, 1985). See "Appendix A The unbiased sample," pp. 388–396.
2. Will Wright, *Sixguns and Society: A Structural Study of the Western* (Berkeley: University of California Press, 1975).
3. See David Chagall, "Can You Believe the Ratings?" in Barry Cole, ed., *Television Today: A Close-Up View. Readings from TV Guide.* (New York: Oxford University Press, 1981), pp. 197–209.
4. Siegfried Kracauer, *From Caligari to Hitler: A Psychological Study of the German Film* (Princeton: Princeton University Press, 1947), p. 5.
5. Kracauer, p. 6.
6. Kracauer, p. 270.
7. See Peter Gay, *Weimar Culture: The Outsider as Insider* (New York: Harper & Row, 1968), and Patrice Petro, "From Lukacs to Kracauer and Beyond: Social Film Histories and the German Cinema," *Cinema Journal*, Vol. 22, No. 3 (Spring 1983), pp. 47–70.
8. See his discussion of *The Cabinet of Dr. Caligari*, p. 67.
9. Kracauer, pp. 3 and 74.
10. "Retrodiction" is a term used by Paul Veyne as a name for historical explanation; see Veyne, *Writing History: Essay on Epistemology*, trans. Mina Moore-Rinvolucri (Middletown: Wesleyan University Press, [1971] 1984), p. 144 ff.
11. Martha Wolfenstein and Nathan Leites, *Movies: A Psychological Study* (Glencoe, Ill.: The Free Press, 1950), p. 13.
12. Wolfenstein and Leites, pp. 13, 16.
13. "Preface to the Paperback Edition," (New York: Atheneum, 1970).
14. Barbara Deming, *Running Away from Myself: A Dream Portrait of America Drawn from the Film of the Forties* (New York: Grossman, 1969), p. 201.

15. Deming, p. 3.
16. For the debate on "mass culture" in the 1950s, see Bernard Rosenberg and David Manning White, eds., *Mass Culture: The Popular Arts in America* (Glencoe, Ill.: The Free Press, 1957) and Norman Jacobs, ed., *Culture for the Millions? Mass Media in Modern Society* (Princeton: D. Van Nostrand, 1959, 1961).
17. See Jim Hillier, ed., *Cahiers du Cinema, The 1950s: Neo-Realism, Hollywood, New Wave* (Cambridge: Harvard University Press, 1985).
18. Andrew Sarris, "Toward a Theory of Film History," in *The American Cinema: Directors and Directions, 1929–1968* (New York: E. P. Dutton, 1968), pp. 19–37.
19. Peter Wollen, *Signs and Meanings in the Cinema* (Bloomington: Indiana University Press, 1969), pp. 74–115.
20. See John Caughie, ed., *Theories of Authorship: A Reader* (London: Routledge & Kegan Paul, 1981), pp. 121–195.
21. Louis Althusser, "Ideology and Ideological State Apparatuses (Notes Toward an Investigation)," in *Lenin and Philosophy and Other Essays*, trans. Ben Brewster (New York: Monthly Review Press, 1971), p. 171.
22. Althusser, p. 162.
23. E. P. Thompson, "The Poverty of Theory or an Orrery of Errors," in *The Poverty of Theory and Other Essays* (New York: Monthly Review Press, 19), pp. 1–210.
24. Raymond Williams, "Base and Superstructure in Marxist Cultural Theory," in *Problems in Materialism and Culture: Selected Essays* (London: Verso Editions, 1980), p. 43
25. Richard Johnson, "Three Problematics: Elements of a Theory of Working-Class Culture," in J. Clarke, C. Crichter, R. Johnson, eds., *Working-Class Culture: Studies in History and Theory* (New York: St. Martin's, 1979), pp. 201–237. See also Stuart Hall, Richard Johnson, E. P. Thompson, "Culturalism: Debates Around The Poverty of Theory," in Raphael Samuel, ed., *People's History and Socialist Theory* (London: Routledge and Kegan Paul, 1981), pp. 375–408.
26. Thompson, p. 23.
27. Raymond Williams, "Means of Communication as Means of Production," in *Problems in Materialism and Culture*, p. 54.
28. John E. O'Connor and Martin A. Jackson, eds., *American History/American Film: Interpreting the Hollywood Image* (New York: Ungar, 1979); *American Quarterly*, Vol. 31 (1979)—six articles were added to the journal's original seven and together published as *Hollywood as Historian: American Film in a Cultural Context*, edited by Peter C. Rollins (Lexington: University Press of Kentucky, 1983); the volumes in the Wisconsin/Warner Bros. Screenplay Series, too numerous to list here, were edited by Tino Balio and published by the University of Wisconsin Press.
29. Jonathan Culler, *Structuralist Poetics: Structuralism, Linguistics, and the Study of Literature* (Ithaca: Cornell University Press, 1975), p. 139.

Thomas Cripps, Professor of History at Morgan State University, has written two books on blacks in film; edited an edition of Marc Connelly's The Green Pastures; *written many articles on film history, one a winner of the Hammond Prize (1962) and another the Thomson Prize (1982); written the script for the prizewinning film,* Black Shadows on a Silver Screen *(1976); and has been a Rockefeller and a Guggenheim Fellow, Resident Scholar in the Woodrow Wilson Center, The National Humanities Center, and the Rockefeller Study Center in Bellagio, Italy.*

THE MOVING IMAGE AS SOCIAL HISTORY: STALKING THE PAPER TRAIL

Thomas Cripps

To begin to study the moving image as a document of social and cultural history we must first grant the obvious—that movies and television "reflect" the sensibilities of their audiences and therefore provide us with a mirror to hold up to society. At the same time, this proposition has been too glibly applied and too literally taken. As we shall see, the joke from another time or culture that is too easily "gotten" may in fact have mislead us. Thus, we must ask the student to press on and ask *how* messages and values have reached the screen: the circumstances of both production and reception by the audience.

The silent negotiation between maker and consumer has been at the center of all decisions as to what shall reach the screen, much as though it were a form of pricing in a marketplace of ideas. This notion embraces, of course, both direct and indirect encounters between filmmaker and audience: that between the filmmaker who accommodated to the politics of irate lobbyists and protesters, and that between filmmaker and the audience in search of amusement (or even between audience and the advertising agency which made the posters intended to catch the eye of the filmgoer). Like the diplomatic historian, W. Stull Holt, who studied Versailles in 1919 in a broad context, compared copies of cables, weighed protocols, and learned encrypting and decoding practices before writing his essay on "What Colonel House Sent and What Wilson Received,"[1] we too must argue from context, challenge the intent of authors, and read over the reader's shoulder in order to take from the film document what it may not wish to give.

The most glib form of hasty judgment made by the student who is inattentive to the trail of paper documents has been the study of past stereotypes, often no more than a means for the present to club the past that is too quickly presumed to be more racist or sexist or whatever than ourselves. But a too readily discovered instance of the apparent racism of one time may lead us to distort or to miss entirely vestiges of formerly malevolent but now merely latent husks of pejorative images.

Take, for example, Biograph's *A Bucket of Cream Ale* (1904), a fleeting, simple vignette, perhaps shown with a dozen similar bits as part of a vaudeville show, and a vivid image that seems to pass on to us an unambiguous kernel of meaning from another time. On its face no more than a single unwavering shot of an encounter in a saloon, the film seems dense with racial meanings easily grasped by any casual observer of American social customs. A bearded old man asks (silently, of course) for a bucket of ale; as he sips from his glass, his waitress, a handkerchief-headed black woman, swigs from his bucket, provoking the old man to anger. He hurls his ale in her face, breaking up in laughter at her sudden discomfiture; she, in turn, with barely a pause, gets the last laugh by dumping the bucket on his head.[2]

Recent students delight in the film for its testimony to the apparently ancient roots of black rage. But at the same time, the figure of the man seems to carry no freight of meaning at all. A spade beard, long clay pipe, too-loudly checked coat, gruff manner, zest for beer, all pass as merely the caste marks of a "white" man. But a glance at George Kleine's *Catalogue* for 1905 (number 289) reveals that he is indeed a stock Dutchman and that we are watching an encounter between two stereotypes, the black one both languid and obstreperous in the manner of all stock plantation matriarchs, the white one both dour and prone to impulsive guffaw. Thus in this frozen moment we see a clash of types built in successive flashes of aggressiveness, ending when the maid—to borrow from the jargon of stand-up comics—tops the Dutchman's topper.[3] But all of this is lost on the overconfident viewer untroubled by vestigial or even lost stereotypes such as the Dutchman in whom no longer are there embedded pejorative meanings. Hence the hasty spectator is able to infer data from a modernist angle—casual racism met by primitive rebellion—but not from a time past in which a polyethnic society was strained by many more intergroup tensions and conflicts.

Yet another case stretched over a quarter of a century, entangling the on-camera persona of Lincoln Perry—stage name, Stepin Fetchit—with his actual life, resulting in the name becoming a shorthand simile for all unctious, black sycophancy. Yet in his own day, Fetchit's image as a performer was elusively ambiguous in that for all of his buffoonery he also represented to blacks a sort of success myth. In his day in the sun, before World War II set loose social forces that restored racial issues to national attention, Fetchit's critics were far from unanimous. In black neighborhoods his name played above the title; he boasted of playing the first ever black lover in *In Old Kentucky*

(1926); he played a semitragic role in King Vidor's *Hallelujah* (1929)
and a combat soldier in John Ford's *The World Moves On* (1934); and
played opposite Will Rogers in a series of Southern, local-color, genre
films. For those blacks who could avert their eyes from his clownish-
ness, Fetchit provided a black model of individual achievement who
earned (and spent) four million dollars, cruised black Central Avenue
in Los Angeles in a car emblazoned "20th Century-Fox Star," and
turned a steady dollar in black vaudeville between movies.[4]

To miss the point that Fetchit was both clown and over-achiever is
to miss much of the social context in which movies were made and
shown, and the omission is readily made because his story runs in a
thin vein through the unindexed black press. In his own day, it surfaced in the often deferential treatment he received. The rise of a
rival was treated as a *coup d'etat*; his wages were taken as evidence of
winning a game that few blacks were permitted to enter; his brushes
with the law seemed like the escapades of an urban Br'er Rabbit. Yet,
only recently have students begun to take up his work on the screen
as a performance in a doubly encrypted code that black and white
audiences read differently, the former regarding Fetchit as a cunning
trickster who had gotten away with something in life and art, the latter
regarding him as a mere clown drawn from a race of clowns.[5] In the
black case, the wily Fetchit must be read in the black press as well as
on the white screen, in other words in the paper trail that Fetchit left
for his fans to follow through an inhospitable white landscape.

Recent feminist criticism, or for that matter, homosexual criticism,
suggest that a politics of film art may embrace any number of as yet
unseen group-centered histories, all of them adding their cautions
against too easily grasping what was on the screen without the aid of
scaffolding taken from the written record.[6] For example, *Miss Lulu
Bett* (1921), a film adapted by William C. De Mille and Clara Beranger
from Zona Gale's "hot" novel of 1920 (rivaling Sinclair Lewis's *Main
Street*) and from Gale's Pulitzer Prize play of the following year, passes
uncited in Marjorie Rosen's *Popcorn Venus* and gets less than two lines
in Molly Haskell's *From Reverence to Rape*, the compendia in the field.
The heroine of the book is the classic maiden aunt who has become
no more than a long-suffering drudge as well as, eventually, a dupe
of the men in her family in a scheme that cruelly trifles with her
feelings. Thus the entire apparatus of the novel—theme, plot, character, incident—settles almost sadistically on reporting her oppression
rather than her recognition of her situation or her decision to break
with it. But in the film, on the other hand, the master scene is a visually
brilliant climax in which Lulu Bett is allowed a flash of rage, a tantrum,
in which she destroys a movie set full of tableware and kitchen ap-
pliances and in the end appears on her way to a good marriage with
the town's prize catch, a local schoolmaster. Hardly a modern notion
of liberation, yet this denouement at least allowed Lulu Bett a freedom
of choice not available to her in the novel.

Clearly, Beranger and De Mille's movie was a stronger assertion of

feminist politics than was Gale's book, an unaccountable transformation until the careful student examines the slim record of events
leading up to the production of the film. What little engine of change
drove this transformation? The answer must begin with Zola Gale
herself, a remarkable figure, a native of Portage, Wisconsin, a graduate of the state university, an adventurer who found her way into New
York journalism and a round of bohemian life, and a rebel whose
book was intended as a response to the ladylike tradition exemplified
by Kate Douglas Wiggin's *Rebecca of Sunnybrook Farm* and Kathleen
Norris's *Pollyanna*. Nonetheless, if the subsequent versions were pos-
sessed of a sharper political edge, who had honed it? Gale had provided the melodramatic heart of the project, anticipating later feminist
criticism that asserted a politics of melodrama in which the genre is
seen as the vehicle through which the outsized and unexpected outcomes bring unaccustomed power to the oppressed. But it was the
theatrical producer, Brock Pemberton, who first broached the idea
of a Broadway play to De Mille and Beranger, his collaborator on a
string of 1920s social dramas. The result was the introducing of Gale's
work to an Eastern, urbane audience and later a national movie audience, both of whom seemed able to tolerate redder meat than the
half loaves and scant victories provided them in Gale's book. In order
to take the fullest measure of *Miss Lulu Bett*, and to see the social step
it represented, we must have examined the record that had been left
before anyone ever considered it movie material.[7]

Even when a historian thinks he knows the social circumstances of
a movie's pedigree, drawn perhaps from personal interviews with one
or more of the principals, he is obliged to corroborate them from the
paper trail. If human memory is a fallible instrument, the memoirs
of filmmakers are exponentially so. In a useful essay on the politics
of postwar filmmaking in Italy, for example, Michael Silverman took
the trouble to seek out and interview Giuseppe De Santis, director of
Riso Amaro (1948). De Santis, in need of completion money, yet re-
buffed by the Italian left, turned to a windfall provided by the European Recovery Program, or "Marshall Plan." The result was a film
that had begun as a probing of the oppressive working conditions
endured by migrant, female rice pickers in the valley of the Po, but
which grew into a more internationally marketable sexy Silvana Magnano star-vehicle. The release print (and many advertising mattes)
focussed on the nubile Magnano. Particular attention was paid to a
sexy shot of Magnano raising her skirt as she enters a waterlogged
rice field, an image which not only diverts the eye from the issue at
hand but, as Silverman charged, provides "the documentable trace of
American capital investment," (which had insisted on a sure-fire financial return).[8] Unfortunately, this delicious revelation of American
fishing in Italian domestic affairs is propped only by an interview with
De Santis rather than, as one might wish, an inquiry into the file in
the records of the relevant government agency.

With World War II, Hollywood was at its zenith as a full-blown

oligopoly of a half dozen major studios, an event that prompted elaborate measures to create and preserve records. Thus the period of the
1940s allows us broader opportunity to resort to the documentary
archive. The story of the U.S. Army's own propaganda film, *The Negro
Soldier* (1944), for example, may be followed in the records of the
Office of War Information, the National Association for the Advance-
ment of Colored People (NAACP), the black press, and any number
of other agencies through to the end of the war by which time the
movie had far outreached the modest goals intended for it by the
Army and had become a weapon of choice of various civil rights organizations. Many feature films that were stridently propagandistic,
including such exemplary or controversial films as *Mission to Moscow,
Wilson*, and *Tennessee Johnson*, reveal the mood of the times not only
through the surviving images on the screen but also the complex and
often stenographically recorded bargaining between the Office of War
Information and the studios, between interest groups such as blacks
and their white allies, and between producers and writers resident on
the movie lots. Without these formerly inaccessible records, historians
were left only with the movies themselves, a few reviewers who addressed a national audience, and the trade papers through which the
industry spoke to itself. The resulting histories, such as Siegfried Kracauer's *From Caligari to Hitler* or Barbara Deming's *Running Away From
Myself* did not lack for historical imagination. Indeed, they might have
been enhanced in charm and insight for want of solid documentation;
but they surely were limited in the sophistication with which they
might address the question of precisely *how* social messages reached
the screen and with what effect.[9]

As an example of how paper records can reveal the conflicting
social/political issues often integral to the production process, consider
Warner Brothers' *It Happened in Springfield* (1946). Although at this
writing it remains accessible only in the Library of Congress and offers
little prospect of classroom use, this film offers a profound instance
of the ambiguous imagery that can result from an internal struggle
between right and left, caution and resoluteness. The roots of the
movie traced far back to the years before the war when, following a
violent racial disturbance in Springfield, Massachusetts, the city set
about designing a curriculum with which to teach its children civility
and respect across ethnic lines. Such sentiments during the war,
embedded in the catch words "unity," "tolerance," and "brotherhood,"
became basic ingredients in the general recipe of American propaganda used to convey a simple version of American war aims. One
of the consultants in the Springfield project, Professor Clyde Miller
of Teachers College, Columbia University, pressed upon Jack Warner
a packet of study-materials, clippings, and pamphlets that momentarily persuaded Warner in 1944 to commit the studio to a heroic
effort to spread the Springfield story in the form of a movie that would
unify Americans and teach them why they were fighting. But when
the end of the war reduced such overt liberalism to apparent irrele-

vancy the new mood helped reduce the scale of the movie and shift its message to a considerably less strident tone. In place of the strong assertion of interracial harmony it easily slipped into a mode which emphasized "the enemy origin" of racism. In order to avoid a possible boycott in "the Southern territory" the script that at first had specified "dignified colored youngsters" shifted its angle so that Chinese pupils got the best lines; on the eve of location shooting in Springfield the producer telephoned a peptalk which warned not to be "too heavy on the colored angle;" and at the final cut when its scale shrank to a mere two-reeler, the studio decided to make a soft theatrical version and a firmer classroom version, the former "without Negroes," the latter including them in the group shots.[10]

By following the progress of production through Warner's correspondence with Columbia University and Springfield, and between the producer in Hollywood and the director in Springfield, the various versions of scripts, casting calls, budgets, and cutter's notes, it becomes possible for the careful student to study the fate of a propaganda of unity and harmony as society's collective need for these civic virtues diminished and as conventional politics of left and right reasserted their divisions after five years of "bipartisan" efforts at preserving national unity. Thus even if the blacks were airbrushed out of the release print, the reader who is privy to the incidental documentation of the birth of the film has access to an illuminating incident in the history of the postwar struggle between the American left and right. Moreover, studying the reception of the film reveals the range of racial opinion and what was at stake for blacks in the incident. Near the political center, a reviewer in an audiovisual film catalogue (itself an interesting wrinkle in the field of mass communication that the war had helped bring to American education) reported that the cautious emptiness of the movie was just what the wary teacher needed. "A natural for your school teachers," it reported, "a neat story which offers information and neatly sidesteps a controversial issue." Even in the black response to the movie the range of opinion extended from faint praise to, among Communists at least, a smart slap at its too gingerly taken steps. *Ebony*, the organ of a new black bourgeoisie, itself partly a creation of the war, praised the movie as "magnificent" and "not too preachy," while on the black left a critic insisted on a tougher line than the soft one that "obviously had no bearing on the Jewish or Negro problem" and even evaded American complicity in racism by imputing its sources to foreign agents.[11]

With UCLA's opening of the 20th Century-Fox Archive to scholars, similar albeit not always as densely documented study is possible for any number of feature films. Darryl F. Zanuck's *Pinky* (1949), for example, often cited as a milepost in Hollywood history and in race relations, came to the screen by way of several weeks of script-doctoring at the hands of officers of the NAACP. The exchanges are recorded not only in the Fox records but in those of the NAACP, as well as in the papers of one of the writers.[12] To use this film as part of an argument in social or political history without reference to these sources would be simply irresponsible.

One of the most compelling examples of a film project that revealed the issues of its times more through the paper record of its creation than through the finished film is *The Birth of a Race* (1918) which began life as a self-consciously black reply to the overt racial chauvinism of D. W. Griffith's *The Birth of a Nation* (1915). Its value for historians both as project and as complete film centers on a complex struggle for control of the idea between a coalition of social activists (both black and white) and a combination of white entrepreneurs. At stake for the scholar is a pathway towards a complex and often neglected aspect of American racial arrangements—that they were a bargain arrived at through endless, even daily, negotiations between unequal forces. Even in slavery times, the process may be seen at work in the slave masters' lifelong complaints of the slowness, ineptitude, and carelessness with tools that marked the slaves' style of labor. In other words, on one side of the table masters insisted on the institution of slavery, but on the other the slaves defined the pace and quality of the work. In one form or another, the bargaining table survived, often misunderstood, down to most recent times. The fate of *The Birth of a Race* provides a case study of its working.

The principals in the enterprise, at first anyway, included two black groups, the youthful NAACP and Booker T. Washington's "machine," as his enemies dubbed his network of connections between his Tuskegee Institute in Alabama and his rich, white Republican friends in Washington and New York. There were also several white groups ranging from philanthropic allies of the blacks to grifters in search of the dollar to be made from a quickie movie. They were united only in their belief that a sequel that rode the slipstream of *The Birth of a Nation* might serve their entangled ambitions to make money and to strike a blow for blacks who felt violated. Even before the idea of responding with a film of their own occurred to them, blacks had faced up to the looming presence of Griffith's epic that dominated American attention in the Spring of 1915: the NAACP by picketing it and lobbying for local censorship as an antidote to its message; Booker T. Washington by refusing to allow Griffith to shoot a conciliatory epilogue on his campus and by disassociating himself from protests against it for fear of raising its fame to a still higher level; and white filmmakers by rubbing their hands together at their financial prospects.[13]

Independently of each other the two black groups opened negotiations with Carl Laemmle's adventuresome Universal Pictures. The NAACP took up the idea first through a quickly formed Motion Picture Committee which had hoped to team with Elaine Sterne of Universal on, as one of them wrote, "the scenario . . . or whatever your call it." By midsummer they had marched boldly from a mere consultant's role in the writing of expository titles to that of a substantive investor in a project that nearly matched Griffith's unprecedented

budget for *The Birth of a Nation*. But in the end so many studio and
NAACP executives "threw cold water" on the idea that Sterne turned
to Tuskegee (and its mailing list of white angels).[14] There too Sterne
felt thwarted and by July told Emmett J. Scott, Booker T. Washington's shrewd secretary, that "she was about ready to drop the photo
play about which we talked because the support she wanted had not
been forthcoming." Through the summer the project wambled: a
writer at Vitagraph proposed a modern version of *Uncle Tom's Cabin*
with which to teach that "prejudice is a conservative reaction and an
ill-founded habit"; Sterne returned to the NAACP with a tabloid version of a script which she had cut from twelve to five reels and retitled
Lincoln's Dream; and Scott went to New York where he met with an
agent of the Thomas Ince studio but quickly cooled toward an idea
that seemed not "a square deal all around." Scott and the Tuskegee
group sifted through a series of lesser firms; and even considered
shooting their own movie on campus based on Washington's autobiography, *Up From Slavery*, a perfect vehicle, Scott thought, for
dramatizing "the strivings of the race climbing up from the tragic
period of slavery."[15]

Representing Booker T. Washington and the Tuskegee supporters,
then, Scott had moved in a single summer from diffidently bargaining
with veteran Hollywood firms toward a position of black cultural na-
tionalism in which nothing less than total black control would suffice.
In this frame of mind he opened negotiations with Edwin L. Barker
of the Advance Motion Picture Company of Chicago. This time he
took a long stride toward asserting a black hegemony over the project.
Not only would *Up From Slavery* provide a sort of ideological control
over the outcome, Scott and Washington also located themselves and
other blacks at the center of eventual distribution by proposing a tie-
in with Washington's publisher, a linkage to six hundred chapters of
Washington's National Negro Business League, a pipeline to the editorial desks of more than one hundred black newspapers which
thereby would "be harnessed to the publicity . . . in the interest of the
photoplay." For his services as a consultant on the project and for
providing "that indefatigable something which I shall call the *colored
man's viewpoint*" Scott asked an only slightly princely fifteen percent
royalty, a monthly stipend, and an expense account.[16] Unfortunately
for all of Afro-America, Booker T. Washington died in November
and Scott alone signed the agreement to carry on, but with a new title
for the production, *The Birth of a Race*.

In the beginning everything bubbled along carrying the team to
new levels of enthusiasm. They printed a glowing, graphically illustrated prospectus and began mailing a newsletter that chronicled their
progress. Their angels included Julius Rosenwald of Sears and Roe-
buck, Governor Frank Lowden of Illinois, Robert Russa Moton (Washington's successor at Tuskegee), Fred Moore of the New York *Age*,
solicitous Southern white men, and numerous black doctors, preach-
ers, and businessmen. Black schoolmen in the South pledged their

support; the famous Harry Burleigh promised to oversee the musical score; Chicago's finest, the Selig Polyscope Company, would do the actual shooting; and the story of the Negro from bondage to freedom would soon be recorded forever—so said the prospectus.

Some footage was shot in 1916 and 1917, but most effort was devoted to finance. But dealmaking takes a long time and things happen; World War I, for example, and the growing temptation to celebrate it rather than the black story. By the spring of 1918 the producers had been at it for almost three years and Barker's little firm was overextended, Selig having already shot $140,000 worth of film, not to mention the money that went toward the glossy promotional materials. By then Selig looked for a way out, Rosenwald and other worthies on the letterhead joined him, Barker's interest was sold into the hands of Giles P. Corey, a Chicago broker soon to be arrested for violating the "blue sky" laws against promoting phoney stocks, and Daniel Frohman, a New York vaudeville producer, took over the filming.[17]

As of this writing we cannot know with certainty how it happened, but the changed sponsorship and the popular attention riveted on the expanding American role in the war clearly conspired to alter the thrust of the movie. Scott's hoped-for survey of Afro-American history suffered from the addition of an epic biblical introduction to which the rest of the movie would seem a mere appendage. To capitalize on the popular headlines of the day, they also added a curiously garbled account of the Great War which managed both to celebrate battle and to preach pacifism (perhaps because the movie had been shot in part at the height of American combat on the Western Front in the middle of 1918, but had been cut in the autumn after the Armistice had been signed).

As far as we can tell, little of Selig's footage about American blacks survived the breakup. The single surviving print of the film includes a preponderance of biblical material, shot (according to the credits) by John W. Noble, mainly in a northern suburb of Tampa called Sulphur Springs Park where a few ruined, Egyptian-styled stone structures still survive. The producer enjoyed a friendly local press and delighted a *Tampa Tribune* reporter who recorded the daily roundup of black and white extras for the streetcar trip out to the park.[18] The World War I footage looks so stylistically different as to hint of having been shot elsewhere (perhaps by another unit or even for another film) and purchased like so much telephone cable. The sweeping infantry charges, some of them at night, silhouetted against the light of flares and artillery bursts, and filmed in wide single-camera setups peopled by seemingly hundreds of troops flowing over the broken ground of a no-man's land anticipated a generation of such scenes topped in 1929 by Lewis Milestone's *All Quiet on the Western Front*. By weighing the approximate allocation of footage to black themes we can reckon, to some extent, the scope of the retreat from racial issues as each new participant carried the film away from the germ of the idea that Scott had put to Washington and his philanthropic white friends in 1915.

Moreover, it becomes possible to assess at least a few of the expectations of the blacks and their allies from the surviving dialogue or expository titlecards which contrast strongly with the visual texture of the images they accompany. The race issue is introduced soon after the Garden of Eden; "the folly of prejudice" says a titlecard, but it is followed not by some harmonious image or the wish for one. Rather, the first vaguely black figure is that of a savage lingering on the fringe of a lighted circle of primitive men, that is, the movie quite literally locates blacks in the darkness outside the circle of enlightenment. This formula persists throughout the film: residual, latent racial liberalism in the subtitle cards, rendered neutral by portrayals of blacks as outsiders undeserving of access to inner values of whites. Moreover, the biblical story is infused with a pacifism that all but excludes the black angle. In Egypt, for example, as the story of the Hebrew captivity unfolds it is as an illustration of the "folly of war." Worse yet, the sole image of blacks in this ancient story is one that was to become a convention in later Hollywood biblical epics—Nubians, black, Negroid, passive, standing on the edge of the frame, away from the central action, silently fanning the Pharaoh and his viziers and courtiers.

Not until more than half-way into the film, as the Old Testament gives way to the story of Christ, do blacks take on a more didactic intent, and even then the racial politics is asserted by the title cards rather than the moving image itself. At least two narrative cards press the case for "equality" as two sharply pointed vignettes underline the idea. In the first one, a benign Jesus is portrayed as the benefactor of "men of all races" as a series of cuts of exotically dressed men of color, no more that static one-shots, passes before the spectator, ending on the head of a Chinese. Moments later, as "equality" is again invoked as a virtue, Jesus has begun the walk to Calvary, and as he falters under the weight of the cross, Simon the Cyrene helps him. Following the example of centuries of painters, he was cast as the black man who momentarily shared Jesus' burden on his way to crucifixion.

Here, fully seventy percent through the existing film, the storyline leaps to the Renaissance and to Columbus, suggesting that America fulfilled the promise of Christian virtue following a millennium and a half of European and Asian and African history so satanic or lacking in virtue as to be beneath citing. If Jesus was the central figure in human history, then with the arrival of America on the stage, only Lincoln could serve as His American embodiment. And surely enough, Lincoln's image reintroduces the notion of "equality" although in a setting entirely lacking in a social or historical context.

Finally, in the last twenty percent of the film the viewer encounters the vividly photographed combat footage. Surely almost all of it must have been done at the same time as the weight of American arms in

Europe was helping to force a turn in the fortunes of the Central Powers toward an eventual Allied victory. By this time, the center of the action and of the theme that Scott had bargained for and Rosenwald and the other philanthropists thought they were paying for, had all but completely eroded away. The film ends with a single, marvelous, touching, anticipatory image of future racial integration. At the "call to arms"—as the title card says—a wide shot of a furrowed field ringed by a few broad trees provides the only clearly established formulation of the original moviemakers' vision of American society. The essential American, the film seems to say, is a stalwart, hardy, individual farmer. A tighter shot catches him, full height, in overalls, at work behind his mule-drawn plow, while a second setup repeats the same milieu except that located in its center behind the white farmer and the plow is a black farmer. The shot that follows remains one of the most sophisticated in early film because of its visual complexity, the technical demands made upon the cutter, and the density of social information that it conveys. The white farmer calls the black farmer to his side and, as they stand erect together, they are both transformed into uniformed soldiers, equally equipped with weapons on their shoulders.

The two figures of the white and black farmers, each in his uniform, violate the basic order of Southern racial etiquette as in a single shot they march off screen side-by-side. The effect, finally, is one of integrating black and white Americans together in a common cause against a foreign enemy. Like Mangano's pulled up skirt in *Riso Amaro*, the sequence provided "the documentable trace" of its investors' original intentions as they had been before the death of Booker T. Washington and the dissolution of the alliance between his surrogate, Emmett Scott, and the white angels who had financed the movie in the beginning. In fact, the scene asserts a politics far in advance of not only what American society allowed blacks but even in advance of Scott's and Washington's wildest expectations. The entire sequence constituted less than two percent of the screen time of the surviving film, yet together with the story assembled from the paper record it conveys an otherwise hidden slice of black life in the "progressive era."[19]

That this account culled from surviving footage and the records of the companies was also accessible to viewers of the time—at least those who knew enough racial history to understand what they were seeing—is indicated in the reviews following the opening of *The Birth of a Race* at the prestigious Blackstone Theatre in Chicago. The writers on *The Chicago Tribune* and a local black paper, the *Broad Ax*, praised it as though celebrating a hometown event, finding it "truly great," "clean, sincere," and "worth seeing" even at an inordinate length. But the trade papers, particularly *Variety*, which had taken the trouble to investigate the circumstances of production, lit into the film not only as an artistic flop but as all but a fraud. Their reporters found that as early as the fall of 1917 Barker, Scott's first partner, had begun to edge him out as a participant and that there was a shift in theme, with the result that the audience was seeing a pastiche of *two* movies, the vestiges of Scott's original idea and those of the succession of parties who followed him. For example, the reviewer caught the disparity between the pious titlecards calling for "equality" and the sequences of combat between white civilization and black savagery. "The spirit of the picture's preachment went glimmering when the producer and scenario writers" linked the two contradictory messages— the lexical pleas for brotherhood and equality as against the visual portrayals of interracial violence.[20]

Moreover, *Variety*'s man caught the wide range in the quality of production that must have derived directly from the changed conditions imposed as control of the cameras passed from Selig to Noble to Frohman. He described the movie Scott regarded as *The Birth of a Race* as a "terrible waste" told in the chunky, barely moving title cards, in which "gorgeous settings run alongside shoddy drops"; pointlessly spectacular scenes ended in cheap stockshots; and a drawn-out biblical epic that "dominates the cheap and uninteresting story" that followed it "as the Rockies would dominate Coogan's Bluff."[21]

As if bad art were not enough of a crime, *Variety* depicted the checkered fiscal career of *The Birth of a Race* as a seamy tale of cupidity complete with backers who bullied some of the investors into buying blocks of seats to help fill the theatre made empty by last minute juggling of dates and houses, and shady stockbrokers hustling the no longer prominent race angle, "largely to the colored folk on South State Street."[22]

From the assembled documents—paper and film—we can see as from no other combination of sources a moment in the history of the essential contradiction in American (or for that matter, any) racial arrangements in which a pariah race coexists with arguments that assert an ideal of parity for all races. From the paper sources the student finds evidence—albeit imperfect and incomplete—of the bargaining of blacks who knew well the arguments for egalitarianism but knew also that insisting on them in a negotiation had been made obligatory by the history that had separated them in law and custom from the dominant race. Taken separately, the film itself or the paper documents can shed only a flicker on an already well known debate. But by studying the two together, the scholar of American racial arrangements in the progressive era must see as with a shock of recognition what W. E. B. DuBois meant when he wrote of "voices within the veil" and of the "twoness" of an American life whose codes of conduct embraced contradictions.

It also must be remembered that when a recent critic praised an anthology because its authors, "utilizing manuscript collections and related materials, took TV scholarship as seriously as any student of the Kansas-Nebraska Act [had done]," he was discussing the research of scholars who had gained access to archives, corporate records, and the like, that had been denied their forbears.[23] To take only one instance in film history of an older work that might have been hardened by access to now available documents, Andrew Bergman's *We're In The Money: Depression America and Its Films* (1971), took up the matter of the threatened censorship of Howard Hawks's *Scarface* (1932) by citing John Keats's *Howard Hughes* (1966), an undocumented, unindexed, popular biography whose own author described it as "hopefully, an interim report." At this writing, on the other hand, Bergman could have access to Hawks's own papers, the corporate record of his studio, as well of the firm which distributed the film, and the records of the Production Code Administration, the agency directly charged with the movie industry's self-censorship of its product.[24]

In another way the paper record provides theorists with tests of, challenges to, or merely illustrations of their theories. For example, a current rage for applying Marxist theory to movies—particularly American ones because of their roots in the highly visible Hollywood corporate oligopoly—often stops short of checking theoretical outcomes against the interoffice memoranda generated by the process of production. The Marxist truism that popular culture always serves the interests of the status quo by, for example, resorting to formulas that provide escape from reality for their consumers and seem always to end happily,[25] is modulated by referring to the record. Without denying or affirming the wisdom of this notion, Nick Roddick, in his *A New Deal in Entertainment: Warner Brothers in the 1930s* (1983), demonstrates through the corporate record precisely how corporate policy, manufacturing procedures, budgetary constraints, and even a profile of audience reception drawn from the studio bookkeepers, contributed to the aesthetics of film and to the politics of happy endings.

For example Roddick traces the formula of the social problem film (a genre often associated with Warner Brothers although constituting only a fraction of that studio's output), not to an ideology embraced by its management but to guesses at audience preference as the New Deal restored American confidence and upon conventional cost-cutting strategies on the sound stages. In the first instance, the demoralizing experience of economic depression drew Americans toward collectivist solutions to their problems, but as confidence returned, Americans resumed their attachment to the more individualistic ideas of John Locke and Adam Smith (although they were not necessarily able to affix these names to the ideas). The plots of some of Warner Brothers movies dramatized these ideas in formulas that presented a social problem as a dramatic situation, reduced it to a human scale by victimizing the hero or someone close to him, and then solved the problem through a combination of individual effort, familial support, and the intervention of a sympathetic member of the establishment such as a judge (who reflects the best of the system, much as the heavy had reflected the worst). Thus the denouement that resolved the problem simultaneously provided a classic Hollywood happy ending. But the ending also derived reinforcement from the press of other forces within the movielots—the need to deliver on time and under budget which obliged producers to avoid tinkering and experiment. In this way the audience's taste for the familiar coincided with the studio's wish for rationalization of production.[26]

Thus the corporate record allows the historian a closer scrutiny from the point of view of the shoproom floor and the accounts office and serves as augmentation of the familiar view from the theatre seat and the reviewer's typing table. Of course every studio in its own way was different in its record keeping procedures, and in preserving its contracts, advertising, interoffice memoranda, story conference minutes, union agreements, drafts of scripts, daily schedules, preview cards, cutters' notes, reviews, fan letters, and box office returns. One front office grouped the records by title, another by categories running from pre- to post-production, and so on; some production chiefs carried their records with them when they left, others did not. Some companies weeded the record before passing it on to university libraries, while others have steadfastly refused to relinquish their archives and at this writing continue to sit on them, often at all but prohibitive warehousing costs.[27] Nonetheless, the record is more accessible to historians than ever it has been.

Having pointed out this growing accessibility of film records, it must be said that the records of American broadcasting networks and their producing arms remain dauntingly closed to outside view. Therefore, except when programming intersects with the protests of an offended sector of the audience, as in the case of the NAACP protest against CBS's *Amos and Andy* television show which generated an imposing file in the NAACP records, the student of broadcast history remains dependent upon published sources such as trade papers.[28] Exceptions to this general rule include an incomplete file of NBC records in the Wisconsin Center for Theatre Research, the odd deposit of personal papers such as the personal donations of scripts by performers or producers, the production files of the Warner Brothers' television series which are part of the larger Warner Brothers collection at the University of Southern California, and the records of J. Walter Thompson advertising agency archived in the agency itself.

Of all the modes of expression on film and television, propaganda holds open the greatest promise of a successful stalking of paper trails in search of fresh meaning. *The Negro Soldier* (1944) was no more than a shameless manipulation by the U.S. Army of the latent patriotism of Afro-America. But the paper record reveals more by leading us from worried Pentagon planners to the film's reception two years later accompanied by the cheers of black activists who imagined rousing uses to which the film could be put after the war as a means of pitching the idea of racial integration. Warner Brothers' *The Charge of the Light Brigade* (1936) may have seemed to be no more than an expression of Hollywood's well-known Anglophilia, leavened by a warning against appeasing Hitler, until Roddick's assertion (supported by the archival record of the producers) that its "broader ideological significance" was its intent to address Americans with the message that "action is right, intrigue is wrong," or more precisely, individual action is the preferred solution to a collective problem. To put the argument as it relates to sponsored films: everyone studies Robert Flaherty's *Louisiana Story*; no one has yet studied Standard Oil's *Louisiana Story*. Thus future scholars must devote more attention to the circumstances of production as a window of access to meaning.[29]

Propaganda films have long been considered compellingly informative about a particular time and place because they are a self-consciously cultivated means of expressing national will or goals or war aims, or at the least, putting the best construction on a nation's accomplishments. Because they are meant to convey the nation's sentiments about itself as ingenuously as possible, propaganda films and their records of production and reception allow an uncommonly close look at the contradictions embedded just below the surface of public life.

The study of a propaganda film along with its paper trail also enables us to feel more urgently the issues that impelled another place and time, minimizing some of the cross-cultural or generational static that usually intrudes into the filmviewing experience. Without access to the paper record, a film's expression of the passions and convictions of an age may seem cross-purposed and murky. Apart from the well-worn paragons of documentary history (*The River* or *Fires Were Started*) drawn from a half-century ago, even a film barely a generation away like *The Battle of Algiers* (1969), may convey little of the radical fire it seemed once to have stoked. Indeed, the latter film that in 1969 had seemed a primer for radicals, shown ten years later to an audience of "business majors," seemed more an occasion to doze than to take up arms.[30]

Such an approach to the film as document of social and cultural history leads to all manner of refinements in understanding. Without this kind of work, the repeated critical acclaim of so-called classic films often masks what they have to teach the careful student. The rhythmic cadences of Leni Riefenstahl's *Olympia* and *Triumph des Willens* and the gossip about her true place in Nazi circles combine to give the films a celebrity that blurs the context from which the student might have learned more important social history. *The Birth of a Nation* enjoys a similar place in film history that has helped to distort its value as a social document; exaggerated accounts of black campaigns to block its showing and of rising Southern white passions as a result of viewing it have passed into legend almost to the exclusion of the actual audience response.[31]

To this caution must be added a warning to probe gingerly into films that may have been made for one purpose but appropriated for other uses. As we have seen; *The Negro Soldier* was such a film, made for a narrowly prescribed goal of minimizing the impact of drafting blacks into the Army, it quickly became an instrument of liberal propaganda.

Scholars embarking on this type of study for the first time should refer to Robert C. Allen and Douglas Gomery's *Film History: Theory and Practice* (1985) which demonstrates how to put the broadest possible construction on the meaning of film history, extending its territory beyond merely new information and critical insights into a search for fresh kinds of documents to be milked for new levels of social meaning. To take only one instance; their inquiry into the social basis for theatre construction decisions and thus of the social dimension of how audiences receive films directs attention to arcana such as fire insurance maps as a means of access onto data that help define the audience with respect to class and neighborhood.[32] In this way, it becomes possible to compare, say, the New York moviegoing experience with that of almost any city for which there are surviving sources in urban geography. Following paths such as these we may anticipate a future in which scholars study local and regional reviewers who have gone largely unread by generations of historians (as though John McCarten in *The New Yorker* and the over-quoted Bosley Crowther in *The New York Times* spoke similarly for the metropolis and for Yazoo City).

Studied in this way, films provide fresh instances of the different ways in which historical sources can document their times and their cultures. With each newly examined moving-image document the scholar is challenged to test the credibility, reliability, and authenticity of the film itself and its paper trail with the same rigor as that brought to bear on any ancient manuscript.

NOTES

1. W. Stull Holt, "What Colonel House Sent and What Wilson Received, Or Scholars Need to Check Carefully," *American Historical Review*, LXV (April, 1960), 569–571.
2. *A Bucket of Cream Ale* (1904) is in the Library of Congress. Surviving records of the Biograph firm are in the Museum of Modern Art.
3. Biograph's *The Fight of Nations* (1907) provides yet another cautionary tale for the dutiful historian. A good half dozen ethnic groups parade across the screen in one vignette after another in stereotypical modes that might seem appalling to a sensitive political liberal, but a trade paper of the day found all the racial pejoratives "well represented." To understand this apparent tolerance of racial pejoratives it must be understood that ethnicity permeated the daily idiom to such an extent that comedians casually advertised for gigs billed as "two hebe comics." To miss this is to miss the meanings of films that are derived from social context. *Fights of Nations* is in the Library of Congress. *Motion Picture World*, March 9, 1907, 9–10. Robert Darnton cautions scholars not to jump to modernist conclusions while studying works drawn from times past in *The Great Cat Massacre and Other Episodes in French Cultural History* (Princeton, 1984).
4. Thomas Cripps, *Slow Fade to Black: The Negro in American Film, 1900–1942* (New York, 1977), V, and XI; interview between Fetchit and Cripps, December 1976; Stepin Fetchit taped memoir in the possession of the author.

5. The idea of a double code, once the property of a small circle of theorists of Afro-American rhetoric, has become a widely accepted currency in a general community of scholars of movies.
6. For instances of this sort of critical particularism, see, for example, Mary Ann Doane, Patricia Mellencamp, and Linda Williams, eds., *Re-Vision: Essays in Feminist Film Criticism* (Frederick, MD, 1984); Richard Dyer, ed., *Gays and Film* (New York, 1984); and John S. Schuchman, *Hollywood Speaks: Deafness and the Film Entertainment Industry* (Urbana and Chicago, 1988).
7. A full account of *Miss Lulu Bett* remains to be accomplished. For the moment, see Harold P. Simonson, *Zona Gale*, 18, "Twayne United States Authors Series" (New York, 1962). Gale's papers are in the Wisconsin State Historical Society; the film is in the Library of Congress. Quite possibly, the film may have stimulated a string of fitfully feminist films by De Mille and Clara Beranger.
8. Michael Silverman, "Italian Film and American Capital, 1947–1951," in Patricia Mellencamp and Philip Rosen, eds., *Cinema Histories, Cinema Practices*, Vol. IV in "The American Film Institute Monograph Series," (Frederick, MD, 1984), 35–46. This essay takes up the concerns of historians but rests this point on only an interview given a quarter of a century after the fact and uncorroborated with a check of, for a start, the files of the European Recovery Administration, Record Group 260, Archives of the United States.
9. See Thomas Cripps and David Culbert, "*The Negro Soldier* (1944): Film Propaganda in Black and White," *American Quarterly*, XXXI (Winter, 1979), 616–40; David Culbert, ed. *Mission to Moscow* (Madison, WI, 1980), 11–41; Thomas J. Knock, "History Written in Lightening: The Forgotten Film *Wilson* (1944)," in Peter Rollins, ed., *Hollywood as Historian: American Film in a Cultural Context* (Lexington, KY, 1983), 88–108; Cripps, "Movies, Race, and World War II: *Tennessee Johnson* as an Anticipation of the Strategies of the Civil Rights Movement," *Prologue*, XIV (Summer, 1982), 49–67, are a few instances of the movement away from the much admired psychological insights of Siegfried Kracauer (Princeton, 1947), Barbara Deming (New York, 1969) and others.
10. Jack L. Warner to Gordon Hollingshead, September 1, 1944, in file 1469, Warner Brothers Archive, University of Southern California; interview with Mrs. Crane Wilbur, August, 1977. A file of correspondence between the studio and Clyde Miller also survives in file 1469; Hollingshead to "Charlie" Einfeld, September 12, 1944 (on *The March of Time*); cast list for *It Happened in Springfield*, and telephone script between Hollingshead and Wilbur, no date; Hollingshead to Warner, copy, December 19, 1944; *Sweet Land of Liberty*, cutter's notes, November 1944, all in file 1469. This conscious exclusion of visible ethnicity from a movie that had begun as an anti-racist tract suggests a Hollywood assimilationist urge for ethnic invisibility. The need to investigate this by pressing the probe more deeply than the film itself may be seen in two ably done surveys of Jews on the screen: Lester D. Friedman, *Hollywood's Image of the Jew* (New York, 1982), and Patricia D. Erens, *The Jew in American Cinema* (Bloomington, IN, 1984), both of which are dependent on imagination and inferences for extra-Hollywood sources, rather than on the interoffice memoranda that might shed more definitive light on this important question.
11. The clippings are cited in Cripps, "Racial Ambiguities in American Prop-

aganda Movies," in K. R. M. Short, ed., *Film and Radio Propaganda in World War II* (London and Canberra, 1983), 145.

12. The 20th Century-Fox records are in process at UCLA; the NAACP Records are now on microfilm through University Publications of America, Frederick, MD.

13. For an account of the making and reception of *The Birth of a Race* see Cripps, "*The Birth of a Race* Company: An Early Stride Toward a Black Cinema," *The Journal of Negro History*, LIX (January 1974), 28–37; and for an account of its rediscovery and deposit in the Library of Congress see Thomas Cripps "*The Birth of a Race*: Lost Film Rediscovered in Texas," *Texas Humanist*, V (March/April 1983), 10–12. On Washington's and Scott's mutual interest in movies and their antipathy toward *The Birth of a Nation*, the "hurtful, vicious play," as Washington described it in Phil J. Allston, copy, April 25, 1915; Rabbi Abram Simon to Washington, April 12, 1915; and Scott to Simon, April 14, 1915, all in box 75, Booker T. Washington Papers, Library of Congress.

14. Mrs. Mary Hallowell Loud to M. C. Nerney, May 12, 1915, and other correspondence in the records of the NAACP, Library of Congress. See Nerney to Charles E. Bentley, May 11, 1915 and June 9, 1915 (for the second quotation); George Cook to Nerney, May 11, 1915; Nerney to William English Walling, copy, May 13, 1915; and Nerney to Joseph P. Loud, copy, may 17, 1915. At first they had discussed a budget in the range of $200,000 with the NAACP contributing 24%, but by June, with the NAACP offering only $10,000, Universal dropped its share to $60,000. See confidential memo from Mary White Ovington, June, 1915.

15. Rose Janowitz to Emmett Scott, July 9, 1915, on dropping the idea; Amy Vorhaus to Washington, July 9, 1915; and Washington to Vorhaus, July 13, 1915, on "prejudice," all in Washington Papers. On the prospects of an arrangement with Ince, see H. C. Oppenheimer to Scott, September 10, 1915; Scott to Mirror Films, copy, marked "personal," October 27, 1915 in Washington Papers; Carl Laemmle, Universal, to Jacob Schiff, November 2, 1915, in NAACP Records; and on *Up From Slavery* as a vehicle, Scott to James Weldon Johnson, August 3, 1915, in Emmett J. Scott Papers, Soper Library, Morgan State University; and Scott to Edwin L. Barker, October 18, 1915, in Washington Papers.

16. Scott to Barker, October 18, 1915, in Washington Papers; Scott to Barker, November 6, 1915, and contract dated December 20, 1915 (roughly a month after Washington's death), in Scott Papers.

17. The famous angels and supporters were listed in the prospectus, a copy of which is in the George P. Johnson Collection, Research Library, UCLA; and in the Julius Rosenwald Papers in the University of Chicago. On the lengthening pedigree of the participants, see George P. Johnson to Curator, Powell Library, UCLA, October 24, 1968; along with issues of *The Birth of a Race News*, I, 3 (July, 1917), (October, 1917), a serial produced as a public relations organ by the firm, all in the Johnson Collection.

18. A clipping file, largely from the *Tampa Tribune*, on *The Birth of a Race* is in the Tampa Public Library.

19. Several years ago, a print of *The Birth of a Race* surfaced in a cowboy museum in Canyon, Texas. A reference print is now in the Library of Congress.

20. *Broad Ax* (Chicago), November 23, 1918; *Chicago Sunday Tribune*, Novem-

ber 24, 1918; *Variety*, October 12, 1917, and March 22, 1918. On the film
itself as played at the Blackstone, *Variety*, November 22, 1918.
21. *Variety*, November 22, 1918. See also *Variety* December 6, 1918. For other
reviews see *Billboard*, March 23, 1919, and undated clippings in the Johnson Collection; *Exhibitors' Herald*, May 1919 (1761); *Billboard*, December
14, 1918.
22. *Variety*, November 22, 1918 and December 6, 1918.
23. James Lewis Baughman, "Thank You for Letting Us into Your Homes:
TV and American History," *Reviews in American History*, XII (December
1984), 601.
24. Bergman, (New York, 1971), 14; and Keats (New York, 1966), vii.
25. See, for example, Theodor Adorno, "Culture Industry Reconsidered,"
New German Critique (Fall, 1975), cited in John Tulloch, *Australian Cinema:
Industry, Narrative, and Meaning*, #11 in "Studies in Society," Ronald Wild,
ed. (Sydney, 1982), 124. As late as 1946, the Jesuit, Gilbert J. Garraghan,
in his *A Guide to Historical Method* (New York, 1946, 47), argued that
despite being "warmly debated" Ranke's nineteenth century ideal of history "wie es eigentlich gewesen ist"—as it really (or even actually) was—
seemed attainable. Today most historians share Hegel's skepticism of the
scholar who "pretends that he is merely receptive, merely surrendering
to the data" (quoted in Robert C. Allen and Douglas Gomery, *Film History:
Theory and Practice* (New York, 1985), 8). Among them are Marxists who
feel as discomfitted by too pat assertions of determinism such as regarding
film as an omnipotent means of "pacifying the proletariat" (quoted in
D. N. Rodowick, *The Crisis of Political Modernism: Criticism and Ideology in
Contemporary Film Theory* (Urbana, 1988), 86. Antonio Gramsci, for example, far from a narrowly simplistic, overdrawn class conflict, imagined
the prospect of "nurturing class alliances" arising out of the stresses of
cultural crises such as wars. As a result, the possibility of a variegated
society, remote from the one-dimensional capitalist culture described by
Herbert Marcuse and other critics the Frankfurt school, and leavened by
alternative minority cultures seemed attainable. Gramsci argued that such
arrangements might undermine established culture and alter political
relations between a dominant culture and its subcultures, thereby establishing a more tolerable basis for a new hegemony legitimized by "the
consent of the governed." (See Walter L. Adamson, *Hegemony and Revolution: Antonio Gramsci's Political and Cultural Theory* (Berkeley, 1980), 100–
01, 148–49, 168, 234.) In its way then *The birth of a Race* invites our
attention as an instance of an antifact of popular culture that came into
being during a cultural crisis that included both urbanization and war
under circumstances that enable a racial minority to begin to assert its
ideology to an audience heretofore inaccessible to it.
26. Nick Roddick, *A New Deal in Entertainment: Warner Borthers in the 1930s*
(London, 1983), 6, 28, 66, 77–78, 87, 99, 126, 183, 200–03, 206, 230,
236, 254, and VIII, for the development of the idea that film form, genre,
and ideology all grow out of the specific social conditions of production.
Tulloch, *Australian Cinema*, passim, makes a similar point with reference
not to production in the main, but to distribution of rival British and
American products which places Australia between two rivals, who in
turn, sold their wares as either exemplars of "civilized" British culture or
"universal" values in American movies, a dilemma to which a few Australians responded by making culture-specific native films including a

genre he identifies as "larrikinism," or a universalizing of a specific working class hero into a symbol for the entire culture—as perhaps the American cowboy became in another context. Much of this argument grows out of Tulloch's investment in the social-industrial theories of the basis of mass culture as put forth by the Frankfurt School.

27. The opening to public scrutiny of formerly private corporate archives must not be taken as an unalloyed benefit. The Disney Archives require permission. Paramount seems to have been weeded; MGM is accessible only through the goodwill of the firm's legal department; and so on— thus demanding a rigorous criticism, both internal and external, of the documents.

28. For a partial accounting of this story see Thomas Cripps, "*Amos and Andy* and the Debate over American Racial Integration," in John E. O'Connor, ed., *American History/American Television* (New York, 1983), 33–54.

29. Roddick, *New Deal in Entertainment*, 237–240. On Flaherty see Arthur Calder Marshall, *The Innocent Eye: The Life of Robert J. Flaherty* (New York, 1963), which tells, for example, a story of a Standard Oil angel that descended on the film, *Louisiana Story*, blessed and supported it without credit, yet without offering a single document in support of the assertion.

30. The two events were observed and reported by Alma Taliaferro Cripps at Stanford and Towson, MD.

31. Thomas Cripps, "The Reaction of the Negro to the Motion Picture 'Birth of a Nation," *The Historian*, XXV (May, 1963), 244–262.

32. Robert C. Allen and Douglas Gomery, *Film History: Theory and Practice* (New York, 1985), 202–207. More than any other work this book proposes a film history that is more than—greater than—either popular anecdotal history or the various schools of contemporary film writing that faddishly rest on potted digests of notions taken from legitimate disciplines such as economic theory, semiology, and psychology.

Carlos E. Cortés is Professor of History at the University of California Riverside. The recipient of two book awards and numerous fellowships, he also received his university's Distinguished Teaching Award and the California Council for the Humanities' 1980 Distinguished California Humanist Award. Among his many publications are Three Perspectives on Ethnicity, Gaucho Politics in Brazil, *and* A Filmic Approach to the Study of Historical Dilemmas. *He is currently working on a three-volume study of the history of the U.S. motion picture treatment of ethnic groups, foreign nations, and world cultures.*

CHALLENGES OF USING FILM AND TELEVISION AS SOCIO-CULTURAL DOCUMENTS TO TEACH HISTORY

Carlos E. Cortés

Films and television programs (moving image media) are valuable social and cultural artifacts. From them we can derive insights into various aspects of times, places, and human experiences. Using them well, we can write and teach better history, in some respects, history that could not be essayed in any other manner.

Yet, it is imprecise to say that historians *can* teach using moving image media. Historians have used, are using, and will continue to use film and television in their classrooms. But how and how well?

An increasing number of teachers are approaching moving image media more seriously as important socio-cultural documents, a trend suggested in the course information obtained as part of this study. The evidence comes in various forms: course syllabi; course examinations; reports and articles about media-based courses (mainly from issues of *Film and History*); and letters from practitioners. Most was collected during the fall of 1984 on the basis of an appeal for history teachers to submit examples of their courses. Therefore, the sample is obviously skewed, reflecting the pedagogical efforts of teachers who also demonstrated the initiative, confidence, and courage to submit their course materials for examination.

Overall, I analyzed descriptions or syllabi of sixty-eight courses involving thirty-nine teachers, mainly university level, but also some at the secondary level. The numerical discrepancy occurs because some professors are represented by more than one course, while other courses were team-taught. Courses can be broken down according to five categories: type, focus, goals, content, and evaluation.

Course *types* varied as to the centrality of moving image media. Although the following system of categorization is clearly arbitrary and there is considerable overlap, three basic types of courses can be discerned. Twenty-four courses used film or television as supplementary material. Twenty-nine courses made film *the* principal source or *one* of the principal sources for examining the course's focal topic. Fifteen courses did not emphasize a specific historical subject, but rather the methodology and problems of using media as a socio-cultural historical document.

As to *focus*, by far the most common kind of course addressed a particular nation or region within a specific time period, using media as a primary or supplementary source. Of the syllabi examined, the most popular regions were the United States and Europe, trailed significantly by Latin America, with Asia and Africa (not to mention Australia) rarely considered. A subcategory consisted of those courses that focused on a specific theme within an area and time period.[1] A few courses were explicitly comparative[2]; others were implicitly comparative, dealing with a general theme without any specific area focus.[3] While these subject area courses dominated, a minority of the courses made film itself the subject: some emphasized the history of film[4]; some focused on the nature of moving image media evidence.[5]

Course *goals* varied, although the degree of differentiation cannot be determined precisely, as only about half of the syllabi or descriptions explicitly stated course goals. Those that did state goals (and implicitly those that did not) usually sought to "help students learn more about" (or gain insights into or develop greater understanding of or get a better feel for) subject X. Some spoke with greater specificity, stating the aforesaid and adding "through the use of film" or some similar rhetoric. Other courses explored the relationship between film and other historical processes, such as politics, social change, foreign policy, and war. In these cases, film became a principal socio-cultural document, either to illuminate the focal topic or to provide insight into the era and nation in which the document was produced; some courses attempted to do both. Certain syllabi contained more explicit statements of film-related goals, such as helping students learn to use film as a historical document, to analyze film as a historical artifact, to understand film and television as instruments of persuasion, to integrate film and written evidence, to comprehend (through visual literacy) the specific film techniques used to achieve certain effects, and in some cases simply to think more critically.

Course *content* varied as to reading assignments, films, the use of guests, and the emphasis on visual literacy. All course syllabi required some reading, although at times this was depressingly skimpy (in some cases one book for a semester course), and various patterns of reading assignments emerged. While all courses required at least one book on the focal topic, only about one third required any books dealing with film and, among the latter, only a relatively small number required books or even articles dealing with media analysis or visual language *per se*.

In terms of media shown, most courses fell into two categories. About one half of the courses used only feature films; the other half used a combination of feature and documentary films. A smattering of courses included other moving image documents, such as newsreels, television programs, and films on visual language and media analysis. By far the greatest number of films were made in the United States, trailed by European films and, considerably further back, by films from Latin America, particularly those of the contemporary "revolutionary" variety. Asian and African films rarely appeared in the reviewed courses.

A few course descriptions indicated the use of guest speakers, occasionally filmmakers, but with mixed results. All professors who evaluated their own courses pointed to the enrichment and alternative perspectives brought to the classroom by such guests. However, a few teachers lamented that guests sometimes dominated the class and stifled discussion by suffocating students with their own interpretations rather than engaging in classroom give and take.

Courses also varied widely in their approaches to developing student abilities in film analysis and visual literacy. Some course syllabi continued no specific references to that topic in stated course goals, assigned readings, films, or class discussion topics. Some syllabi proclaimed visual literacy or increased ability to analyze films as a goal, but this was not always reflected in the listed course content of readings or daily classroom topics, except by indicating that students were to write film critiques. Less than one fourth of the course syllabi specified class periods, films, books, or articles on media analysis per se.

However, syllabi cannot be taken at face value. Some professors who do not specify books or class periods on film analysis per se may do an excellent job of developing these skills throughout the course. Conversely, the fact that some professors assign books on visual language or set aside class periods to discuss strategies of film analysis or methodologies for using film as a historical document does not guarantee that they do it well. Yet film-and-history teachers *appear* to place a relatively low priority on training in visual language, at least as suggested by the absence of assigned materials or class periods on that topic. This may mean that most teachers who use film feel that it takes no special skills to analyze a moving image document and that students merely need to apply general critical skills or historical thinking.

Finally, as in every course, there is the question of the *evaluation* of student performance. Most courses included a final examination; some had midterm examinations. Most courses required some kind of paper, usually short film analyses (two to five pages), but sometimes papers on a topic in which students were to integrate film and assigned readings; occasionally there was even a research paper, in which film was to be part of the evidence. A handful of courses included less traditional forms of assignments (required or optional), such as scripts, videotapes, or private journals.

TEACHING IMPLICATIONS OF SCHOLARLY ISSUES

Historians who use moving image documents face all of the problems of evidence common to any historical scholarship or pedagogy. However, such media present special analytical problems, while their use as socio-cultural documents adds an additional dimension of challenge. These problems cannot be avoided by those engaged in using moving image media for historical scholarship. For teachers using such media, these issues should be considered in planning courses and, where appropriate, should be addressed explicitly in the courses. These problems can be examined within the context of the three categories provided in this book's introduction: content, production, and reception.

Take, for example, one scholarly *content* issue that has pedagogical implications: authenticity of source. Were all films "original editions" (or at least authentic copies of the master film or tape), then historians could depend on "seeing is believing" as a form of authentication. No such luck. Films may be released, re-edited, and re-released in severely modified form, making it difficult for scholars to know if they are truly dealing with an original source, a valid copy, or a modified version. Following are two examples that demonstrate that "seeing" may involve more or less than the original.

On the more side, take the World War II-made film, *The North Star*, which praised the Russian peasant for opposing the German war machine. After all, the Soviet Union was our ally when the film was made. Then the rise of the cold war quickly antiquated the film, making it inappropriate for general release in its original form. To make it acceptable for continued showing, it was re-released as *Armored Attack*, with modifications mitigating its positive view of the Soviet Union. Unless informed by a knowledgeable teacher, students would probably be unaware of the fact, nature, and reasons for the drastic modification of the original document.

On the less side, feature films shown on television may well be shortened, sometimes slightly and delicately, sometimes massively and brutally. This may be done to fit available time slots (for example, if you have a strong stomach, try to sit through the mini-*Citizen Kane* currently polluting the television airwaves). Film editing for television may also remove jarring language, graphic sex, and gratuitous violence. Such restraints are eroding, however. Even the dreaded "f" word sometimes survives unscathed, as in some local telecasts of such heavily scatological films as *The Deer Hunter*. In addressing content, teachers need to be certain of the authenticity (or lack of it) of the films that they show or assign (particularly on television), while students need to be aware of the possible heavy hand of latter-day editing.

Authenticity of source is only one of the myriad content-related scholarly issues with pedagogical implications. Other content issues, particularly those specifically related to the development of student understanding of the moving image media, will be discussed later in this chapter.

The area of *production* raises a number of pedagogically important scholarly issues. For example, there is the question of *intent*, particularly problematic when addressing feature films or fictional television. Creators make media for a reason. They may simply want to entertain, earn money, or just have the pleasure of making a film. On the other hand, they may have more instrumental, maybe even propagandistic, goals in making these films or television programs: to raise awareness of societal issues; to criticize aspects of societal or international behavior; to spread moral or ethical instruction; to reinforce or modify values or attitudes toward societal groups or foreign nations; to support or oppose aspects of foreign policy; or to promote social action, maybe even revolution.

How can historians be certain of creator intent? Scholars sometimes fall into the trap of definitively asserting intent on the basis of viewed content, as if the results "proved" the goals. Yet filmmaker intent does not always translate into content, particularly as this content is perceived and interpreted by diverse audiences. Both teachers and students must demonstrate restraint, therefore, when attempting to tease filmmaker intent from film content.

Take one example. Francis Ford Coppola's *The Godfather* combo (Parts I and II) struck many viewers—including many Italian-American viewers—as a stereotypical calumny against Italian-Americans. Yet Coppola intended the films as a multilayered insider's vision of Italian-American life, of which violence was only one part, with the Mafia serving as a metaphor for the excesses and amorality of U.S. capitalism. As a compromise, when NBC televised the rearranged combo as *The Godfather Saga*, the network led off with a posturing disclaimer that "it would be erroneous and unfair to suggest that they are representative of any ethnic group" (interestingly, this disclaimer was cloned for Brian DePalma's violent Cuban-American remake of *Scarface* and Michael Cimino's similarly violent Chinese-American *Year of the Dragon*). By introducing students to the topic of intent, using such sources as interviews with filmmakers, teachers can challenge students to compare stated intent with resulting film content.

This brings us to another production-related problem—the external limitations imposed on media creators. Those limitations can be societal, from Federal Communications Commission restraints on television content to moral pressures from protest groups. They can be economic, ranging from financing and production choices to the overriding (or maybe sole) desire to make money by attracting audiences and, in the case of television, advertisers. The limitations may be film sources, such as novels and theatrical pieces (although these can be adapted), and sometimes history itself (although television docudramas have demonstrated that even documented facts lay only a light restraining hand on "artistic freedom"). There certainly have been industry restraints, such as the now-defunct Motion Picture Production Code (Hays Code). Additionally, film audiences themselves provide a commercial restraint on filmmakers who try to predict audience tastes and shape movies that will sell tickets. In other words, just as it is difficult to infer intent on the basis of content, even an accurate identification of intent does not mean that media makers enjoy total freedom to carry through their intent. A recognition of these limitations should influence students to temper their judgments, while readings and lectures about the societal and media industry milieu in which a film or television program was made should lead to richer student insights.

Finally, there is the issue of *reception*. Filmmaker intent does not always translate into content, and content does not always have the creators' desired impact. In some cases, such as television's "All in the Family" or its more virulent movie counterpart, *Joe*, the content had polarically different effects on different audiences. Put another way, once the creators' efforts become encapsulated on film or videotape, they lose control. At that point the audience takes over, doing what it will with the frozen content.

This audience includes teachers and students in courses using film and television to study history. In receiving these media, they will interpret content. Yet both teachers and students need to recognize that their interpretations are individual, maybe idiosyncratic, responses, rooted in a particular time and place. They should not project *their* responses onto other audiences, particularly those of another era and cultural setting.

PEDAGOGICAL CHALLENGES

Aware of the basic scholarly issues concerned with the content, production, and reception aspects of the moving image media, teachers still need to face other critical but exciting pedagogical challenges. The first challenge, quite simply, is getting students to think seriously about the media. After years of being conditioned to viewing media as basically a conduit of information or a pipeline of entertainment, students often have difficulty recognizing the immense possibilities of moving image media for deriving serious socio-cultural insights. They need to be convinced of the importance of addressing media analytically, not as simple deliverers of entertainment and information, spelled Truth, but as media people's creations and interpretations. These misconceptions can easily occur, particularly in the face of such popular blenders of fact and fiction as television docudramas and so-

called fictional documentaries, two media forms that implicitly reinforce the concept of "history-as-story-telling" by pandering re-creation
as history in forms ranging from *State of Siege* to *Midnight Express* and
from "Peter the Great" to "The Atlanta Child Murders." Therefore,
teachers need to work with students to internalize the predisposition
for applying the same critical standards to moving image documents
that they would apply to any other types of historical evidence.

Attitude, unfortunately, does not automatically translate into ability.
Many students simply do not know how to critically analyze a piece
of evidence, written or otherwise. Students need some of the special
skills of moving image media analysis if they are to do a good job of
assessing those elements and techniques that give moving images their
impact, including the power to stir and delude. What techniques enable films and television programs to become particularly effective
interpreters of society, deliverers of messages (including obvious
propaganda films), contributors to image building (such as popular
images of ethnic groups), critics of societies or activities (like war), or
even catalysts for action? How is television news produced and how
does this influence the ways that news is presented on television? What
television advertising techniques have proven particularly effective
and how have they drawn upon and manipulated social and cultural
values?

The pedagogical challenge: to help students develop visual literacy
and some understanding of media techniques in a reasonable amount
of time. About one third of the surveyed courses required the reading
of at least one book on film, while about one fifth set aside at least
one session to deal specifically with the general topic of film, visual
literacy, or media analysis techniques.[6] Clearly teachers should devote
more effort here.

Assuming that students have learned to take film seriously, to analyze critically, and to understand visual language and moving image
media techniques, the question becomes, what next? Teachers need
to plan carefully in order to help equip students with sufficient factual
knowledge so they can begin to analyze the visual material validly and
effectively. Functioning as scholars, good historians search for and
consider evidence until they feel confident that they can test hypotheses, reach conclusions, suggest causation, and create a convincing narrative. However, when they function as teachers, historical
scholars find that involving their students in a similar analytical quest
differs in at least two significant respects.

Students have far less background knowledge on the topic and evidence to be considered, and they certainly have far less time to devote
to their work. How can the history teacher compensate for the students' lack of background knowledge within the span of a quarter or
semester, while also considering the limited amount of time students
can reasonably devote to the course? The importance of planning is
crucial here. To be most effective, the teacher should support the

showing of any film with lectures and carefully selected reading materials concerning both relevant media history and the specific socio-cultural subject and context of the film.

For example, for a course on the history of the United States during the 1960s, the teacher could select from a number of films and books that address important issues of that decade. The changing situation of women could be engaged through the feature film, *Rachel, Rachel*, combined with the reading of Betty Friedan's *The Feminine Mystique*. Godfrey Hodgson's *America in Our Time* could be paired with *Save the Tiger* as a launching pad for considering the cultural and moral quandries that surfaced during that era. Ethnic self-assertion, in both society and film, could be addressed with such films as *Super Fly* and books as *The Autobiography of Malcolm X*. Of course, there is the war in Vietnam. After assigning conflicting written interpretations of the war, the teacher could show conflicting film interpretations, such as the documentary, *Hearts and Minds*, and the feature film, *The Green Berets*, while requiring that the students evaluate both films seriously as historical documents.

In addition, one or two documents relating to media history might be included. For example, when using films made from the 1930s through the 1960s, the Hays Code makes a fascinating background source, as well as being interesting in itself as socio-cultural history. After reading it, students would be far better prepared to conduct a more sophisticated analysis of the dramatic changes represented by films of the 1960s (when movie married couples began to share single beds and where, at least occasionally, film crime would pay, as in *The Thomas Crown Affair*—both absolute no-no's under the Hays Code).

Such planning is critical, whatever the use being made of moving image media. For the analysis media propaganda, students need some background on the social and cultural forces at work at the time that the film or television program was made. In this way students can begin to consider the themes and techniques by which the media tried to manipulate contemporary hopes, fears, and values for their desired effect. Maybe such an approach can help students become more adept at dealing with advertising, political commercials, and various forms of propaganda that are trying to influence society.

There is also the special issue of stereotyping in the moving image media. In recent years, particular attention has been devoted to the significance of the media in affecting the public images of foreign nations, ethnic groups, and women, as well as other societal groups.[7] Teachers could address this issue by combining the showing of *The Birth of a Nation, Guess Who's Coming to Dinner?*, and *Hollywood Shuffle* with the reading of Tom Bogle's *Blacks, Coons, Mulattoes, Mammies, and Bucks: An Interpretive History of Blacks in American Films*. They could have students read Allen Woll's *The Latin Image in American Film* and watch *Viva Zapata!, El Norte*, and *Stand and Deliver*, or read Eugene Franklin Wong's *On Visual Media Racism: Asians in the American Motion*

Pictures and watch *Broken Blossoms, The Bitter Tea of General Yen*, and *Chan Is Missing*. They could link Mollie Rosen's *Popcorn Venus* with the screening of *The Heiress, Julia*, and *Working Girls*.

THE CHALLENGE OF UNDERSTANDING

All of the foregoing challenges—predisposing students to take moving image media seriously, developing student visual literacy and skill in critical analysis, and careful course planning—meet their final test when students come to grips with the media itself. The final challenge, then, involves improving student understanding of history using film. This incorporates a variety of issues, but let us look at just five: values; cultural differences; surface versus subsurface messages; reflection versus refraction; and emotional response versus rational analysis.

The first understanding issue is the *clash of values*. A teacher screens a moving image document as part of a course. There are values intrinsic to the time and place upon which the document focuses, as well as time and place in which the document was created. The document makers had values and operated within a context of values, some embodied in laws, codes, or other forms of restriction or injunction. Moreover, the document was made for viewers of a particular period and sometimes of a particular place. In a course, however, the film or television program is being shown outside of the originally intended context, and to students who bring their own values, as well as assumptions drawn from the values and norms that surround them.

This was brought home to me in 1981 when I showed *Rachel, Rachel*. In that film, set in a small town, Rachel and a former high school friend slip off into the woods and make love on a blanket. Some students concluded from this evidence that he was a cheapskate because he did not take her to a motel. I had a major task convincing these urban Southern California college students of the "me generation" that traditional small-town values of the early 1960s would have precluded such public displays of premarital sex, particularly by a female teacher, that the news of their entering a motel would probably have raced through the town, and that Rachel might well have been fired before she got home.

Second is the problem of *cultural difference*, a problem that surfaces when students grapple with films about foreign cultures, particularly films made within foreign cultures. The differing values, dilemmas, issues, and even social categories in these cultures can be obstacles to student understanding of such films. Intellectual knowledge of dictatorships does not necessarily lead to an emotional understanding of actions taken within the ambience of such repressive societies; for most American students, dictatorship is merely a label or exotic construct for a form of government, not a part of their personal experience. The close and sometimes inseparable relationships between government and religion in many nations, particularly in the Middle East and Latin America, defy comprehension for students conditioned by the First Amendment. Possibly even more difficult for students to address is the fact that the meaning of race and the assignment of people to racial categories vary from country to country, and that in some countries, particularly those with complex, historically rooted patterns of racial mixture, people can change their racial category through acculturation, the modification of their economic fortunes, or even by movement from village to city.

Third is the question of *surface versus subsurface messages*. General knowledge of an era or even tremendous skill in visual language will not necessarily enable students to grasp the more subtle or esoteric subsurface messages of moving image media. Students should have no problem spotting the anti–cold war elements of *Dr. Strangelove*, but without teacher prompting will they know of the flouridation controversy that provides the impetus for Sterling Hayden's actions in launching a bomber attack on the Soviet Union or will they so readily grasp the cold war features of the original *Invasion of the Body Snatchers*? They probably can determine that the 1947 *Crossfire* suggests the World War II-spawned growth of opposition to prejudice and renewed willingness to question U.S. societal practices. But how will they know that this admirable film backed away from the original novel, *The Brick Foxhole*, by replacing its critique of homophobia with the more socially acceptable criticism of anti-Semitism. And I would even bet Sky Masterson that students would not be able to hypothesize that *High Noon* and *On the Waterfront* were dueling metaphors for the Hollywood war over the House Un-American Activities Committee's hearings. Yet *High Noon* provided a metaphorical critique of most Hollywooders (the townspeople) for turning their backs on their industry brethen (Marshal Will Kane) who stood up to the committee, while *On the Waterfront* defended the act of naming names, if such naming was done with the intent of ridding the industry of corruption (read Communism).

Fourth is the issue of *reflection versus refraction*. To some degree (sometimes even a very small degree), moving image documents "reflect" the era, locale, and ambience in which they were created. But more extensively, film and television "refract" the world around them, with media creators forming the prism through which that world finds expression in these documents. With creators, then, as intermediaries between society (writ large) and product, moving image documents become more refractions than reflections of society. In order to avoid a banal and simplistic use of these documents simply as direct socio-cultural "reflections"—a common error in media analysis—teachers need to address the individuality of the creators, including their goals in creating a specific piece of media. Moreover, teachers and students should assess the extent to which a moving image document reflects that time and place and the degree to which that same document mediates and refracts that time and place through the prism of the creators.

For example, revolutionary films certainly reflect the existence of

desires for major social change. In addition, they refract specific societies by presenting societal visions as mediated by the document
creators. Films by Frank Capra, Stanley Kramer, Sylvester Stallone,
Cheech Marin, and Spike Lee may to some extent reflect the time and
place in which they were made, but their films challenge viewers to
discover that reflection, precisely because their films also contain the
results of their creators' refractions, not simple reflections. While no
methodology exists to scientifically separate media reflections from
refractions, teachers using film to help students understand a time or
place need to encourage them to be aware of and grapple with this
tightly woven connection.

The reflection-refraction dilemma relates closely to the fifth issue,
emotion versus analysis. Take the Bolivian film, *Blood of the Condor*, whose
subject matter includes a critical depiction of the supposed role of the
Progress Corps (an intentionally transparent pseudonym for the Peace
Corps) in the sterilization of Bolivian Indian women. I personally
found the film to be both satisfying aesthetically and moving emotionally. At the same time, I considered the film to be manipulative
and historically distorting, based on my own knowledge of the subject.
Thus I could move back and forth between reacting emotionally and
analyzing critically. Not so my students, most of whom were captured
by the emotion-producing artistry of the filmmaker and readily accepted his depiction as re-created truth.

Thus the socio-cultural significance of films goes beyond whether
or not they are historically accurate or aesthetically pleasing. It includes their emotional power to "sell" the media creators' interpretations of the world. *Blood of the Condor* reflects the existence of social
tensions and the opposition of some sectors of Bolivian society to class
oppression, military brutality, the exploitation of Indians, and U.S.
influences on Bolivia. In addition, it provides a fascinating refracted
portrait of Bolivia. Whether factually accurate or not, whether or not
it passes critical muster as film art, *Blood of the Condor* stands as an
important socio-cultural document because it refracts Bolivian life and
does so convincingly and effectively. Moreover, as one of the few
Bolivian films to gain international release, it has reached international
viewers who may have never read a substantive work about that nation.
Therefore, it may function, in a sense, as some viewers' main or only
"textbook" on Bolivia.

The socio-cultural significance of Costa-Gavras's films lies not in
their historical accuracy (most viewers will not be in any position to
evaluate accuracy) or whether or not they are great film art (although
artistry influences their capacity to engross and move audiences).
Their socio-cultural significance consists of their documenting of the
existence of a coterie of socially committed filmmakers, their presentation of these filmmakers' social criticisms, and their potential for
being accepted by some viewers as fact. For example, *Missing* may be
the most powerful socio-cultural critical document of the post-Allende
military dictatorship period in Chile, just as Alan Parker's *Midnight*

Express may be the most powerful publicly disseminated image of Turkey in recent decades, irrespective of the factual accuracy or inaccuracy of these films.

In other words, the socio-cultural significance of moving image documents as contributors to historical understanding or misunderstanding—by the general viewing public, by students in history courses, and by historians themselves—lies not merely in the intellectual testing of their historical veracity or the debate over their place in the pantheon of film art. It rests upon the evidence that may be extracted from them about the time, place, and topic on which they focus, the nature of their creators, the refraction of the societal milieu in which they were made, and their potential impact on different audiences. By addressing these and other challenges to student understanding, history teachers can bring additional intellectual stimulation to their classrooms through moving image media.

MOVING IMAGE MEDIA: A POTENTIAL SOURCE FOR ALL HISTORY COURSES

The moving image media have the potential, then, to enrich most history courses, be they general history courses or courses focusing more specifically on the media themselves, such as film-and-history courses. The issues and challenges discussed above suggest the richness, excitement, and pedagogical possibilities of addressing these sources as socio-cultural documents. Teachers should consider these issues as they integrate those media.

Well-planned courses already address some of the challenges presented above. For example, students in history courses are developing knowledge of specific historical subject matter, which in turn could help to provide some context for analyzing the selected media. On the other hand, teachers may need to increase their emphasis on examining the milieu in which these moving image documents were created and on providing students with a synthetic but vital introduction to media analysis and visual literacy.

As powerful and revealing socio-cultural documents, films and television deserve the attention of scholars and teachers. Used well, with sound preparation and imaginative implementation, moving image media can help make history an even more engrossing area of study for students of an increasingly media-influenced world.

NOTES

1. Courses on specific themes within a delimited geographical locale and time period included The American Dream on Film, Women in American Film, Violence in America, The 1960s in Film, American Sexuality, Changing American Values, and Image of the West, all of which focused on the United States, as well as Film as Revolutionary Weapon, which focused on Latin America.
2. Among the courses with explicitly cross-cultural comparative frameworks

were Imperialism in Film, Race and Ethnicity in the History of the Americas, and The Feature Film as Historical Source: A Study of Human Dilemmas (Economic Dislocation and Human Migration; The Conflict between Law and Justice), as well as three courses that dealt principally with the issue of war: War through Film; Modern War and Its Images; and Politics and the Film (which addressed World War II, the cold war, the Korean War, the War in Vietnam, and Weimar Germany).

3. Among courses that tended to be more implicitly comparative, treating a general theme without any specific area focus, were four courses on World War II through film, with one of the courses concentrating on the Holocaust.

4. Courses that emphasized the history of film itself included The Social History of American Movies, History through the Newsreel, and Cinema and Society: Motion Pictures in American Society, 1945–1960.

5. Courses that placed their major emphasis on the nature of film as socio-cultural evidence included Film and History, The Film as Social and Intellectual History, Hollywood as History, Movies and Modern American Society, British Film Propaganda During World War II, and two courses dealing with the Soviet Union—Hollywood and the Russians and The Film as Social History: Russia and the Image of Communism in America, 1917–1964.

6. One excellent effort to address the challenge of developing visual literacy was the worksheet developed by John E. O'Connor of the New Jersey Institute of Technology to train students about editing and shot analysis, using the documentary film, *The Plow That Broke the Plains*. O'Connor discusses his approach in his American Historical Association pamphlet, *Teaching History with Film and Television* (Washington, D.C.: American Historical Association, 1987).

7. I am currently working on a three-volume study of the history of the U.S. feature film treatment of ethnic groups and foreign nations (volume one on ethnic groups, volume two on foreign nations and world cultures, volume three on interracial love), drawing upon my Ethnicity and Foreignness in Film Computer Data Bank in the University of California, Riverside's, Laboratory for Historical Research. See Carlos E. Cortés, "The History of Ethnic Images in Film: The Search for a Methodology," in *Ethnic Images in Popular Genres and Media*, special issue of *MELUS, The Journal of the Society for the Study of the Multi-Ethnic Literature of the United States*, XI, 3 (Fall, 1984), pp. 63–77.

FRAMEWORK 3:
ACTUALITY FOOTAGE AS EVIDENCE FOR HISTORICAL FACT

Certain historical subjects require the study of moving image sources for the specific factual information they contain. Historians who pass over the film and television sources on these topics simply fail to deal responsibly with their subject area. By factual content we mean here not the general information about social and cultural values noted above, but significant, detailed, and specific facts about historical events and individuals that could not be known (or known as fully) in any other way. What was it like, for example, to see and hear a speech presented by Franklin D. Roosevelt? Was his personality as magnetic and his style of speaking as moving as we are told? There is no better way to approach that experience than to study a film of FDR at the podium.[1]

As factual sources, moving image materials can present both wonderfully rewarding and terribly frustrating experiences. The unique value of film and photographic images is that they sometimes capture details of information which even the cameraman was unaware of—details that may even have been invisible to the human eye. It is possible, for example, to blow up a photograph or a film frame to reveal the hands on a clock or the date on a wall calendar, details that would have been so small or so far away as to be invisible to the cameraman. To the extent that a photograph or a film frame can "stop" the action going on in front of the camera, it can also offer unique evidence depicting events that passed too quickly to be perceived by the human eye. Sometimes this information is immediately evident in the image itself (one thinks of the stroboscopic images made over the years by Harold Edgerton at MIT), other times it must be coaxed out of the image by some special process such as computer digitalization and enhancement. This was the procedure used to prove that it was the failure of an O-ring in the *Challenger* booster rocket that led to the 1986 Space Shuttle explosion.

Films are often frustrating as sources for factual information because of the limitations imposed by the nature of the photographic process and by visual language. Those who saw from the first the significance of photography and later motion pictures for the study of history were thinking most directly of the factual record that the camera could provide. What Civil War scholar would not trade in his new word processor for a three-minute piece of film taken that April night in Fords Theater? Yet several modern counterpart situations raise doubts about the extent to which even such a find as that would

169

alter our real knowledge of John Wilkes Booth's infamous moment in history. The Zapruder "home movie" film of the Kennedy assassination offered wonderful evidence to the Warren Commission about the way the president's body reacted when he was hit. Twenty-five years later experts are still reprocessing and manipulating the footage to try to learn more from it. The number of frames exposed between each shot told them how quickly the gunman had to reload. But even such a record as this did not tell all we want to know. If only Mr. Zapruder had aimed his camera at such an angle that we could see whether or not another assassin was shooting from the grassy knoll.

The televised images two days later of Jack Ruby's killing of Lee Harvey Oswald were even more startling; the entire nation watched the event. This is one of this author's earliest memories of having seen an "instant replay," as Ruby's crime was committed over and over again in the days that followed. Almost twenty years later, when John Hinkley fired at Ronald Reagan, things had not really changed much. The camera catches the confusion that the gunshot sets off in the presence of a world leader. Secret Service agents jump to protect the president and seize the gunman. As Press Secretary James Brady collapses to the pavement, another camera captures the expression of pained surprise on Reagan's face as he is pushed into the waiting car. As quickly as possible the networks suspended regular programming and turned to a minute-by-minute account of the events as they transpired in Washington, punctuated again by repeated replays of the shooting itself.

These few examples illustrate two of the central problems involved in using the moving image as factual resource. First, there are inherent limits to the information that can be recorded by a camera, even a moving camera. The photographer must always have just one point of view. A different angle, a different composition, a wider angle lens, moving the camera from right to left, any one of these may have allowed the grassy knoll to be included in the Zapruder footage, but it was not to be. Viewers who watched the replay often enough, with the help of a superimposed arrow to draw their attention, were able to see Ruby push his gun toward Oswald as he pulled the trigger, but the ordinary viewer could not identify the killer from that footage alone. Ruby was arrested because the police caught him red handed, and although the footage might surely have been used against him if a trial had ever been held, it would have been the testimony of first-hand witnesses, not the recorded images that would have convinced the jury of Ruby's guilt.

This leads us to the second problem: there are almost always more complete and more reliable sources. Effective as such images are at conveying the electricity of a split-second experience, it is the historian's role to analyze such events in a broader context. Imagine the scholar thirty years from now who sets out to research the attempt on Reagan's life. Certainly the court records of Hinkley's trial and the related studies of his background and personality will provide more information about his motives than the picture of his gun being wrenched away. Surely the medical records of those wounded will provide fuller and more reliable evidence on the direct results of the attack. In the rush for their story the TV news people had mistakenly reported Brady dead, an error which struck the ABC anchorman with anguished frustration as he openly complained to his colleagues: "Why can't we get this right?" For more searching analysis one would expect scholars to refer to the heated (if unproductive) debate on gun control that ensued in Congress, to the public opinion polls that showed how the popularity of the stricken president had been bolstered, or to the flurry of editorials following Hinkley's acquittal that questioned the justice of the insanity defense in American law. A historian of the Reagan presidency would surely be missing something if he had not seen the visual record of the shooting, but for the questions outlined here, the TV record would provide precious little new evidence.

The most obvious such factual resources are the newsreels. Since early in the century, movie audiences in Europe and America received weekly visual reports on world events. More directly than any other collections of moving images, newsreel archives contain the raw material for historical scholarship. But the newsreels were notorious for faking footage with battleships in bathtubs, and any scholar must beware.

Films impart factual information both explicitly and implicitly. There are two explicit ways. The first is within the image itself; when actuality footage (photographs of actual people and events rather than actors and reenactments) reveals a piece of information directly. The newsreel pictures are the best direct evidence we have about Bobby Thompson's famous home run that won the National League pennant for the New York Giants in 1951—the next best account relies on an observer's memory and talent to describe in words, and after that we get into hearsay. The second is when an image (or the production of which it is a part) becomes itself a factor in shaping historical events. The events of any modern political campaign, for example, are influenced by the television commercials for (or against) a political candidate, making each commercial itself a piece of solid explicit evidence. Likewise, a newsreel or TV news story can become a stimulus to other events, making it as much an explicit force in history as any written document.

There are also specific types of relevant historical information which films impart only by implication. For example, a German newsreel story about the war on the Eastern Front might present explicit evidence (however questionable) in its images of troops in action there, but it also presents implicit evidence regarding the ways in which the leaders of the Nazi propaganda machine wanted to characterize those events to the German people. Robert Herzstein's essay to follow offers interesting examples of explicit and implicit analysis based upon his own extensive research on German newsreels and documentaries.

The O'Connor essay in this section focuses on nonfiction television. Critics often fault TV news, as they faulted the newsreels, on questions of completeness and accuracy. The controversies over the editing of TV news documentaries such as "Selling of the Pentagon" (1970) and "The Uncounted Enemy: A Vietnam Deception" (1982) have echoed through the halls of Congress and the federal courts. Knowledge of how each editing decision was made and access to the outtakes would be necessary for the fullest factual analysis. Yet, having all the raw footage on the reel before us would still not constitute the "complete story." The concept of accuracy presents difficulties as well. There are certain historical facts which are incontrovertible: Kennedy was shot and *Challenger* did explode. But beyond this most basic level, perception is always subjective. Even though we consider a film or TV program to be nonfiction, we should not think of it as a simple shell which can be cracked open to reveal some objective truth.

It is not our business as historians to tell journalists how they should do their work, but to teach our students how to evaluate what they see. In terms of the Hinkley/Reagan assassination attempt, while the historian would be foolish indeed to ignore the additional dimension that the moving image might provide, the "electricity" of the moment, the look on the president's face, the image of Brady's collapse to the pavement, may be less important than the other issues noted above. We can expect that a moving picture record from 1865 would prove unsatisfactory in answering certain of our questions about Lincoln's murder. However, compelling as it may seem, there can be no single form of evidence that tells us *everything* that we want to know. If film or video provide any kind of "window on the past," the view through it is fuzzy indeed.

When we look for explicit factual information in moving image documents, audience reception is important in that the film tells us what facts viewers knew—or thought they knew. In this last connection, even if we know a newsreel story presented as fact was false, it can be a worthwhile source for documenting what people may have mistakenly thought to be true.

Aside from the ubiquitous evening newscast on television, most people see factual film footage as part of a larger documentary film. The most obvious type is the historical compilation film discussed in detail in framework 1. Constructed from pieces of film collected from newsfilm and other archives, they often use a narrator to tie the pieces together, or intercut archival footage with present day interviews with participants, eyewitnesses, or academic scholars. A viewer is at great peril when trying to draw conclusions of fact based upon actuality footage which has been selected and reedited into a compilation film. Documentaries which focus on issues and events contemporary with the production may be more valuable for factual information because the actuality footage in them is characteristically photographed precisely for that production and might otherwise not be available.

Newsreel and TV news may endeavor to inform more or less objectively, but it should be evident that complete objectivity is impossible. If not the bias (intended or otherwise) of the footage itself, then the sensibilities of the newsperson (often a composite of producer, reporter, film editor, and anchor) invariably slant every story in some way. At a recent televised conference on advocacy journalism, newsman and critic Hodding Carter caught himself saying that newspeople seek for "truth." He quickly corrected himself by explaining that the best that they can aim for is "an accurate rendition of whatever seems to be reality at the moment."[2]

Documentary filmmakers in contrast, most good ones anyway, whether they work in film or television, endeavor consciously to transcend objective reality, to move their audiences emotionally, and/or to lead them toward one or another conclusion. As originally conceived by John Grierson, documentary films were intended to have a socio-political purpose. He began in Great Britain in the early 1930s to produce films for the Empire Marketing Board which would help people from various areas of the then still far-flung British empire better understand one another. Grierson himself wrote in 1933: "I look on cinema as a pulpit, and use it as a propagandist." Whether motivated by the sought-for objectivity of the newsman or the thoughtful purpose of the documentarist, each creative choice that a filmmaker makes, while it does constitute the essential core of the medium's artistry, also creates a puzzle for the historian who seeks to study the film for its factual content.

Documentary film analysis for factual information must be different from analysis for social and cultural history as described in framework 2 above. There the attention was on studying the values inherent in the point of view of the filmmaker and on trying to reconstruct the varieties of consciousness which different groups of historical spectators might have brought to the viewing of the film or taken with them as they left the theater. Here the important element is the studying of the factual content of the individual shots, taking care not to let the bias of the filmmaker (the values that may have led him to light a scene in a certain way or to compose a shot in a certain way or from one or another angle) influence our observation of the factual content. The first step, therefore, must be to identify that point of view and how it is supported by the filmmaker's art. Special care must be taken with regard to editing. So much of the meaning in a documentary film comes from the juxtaposition of images. The effort here must be to take each shot as a unit of study and not let the fact that it is cut against any other shot influence our factual analysis.

One can conceive of historians making effective use of many documentary films addressing issues which were current at the time the films were made. Scholars should turn to these as factual references with the same care in judgment they would apply to any written source reporting on their contemporary events from the past. Robert Flaherty's *Nanook of the North* (1922), a film which is unreliable for many specific facts (many of the scenes were purposely enacted or reenacted

for the sake of the cameras), is wonderful for an overall impression—
one perceptive view (albeit "a view") of what Native American life was
like in the great north near the end of the frontier period. The films
of Frederick Wiseman provide several other interesting examples.
Wiseman has produced an extended series of cinéma vérité documentaries which closely examine American institutions as diverse as
an Anglican seminary and a downtown police department. The historian of education, for example, might very profitably view Wiseman's *High School* (1968) to get a feeling for the dynamics of the
American high school in the 1960s. The military historian might benefit as much from studying his *Basic Training* (1971) or the historian
of American consumer practices from *The Store* (1983), a close-up look
at Dallas's Neimann-Marcus. Among the institutions Wiseman has
studied with his camera, perhaps the most interesting is the mental
hospital profiled in *Titicut Follies* (1967), because there are so few visual
documents like it. The scholar must be sensitive not to accept Wiseman's view as more truthful than another source just because it is
constructed of actual images. Conversely, the scholar who wrote without attention to the facts captured by Wiseman's camera would clearly
be missing something. Peter Davis's *Middletown*, a six hour documentary study of life in Muncie, Indiana, produced for public television
in 1982, should become a factual resource on the early 1980s just as
respected as the Lynd's famous 1929 book of the same name (minus
the visual dimension), which made Muncie a touchstone for historians
and social scientists of several generations.

Television news as factual resource is equally problematic. One particular difficulty is access to national television news coverage before
1968 when the Vanderbilt Television News Archive began regular
taping of the three networks. This is not to mention local news coverage, which is all but impossible to study in any comprehensive way.
At present there are efforts underway in a few places to preserve local
news programming and archive it for scholars' future reference. Even
if access were easily available, scholars must remain sensitive to the
limitations of TV news as factual resource. While at first glance it may
seem that the images are inherently more factual than the written
accounts that find their way into newsprint, moving image scholars
know that all images are interpretive as well. On the other hand, as
Daniel Boorstin established so convincingly in *The Image: Or What
Happened To the American Dream*,[3] our news today is largely made up
of "pseudo-events." In a world driven by public opinion, what "really
happened" may not matter as much as what got reported and how.
Television *is actuality* for masses of people, and in an important sense,
analytical problems of reception notwithstanding, this transforms it
into historical fact. At Columbia University, a current project takes
Soviet television news off a satellite and studies it for insight into both
Soviet policy and what the Soviet people know. Again, this demands
that scholars take care when they generalize about audience perceptions. Aside from the absence of an institutionalized opposition (im-

mediate critical analysis of a presidential speech, for example), why should we presume that Soviet audiences are any more or less naive than American ones in blindly accepting their government's interpretations of issues and events?

Gerald Herman's essay focusses on the study of film as factual source material in the history classroom. Note especially the student production projects he describes, and how they center on the historical issues at hand.

SUMMARY

To summarize, then, let us consider the special concerns that arise in the study of moving images as factual sources.

Content

As far as content is concerned, for the vast majority of historical subjects that a scholar might study, there will be far fuller and more reliable factual sources than films. However, for those subjects which do lend themselves to (or even demand) film study for the establishment or verification of specific facts, only unedited actuality footage will fully qualify. Few are fortunate enough to find the complete newsreel files for an event (the published story as well as the outtakes or film shot but not included in the finished story). Scholars forced to work from footage incorporated in a compilation film must tread with particular care. As with the quotation of any source, it is always best to get back to the original context.

Production

Some, but surely not all, filmmakers set out to make a film that is factually informative. It is important to inquire into the purposes and biases of the filmmaker and cameraman which may have led them to photograph, to select, or to edit footage in a particular way. In some cases, as with newsfilm in a totalitarian country or with propaganda documentaries, the intent of the filmmaker is itself the factual information that you are trying to deduce. As noted elsewhere in this book, there are ways to get at the production background of factual films. There are full biographies of such documentarists as Flaherty, Grierson, and Lorentz, numerous articles on others such as Wiseman. On the production of newsreels there are general studies such as Raymond Fielding's *The American Newsreel* (Norman, OK, 1972) and more focussed ones such as Anthony Aldgate's *Cinema and History: British Newsreels and the Spanish Civil War* (London, 1979) which are sure to prove helpful. Considerable literature also exists on the institution of television news and the ways in which decisions are made regarding what gets reported and how. As with any other form of analysis, if such production information is not available, be sure to couch your conclusions more tentatively.

Reception

In terms of reception, factual analysis of newsfilm (in conjunction with press reports and other sources) allows some estimation of what the public knew or thought they knew at any particular time. Such sources as the *Television News Index and Abstracts*, published monthly by the TV News Archive at Vanderbilt University, can be helpful in establishing such information. It is important, however, not to presume that the audience is totally naive and impressionable. Scholarship has raised important questions about the extent to which populations are taken in by propaganda, especially when characterized by blatantly falsified reports. There is the question about how much the public, even in a free society, accepts the interpretation of events presented them in the news. Finally, the conditions of the reception of television news present particular problems. As news programs assume more of the trappings of entertainment programs, and program flow is carefully designed by specialists in the industry to lead audiences from one program to the next, it is unclear what influence such media context has on the public's perception of issues and events.

NOTES

1. Film researcher William Utterback is working on reconstituting some of the most important of FDR's speeches in videotape. He is collecting footage and soundtracks from various sources and putting them together so that one does not only see and hear a few sentences of a longer speech, or the speech as edited for distribution in the newsreel, but so that one can see and hear the entire speech from start to finish.
2. Carter spoke at a Georgetown University Conference on Advocacy Journalism televised over C-Span on January 22, 1985.
3. (New York: Atheneum, 1962).

Robert E. Herzstein is Professor of History at the University of South Carolina where he teaches courses on the diplomatic and political history of contemporary Europe. He specializes in the history of the Nazi era. He is the author of six books including: The War That Hitler Won (1978 and 1987) Waldheim: The Missing Years (1988), and Roosevelt and Hitler: Prelude to War (1989).

NEWSFILM AND DOCUMENTARY AS SOURCES FOR FACTUAL INFORMATION

Robert E. Herzstein

Newsfilm can provide the historian with factual information not otherwise available. As a student of the Nazi era I draw most of my examples from that period. In each instance, however, the principles dictating my selections have broader applications.

In February 1942, the Nazi *Deutsche Wochenschau* newsreel contained footage of Adolf Hitler paying his last respects to Dr. Fritz Todt, the late munitions minister of the Third Reich. This final farewell to an old Party comrade took place in the solemn yet gaudy "Mosaic Room" of the New Reich Chancellory. The "Führer" looked sad, but despite the recent Soviet offensive on the central sector of the Eastern Front, he appeared to be healthy and vigorous. In the late summer of 1944 the same newsreel series showed the world a different man, stooped, with heavy bags under his eyes. For twenty years historians and popular writers have argued about the exact nature of Hitler's illnesses. The diaries of one of his physicians, Dr. Theo Morell, tell us more about his patient's digestive hypochondria than they do about the causes of Hitler's physical deterioration. The film footage is unambiguous, while the written testimony, both medical and personal, is contradictory and incomplete. The films may not yield the secrets of causation, but they indubitably establish a physical fact.[1]

In case of President Franklin D. Roosevelt, newsfilm establishes a somewhat different, though related fact. Newsreel footage makes clear the deterioration in the president's health between 1941 and 1945, while written sources, at least until the spring of 1944, are ambiguous. Newsfilm also makes the historian aware of the medium's power in another sense. The "Gentlemen's Agreement" by which the media would not reveal FDR's polio-induced infirmities, could not conceal his physical condition. Yet few people who saw the late Roosevelt newsreels seemed to sense that they were looking at a dying man.

They had been conditioned by years of carefully edited newsfilm and saw a leader, not a mortal being, on the screen. This was true of those who loved FDR and of those who hated his "gaudy guts." In this instance, newsreels are a valuable resource for the historian of social psychology.[2]

Like literate sources, newsfilm is open to diverse and controversial interpretations. It may establish a fact that would otherwise be disputed, yet the establishment of that fact can lead to further argument.

The instance of the Zapruder film of the assassination of President John F. Kennedy in Dallas on November 22, 1963, comes to mind. The film establishes certain facts, among them the movements of the victim's body and the actions of other victims, witnesses, and participants. At the same time, the film has fueled debate among historians and conspiracy buffs, since the actions depicted on the screen are subject to diverse causal interpretations.

Where does the historian find major newsfilm resources? A few examples provide some sense of the magnitude of various collections. Copies of valuable German newsreels from the prewar, wartime, and postwar eras are in the Film Division of the Library of Congress, in the Audio-Visual Department of the National Archives, both in Washington, D.C., and in the West German Federal Archives in Koblenz. Much of the Movietone News collection (Twentieth Century Fox) is housed at the University of South Carolina in Columbia, S.C. The Hearst newsfilm collections are available to researchers at the UCLA film library. Other newsreels remain the exclusive property of commercial firms, such as the Sherman Grinberg Company in New York City.

Newsfilm represented the first mass medium not tied to the printed word, preceding commercial radio, sound features, and television by five, ten, and thirty years, respectively. Historians who neglect this precious source may miss important aspects of the events described by the print media and archival sources. One thinks of the funeral of Queen Victoria in 1901, or the assassination of King Alexander of Yugoslavia over three decades later. No print source can provide an equal sense of the gestures, movement, and reactions of participants.

No print source can provide the historian with a total understanding of the political leader's manipulation of the medium. Yet this manipulation is an essential fact of our century. When one sees Mussolini speaking English to an American audience (thanks to an early Fox sound newsfilm), one understands his boast regarding the manipulative potential of the sound newsfilm.[3]

Historians using printed sources, such as diplomatic dispatches, try to determine authenticity, motive, and effect. Newsfilm presents similar challenges. Unlike many print sources, however, newsfilms were intended for a mass audience, often with the purpose of robbing their viewers of their autonomous judgment. Yet this judgment is precisely what the historian must retain when evaluating newsreel sources. Before selecting analytical criteria, the historian must be aware of this basic contradiction: he is trying to be an objective evaluator, but the original newsfilm audience saw the movies in an entirely different context.

The researcher sits alone at his machine, intently listening to the soundtrack through earphones. He is isolated, and his autonomous judgment is generally intact. When he researches the impact of newsfilm, he culls through reviews, theater attendance figures, and other dry data. He is detached and objective. Yet the original audience had an entirely opposed experience. One example will illustrate this important point.

In the summer of 1975, while researching my book *The War That Hitler Won*, I had occasion to view the Nazi epic *Kolberg* (a sort of Goebbels's version of *Gone With the Wind*) on a tabletop Steenbeck viewing machine at the Library of Congress. The facilities were adequate (they have since greatly improved), but something was missing. Then I journeyed to the International Museum of Photography in the Eastman House in Rochester, New York, where I viewed the same film. This time, however, I was sitting in a small theater watching the film on a large screen. Although I was not part of a large audience, the impact of the film upon me was entirely different.[4]

The researcher examines film in an atmosphere akin to that of the television audience. He is not part of a crowd, and the screen is tiny in comparison to the huge silver screen of the movies. The viewer is much like Nicholas Pronay's newspaper reader: "... in newspapers, the *reader* decides which articles to read; when to stop and if necessary re-read a passage; and he can even compare side by side two different ... versions."[5] The methodology of the historian analyzing newsfilm puts him in the company of newspaper readers or of television viewers who can switch channels on the evening news, something beyond the range of newsreel audiences in 1935. He lacks the pressure of the crowd, of the collective suspension of disbelief. There is nothing that he can do about this, but he should be aware of the dilemma.

With this caveat in mind, we can examine some fundamental questions facing the historian using newsfilm. The first concerns the concept and purpose of the newsreel. How did its producers assess its social role and its importance? The thin line between newsfilm and propaganda was frequently crossed. Hitler, in discussing the *Deutsche Wochenschauen* newsreels declared that "For the sake of the future, it is important to preserve the newsfilms of the war. They will be documents of incalculable value."[6] Dr. Paul Joseph Goebbels, Hitler's minister for popular enlightenment and propaganda, had this to say: "The 'German Weekly Newsreel' is an incomparable contemporary document such as no other nation in the world has ever brought forth."[7] Fairly warned that this document was to meant to influence behavior rather than to inform, the historian proceeds with the task.

The researcher must then determine who chose the themes for the newsfilm, and why. The motives may be largely commercial, as in the case of Movietone News until the Second World War, or mainly political, as in the Italian wartime newsfilms called "Luce".[8] An important question concerns the manner in which the firm obtained the film footage. In the case of wartime films, in both democracies and totalitarian states, one must understand the censorship process.

Nor should peacetime censorship escape our scrutiny. In the United States self-imposed censorship (in the form of blue laws, perceptions of sexual morality, patriotism, fear of lawsuits, or government imposed restrictions) played a major role in newsfilm. American newsfilm of the 1930s was a form of filler entertainment, and it tended to avoid controversy. German newsfilm informed its viewers of the glories of the Third Reich. Neither medium existed to provide useful information to citizens. The German purposes were more nefarious, but we should understand that neither society saw the revolutionary new medium of sound newsfilm as a means of providing accurate information to the public. Oscar Levant joked about newsfilm as a series of catastrophes followed by a fashion show.[9]

Historians must realize that in many cases the outtakes are as interesting as the newsreels, perhaps more so. Outtakes refer to newsfilm footage that was developed and retained, but not used in the finished newsreels shown to the public. A newsreel may contain some brief, staged footage of a Fascist youth demonstration for Mussolini, against the annoying backdrop of the staccato voice of an American commentator, all to the accompaniment of a musical overlay alien to the Italian participants. The outtakes, by contrast, may consist of hours of film, without narrative or phony music. The participants are less conscious of the medium, if they pay any attention to it at all.[10]

We have an extraordinary outtake of President Franklin D. Roosevelt that violated the "Gentlemen's Agreement." He is clearly seen moving his crippled legs. In another violation of that pact, the president bestows a medal upon a kneeling General Wilbur. These outtakes, if used, would have betrayed FDR's infirmity to the wartime American public. In these cases newsfilm establishes historic facts as they are made explicit on the screen. There are no print sources that document these events. Print sources may tell us about the medal, but not about the general on his knees. Other film sources show how FDR solved this problem: he sat on the back seat of a motor vehicle, while the honoree stood by to receive the decoration.[11]

Even where these film sources provide unique information, they cannot be used in isolation. The historian must cull what knowledge he can from all sources. For example, print sources may give us a good idea of what Adolf Hitler was saying at the funeral of Fritz Todt.[12] They may provide us with information about the reasons why FDR bestowed medal upon General Wilbur. Too often, however, our monographs and textbooks rely upon one single medium, usually print/archival. A related example may prove helpful. In my research on the wartime career of Dr. Kurt Waldheim I needed to examine his role as an interpreter for the German liaison unit attached to the Italian Ninth Army and to the Italian XIVth Corps. I was particularly concerned with his participation at a conference held near Podgorica, Yugoslavia, in late May 1943. The World Jewish Congress provided me with a photograph of some of the participants, including Waldheim. Through archival research I later discovered German and Italian accounts of the meeting. Part of the truth could be found in the picture, part in the German records, part in the Italian archives.

Many other print sources make the historian's use of newsfilm more productive. In the case of Germany, one can use the top secret reports of the Security Service of the SS in order to better understand popular reaction to the newsreels. The Propaganda Ministry maintained records of gross receipts for movie theaters, as well as attendance figures. In the case of Movietone News, one might examine the procedures leading to the release of some of the Pearl Harbor footage in March 1942. The paper trail would lead to the War Department, but some valuable insights may be yielded by Fox's own files.

Despite these worthy efforts, the historian using film is analyzing something that was meant to be received and absorbed. It is very hard to think one's self back into the emotional, collective personality of an audience in 1942. We can learn about reaction to newsfilm and describe it, but we cannot really feel it.

We are on more secure ground when it comes to authenticity. We can learn about the creative use of camera angles and composition, about the collapsing of time and the use of visual juxtapositions, and the application of voice overlays and musical composition. Our newsfilm sources, after all, were the work of many hands. There was a lot of fakery in newsfilm, and some feature films even included footage from newsreels— or so it appeared. Some of the exciting if brutal footage of the Italian-Ethiopian War was staged and re-staged until the participants got it right. Hitler did not do a jig in front of the railway car near Compiegne. The depiction of the funeral procession of the Nazi "martyr" Horst Wessel in the 1933 feature film *Hans Westmar* was not taken from newsfilm, as many believed. Yet even fakery, if detected, yields interesting material to the historian. Who faked the film, and for what purpose? If Italian censors in 1936 wanted Italians to see the war in a certain light, that too is important to the historian.

An incisive work on newsfilm as a historical source is the 1970 volume by Günter Moltmann and Karl Friedrich Reimers, *Contemporary History in the Film and Sound Document*.[13] The editors, directors of an ongoing seminar at the University of Göttingen in West Germany, have been examing film and televsion as a source for the historian since the winter semester of 1964–1965. Moltmann makes the point that historians and social scientists are coming to see film as an important pedagogical tool, but have been slower to understand its research possibilities. He suggests several uses for this invaluable resource.

Film, Moltmann argues, can provide a unique sense of the atmosphere of an era, event, or personality. These qualities seldom appear in written documents, at least not in terms of their total impact. The historian studying the Holocaust reads German documents that use terms like "putting aside," "deportation," and "evacuated to the East." These were Nazi euphemisms for mass murder of the Jews.[14] The same historian, examining Nazi propaganda films like *The Eternal Jew* and *Jew Süss*, as well as American newsfilm on the concentration camps in 1945, better understands the print documents.

Film alone can give the historian an awareness of the leader's rapport with the crowd. One can read descriptions of Roman crowds hailing Mussolini as he speaks from a balcony jutting out over the Palazzo Venezia. One can read the text of a Hitler campaign speech delivered in the vast Berlin Lustgarten in a 1932 campaign. Yet national and political characteristics emerge most clearly on the screen: the *stile fascista* of the Italians, the stolid, disciplined Germans singing the "Deutschlandlied." Printed sources do not yield this kind of knowledge, which is particularly important in examining foreign cultures. Even if an Italian or German participant wrote down his reactions to these spectacles, he might have omitted or taken for granted aspects of behavior that are important to us.

Other film treasures bear out Moltmann's concept. The 1932 German print media, particularly the leftist press, gives the impression that vast rallies of anti-Fascists were the order of the day. Indeed, they were. They are invariably described as "successful," "determined," etc. Here newsfilm is invaluable. We can see a rally in Berlin, with a large but desultory crowd, a pompous, middle-class type speaker, pedantic as many a professor, in sum, a staged rally without real enthusiasm. Then we look at one of Hitler's Nazi rallies, and the whole atmosphere is different. People seem younger, more enthusiastic. Film alone cannot explain the failure of the German left and the victory of the Nazis, but it yields secrets that the print media of that era do not.[15]

Hitler's entire career before 1933 rested upon his ability to move audiences with his rhetoric. "In the beginning was the Word," or so proclaimed Nazi propagandists, and they were right. The communion between "Führer" and Volk cannot be understood by reading speeches or press clippings. Only film can help us here. We can read the speeches and wonder about their prolixity, repetitiveness, their pedestrian thoughts, and weak grammar. Yet when we look at newsfilm and see the mating ritual that transpired between crowd and "Führer," we can at least understand the appeal—or if not understand it, at least feel it. And that is crucial.

Reading an FDR "fireside chat" does little for the historian, but listening to the tapes helps us to understand how his voice comforted so many Americans. For the historian of three important twentieth century figures, moving image media are essential sources. In Hitler's case we look to newsfilm; in FDR's it is newsfilm and radio; in Ronald Reagan's, it is feature film and television.

To be more specific, newsfilm alone can convey "mimicry and gestures, comportment and demeanor," which rarely emerge in printed documents. Hitler's gestures, his gaze, his body language, these are the explicit facts that emerge from newsfilm, not from archival print sources. Newsfilm such as *Für Uns*, a 1936 documentary depicting the commemoration of the sixteen Nazis killed in the Beer-Hall Putsch, captured one powerful performance. The solemn faces, the somber music, and the neoclassic setting make the Nazi death cult accessible to the historian. Print sources, while of supplementary value, fail to reveal fully a past which is so alien to us and to our values.[15]

Für Uns or *For Us* was conceived by Nazi party film experts as an elitist tribute to a single leader. It was an esoteric product, intended only for those initiated into the cult of death, national immortality, and resurrection in the solemn ceremony of November 9. While depicting a real event, *Für Uns* was newsfilm at its most contrived. A brief analysis shows how the historian can use this newsfilm as a source.

Für Uns consists of the procession (filmed in 1936) to the new tomb of the sixteen "martyrs" which the Nazis had dedicated the year before. The procession is somber in mood, but relentless in its march to the Eternal Watch. Respectful citizens line the route.

Nazis who wear the *Blutorden* or Blood Order march in the first row. The music conjures up memories of the Time of Struggle, when heroes such as the sixteen fell in order that Germany might rise again. The procession consisted of *Alte Kämpfer* or Old Fighters, men who wore the Golden Party Badge as proof of their suffering under the Weimar Republic. The living heroes stepped out of the present in order to march to the past.

Their purpose became apparent when they reached the Ehrentempel, which housed the remains of the martyrs. Hitler placed his wreath before their collective tomb. The names of the fallen were called out, one by one. The assembled SA units shouted in unison, after the calling of each name, "Hier!," which meant that the dead had arisen. The intonation of the "Horst Wessel Lied" ended the ceremony. A slogan provided the final backdrop as the film fades: "You Have Conquered After All."

Für Uns is excellent example of the ways in which we can use Moltmann's categories. The film enables us to analyze mood, setting, gestures, symbols, and music in the context of a historical event. The event is described elsewhere, in the print documents, but these sources give us little or no information about atmosphere, physical environment, facial expressions, and spatio-temporal context. We can probably discover what the temperature and cloud conditions were in Munich on that day in 1936, but only through this film can we see how they affected the ceremony. This gives us *actuality* in the true sense of the word.[16]

Newsfilm can provide us with many other examples of implicit information, drawn from the "dog that didn't bark" school. No German theatergoer saw anything on his newsreel screen depicting the German battle for Stalingrad in the winter of 1942–43. He could hear about it from military communiqués broadcast on the radio, or even read something about it in the press. Goebbels was convinced that film was the most powerful medium of our time, and so he suppressed visual evidence of the Sixth Army's debacle.

In 1943 and 1944, as the German Army retreated in Russia, German military communiqués spoke of "rectifications of the front." Goebbels's newsfilms devised two other forms of obfuscation. The newsreel audience would see a large map of a small region in Russia. It consisted of towns and villages with obscure names, and it was not clear where the region was in relation to the rest of the front. Combat scenes then appeared on the screen. The Wehrmacht invariably did well, or at least held its ground. Since few people knew where the depicted battle had taken place, or exactly when, there was no way of proving that the front had moved far to the west. Another trick was to show the battle scene, then have the commentator intone the past tense : "The fighting German Wehrmacht had held the town against overwhelming Soviet armored attacks . . . " Newsfilm censorship is the historian's guide to a totalitarian elite's perception of the people's vulnerability to defeatism.

Historians can make use of another type of newsfilm/documentary, one that employs staged footage. These films sometimes combine actual newsfilm with reenactments. They can be useful to the historian if he examines them in terms of their original purpose. Consider, for example, *The Eternal Jew.* Released in Germany on November 28, 1940, the film was a prelude to the final stages of the Holocaust. We know from print sources that Hitler and much of the Nazi elite did not consider the German nation tough enough to accept an explicit revelation of the "Final Solution of the Jewish Question." People had to be led to the truth in a very gradual way. These Nazi leaders believed that the German people must at first be a silent and complicit partner in the destruction of the Jews. The nation, poisoned by centuries of Jewish liberalism, "Jewish Christianity," Marxism, and "humanist drivel," must learn to see the Jew as the Nazis saw him, and react accordingly.[17]

Der Ewige Jude or *The Eternal Jew* made use of staged scenes of kosher slaughtering rituals. The torture of innocent animals, of concern to Germans as diverse as Richard Wagner, Adolf Hitler, and Heinrich Himmler, revealed Jewish depravity to the German people and to the nations of Europe. The historian must realize that the Nazis could have filmed a real scene of kosher ritual, but chose to produce a caricature, just as they themselves were caricatures of all past anti-Jewish movements. In this sense the film is a unique guide to the educational policies of the regime and to its view of the limitations of the German people. Hitler did not need a faked scene in order to reach his conclusion about the Jews, but the German people would have to be jolted onto a higher plateau of consciousness.

Documentary films, which often consist of large amounts of newsreel footage, can be important sources of factual information. The problem is that this footage has been taken out of its original context, and placed in a brand new setting, one determined by the director or auteur. Therefore, it is essential to understand the filmmaker's point of view and not allow it to influence factual analysis. Yet these compilation documentaries can yield important ideas.

In *Lowell Thomas Remembers Benito Mussolini* (1977) the narrator is looking back three decades after the death of the Duce. His tone is not laudatory, but the documentary provides us with important information about American perceptions of fascism over the years. Scenes dating from the late 1920s or early 1930s reveal that the American commentators had some favorable things to say about the Italian regime. The narrator gives the impression that the Italians were delirious with joy when Mussolini escaped an assassination attempt in 1926. Fascist reenactments of the March on Rome are treated with respect.

By the time of the war everything has changed, and there is no mercy for Mussolini, even as his dead body is pelted with refuse by a Milan mob. By the sequential use of contradictory newsfilm testimony, Thomas has provided useful (if selective) information about changing American views of fascism.[18]

Night and Fog (1955), directed by Alain Resnais, presents the historian with other problems and opportunities. Resnais offers still and moving images depicting concentration camps such as Mauthausen and Auschwitz. He flashes back and forth between past and present, interspersing film clips of postwar trials. The narrator raises somber questions about moral responsibility and the possibility of another Holocaust. These inquiries force us to rethink the context of the Holocaust footage: are we looking at historical events or at examples of unchanging human potential? We see more than the event depicted, but we may also see less. Resnais has commented that his film was really a protest against the Algerian War, and in this sense he took the Holocaust out of history and used the death camp footage as a political prop. The historian moves onto difficult terrain, but the journey is worthwhile.

Documentaries conceived in tandem with the event they portray may offer unusually complete newsfilm footage. The historian, however, must be aware that the event itself may have been tailored to the specifications of the documentary. Leni Riefenstahl's *Triumph of the Will*, depicting the 1934 Reich Party Rally in Nurnberg, changed the nature of the event. She tells us that "The preparations for the Party rally were made in concert with the preparations for the camera work."[19] Here the political event, a form of national communion, was adapted to a mass medium. In our age of television this is common.

Although the speeches were, with one exception, of little importance, *Triumph of the Will* is a vital resource for the historian. No other film can lead us so well to the secrets of Nazi propaganda. The banners, Albert Speer's "vault of light," the music, the crowds, the clever camera angles and photographic novelties create an impression of overwhelming strength. It is not just a film about the Party rally, it is a document about the self-image of the Nazi elite. In this sense, and in this sense only, one can accept Riefenstahl's perverse conclusion that *Triumph of the Will* is not propaganda, but is a documentary.

NOTES

1. Ufa-Tonwoche 598/42: see the "Guide to German Newsreel Series Entitled Deutsche Wochenschauen . . . made by UFA, Berlin," in the Hoover Institution, Stanford University. p. 14, no. 1. Also, see Heiner Schmitt, comp., *Verleihkopien von Dokumentarfilmen und Wochenschauen 1895–1945 im Filmarchiv* (Koblenz: 1977).
2. Movietone News Collection (MTN) at the University of South Carolina, 48–391, frames 18:18 to 19:38, and 52–859/860, frames 4:37 to 5:15, and 29:50 to 30:07.
3. Raymond Fielding, *The American Newsreel 1911–1967* (Norman: 1972), pp. 164–165.
4. See *The War that Hitler Won: Goebbels and the Nazi Media Campaign* (New York: 1987), pp. 320–321.
5. Nicholas Pronay, "The Newsreels: The Illusion of Actuality," in Paul Smith, ed., *The Historian and Film* (Cambridge: 1976), p. 111.
6. Adolf Hitler, *Hitler's Secret Conversations 1941–1944* (New York: 1953), pp. 69, 75.
7. Joseph Goebbels, *Unser Wille und Weg* (1940), p. 103.
8. There is an excellent selection of the wartime *Luce* series in the Film Division of the Library of Congress, Washington, D.C.
9. Fielding, *The American Newsreel*, p. 228.
10. MTN 24–612m frames 49:37 to 50:42. This collection contains several hours of outtakes picturing Mussolini and Fascist crowd scenes.
11. MTN 48–435, frames 35:57 to 37:18.
12. See Max Domarus, comp., *Hitler Reden und Proklamationen 1932–1945* (Wiesbaden: 1973), 2 vols.
13. Günter Moltmann and Karl Friedrich Reimers, eds., *Zeitgeschichte im Film- und Tondokument* (Göttingen: 1970).
14. See Raul Hilberg, *The Destruction of the European Jews* (Chicago: 1967), p. 652.
15. MTN 15–207, frames 30:46 to 34:50.
16. There is a good print of *Für Uns* in the Library of Congress.
17. Herzstein, *The War that Hitler Won*, pp. 309–310.
18. This film should be used in conjunction with the excellent work by John P. Diggins, *Mussolini and Fascism: The View from America* (Princeton: 1972), especially chapter twelve.
19. Siegfried Kracauer, *From Caligari to Hitler: A Psychological History of the German Film* (Princeton: 1947), p. 301.

John E. O'Connor, the editor and principal author of this volume, is Professor of History at New Jersey Institute of Technology and Editor of the journal Film & History. *His books on early Amerian history and on the historical study of film and television include:* William Paterson: Lawyer and Stateman, 1745–1806 *(1979),* Film and the Humanities *(1977),* American History/American Film: Interpreting the Hollywood Image *(1979),* American History/American Television: Interpreting the Video Past *(1983),* I Am A Fugitive From A Chain Gang (1981), *and* The Hollywood Indian *(1983). O'Connor designed the NEH funded project entitled "The Historian and the Moving Image Media" which he directed for the American Historical Association. This book is an outcome of that larger project, as are his 120 minute* Image As Artifact *video compilation and the pamphlet* Teaching History With Film and Television *(1987), both cross-referenced to this book and both published by the American Historical Association.*

HISTORY AND THE REALITY OF NONFICTION TELEVISION

John E. O'Connor

Sitcoms, soap operas, and game shows notwithstanding, much of what appears on commercial television qualifies in some way as nonfiction. Rather than actors and actresses reading lines written for them by Hollywood professionals, nonfiction television is based on images of actual events and of people playing themselves. In a superficial way, TV coverage seems to provide a flawlessly accurate record of such things. Football field officials and baseball umpires may disagree about a play, but viewers have the video record shot in closeup and poised for instant replay. In a more pertinent sense, of course, all televised events are mediated—transformed into a new reality.

The selection from *Für Uns* in the video compilation offers an interesting example of how an event can be transformed into a new reality in propaganda film. Paid political broadcasts and political and other commercial messages might qualify as comparable propaganda. To the extent that it sought to play upon the emotions of viewers, Richard Nixon's "Checkers" broadcast of 1952 is a good example. But most nonfiction programming on commercial television is not so pointed: It can be classed as journalism of one kind or another (nightly news, news documentaries, news magazine shows) and as such, it should be held to a different standard. Although it is also entertainment and must compete for audience with purely entertainment programs, network news largely accepts the standards traditionally set by print journalists. As unattainable as complete accuracy and objectivity may be, journalists do strive for them, trying (with mixed success) to minimize the influence of personal bias. On the level of intended objectivity, therefore, the ways in which nonfiction television mediates what it shows and the new realities it creates are in some ways predictable.[1]

As any candidate will testify, recent political history cannot be written without close reference to television. Partisans will always question the accuracy with which television reports issues and events and the relative importance relegated to one issue over another, but regardless of how truthfully TV reflects the reality of the world, the televised reports assume a central importance themselves—they become reality as far as the perception of much of the public is concerned.

An interesting example of the role of television in the electoral process is to be found in a study by Gregory Bush, illustrated with relevant TV news clips from the Vanderbilt Television News Archive.[2] Bush's work concerns the Edward Kennedy campaign for the 1980 Democratic presidential nomination, focusing on the November 4, 1979, hour-long "CBS Reports" broadcast "Teddy" and on several damaging news stories, especially one in which Kennedy is criticized for coming out against the Shah of Iran.

The prevailing atmosphere of the 1980 primary campaign was shaped by the Iranian hostage crisis and complicated by the deposed Shah's presence in the United States for medical treatment and by President Carter's "rose garden" strategy. The "CBS Reports" special, broadcast the week before Kennedy's formal announcement, had damaged him from the outset. He didn't seem to have the answers to critical questions, and the sense of an energetic candidacy was undermined by the visual texture of the program; a dynamically edited introduction on Kennedy as the inheritor of his family's mantle was followed by an hour of two talking heads.[3] Then, on November 30, candidate Reagan had made a comment to the effect that the Shah should be granted permanent asylum: "He certainly was as loyal an ally of this country as this country ever had." Although such a statement clearly might have telegraphed the message to the Iranians that there was still much support in America for the Shah and his policies, thereby conceivably undermining whatever sensitive negotiations might be underway, the network newscasts made no critical comment on Reagan's remark and the story was lost in the flow of other news.

In contrast, when Kennedy responded to the Reagan comment in a December 2nd interview in San Francisco, suggesting that because of his cruel regime the Shah might not deserve asylum, reporters pushed him on the question. CBS played up their December 3rd report of Kennedy's comment (reproduced for close study in the video compilation) by inviting other candidates and spokespersons of both political parties to comment. All of them were negative to the senator.

Constructing a news story in this way is a standard procedure in modern news practice; in effect it manufactures a major story where there might not otherwise be one. It might be argued that Kennedy's involvement made the difference, either because of the long standing public fascination about Kennedys and the presidency, or because Kennedy's campaign seemed hotter than Reagan's at the moment. Regardless of the rationale, once the airing of the CBS broadcast had shaped the basic framework of the story—establishing, for example, that the senator's aides had been caught by surprise by his off-hand comment—it was picked up by radio, newspapers, and newsweeklies. As it happened, an incident which might have been substantially overlooked (as had the Reagan comment of a few days before) eventually became a major source of difficulty for the Kennedy campaign *because* of the way it was first covered on television. The point is that the study of this campaign by future scholars cannot fail to include a study of this piece of video evidence.

Common to both print and electronic journalism today is the agressive newsman, driven by the daily challenge to come up with a new and interesting report and tempted therefore to "create" a story by goading a candidate or pumping people for on-camera responses to some statement or event. The phenomenon was first fully described by historian Daniel Boorstin in *The Image: Or What Happened to the American Dream.*[4] The everpresent intrusion of the television camera puts particular pressure on a national candidate. Consider the political damage done to George Romney in 1968 by an off-hand comment about brainwashing, to George Muskie in 1972 by an unfortunately timed New Hampshire tear, and to Gerald Ford by a gaffe in a campaign debate about which countries constituted the "eastern block."[5]

A second way in which television is essential in understanding the nature of recent political history is as a campaign tool consciously applied by the candidate and his staff of media consultants to influence voter behavior. The media influence of the incumbent is particularly important here, the office holder having more opportunity to orchestrate what almost three decades ago Boorstin referred to as "pseudo events"—news conferences, "photo opportunities," and other occasions designed for the sole purpose of winning media exposure. The 1980s have seen this political manipulation of the "unpaid media" (as opposed to advertising) raised to the level of an art form.

The 1960 presidential campaign was one in which no incumbent was running, yet it represents a watershed in the polical use of the media because of the famous Kennedy/Nixon debates—not news coverage *per se*, and not really a "pseudo event," but one carefully planned as far as possible by each of the candidates to present them in what they thought to be their best light. There are more comprehensive and more in-depth sources for information on the different positions taken on issues by the Nixon and the Kennedy campaigns. But the videotapes of the debates are important to historians for more than the words that can be quoted from them. The fact that these debates were televised and were viewed by a huge audience is what made them significant, and to a large extent that significance was based less on the words spoken than on the physical appearance and the presentational style of the speakers. Had Nixon not just been released from the hospital, had he gotten better advice on make-up and how to behave before the camera, the outcome might have been quite different. As it was, the polls indicated that a greater percentage of those who listened to the debate on the radio thought Nixon had won it.[6] Twenty years later there would be an actor in the White House.

The development of television as a political tool is closely examined by Edwin Diamond and Steven Bates in *The Spot: The Rise of Political Advertising on Television*.[7] Diamond and Bates offer scores of interesting examples of the ways in which the subtle (and not so subtle) persuasive powers of the moving image have been orchestrated in television commercials to manipulate voters' opinions—selling candidates as though they were soap powder. Here we have potential for the most direct danger of visual propaganda in a democratic society. The close analysis of individual commercials and overall campaigns must be key to any understanding of the dynamics of electoral politics since 1960—analysis concerned less with the truthfulness of the statements or political promises made than with the television commercial itself as central factual evidence, at least as important as the text of a campaign speech or promotional poster for the study of political strategy and voter behavior. Although Eisenhower was the first to use television commercials in his presidential campaign, Tony Schwartz's "Daisy Spot," produced for the 1964 Johnson for President campaign, was the first to make full creative use of the television medium. While it presented no new information, the "Daisy Spot" used images and sounds expertly. It led viewers to draw conclusions about Barry Goldwater based upon ideas that were already abroad in the political environment of the day, at the same time that it evoked a powerful emotional response (see the video compilation).[8] By the 1988 presidential contest, researchers were noting a backlash from viewers in response to negative advertisements, but the election of George Bush seemed to reinforce the obvious. However cynically it may avoid the substantive issues, the campaign which orchestrates itself effectively in terms of television has a tremendous advantage.

Thus far we have concentrated on presidential politics. Other issues and events have been forced upon the national consciousness by specific TV news reports. While conclusions may remain impossible to prove incontrovertibly, the influence of certain stories seems self evident. Consider the interest spurred in America in the winter of 1984–85 concerning the famine in Ethiopia. Regretably, starvation in that region is nothing new. In the early 1970s, hundreds of thousands of people died there under similar conditions, but an America preoccupied with Vietnam and the Nixon White House took little notice. Information about the current plight of the Ethiopians was available long before it was widely reported. In the fall of 1983 *Denver Post* photographer Anthony Suau brought back a series of powerful photographs which, while they won him a Pulitzer Prize, were only carried by a few newspapers. Notwithstanding verbal reports or the shocking still photographs of the stricken people which had been available as much as a year before, it seems to have been *because* one three-minute news story produced and first broadcast by BBC on October 22, 1984, was taken off the satellite and aired the next night in the United States that the attention of the American people was finally drawn to the issue. It was television that delivered the "slap in the face" that woke the public to the situation.[9]

Such a sequence of events cannot be predicted, of course. The same story with different images, the same story framed by different leading and following stories, the same story received by an audience in a different frame of mind—any or all of these and a myriad of other factors may have altered the impact. But, as was the case with Edward Kennedy's comments on the Shah of Iran, once the Ethiopian famine was highlighted on television, more detailed reports showed up in the newspapers and cover stories appeared in the weekly news magazines. All the networks and news agencies sent camera crews to Africa to record the gruesome sights and even Suau found a market for the pictures he had not been able to sell before the TV broadcast had opened up the story. Gradually the news coverage expanded to include the relief efforts of various agencies and individuals. A Congress partly influenced by the communist ties of the Ethiopian regime and likely to have been content with sending minimal aid, was driven by public outcry to respond more forcefully. Scandals were reported regarding certain charity groups which collected funds for African relief but did not deliver. Eventually rock music stars began sponsoring fundraising spectaculars with reporters everywhere and cameras popping. One might well question whether the evidence is strong enough to actually prove that one TV news story set all this in motion, but future historians who address the subject of America's response to world hunger cannot reasonably ignore this video document.

Analysing news stories as historical documents must include the three essentials noted in the introduction to this volume: a close study of the images themselves, an awareness of the factors that influenced (or may have influenced) the story's production, and a sensitivity to the various factors which influenced the story's reception.

CONTENT

It is an often repeated truism that the transcript of an entire thirty-minute newscast would not fill the front page of *The New York Times*. Almost any paper would do, of course; the point is not to boast about the detail of newspaper coverage but to dramatize the fact that time limitations make it impossible for TV news to be any more than a headline service.

Other comparisons can be made between newspapers and television news. Unlike the newsreels, for example, as the production of television news developed in the 1950s, it did adopt many of the professional standards of print journalism. In some ways developing television news standards have become stricter than those of the print media, partly due to the demands of government licensing and regulation. (See the reprinted pages from the CBS News Standards reprinted in the study guide to the video compilation.)

As with any moving image document, the form of a television newscast is as important as its content. Stories that lead the newscast are usually considered the more important, but there may be other factors such as the timeliness of a breaking story or the dramatic nature of a set of images which producers use to grab and hold the audience. The ways in which stories are paired with one another and the ways they are related to commercials invariably influence meaning. When editors define stories as topical and link them together thematically, the organization often gives emphasis to one or another aspect of each item. Many stories, of course, are left out altogether.

Individual news stories also have a beginning, a middle, and an end. The way a story is introduced, the choice of supporting statements and the strategies in which they are presented, the tone of the reporter's close—have a combined effect. The structure of a news story seems so natural and familiar to us that we may need to be reminded that every story is an artificial construct, as a look at any journalism textbook will confirm. In the 1940s and early 1950s the news looked very different than in the 1970s and 1980s. Although a broadcast might include film (usually sixteen millimeter silent film) from many locations, the commentary over it was read live from the studio by the same voice that read all of the stories (a person not yet called the anchor). Audio tracks were commonly recorded in the field for radio news, but not yet for television. It was not unknown to have music and sound effects layered over the images as they had been in the newsreels.[10]

One mark of the transformation to the story structure with which we are familiar today is a February 1953 memo Av Westin penned to his CBS News colleague Douglas Edwards. Westin asked: "why not 'take' the audience—eyes and ears—to the news site by 'switching' to the television reporter who is there? He would describe what's going on, just as the commentator would—but with the added advantage of being on-the-spot." Westin was aware that the format he was suggesting would "bring a new illusion" to the coverage of the story.[11] There is no real evidence that Westin deserves special credit for the idea. It was only a matter of time before something like this would be tried. The Westin memo does, however, provide a vivid reminder that every story represents some "mediation" of the news information. No where is that mediation clearer than in the editing of the typical TV news interview. Few untrained viewers are aware of the fact that every interview that is longer than a single shot is likely to have been condensed—reduced in length by editing out some of what was said before the camera. The reason viewers are unaware is that an editing device called a cutaway is used to hide the omission. Because they have been called to account on occasion, news producers have become very sensitive to problems inherent in the editing of news interviews.[12]

As with newsreels, visual language is important in analysing the content of television news. Just as newsreel companies spared FDR the indignity of having his physical infirmity displayed on the screen,[13] so New York television newsmen gave Mayor Abraham Beame the benefit of never shooting him from a high angle which would have accentuated his diminutive height and made him look foolish in comparison to the other newsmakers with whom he was photographed.

For another example of the way in which visual language influences the meaning in TV news, consider the CBS Evening News broadcast of March 17, 1986. The newscast included the first in a series of reports by Peter VanSant on air travel and the airlines. The story started with comments regarding FAA findings of violations of maintenance procedures by Eastern, American, and Peoples Express airlines. The story then shifted to a discussion of deregulation and how the shortage of experienced air traffic controllers was contributing to a growing frequency of "near misses" at metropolitan airports. As the reporter spoke, viewers watched a series of planes stacked up in a landing pattern looking as though they were close enough to touch one another. The impact of the image was frightening, at least for those who were unaware of the way in which a telephoto lens foreshortens the image it captures. Bringing the planes closer and collapsing the distance between them made for an effective shot, but it also manipulated the reality of the situation in a way few casual viewers would understand. Once you start looking for them the examples are endless.

PRODUCTION

Much has been written in the last decade toward an understanding of the institutions responsible for producing television news. Some of the many books on the subject, such as Edward Jay Epstein's *News From Nowhere* (1972) and Herbert Gans's *Deciding What's News* (1978), focus on the decision-making processes various news organizations use to establish what is newsworthy and what is not. Ron Powers's *The Newscasters* (1977) deals more broadly with television news institutions and practices, stressing the involvement of media consultants in the effort to build audience ratings. Peter Braestrup's *The Big Story* (1977) concentrates on the coverage of one subject, the 1968 Tet offensive in Vietnam. Av Westin's *Newswatch* (1982) is just one example of a growing genre of newsroom reminiscences, while Barbara Matusow's *The Evening Stars* (1983) focuses on anchorpersons as media celebrities.

It is important for the historian looking at a news source to have some idea of what happens behind the scenes. The books noted above

offer countless insights into politics and personalities. Consider the
simplest technicalities involved in putting the show on the air. Anchorpersons sit at their desks with scripts that have been written to precise
time requirements. There is always some flexibility built in, but each
video report from the field (usually a tape photographed and edited
earlier in the day) must be cued several seconds before the machine
can display it on the screen. The script details exactly what is said,
who says it, and when. The typed script is important for participants
(a dozen or more of them including producers, director, camera people, sound engineers, videotape and special effects operators) to follow
along, but at the point that they speak into the camera, the news reader
is actually reading from a teleprompter. This seems obvious when we
think about it, but we don't think about it. The technology is such
that the commentator can look directly into the lens and see the teleprompter readout reflected on a glass plate without averting his eyes
even slightly. The camera shooting from the other side of the tilted
glass plate sees none of it. The goal is to create an impression of natural
face-to-face communication, but there is nothing natural about it.

In terms of production values, one factor upon which all critics and
scholars agree is that TV news, in America at least, is first and foremost
a visual medium. The availability of good pictures is among the first
considerations in deciding what gets reported and how. The Ethiopian
famine story provides a clear illustration. How was the important
decision to air that story made? A few weeks later NBC news focused
on just that question in one of a series of advertisements for their
news operation. Tom Brokaw sits reclining on a couch in the advertisement as he explains that when those pictures came over the satellite, people in the office were moved to tears. "There was no
question," he said, "that that story would go on the air that night no
matter what else did." Brokaw continued, "We've been given a lot of
credit at NBC for being the first to present that story, but in fact the
Ethiopian story put itself on the air." The advertisement did not address the important implied question: would NBC have run a story
about the famine, or stressed it as they did, if all they had were statistics
in place of such overwhelmingly dramatic pictures?

Much analysis of TV news concentrates on its role as an "agenda
setter." As the logic goes, because the time limitations of a thirty-
minute broadcast demand that news choices be extraordinarily
selective, public attention is focused on those choices. Besides the
availability of good pictures, what else goes into such a decision? Conservative critics such as Spiro Agnew and Edith Efron[14] attacked TV
news for harboring a liberal bias. As Herbert Gans put it in 1979:
these critics "attacked the news media for their coverage of ghetto
disturbances and the anti-war demonstrations, maintaining that these
stories, by publicizing dissent, had negative implications for the status
quo."[15] In response, Gans suggested a series of "enduring values"
which he argued were shared by the American news establishment
and which invariably influenced the judgments that journalists made.

They tended, he claimed, to be characterized by a belief in: ethno-centrism, altruistic democracy, responsible capitalism, small-town pas-toralism, individualism, and moderatism.[16]

While most journalists may admit that no one can be completely value-free in the decisions they make, they categorically deny that they consider the liberal or conservative implications of a news story. This controversy, perhaps first drawn in sharp relief by Spiro Agnew in 1969, has been fostered by conservative spokesman such as Senator Jesse Helms and organizations such as Accuracy in Media, and to some extent their charges have been supported by independent scholar-ship.[17] A controversy such as this is not likely to disappear quietly and someday it will make an interesting historical subject. It is a sharp reminder that a historian using news reports for the facts they contain must remain conscious of the forces behind the scenes.

While we cannot develop many of them here, other production factors include the influence of changing technology on the creative options which TV news may consider for any particular story. The availability of portable videotape technology in encouraging on-the-scene reports is a good example, as is the the role of satellite transmission in accentuating (perhaps too much) the importance of immediacy in reporting. The use of new computerized graphics tech-niques for representing otherwise unavailable images came in for com-ment from President Reagan in January 1985. Reagan complained about how such imaginative computer-generated graphic images in-tended to represent the still undeveloped concept of a so-called "Star Wars Defense," in fact misled the public into thinking that research had already established that such weapons were possible, what they would look like, and how they would work. "You've already got a picture of the weapon, and I can see it shooting missles down, and it looks so easy," Reagan explained.[18] An alternative view might suggest that such lifelike images supported the president's belief in the prac-ticability of a technology which many experts had (and have) grave doubts about. In either case, a significant public perception is created out of whole cloth. Admittedly, such graphic tools do make it easier for TV news to deal with important analytical issues (in economics, for example) which have often gone underreported on TV because of the difficulty of visualizing them.

RECEPTION

When one gets beyond the most elemental factual question (did or did not the person charging police brutality have a black eye to show for it?), the matter of audience response to newsfilm becomes as im-portant as it is with any other moving image. We should want to know how many people watched and if possible something about why they watched.[19] The demand for news information is nothing unique to our time; people have been interested in what's new since the begin-nings of civilization.[20] Presumably television viewers do not voluntarily submit themselves to something from which they do not derive some pleasure. But what is the source of that pleasure? Is it a passion for information that Robert Stam has called "epistemophilia,"[21] the enjoyment of following the exchange between the anchorpersons and the field reporters, a voyeuristic fascination with the misfortunes reported, or the assurance of stability that usually comes from the combination of news stories and the friendly sign-off?[22]

At times the numbers of people who watched matter less than whether or not a particular individual did. In *The Powers That Be*, David Halberstam made much of the contention that Lyndon Johnson's 1968 decision not to run for re-election could be directly traced to his viewing of Walter Cronkite's special report from Vietnam at the end of February of that year. As Halberstam argued, Johnson was shaken by the commentator's pessimism about the war and reasoned that "if he had lost Walter Cronkite he had lost Mr. Average Citizen."[23] Yet, David Culbert studied Johnson's calendar for the day of broadcast to establish the liklihood that he had not watched the program, at least not at the time that it was originally aired.[24] Another interesting case is recounted by ABC reporter Roger Sharp, who remembers getting a call from the White House one spring day in the midst of the 1980 primary campaign (a time when he was covering local news for the ABC flagship station in New York) requesting him to meet President Carter and his entourage in Philadelphia. Sharp was given the opportunity to interview the president without other reporters present and asked questions on a number of topics, with the understanding that the one story Carter was particularly interested in getting out was his avowed intention not to sell spare fighter airplane parts to the Arabs. When the show aired on local New York news that evening, only one viewer mattered. Before Mayor Ed Koch would agree to campaign for Carter among Jewish voters in the Florida primary, he demanded that the president go on the public record with the assurances he had given only privately up to that time. The message of that broadcast was clearly more important for Mayor Koch than it was for the hundreds of thousands of others who may have seen it. Within a week he was shaking hands in Miami.[25]

In drawing hypotheses about the impact of a news story on its audience, as much care must be taken to appreciate the dynamics of general cultural values as with evaluating the reception of any feature film. When studying the Ethiopian famine story, for example, we must understand that the images of babies with bloated bellies must have had a peculiar impact when broadcast at 6:00 or 7:00 PM (depending on time zone), just at the moment millions of American familes were scraping from their dirty dinner plates enough food to maintain each one of those starving children for at least another week. Moreover, the images of children passively accepting buzzing clusters of flies around the mouth, nose, and eyes have special meaning in a culture like ours with such different standards of personal hygiene; the Ethiopian famine story was preceded by commercials for Remington electric razors and Polident denture adhesive.[26]

In addition, we must remain aware of the broader media environment within which viewers perceived the story in question. In other cultures, where news information may be more at a premium than it is in the west, people may watch news broadcasts more avidly. At least part of the reason that so many of the Soviet people watch their national nightly news is because it comes on at 9:00 P.M. all across the Soviet Union and supersedes all other programming. In Europe and America the line between entertainment and news programming is not so clear. During 1986 network news organizations juggled their time slots precisely so that their major news programs would not all appear at the same hour. The changes were based on a desire to compete for viewers, but more important was the competition for the advertsing dollars that could be made from popular game shows like "Wheel of Fortune" which were scheduled against the competitors' nightly news offerings. The slick promotion which masks the ways news mediates issues and events by encouraging the viewer to think of himself as an "eyewitness"; the efforts to get audiences to personally identify with friendly anchorpeople; the ever-present commercials which provide both the structural pacing and a persistent ideological tone for each news program, all place people's perception of TV news squarely in the context of the larger media environment.

Finally, an analysis of the reception of a news story must also consider the climate of news information. For example, in October 1984 the Reagan administration was doing all in its power to project an image of an economy rebounding from the recession of eighteen months before. At that earlier time newspapers had carried a flurry of stories about people living in their cars or in tent villages of the unemployed on the outskirts of major American cities (not altogether dissimilar from the ad hoc camps of homeless and starving Ethiopians). TV news stories had compared the travels of unemployed in search of work to the migrants of the Great Depression, noted the meagre diets of the children, and reported the efforts of some local welfare agencies to move such people along to some other jurisdiction. It was not that unemployment had gone away by election time 1984, but it had been reduced and was less central to the national consciousness than it had been a year or two before. In the context of this news environment we can assume that viewers reacted to the Ethiopian story differently than they would have if it had been aired early in 1983. Perhaps other factors were significant as well in stimulating the public to respond in such an animated way. People may have been moved by remembered images of earlier famines in Biafra and Bangladesh. Others may have been motivated by a nostalgic longing for the social activism of the 1960s in the wake of Walter Mondale's less-than-stirring presidential campaign and Ronald Reagan's second landslide victory at the polls. Difficult as they are to measure, cultural

values, the media environment, and the climate of news information
are essential elements in studying the reception of any newsreel or
news broadcast and in understanding its role in the shaping of public
opinion.

The same techniques of close analysis should be applied to "news
documentary." In contrast to the historical compilation documentary,
the news documentary characteristically addresses a topic of current
public concern. Because they are produced not by independent (and
often ideologically committed) documentary teams but by television
news organizations, these programs carry the presumption of higher
standards of professional journalistic integrity. Television news documentary has gone through a transformation during its thirty-five to
forty year history. There was a tendency in programs such as "Harvest
of Shame" (1960) and "Hunger in America" (1968) to address such
subjects as the working conditions of farm labor and the undernour-
ishment of the American poor with at least some of the same reformist
fervor that characterized the origins of the documentary film movement in Britain. Over time, however, as Daniel Leab has suggested
earlier in this volume, much of the passionate tone of television documentary has been dampened by concern about avoiding troublesome
controversy. The word "documentary" itself has been watered down
to refer to almost any type of nonfiction program. It might be argued
that CBS has faced the most public of controversies, over documentaries such as "The Selling of the Pentagon" (1970) and "The Uncounted Enemy: A Vietnam Deception" (1982) because among the
three commercial networks they have been the most consistently committed to the documentary form. In the 1980s pre-eminence in the
field is clearly shifting to public broadcasting.

Good documentaries are those which translate a solid and thoughtful understanding of a social and/or political problem into clear arguments for responsible public action. In addition to information,
they communicate urgency and attempt to focus popular concern.
Their recommendations need not be detailed or partisan, but their
conclusions must be based on a clear understanding of the issues and
they must be intellectually defensible. Beyond this, the art of documentary is in the ability of the filmmaker to use the tools of the medium to move the viewer—to go beyond the intellectual correctness
of the argument to involve the viewer psychologically and emotionally
in the cause being presented. A documentarist seeking to touch
American audiences with images of the Ethiopian famine, for example, might use images of flies crawling on the faces of passive children purposefully to shock American audiences into responding, even
though the children's acceptance of the insects may have had little if
anything to do with their real hunger.

The unanswered question is where the line should be drawn between the artistic use of the medium for emotional involvement and
the journalistic values of accuracy and objectivity. The children were
starving, and they did have flies around them. In terms of accuracy,

it would have been unconscionable for the cameraman to try to shoo the insects away. Perhaps the view of journalism that argues for objectivity above all is too naive. However objective they may try to be, it is natural for reporters to have personal biases, and they are often unconscious and unintended. In studying a documentary film for its factual content our aim is not to pass aesthetic or journalistic judgment on the program itself (as might be the case in the fourth framework for inquiry discussed in the next section of this book), but to sensitize ourselves to the ways in which facts and opinions are conveyed.

Consider Edward R. Murrow's famous "See It Now: Report on Senator McCarthy" (1954), arguably one of the most famous image artifacts in the history of television documentary. Excerpts from it are included in the video compilation. Murrow and co-producer Fred Friendly effectively destroyed McCarthy's credibility by carefully selecting pieces of film from the archives and presenting them in a context which showed the senator contradicting himself. As the program progressed, Murrow attacked McCarthy directly, charging him with violating constitutional guarantees and exploiting America's current climate of fear for personal political gain. The program was bold, convincing, and based upon rock solid evidence. But part of the reason it drew as much attention as it did was the way it used dramatic structure (the idea of McCarthy answering himself), visual language (a number of very unflattering images of the senator), and editing (at one point comparing McCarthy visually with a heroic George Washington) in addition to logical argument. At least one critic at the time was troubled, not because the program was too hard on the senator, but because it was was called a "Report on Senator McCarthy," and thus carried the allusions to objectivity that one would expect of a news "report" over an editorial or commentary.[27]

Whether a journalistic critic or not, every scholar of the McCarthy period should study this film, and be aware of the subtle filmic ways in which it undercut McCarthy's position. As with the Kennedy/Nixon debates, the "Daisy Spot," and the Ethiopian famine coverage, it is simply insufficient to read the verbal transcript. The production background and reception history of the show are important too. One should be aware that Murrow's anti-McCarthy attitudes were very well known, that this was a program which the production staff had planned for more than a year, and that—effective as it was in winning public attention—a significant percentage of people took the program (as McCarthy suggested) as proof that Murrow himself was a communist.

* * * *

Many of the examples offered in this essay, especially those dealing with television news, have been described in hypothetical terms which are likely to concern historians in the future. In part because the material is so recent, historians have made little use of TV news to date. But this will change. If future historians are to have access to evidence we must preserve it for them now. This was the rationale for the establishment of the Vanderbilt Television News Archive which, since 1968, has videotaped the nightly news output of the three major networks. Such a resource deserves financial and legal support as well as regular use. More recently Purdue University has established an archive of all C-SPAN (Cable Satellite Public Affairs Network) programming which, like the Vanderbilt collection, is available through loan of videotape copies.[28]

Local news is important as well. Perhaps not all of it can or should be saved. But it is essential, even if only for a clearer understanding of the broader information environment in which a national or international story is understood, that there be some examples of the ways in which local and regional news organizations covered both their own and national news.[29]

Vanderbilt preserves the news as it was broadcast. The archives of the networks and stations themselves often extend to the outtakes which were not used on the air, but these collections are usually inaccessible to underfunded researchers. A number of other regional collections hold this type of material but they are usually spotty and incomplete.[30] Newsreel outtake material is accessible at the National Archives (for Universal Newsreel) and at The University of South Carolina Newsfilm Library (for Movietone).[31] For certain specific factual questions the outtakes may be crucial, but most scholars should find the broadcast stories as much if not more helpful. Archives which retain the individual pieces of film or video footage but not the entire news broadcasts (with anchor commentary, commercials, etc.) are of limited value.

Nonfiction television is now, and will be more so in the future, a crucial factual resource for historians. As this essay has tried to show, the use of that source demands special care and special attention to visual language. Perhaps most important is the recognition that the mass media in the twentieth century have created a new electronic environment in which reality may be defined by what gets reported on television and how. Future historians cannot ignore what has happened in that electronic environment.

NOTES

1. For an interesting survey of the issues of concern see Elayne Rapping, *The Looking-Glass World of Non-Fiction TV* (Boston, South End Press: 1987).
2. "Edward Kennedy and the Televised Personality in the 1980 Presidential Election," in John E. O'Connor, ed., *American History/American Television: Interpreting the Video Past* (New York: Ungar, 1983), pp. 328–362. The key news story is included in the video compilation.
3. *Ibid.*
4. (New York: Atheneum, 1962).
5. For further analysis of television and politics see David Broder, *Changing of the Guard: Power and Leadership in America* (New York, Simon and Schuster: 1980), Austin Ranney, *Channels of Power: The Impact of Television on*

American Politics (New York: Basic Books, 1983), and *Television and Political Life: Studies in Six European Countries*, (London, Macmillan, 1979).

6. See Kathleen Hall Jamieson's *Presidential Debates: The Challenge of Creating and Informed Electorate*, (New York: Oxford University Press, 1988) and her *Eloquence in an Electronic Age* (New York: Oxford University Press, 1988).

7. (Cambridge, Mass.: 1984); See also Edward W. Chester, *Radio, Television and American Politics* (New York: 1969).

8. Another valuable source for the study of political commercials is the Political Commercial Archive at the University of Oklahoma which for a small fee to cover costs will lend compilation reels of political commercials to scholars and teachers for use in their work. An interesting moving image source is "The Thirty Second President," one program in the PBS series "A Walk Through the Twentieth Century With Bill Moyers."

9. For an interesting analysis of the situation see David Marcus, "Moving Pictures: How Photographers Brought The Ethiopian Famine to Light in the Shadow of Television," *American Photographer* (May, 1985) pp. 50–53. See also the three part ninety-minute television documentary "Consuming Hunger" (1987) which details the coverage of the famine story from start to finish.

10. Brian Winston demonstrated all this in an analysis of the CBS News with Douglas Edwards for April 7, 1949, at an IAMHIST conference in London in July 1987.

11. Av Westin to Douglas Edwards, February 20, 1953, Westin Papers, Wisconsin Center for Film and Theater Research, State Historical Society of Wisconsin.

12. Pages from the CBS News Standards on the filming and interviews have been reproduced in the study guide to the video compilation. Several of the video selections illustrate the practice. For more on the cutaway see Chapter V.

13. Outtakes from Movietone newsreel which illustrate the point are included in the video compilation.

14. See Efron's *The News Twisters* (Los Angeles, Nash Publishing: 1971).

15. Gans, *Deciding What's News*, p. 40.

16. For a brief updated survey of TV news production values see Carlin Romano, "What? The Grisly Truth About Bare Facts," and Michael Schudson, "Deadlines, Datelines, and History," in Robert Karl Manoff and Michael Schudson, eds., *Reading the News* (New York, Pantheon, 1986).

17. See for example Peter Braestrup, *The Big Story: How the American Press and Television Reported and Interpreted the Crisis of Tet 1968 in Vietnam and Washington*, two volumes, (Westview Press, 1977). For a contrasting Marxist interpretation which sees British television news as the bare-faced expression of capitalist ideology see the several works of the Glasgow Media Group, *Bad News* (London, 1976), *More Bad News* (London, 1977), and *War and Peace News* (Milton Keynes, 1985).

18. *The New York Times*, January 10, 1985.

19. On this last point see Lawrence Lichty, "Video vs. Print," *The Wilson Quarterly* 6 (Winter, 1982), pp. 49–57. See also Shanto Iyengar and Donald R. Kinder, *News That Matters: Television and Public Opinion* (Chicago, University of Chicago Press: 1987); and John P. Robinson and Mark R. Levy, *The Main Source: Learning From Television News* (Beverly Hills, Sage: 1986).

20. See Mitchell Stephens, *The History of News* (New York, 1988).
21. Stam coined the phrase in a presentation entitled "The Pleasures of Instant History: Television News and its Spectator" at a conference on "Television and History" at the National Humanities Center in North Carolina in April 1987.
22. On the rituals of news viewing see Daniel C. Hallin, "Network News: We Keep America on Top of the World," in Todd Gitlin, editor, *Watching Television* (New York, 1986), pp. 9–41.
23. (New York, 1979), p. 514.
24. David Culbert, "Johnson and the Media," in Robert A. Devine, ed., *Exploring the Johnson Years* (Austin, Texas, 1981), pp. 223–227.
25. Sharp told the story at a conference at William Paterson College in 1981.
26. Vanderbilt Television News Index and Abstracts, October, 1984, pp. 2074–75.
27. See John E. O'Connor, "Edward R. Murrow's 'See It Now Report on Senator McCarthy': Image as Artifact" in *Film & History*, Vol. 16 (September, 1986), pp. 55–72. This article is reprinted in the guide to the video compilation.
28. For further information contact The Vanderbilt University Television News Archive, Vanderbilt University Libraries, Nashville, TN 37203; or The Public Affairs Video Archives, Purdue University, Stewart Center G-39, West Lafayette, IN 47907.
29. In January 1984 the Newark Public Library established the New Jersey Television News Archive, the first local/regional effort operating on the Vanderbilt model. Write them at 5 Washington St., Newark, NJ 07102.
30. As yet there is no complete list of TV news archives, but there is a national organization in which they are represented, and work on a national catalog is underway. For information write The Film and Television Archives Advisory Committee at The National Center for Film and Video Preservation, c/o The American Film Institute, P.O. Box 27999, 2021 North Western Ave., Los Angeles, CA 90027.
31. Examples of newsreel outtakes from both collections are included in the video compilation.

Gerald Herman is a tenured Assistant Professor of History at Northeastern University in Boston, teaching media literacy and production courses on both undergraduate and graduate levels. He edited the media chapter in The Craft of Public History *(Greenwood, 1983) and has written extensively on issues related to the media and history. Currently he is working on a media guide for use in world civilization courses. He has produced two video-based history of western civilization courses that were recently nominated for the Charles A. Dana Award and has served as consultant in the production of both documentary and dramatic films.*

DOCUMENTARY, NEWSREEL, AND TELEVISION NEWS AS FACTUAL RESOURCES IN THE HISTORY CLASSROOM

Gerald Herman

Over the past decade both the sensibilities and conditions surrounding the availability and use of nonfiction media have changed significantly. On a theoretical level, historians have become more sensitive to the problematic nature of all discursive sources and media and therefore less concerned with the uniqueness of the particular difficulties associated with nitrate-celluloid/electronic materials.[1] At the same time researchers,[2] teachers,[3] and students[4] alike are becoming more cognizant of the dimensions, divisions, and directions of the history and media field. Historical documentaries, docudramas, melodramas, and "miniseries" on television and in the movies have proliferated. At the same time, questions have been raised concerning the accuracy and objectivity of news and documentary reporting, particularly surrounding the Vietnam War.[5] All of this enhances the ability of students and teachers alike to deal with the issues surrounding the nonfiction media at the same time that the pressure to confront such issues has increased. Finally, the last decade has witnessed an explosion in the amount and range of film/video materials as well as of ancillary documentation for film study available to researchers and teachers. The archival and copyright situation for at least some of these materials has also worked to increase their availability.[6] And the nearly universal spread of videocassette technology has made nearly "constant access to mediated materials"[7] a reality. For all these reasons, the use of nonfiction historical media in the classroom has become a much more complex and exciting endeavor. Making use of this expanding array of resources, approaches, and technologies, historians have proceeded beyond the "stimulation"[8] and "illustration"[9] modes of nonfiction media utilization to a variety of more sophisticated analytic dimensions. The first level of analysis treats film and video as source material and investigates the content they offer rather than merely accepting their flow of narrative images at face value. The argument concerning the extent to which these media represent "primary" or "secondary" sources on past events[10] goes on with even greater urgency as the "video" uncut cinematic sources of documentary and newstories appear to be even less available than were those of the newsreels.[11] Using the "freeze frame" technologies of film projectors and especially video players, history teachers have undertaken detailed analysis of what the news and documentary media show of the events they recorded. In 1973, the British Open University, as part of its "War and Society" Third Level Arts course, developed supplementary print materials to "footnote" the film sources for the programs.[12] By the mid 1970s Marc Ferro had published his two volumes on the Russian Revolution, employing newsreels as primary sources for analyzing the popular response to certain public revolutionary events.[13] "Visual facts" also played a major part in Richard Ellison's nationally broadcast thirteen part television course, "Vietnam: A Television History" (1983).[14] The most sophisticated course that I know of that has attempted, since 1972, to introduce students to the possibilities and problems associated with using film as historical source material is Kenneth Ward's "Film, Sound, and Historical Analysis" at the New University of Ulster.[15] In the United States, a model for such courses has also existed since the early 1970s.[16]

Teachers have also concentrated on the kinds of events that nonfiction film and video makers have deemed worthy of coverage and the ways in which the content of their products reveals their attitudes and biases. This form of analysis is most often undertaken with respect to "propaganda" films or video[17] and many of the courses or units offered on this subject focus on the interwar European dictatorships or the Second World War for their subjects.[18] Such courses have also begun to realize that, despite the absence of centrally directed propaganda imperatives, documentaries and newsreels produced in the Western democracies also contain biases of comission or omission, reflecting the attitudes of their producers:

> Look at enough news film, in fact, and one begins to feel that the most constant image of the 1930's is of a mounted police charge into an unarmed street crowd. But I realize as I write this, how little real idea I have of the facts.[19]

By comparing the newsreel or television news of important events to print journalism and historical accounts, it is possible to identify the content biases and omissions—what was or was not considered important enough to record—by filmmakers.[20] In addition, the comparison, in classroom situations, of cinematic to other sources or to historians' accounts have yielded interesting information about the manner in which those other accounts reported such events. The comparison of newsreels and documentaries from different producers on the same or related subject—especially if they represent different ideological or national viewpoints—has also been suggested[21] as a way of uncovering the filmmakers' attitudes.

"Actuality" films and videos have also been used either alone or in combination with other materials as sources for ethnographic readings of particular periods, cultures, events, or themes.[22] In exploring the "consciousness" of a particular time and place, the range of actuality film/video sources employed by historians has grown tremendously, encompassing not only newsreels, documentaries, and compilation films/videos, but also private and government informational (educational) productions[23] and commercials.[24] The major problem in utilizing this material heretofore, except in courses dealing with contemporary history, has been that their preservation has been, except for government-sponsored films, haphazard at best and retrieval difficult, if not impossible.

Content analysis, however, only partly explains the messages of film and television. Both in their scholarship and in their classes, film and video historians are devoting considerable time to its other dimension—the various kinds of cinematic analysis. This analysis takes many forms, beginning with the interrelationship between the camera and its object. Since for much of its history, the camera was a cumbersome device that needed "set-up time" for both picture and sound, the normal newsreel or documentary opportunity was neither spontaneous nor camouflaged from its subject. The observer and the observed therefore accommodated each other in what a later period defined as staged "media events." In viewing the results, it is necessary to bear in mind that these are the records of "actors on public stages" offering themselves in ways designed to conform to current conventions and to portray themselves as they wished history to remember them. Similarly, what the lens sees and the film records, the manner of processing, the editing conjunctions, the relationships of visual and audio tracks, and the final assembly are all subject to an "iconic code." This subtext, long understood to be a central element of fictional film, has been more recently made a part of courses related to actuality film/video.[25]

Beyond reading the structure of individual productions, students should also be helped to understand the genre within which the film or video maker works and which provides many of the conventions of form, structure, and language for individual works. To ignore these conventions might lead to faulty conclusions with respect to the intent or methodology of individual film-or-video makers.[26] The Averell W. Harriman Institute for Advanced Study of the Soviet Union at Columbia University receives continuous Soviet television signals from

Russia's Molniya polar satellite system. For the first time, Soviet television transmissions are being viewed by scholars and students in context. According to the Institute's assistant director, Jonathan Sanders, "we see this as a window into the popular culture of the nation . . . There's an awful lot that we can learn about them from their televsion."[27]

The earliest warnings about taking nonfiction film seriously as a source of historical information stemmed from the ease with which the cinematic record could be faked or falsified.[28] To reduce the danger of being so deceived, scholars and teachers have learned a variety of contextual and technological detective skills—good sense and media-history memories, and a discerning eye to spot the different sources that are often combined in actuality film or video. Since nonfiction film/video can contain original and stock ("file") newsfilm (tape); original, other contemporary, narration or commentary, recreated, or musical sound; staged re-creations by actual participants or by actors; and/or scenes from other films or tapes, much time and effort has been spent by scholars and students with the films (tapes) and attendant documentation to "disassemble" these productions to determine their validity as sources or as historical interpretations.[29] Students often have a great deal of fun discovering pieces of acted films in supposedly genuine documentaries by beginning to ask themselves questions about how a cameraman could have been shooting from a particular angle, by discovering sound tracks before sound was in regular use, or by simply finding an all-too-familar scene from a movie in the newsreel or compilation under consideration.[30]

The context, cinematic, and source analyses of actuality productions represent the "inside" element of film/video studies. The external factors also must be understood if the complexities of creation and impact are to be properly assessed. On the production side, there has been an explosion of scholarship and a growth of teaching about the people and institutions that produced and distributed these works— motivations, procedures, ideologies, and relationships among themselves and in connection to the surrounding world.[31] Without understanding the informal middleman role played by Max Winkler in "rationalizing" the German film industry, the timing and extent of Nazi control over individual German movies would remain obscure.[32] Similarly the seemingly impromptu zeal that impelled the major Hollywood studios to make pro-Russian movies during World War II becomes much clearer once one understands their (particularly Jack Warner's) relationship to the Roosevelt administration.[33]

On the distribution-reception boundary lie a number of scholarly and teaching issues including the role of such outside forces as the National Board of Review, sponsoring organizations, government censorship and/or sponsorship in determining the terms of release and distribution (in many instances their control exists at the production level as well),[34] and the structural context (scheduling, surrounding stories, or commercials) of the viewing of the material itself.[35]

Finally, some of the most difficult and subtle issues for study by scholars and students involve the reception of the productions.[36] The questions asked here are difficult to answer except in the most general manner, but much research continues. Students can be made aware of these issues by studying this literature and by analyzing for themselves the reviews of particular films or videos in ideologically diverse publications as well as the audience and revenue data associated with them. These topics include production distribution data, audience size and composition, the sociology of attendence, the psychology of audience response to the production, and questions concerning film's impacts on the public both rationally and in the affective domain, both immediate and long-term (especially when sequels are generated from the initial production). And how did such responses, in turn, affect policy makers on the particular issues?[37]

At the other end of the instructional spectrum from the stimulation effect is the attempt to involve students in the actual production process. As advisors to productions or as film/video-makers themselves, historians have attempted to provide ancillary materials and/or study guides so teachers can maximize the utility of their products.[38] The productions themselves have become more varied and complex, including not only traditional compilation productions, but also modules or "raw materials" which students must interpret or may even manipulate for their own purposes.[39] Student interns or assistants are often employed in the production of such projects.

Beyond this, some courses actually involve students in media production or production simulation as part of their regular coursework.[40] The graduate course in media production in history "History and Media" that a production expert and I teach together for the department's master's degree program in Historical Agencies and Administration is designed to give students "hands on" experience in dealing with nonwritten historical materials in the two chief and interconnected ways that historians encounter them: in the collection, analysis, and evaluation of materials and productions that already exist; and in the scripting, assembling, production, and distribution of historically valid materials from their own research. Dealing with the first of these, students begin by reading a variety of articles on historical media, their sources, collection, and evaluation. They then hear and see excerpts from the range of materials and productions using historical data or media now available, which we analyse as a group to get students used to "reading" such presentations on their many levels. Each student then chooses a movie currently in mass distribution in the Boston area or scheduled for televised showing by one of the local stations and writes a short review of its use (and/or abuse) of its historical subject or material.

At the end of this unit, the students are confronted by a copyright-cleared Universal newsreel series on the Berlin Blockade which I obtained from the National Archives with the kind assistance of Richard Myers. The video tape I received contains both the finished productions and the "outtakes"—the film shot for the subject but not actually used. Before the class began, I had worked with a television editor to disassemble the film itself into its raw film and sound components on video tape and to reassemble the original footage from which the film was made (since the outtakes do not include the film actually used in the production).[41] The students are presented with the topic of the newsreel and asked to construct their own "historically-valid" newsreel from the raw footage. When they are done with their research, analysis, and editing, their product is compared to the finished Universal newsreel segments. From this exercise, students learn about the liberties taken with historical materials—the creative use of stock footage, for example—as well as the variety of ways in which prejudices of various kinds can be embedded within the text, pictures, music, or the juxtaposition of all three.

While this is going on during the first half of the twelve week quarter, the students have agreed upon both a topic (deemed possible from available sources by the instructor) for their own production and by a process of target audience and topic analysis, the medium most appropriate to its presentation. They have selected a producer from among themselves, divided the activities involved in producing their topic into discrete tasks, and set themselves up as a production team. Individual students become historical researchers, visual and audio materials researchers, location and interview source searchers, and scriptwriters. Each individual must act, in the performance of these tasks, as if he or she were involved in an actual noncommercial production—writing requests for copywrite clearances, obtaining various permits, and executing appropriate releases. Even a mock budget is produced and the process of compromise based on cost or availability is fought through.

The research group then reconstitutes itself into an actual production team with individual students becoming the various crew members: audio assembly and insertion specialist, still photographer and inserter, film assembler and inserter, onscreen talent or interviewer, camera crew, director, and postproduction editor. The department provides the equipment, an engineer and technical director, and general supervision and training. The object of the exercise is neither to create a fully professional production nor to train a fully professional crew. Its goals are to give these present and future historical administrators and public historians insight into the nature and variety of the tasks involved in media production and to familiarize them with the process they would have to oversee if they want to produce such materials for their own archives or agencies. This is not to say that the product of their endeavors is completely unimportant or amateurish. A recent class produced an electronically cued slide taped history, using material from Northeastern's Oral History Archive, of the shoe industry in Lynn, Massachusetts, which was later used by one of the local historical societies as an introduction to its exhibit on the same subject. Another class developed a video on Irish immigration to Boston involving interviews with new arrivals which is now used by our Irish Studies Program. A third class made a video compilation exploring the period of Amelia Earhart's life that transformed her from an advertiser's gimmick into a true aviation pioneer. The tape, called "From Passenger to Pilot," is based on an interview done by the class with Amelia Earhart's sister, Muriel Morrissey. Still another class completed a video project entitled "Here to Stay: Women in the Trades." And most recently, a multi-media/video survey of Boston's historical resources was produced for use as part of Northeastern's freshmen orientation.

Though by no means comprehensive, this survey seems to me to present the major directions that school-based education in nonfiction film and video is currently taking.

As to the future, I can do no more than extrapolate from what I see as the current frontiers of the field. I believe that the following four trends will continue. First, I think there will be an even greater availability of both media-based and print materials for students and scholars alike. The materials will continue to be made available through the university, public, and private archives, because their private and corporate holders find the cost of maintaining them too expensive and the tax benefits of releasing them too lucrative. The materials will be more accessible because of the rapidly decreasing cost of video and computer technology[42] and because of expanding satellite-based distribution systems. The latter will greatly facilitate crosscultural study as well.

Related to this is the tendency toward increased pooling of these resources through the expansion of networks, consortia, and cooperative computer-based cataloguing services, such as the Princeton University-University of Southern California sharing of the Warner Brothers Archives.[43] Furthermore, I believe that simplified and inexpensive machinery and materials will continue to become available to allow students themselves to manipulate and compile audiovisual sources into historical interpretations in the same way as print primary sources.[44]

Finally, at the other end of the cost spectrum, the combination of videodisc and computer technology, combined with "idiot proof" videocassette recording equipment,[45] should allow the development of precisely defined historical problems in multimedia and moving image formats for students. Combining all this technology with print primary and secondary sources will enable students to manipulate and construct their own "solutions" to historical problems and actually play them back to their teachers and peers as integrated compilation videos. Once historians or multi disciplinary teams with appropriate skills get into the business of producing these, it will be a very exciting time indeed for teaching media and history.

NOTES

1. See Wolfgang Ernst's report of the joint *Hochschule für Fernsehen und Film* (Munich) *Akademie Für politishe Bildung* (Tutzing) seminar on Mass Media

and contemporary history entitled "Distory: Cinema and Historical Discourse" in the *Journal of Contemporary History* (vol. 18, no. 3, July, 1983), pp. 397–409.

2. See R. C. Raack, "Historiography as Cinematography: A Prolegomenon to Film Work for Historians," *Journal of Contemporary History* (vol. 18, no. 3, July, 1983), pp. 411–438.

3. This sophistication can be seen in articles like Paul H. Scherer "New Approaches to the Teaching of Film History," *The History Teacher* (vol. 16, no. 3, May, 1983) pp. 371–382 and in textbooks such as Robert C. Allen and Douglas Gomery, *Film History Theory and Practice* (New York, Knopf, 1985).

4. e.g., Richard S. Geehr, ed., *Soviet History and Film, an Undergraduate Student Perspective by the Students of Bentely College* (Lexington, Mass., Ginn Custom Publishing, 1980).

5. e.g., Alex S. Jones, "The Westmoreland Trial Draws Attention to the Tricks of the Filmmaker's Trade: Sometimes, It Seems, The Camera Does Lie. Here's How," *The New York Times*, Sunday, February 17, 1985, E p. 8.

6. Such events as the settlement of the CBS. copyright infringement suit against the Vanderbilt University Television News Archive, allowing that archive to continue operation, and the growth of archival collections of newsreel and documentary materials (Universal Newsreels at the National Archives, Hearst at U.C.L.A., a broad selection of radio and television materials at the Museum of Broadcasting, ABC. newsfilm and outtakes at the Sherman Grinberg Libraries in New York, NBC. materials at the Wisconsin Center for Theater Research, the CBS. News Archive at New York, and Fox Movietones at the University of South Carolina) and of large amounts of paper documentation for those materials, have greatly increased the sources for nonfiction media study in recent years, though these are partially offset by problems of underfunded preservation, unstable or deteriorating film and video stock, and tragedies such as the National Archives fire at Suitland, Maryland.

7. Roger Eatwell, "Film, History and Politics in British Higher Education," *Historical Journal of Film, Radio, and Television* (vol. 2, no. 2, 1982) pp. 201–202.

8. This "stimulation effect" is sometimes achieved by surrounding history courses with extracurricular film festivals (e.g., the West Virginia University History Film Forum, described in *Film and History*, vol. XI, no. 1, February, 1981, pp. 14–15) and is sometimes achieved by using films to introduce or punctuate units within courses themselves (e.g., Introduction to American Civilization two semester course at Brookdale Community College described in *Film and History*, vol. III, no. 1, February, 1973, pp. 9–12 or the "History of Civilization since 1660" at the University of South Alabama described in *Film and History*, vol. IV, no. 4, December, 1973, pp. 4–8). Film distributors sometimes and television networks often try to enhance the size of audiences for documentaries and docudramas (especially in its miniseries form) by soliciting educators, through printed guides, to assign or encourage viewing.

9. Using nonfiction motion pictures as "historical illustrations" normally takes one of three forms: (1) illustration of particular periods or events (*e.g.*, "Movies and Modern America" at the State University of New York at Buffalo described in *Film and History*, vol. V, no. 2, May 1975, pp. 16–

18, 20); (2) illustration of historical themes or great ideas (*e.g.*, "The American Dream on Film" at the University of Delaware described in *Film and History*, vol. III no. 3, September, 1973, pp. 17–18 or "Issues in Western Civilization: The Individual in Society during Revolution" at Temple University described in *Film and History*, vol. II, no. 1, 1972, pp. 15–19); or (3) illustrative comparisons on which to base analyses of fictional or "docudramatic" materials. The techniques for the latter are those designed for a course called "The Age of the Democratic Revolution in Europe and America 1750–1850" at California State University, Hayward—though there art slides and documentary prints and photographs rather than nonfiction film, which did not then exist, were used as the comparative sources—described in *The History Teacher*, vol. VI, no. 2, February, 1973, pp. 281–294, or the general approach to teaching American labor history suggested by Daniel Leab in the *IAMHIST Newsletter*, no. 12, Winter 1981/82, pp. 54–60.

10. J. A. S. Grenville, *Film as History: The Nature of Film Evidence* (Birmingham, U.K., 1971) Report on the "Conference on the Use of Audiovisual Archives as Original Source Materials," *The History Teacher* (vol. VI, no. 2, February, 1973), pp. 295–321. Martin A. Jackson "Film as a Source Material: Some Preliminary Notes Toward a Technology," *Journal of Interdisciplinary History* (vol. IV, no. 1, Summer, 1973)- pp. 73–82 and Karsten Fledelius' introduction to and Jack Duckworth's article in section two of Karsten Fledelius, Kaare Rübner Jørgensen, Niels Skymm-Nielson and Erik H. Swiatek, eds., *History and the Audio-Visual Media: Studies in History, Film and Society 1* (Copenhagen, 1979).

11. Pierre Sorlin, *The Film in History, Restaging the Past* (Totowa, New Jersey, 1980), pp. X-XI.

12. *Archive Film Compilation Booklet* and *Supplementary Material* A301, both published by the Open University in 1973. An introductory film entitled "Archive Film in the Study of War and Society" narrated by Arthur Marwick was also developed to orient students with respect to these sources.

13. Marc Ferro, *The Russian Revolution of February 1917* (Englewood Cliffs, N.J., 1972), and *October, 1917* (London, 1976). Ferro had suggested this use for newsreel film in a 1968 article "1917: History and the Cinema" in the *Journal of Contemporary History*, 4 and has created a general typology for historical films in *Cinema and History* (Detroit, Wayne State University Press, 1988).

14. Steven Cohen, ed., *Vietnam Anthology and Guide to a Television History* (New York, 1983), "Preface: 'Vietnam as Telehistory' " by Richard Ellsion, p. 3.

15. K. E. Ward, "Film, Sound and Historiccal Analysis—A Course in Film and History," *University Vision* (no. 12, December, 1974), pp. 50–56.

16. William Hughes, "Proposal for a Course on Films and History," *University Vision* (no. 8, January, 1972), pp. 9–18.

17. Richard M. Barsam, *Filmguide to 'Triumph of the Will'* (Bloomington, Indiana, 1975) is an excellent example of this.

18. Richard Taylor's course at the University College of Swansea (U.K.) entitled "Public Opinion and Propaganda" (based, presumably on his own work in the field, *Film Propaganda: Soviet Russia and Nazi Germany and The Politics of Soviet Cinema 1917–1929*) is an excellent example of this, as are both the course taught at the University of Bath on "Political Propaganda in the Twentieth Century" and Martin Pernick's course entitled "Sickness

and Health in Society: 1492 to the Present" at the University of Michigan which uses both actuality and fictional film to explore popular attitudes about Medicare and public health at the times they were made, irrespective of the films often historical subject matter. This use of the films is described in "Thomas Edison's Tuberculosis Films: Mass Media and Health Propaganda," *The Hastings Center Report*, 8 (June, 1978), pp. 20–27. In K. R. M. Short and Karsten Fledelius, ed., *History and Film: Methodology, Research, Education: Studies in History, Film and Society 2* (Copenhagen, 1980) articles by Stig Hornshøj-Møller on course use of *"Der Ewige Jude,"* by Carsten Jørgensen on Nazi Spanish Civil War documentaries, and by Stanisaw Ozimek on Nazi film coverage of the 1939 Polish invasion, provide other examples of this analytical mode.

19. Penelope Houston, "The Nature of Evidence," *Sight and Sound* (London, British Film Institute, vol. 36, no. 2, Spring, 1967), p. 92.

20. In Britain, Nicholas Pronay has been concerned with this issue, among others, in such BBC education projects as "Propaganda with Facts" and in his teaching at the University of Leeds. Pronay is a co-author of *The Use of Film in History Teaching* (London, the Historical Association, 1972).

21. See Peter C. Rollins "Ideology and Film Rhetoric: Three Documentaries of the New Deal Era (1936–1941)," *Journal of Popular Film and Television* reprinted as chapter 3 of Peter C. Rollins, ed., *Hollywood as Historian, American Film in a Cultural Context* (Lexington, Kentucky, 1983). See also Robert E. Herzstein, "Crisis on the Eastern Front, 1941–'42: A Comparative Analysis of German and American Newsreel Coverage," *Film and History* (part I, vol. XIII, no. 1, February, 1983) pp. 34–42, (part II, vol. XIII, no. 2, May 1983) pp. 1–11. In addition to the large number of committed films made to support the various sides of contemporary controversial issues, historical documentaries on the same subject, presented from a variety of ideological or national viewpoints, are available for teachers to assign for comparative analysis. Examples include the Russian Revolution ("Nightmare in Red" (NBC) versus "The World Turned Upside Down" (BBC)), the Battle of Russia ("Operation Barbarosa" (BBC) versus "Barbarosa, June-December, 1941" ("World at War," Thames)), and the Tet Offensive of the Vietnam War ("Tet" ("Vietnam, a Television History," PBS) versus "Televisions's Vietnam: The Impact of the Media"). In my undergraduate film course "History through Film, Film through History," I show feature films on single historical subjects (such as "the Charge of the Light Brigade" or the "Gunfight at the O.K. Corral") made at different times, and ask students to analyse and assess their differences in interpretations.

22. Arthur Marwick has undertaken the most systematic use of this sort in his *Class: Image and Reality in Britain, France, and the U.S.A. since 1930* (London, 1980). Kenneth Short of Westminster College, Oxford teaches a course on "Film Evidence for Twentieth Century History" exploring the manner in which film has been used to communicate policy and the ways in which it can be used to help understand the values and mores of the period from 1915–1945. In the United States courses like "Modern War and its Images" at the University of Maine at Portland-Gorham (*Film and History* (vol. III, no. 3, September, 1973), pp. 12–16) "War: Illusion and Reality" at Skidmore College (*Film and History*, (vol. XII, no. 2, May, 1982) pp. 36–43), and "Women in American History" at Lowell State

College (*Film and History* (vol. IV, no. 4, December, 1974), pp. 12–15, 20) are rather elementary examples of this approach.

23. Richard D. MacCann, *The Peoples' Films: A Political History of U.S. Government Motion Pictures* (New York, 1973), K. R. M. Short and Stephan Dolezel, eds., *Hitler's Fall: The Newsreel Witness* (London, 1988), and Daniel J. Perkins, "The Sponsored Film: A New Dimension in American Film Research," *Historical Journal of Film, Radio, and Television* (vol. 2, no. 2, 1982), pp. 133–140. Iowa State University has established an American Archive of the Factual Film and its film students are compiling indices for it.

24. Joseph Corn "Selling Technology: Advertising Films and the American Corporation" *Film and History* (vol. IX, no. 3, September, 1981) pp. 49–58.

25. See the methodolgical section of Short and Fledelius, *op. cit*, especially the articles by J. M. Peters and Karsten Fledelius and the Jens-Erik Martinussen application of Fledelius's mode of analysis to "Hué in Memorium, February, 1968." Judith Gane's article in the second section of Fledelius, Jørgensen, Skyum-Nielsen, and Swiatek, *op. cit*, is also useful. Fledelius has also expounded his structural approach to documentary analysis in an article entitled "Film Analysis: The Structural Approach" in M. J. Clark, ed., *Politics and the Media* (Oxford, 1979). Other explorations of nonfictional film/video analysis can be found in chapter 6 of Bill Nichols, *Ideology and the Image: Social Representation in the Cinema and Other Media* (Bloomington, Indiana, 1981) and in Robert Stam, "Television News and its Spectator" in E. Ann Kaplan, *Regarding Television, Critical Approaches— an Anthology* (American Film Institute, 1983), pp. 23–43. Vincent Porter describes a joint history-film studies postgraduate course at the Polytechnic of Central London that employes these analytic techniques in an article in the *Historical Journal of Film, Radio and Television* (vol. 3, no. 1, March, 1984), pp. 76–81. The 1985 Ohio University Film Conference on "Narrative/non-Narrative" included a session called "Re-thinking Documentary" on the "ontology of the documentary image."

26. See Thomas W. Bohn and Lawrence W. Lichty, "'The March of Time:' News as Drama," *The Journal of Popular Film* (vol. 2, no. 4, Fall, 1973), pp. 373–387.

27. Neil Hickey, "Moscow on the Hudson-via Satellite," *TV Guide* (January 19, 1985), p. 26. Inside the Soviet Union, D. Barschevsky has written "The Means of Expression in Documentaries as Influenced by the Methods of Mass Media," in *Problems of the History and Theory of Cinema* (VGIK Proc. Issue II, 1972) pp. 23–43.

28. See Jay Leyda, *Films Beget Films: A Study of the Compilation Film* (New York, 1964) and Nicholas Pronay, "The Newsreels: The Illusion of Actuality," in Paul Smith, ed., *The Historian and Film* (Cambridge, U.K. 1976), pp. 95–119. Newsreel "tricks" were so commonplace a popular perception during its heyday that MGM made a screwball comedy about it in 1938. The film was called *Too Hot to Handle* and starred Clark Gable and Myrna Loy. The controversy among historians emerged from two British mid-sixties TV documentary series entitled "The Great War" and "The Lost Peace."

29. See Peter Rollins, "Document and Drama in Desert Victory," *Film and History* (vol. IV, no. 2, May, 1974), pp. 11–13, Stig Hornshoj-Møller's

article on the use of *"Der Ewige Jude"* (1940) to teach students source criticism (Short and Fledelius, *op. cit.*), V. M. Magidov, "Film Documents: Problems of Source Analysis and Use in Historical Research," *Istorya* SSSR (I, 1983) pp. 92–103 translated and reprinted in the *Historical Journal of Film, Radio and Television* (vol. 4, no. 1, 1984), pp. 59–72, and William T. Murphy, "The Method of 'Why We Fight,' " *The Journal of Popular Film* (vol. 1, no. 3, Summer, 1972), pp. 185–196.

30. Three of John O'Connor's moving image teaching units for the New Jersey Humanities Council—Pare Lorentz's "The Plow that Broke the Plains," Edward R. Morrow's "See it Now: Senator Joseph R. McCarthy," and Alain Resnais's "Night and Fog"—provide excellent resources for teaching students to deal with documentary film and video in a critical manner. "The Plow," with its original ending restored, and excerpts from the McCarthy "See it Now" are included on the video tape/disc "Image as Artifact" package (American Historical Association, 1988) along with supporting print materials. The analysis of "Night and Fog" by Charles Krantz appears in *Film & History* (Vol. XV, no. 1, February, 1985), pp. 2–15.

31. Manchester (U.K.) University offers a course entitled "Hollywood" which covers much of this territory (Eatwell, *op. cit.*, p. 202).

32. Marcus S. Phillips, "The Nazi Control of the German Film Industry," *Journal of European Studies* (vol. 1, 1971), pp. 64–65.

33. Colin Shindler, *Hollywood Goes to War, Films and American Society, 1939–1952* (London, 1979) pp. 57–62.

34. See, for instance Nicholas Pronay and D. W. Spring, eds., *Propaganda, Politics and Film 1918–'45* (London, 1982), "The Political Censorship of Films in Britain between Wars," by Nicholas Pronay, pp. 98–125.

35. One of the unique elements of David Culbert and Peter Rollins's revisionist video on the American media's coverage of the 1968 Tet offensive, "Television's Vietnam" is their inclusion between the news stories of the commercials shown at that time. See Peter C. Rollins, "Television's Vietnam: The Visual Language of Television News," *Journal of American Culture* (4, 1981), pp. 114–135. The film has been shown in many classes both in journalism and history.

36. Nicholas Pronay, "The Moving Picture and Historical Research" *Journal of Contemporary History* (vol. 18, no. 3, July, 1983). M. Taylor, *British Propaganda during the First World War, 1914–1918* (London, 1982), and Nicholas Reeves, "Film Propaganda and its Audience: The Example of Britain's Official Films during the First World War," *Journal of Contemporary History* (vol. 18, no. 3, July, 1983), pp. 463–494 are good examples of research in this field. Jeffrey Richards's course at the University of Lancaster on "The Cinema and Society in Britain, 1930–1970" deals with some of these issues. An Archive of Mass Observation has been established in Britain.

37. The British Inter-University Consortium film on "Munich" by J. A. S. Grenville and Nicholas Pronay is especially concerned with this. A fascinating, if troubling, contemporary variation on this theme is the apparent confusion between the "real" world of policy and action and the "reel" world of movie roles in the mind of President Ronald Reagan investigated by Michael Paul Rogin in *Ronald Reagan, The Movie and Other Episodes in Political Demonology* (Berkeley, 1987), pp. 1–43.

38. For the Open University materials, *Supra*, fn. 12, for "Vietnam: A Television History," *Supra*, fn. 14. The Cadre Films historians have put together a set of papers on their first four productions *Goodby Billy: America Goes to War, 1917–18*, *The Frozen War: American Intervenes in Russia, 1918–'20*, *Storm of Fire: World War II and the Destruction of Dresden*, and *Will Rogers' 1920s: A Cowboy's Guide to the Times*. Additionally, a study guide to the last of these has also been printed. Nor are such ancillary materials limited to the print medium. The Thames Television producers of "The World at War" series deposited the oral histories that formed the spine for each epidode at the Imperial War Museum. Similarly, the full interviews for "Vietnam: A Television History" were turned over to the Harbor Campus of the University of Massachusetts for the use of future researchers and students. In addition, the ancillary materials for the latter included an audio cassette of "Voices of the Vietnam War." In Short and Fledelius eds., *op. cit.*, R. C. Raack reports on what appropriate educational packages might look like. British members of the Inter-University Film Consortium including Tony Altgate and Nicholas Pronay ("The Spanish Civil War" and "Munich" among others), Dutch historian Rolf Schuursma ("Anton Mussert"), and the late Danish historian Niels Skyum-Nielsen are also involved in this activity. Much more needs to be done by historians to provide raw materials and critical guides to both current and past film/video presentations. Currently this field is dominated by consulting firms paid by producers or networks to help sell their wares to educational audiences.

39. The Educational Services unit of the U.S. National Archives created boxes of materials including pictures and audiotapes for school use on specific topics, the British Historical Association's Secondary School Project has produced materials entitled "History through the Newsreel—the 1930's" (See Nicholas Pronay's report on this in Fledelius, Jørgensen, Skyum-Nielsen, and Swiatek, *op. cit.*), the BBC produced a series of "Scrapbooks," and Peter Boyle has produced a set of "chosen" cold-war newsreel extracts and a teaching guide (see his report in Fledelius *op. cit.*).

40. *Supra*. endnotes 16 and 17.

41. An example of this is presented on the "Image as Artifact" tape/disc set (*Supra.*, endnote 30) with supporting print materials.

42. One company, the Corporation for Entertainment and Learning, Inc., has recycled a collection of films and videotapes it originally accumulated as a resource for local television news into a 2,217 unit *Video Encyclopedia of the 20th Century* for use in schools. In addition to its 75 videocassettes or discs, the collection includes a five volume master index and a background reference volume. Based on this collection, C. E. L. produced "A Walk through the Twentieth Century with Bill Moyers," which, after its broadcast on PBS, became its largest selling video documentary series.

43. Northeastern University has recently joined a Boston-area consortium to acquire fifty-four Nazi-era feature films from the *Deutsche Instut Für Filmkinde*.

44. Using contact prints and inexpensive audiocassettes as their basis, these packages would be inexpensive to produce.

45. This technology, with which the Digital Equipment Corporation (in a system called Ivis) and others are already experimenting, combines com-

puter speed with instant search and retrieval capacity which only videodisc currently has. The "Image as Artifact" set (*Supra*, endnote 30) on videodisc offers the additional benifit of having historical commentary on a second simultaneous audio track that can be accessed at will. The tape version provides this material on an accompanying audio-cassette.

FRAMEWORK 4:
THE HISTORY OF THE
MOVING IMAGE AS
INDUSTRY AND ART FORM

The art forms of film and television and the industries which produce them are arguably among the most significant twentieth-century institutional subjects available for historical study. We may not be able to demonstrate in a specific or clinical way the impact that these media have had on culture, but it is safe to say that they rank with such other hard-to-quantify forces as the factory system and the automobile. They deserve the critical attention of historians, not only because of their effects in what we might term the mainstream of history, but also because of their importance as art forms and media per se. A few valuable and influential studies have laid out the groundwork for such work, among them Garth Jowett's *Film: The Democratic Art* and Robert Sklar's *Movie-Made America*. There is also the *Historical Journal of Film Radio and Television* which specializes in work by historians about the history of the media. Still, even if there have been solid first steps in the historical analysis of moving image art and institutions in their own right, there has yet to be a recognition of the importance of that institutional history within the mainstream of historical study. It is one thing for an author to refer to a film (such as *The Grapes of Wrath*) or to the popular image of Hollywood (in the Roaring Twenties, for example) to help characterize a period. It is quite another for a historian to recognize the importance of self-regulation and censorship within the American film industry as a characteristic in American economic life. Of all the textbook treatments of American history available, none does justice to the mass media as an industry, an art form, or a force in modern civilization. Garth Jowett's essay to follow addresses this important concern.

Part of the difficulty in addressing the history of media arts and industries is that, in addition to traditionally trained historians, the field is claimed by two other distinct academic disciplines—communication studies and film (or cinema) studies. Each has its own journals, its own professional societies, and its own networks of personal associations. Seldom do they exchange ideas with one another or with their colleagues across the campus in the history department. Much of the work in communications studies is based in social science research techniques and relates to audience impact. Jowett's essay also surveys some of the most important examples of this work which

should be readily accessible to historians. Bringing historians and cinema studies people together is a bit more complex.

There has been a continuing and appropriate distinct between what
has been commonly known as "film history"—the popular and nostalgic anecdotes about the public and private lives of the Hollywood
stars and their studios—and the more serious analytical work of traditionally trained historians. It is wrong to presume, however, that
historians were the only ones who were dissappointed with that product. Although fan biographies and pictorial "histories" continue to be
published, the field of "film history" has been transformed significantly over the past decade as specialists trained in cinema studies
turned to developing a substantial body of scholarship on the historical
analysis of film and television.

A gulf continues to exist. It can be traced largely to the complex
theoretical methodology and related terminology which cinema studies scholars bring to their work—the methodology of linguistic and
literary analysis, Marxist cultural studies, and psychoanalysis. It has
been argued that such reliance on privileged and technical jargon is
unnecessary, but cinema scholars retort that it is important in identifying the ways in which their work—work in an area only recently
recognized as an academic discipline—differs from what went before.
Some of this new work has been taken to extremes; a few film theorists
have carried their search for hidden meaning in film images so far
as to claim that a text *never* means what it actually says. Total reliance
on internal analysis has led some scholars to devalue or totally ignore
external evidence such as found in the "paper trail." Moreover, as
Robert Hewison noted in *Too Much: Art and Society in the Sixties, 1960–
75* (1987), if driven to their ultimate conclusions, the logic of such
influential thinkers as Louis Althusser and Michel Foucault is "that
man had no control over the ideological structures which formed his
perception of the world, and which he existed solely to reproduce."
Perhaps the ultimate critique of those committed to the extremes of
theoretical analysis was E. P. Thompson's attack upon them in *The
Poverty of Theory* (1978) as a "bourgeois *lumpen* intelligentsia." Hewison
takes a more measured view. It would surely be a mistake to reject
all recent theory because some have pressed it to the extreme. We do
not have to see individuals as deprived of free will or "powerless
against intervening ideological structures" in order to recognize that
"there is a connection [an unconscious as well as a conscious connec-
tion] . . . between what is written or painted or performed, and the
material conditions under which it was produced."[1]

Bridging the gap necessary to understand historical articles published in such important current cinema journals as *Wide Angle, Cinema
Journal, Screen,* or *Quarterly Review of Film Studies* will be easier for
those historians who are conversant with recent trends in the philosophy of history. The work of thinkers such as Hayden White and
Michel Foucault have been central to these new historians who were
trained first in cinema studies. In a significant way, Janet Staiger's

essay in this section represents an intellectual history of the current film history movement, tracing its roots in linguistic, literary, economic, social, psychological, and historical theory. Any scholar unfamiliar with the basic terminology or patterns of reasoning which much of cinema studies scholarship takes for granted today would do well to study her essay before launching themselves into that current literature.

Art history is another field which should inform this kind of historical investigation. One crucial distinction between the study of painting and the study of photography or film is that a painting is unique and therefore elite, whereas the technology of photography has opened images up both to ready duplication and to questions about whether or not they qualify as art.[2] Notwithstanding such an important distinction, however, there are striking resemblances between the new directions in art history over the past decade and the development of serious scholarship regarding film as social and cultural artifact. One basic theme in art history has been stimulated by the recognition that styles in painting (and sculpture and architecture, etc.), rather than being strictly formalistic extensions of earlier styles, are invariably related to other forces in the society. This can be seen in Samuel Edgerton's *Renaissance Rediscovery of Linear Perspective*, which demonstrates in detail how the new style in drawing came to represent a "visual metaphor" for many aspects of the contemporary culture of Florence, from the increasing rationality in banking and commerce to the growing political dominance of the Medici family.[3] For a closer consideration of particular works see the *Art in Context* series, edited by John Fleming and Hugh Honour, which interprets individual paintings using all the tools of the art historian, but does so in light of then current political events and social and economic trends. This is the obverse side of the framework for investigation discussed above under framework 2. We may study films for what they can tell us about the social and cultural values of the time, but those who are primarily interested in the close historical analysis of a film itself, or a genre of films, should be using the social and cultural history to help them understand the work of art.

Douglas Gomery and Robert Allen's *Film History: Theory and Practice* (New York: Knopf, 1985), provides a long awaited and very useful manual for film history research. Scholars interested in pursuing this framework for analysis should surely study Gomery and Allen's work. In addition to providing a solid and readable introduction to the nature of film history research in published sources, in film archives, and in manuscript archives relating to the industry, *Film History* offers several interesting models for "doing film history" and a comprehensive bibliography. The core of the book is a survey of four "Traditional Approaches to Film History," each with a short illustrative case study. Their discussion of (1) aesthetic film history, for example, spells out the "masterpiece tradition," which has marked much of the discussion of films past, and goes on to treat recent trends toward a history of changing film style, modes of production, and concepts of authorship, as they have related to the evolution of film art. The section on (2) technological film history concentrates on the connections between economic and technological innovation and includes a review of Gomery's interesting work on the coming of sound. In arguing the importance of (3) economic film history, they stress that "no film has ever been created outside of an economic context" and go on to offer a model for industrial analysis of Hollywood. Finally, under the rubrik of (4) social film history they adapt the basic questions raised by Ian Jarvie in his *Movies and Society*: Who made movies and why? Who saw films, how and why? What has been seen, how and why? And what has been said about the movies, by whom and why?

If Allen and Gomery's work is taken as the "how to" manual for a new and comprehensive approach to the research and writing of film history, then another book, David Bordwell, Janet Staiger, and Kristin Thompson's *The Classical Hollywood Cinema: Film Style and Mode of Production to 1960* (New York, Columbia University Press, 1985) provides a fine model for successful work in the field. In fact, in some ways the real accomplishment of *The Classical Hollywood Cinema* is to show in the context of a study flawlessly researched in both filmic and non-filmic sources that all four of Allen and Gomery's "traditional approaches" can and should be addressed together. Bordwell, Staiger, and Thompson's work represents at once the aesthetic, technological, economic, and social history of the classical Hollywood cinema, demonstrating the complex ways in which they are inseparable from one another. In addition, this book transcends the "masterpiece tradition" by basing its conclusions not on the rare and unusual aesthetic gems, but on the "typical" Hollywood product (isolated in a sample of one hundred films which the authors traveled to various archives across the country to view and analyze).

As the work of Gomery and Allen and that of Bordwell, Staiger, and Thompson make clear, the history of film and television is on one important level a history of technology.[4] The evolving technology of the media provides such an easy gauge of industrial development, however, that historians must be particularly careful to avoid the pitfalls of technological determinism. Reaching the same conclusions as recent scholars in the broader history of technology, Raymond Williams presents this point clearly in his *Television: Technology and Cultural Form*. We have a tendency, he argues, to presume that the technology itself arose, as it were, accidentally, as the simple result of scientific and technical research. What gets researched and what gets developed, however, are as much determined by social, cultural, and economic forces as by anything else.[5] Why have the developers and innovators in the field of personal computers assumed as their display device a monitor that by its looks is indistinguishable from the ubiquitous television set?

In attempting to analyse the impact of a technology historians must avoid the temptation of oversimplified assumptions as well. Most of what has been written about the earliest experiences of audiences with moving pictures, for example, stresses the great novelty involved—women raising their skirts in the front row to protect them from the ocean waves, people screaming as a locomotive seems to come directly toward them off the screen. Aside from the likely exaggeration that characterizes most such reports, we should also remember that there had been a long history of screen practice predating the invention of the actual moving picture. Sometimes magic lantern shows (a technology which can be dated back several centuries) even included mechanically manipulated moving images on the screen.[6] To reconstruct the impact that a technology is presumed to have had, we must carefully reconstruct the larger pattern of experience within which people perceived the innovation.

While the very newness of a technological innovation may captivate a culture for a time, the form in which that new technology catches hold more permanently is surely a determination of that culture and its economic system. As Warren Susman put it, "we should be thinking 'ecologically' in terms of a total, interacting environment."[7] Why feature-length films as we know them, for example? Why half-hour television programs? Why sitcoms? Why soap-operas? The introduction of a new technology into any culture must be understood in the context of other cultural forces at the time—including other media. Certainly the shape of television as an industry was directly influenced by the structure of radio broadcasting —including preexisting corporate entities, a preexisting reliance on advertising as the source of income, and a preexisting pattern of government regulation. Still, the technology itself can be a powerful factor. Consider the influence of the now common home video recorder on the predictability of television advertising returns. What does "prime-time" mean in terms of fixing the price for a minute of television advertising now that many people record their favorite shows, watching them when they want to and fast-forwarding the tape past the commercials?

Anthony Aldgate's teaching experience in Britain's Open University is quite different from the typical American classroom. His essay in this section strongly reminds us of the importance of maintaining the goals of our history courses when we turn to visual analysis.

SUMMARY

To sum up, traditional historians tend to neglect the close analysis of the visual image. Cinema studies scholars may too often rest on their theoretical base, doing injustice to the broader historical context of their discussion; those in communications studies may be too limited in their concern with what can be quantified. We must find ways to integrate the research in the collateral fields of communications and cinema studies into a comprehensive approach to the history of mass media art and industries. Garth Jowett's and Janet Staiger's essays to follow should help to foster that integration.

Content

In the first place, studying the content of a moving image document in the context of framework 4 involves the recognition that a careful viewing of the films themselves provides important evidence for film history. Until recently few film historians have tried to do more than summarize plots and general stylistic elements in the films they discussed. Moreover, most of those films were the ones recognized as "masterpieces" and seen most widely in 16mm rental prints and on TV. At least in part this has been due to the inaccessibility of film archives and the special projectors or viewing tables necessary for close visual analysis. Another factor has been that in the past ten to fifteen years those film scholars most interested in closely studying the image itself were often applying thoroughgoing theoretical models which were (and are) at their root antihistorical. Perhaps the most important contribution of the film historians discussed here and in Janet Staiger's essay to follow is that they are able to apply important aspects of film theory to their work without losing sight of their ultimate objective—to research and write the history of cinema and television.

Production

Understanding the mode of production is central to the study of film history. To some extent this is technological history and to some extent economic; both of these factors and other dominant industrial practices invariably influenced the ways in which films looked and the messages they delivered. For certain historians, the measure of a great film is the extent to which it takes advantage of the technological opportunities available at the time of its production. Gomery and Allen argue persuasively that this is an unsatisfactory approach, because there are often jumps and gaps in the relation of technology to film style. This is brought home perhaps most clearly by David Bordwell's treatment of the development of deep focus techniques in relation to *Citizen Kane* (1941); not only was the technology available long before (some of it thirty years before) Gregg Toland began to work with Orson Welles, but once the flurry of interest concerning Toland's creative use of the technique had passed, its use never became the dominant mode.[8] Gomery and Allen's outline of Hollywood's industrial market structure and economic performance is also instructive.[9] A recent review of the Bordwell, Staiger, and Thompson book noted that a decade ago, film historians might argue that it was too much to try to study the paper archives on the industry in any comprehensive way because the "documents for this kind of cinema history either do not exist, cannot be examined impartially, or are highly suspect." "As if in some way," the reviewer noted, "this were not true of all historical documents." Today serious film history cannot be conducted without getting into the archival record of the industry.

Reception

Finally, to study reception, scholars of film history must devote special attention to the promotional efforts of film distributors. The way a film was advertised to the public may offer insight into the way the public responded to it. The study of moviegoing is a part of social and cultural history, but in a slightly different way it is the consumption side of industrial history as well. How was that experience controlled by the producers and distributors? How much of it had to do with matters other than the films themselves, such as the offering of air conditioning or the sumptuous design of movie palaces? Most of the discussion here has been about film, but the history of television audiences is important as well. Perhaps no other industry is able to be so immediately sensitive to the whims of popular opinion as perceived in the daily and weekly audience rating reports on their programs.

NOTES

1. *Too Much: Art and Society in the Sixties, 1960–75* (London, Methuen, 1987), pp. 287–89.
2. The key reference on this issue is Walter Benjamin, "The Work of Art in the Age of Mechanical Reproduction," in Hannah Arendt, editor, *Illuminations* (New York: Harcourt, Brace and World, 1960), pp. 219–253.
3. (New York, 1975). For a beginning survey of this trend in art history scholarship see Svetlana Alpers, "Is Art History?" in *Daedalus* (Summer, 1977) pp. 1–13. A recent important addition to the scholarship is Michael Baxandall's *Patterns of Intention: On The Historical Explanation of Pictures* (New Haven, 1985).
4. Note particularly the continuing work of Raymond Fielding, *A Technological History of Motion Pictures and Television*, third edition (Berkeley: University of California Press, 1979), and such recent publications as Barry Salt, *Film Style and Technology: History and Analysis* (London, 1983); *Cinema and Technology: Image, Sound, Colour* (London, 1985), and Theresa DeLauretis and Steven Heath, ed., *The Cinematic Apparatus* (New York, 1980). Work has continued on the technology of television as well. See Joseph H. Udelson's *The Great Television Race: A History of the American Television Industry, 1925–1941* (University of Alabama Press, 1982), and Brian Winston, *Misunderstanding Media* (Cambridge, Mass., 1987).
5. *Television, Technology and Cultural Form* (New York: Shocken Books, 1975), see especially chapters one and two.
6. One young film historian doing especially interesting work in this area is Charles Musser. His "Towards a History of Screen Practice," unpublished paper presented at the Society for the History of Technology annual meeting at MIT in 1984, traced the projected moving image from the sixteenth century to the twentieth, making dramatically clear why accounts of the responses of early film audiences could not ignore this "prehistory" of the cinema.
7. *Culture as History*, p. 253.
8. In Bordwell, Staiger, and Thompson, *The Classical Hollywood Cinema*, pp. 341–352.
9. *Film History*, pp. 138–143.

Garth Jowett has a Ph.D. in History from the University of Pennsylvania, and is a Professor in the School of Communication, University of Houston, where he served as Director for five years. His special interests are the history of communications, propaganda, and popular culture. He is the author of Film: The Democratic Art *(Little Brown, 1976), a detailed history of movie-going in America, as well as* Movies as mass Communication *(Sage, 1981), and* Propaganda and Persuasion *(Sage, 1986) with Victoria O'Donnell. He has recently completed a book on culture and communication, and his work in progress is a social history of television.*

MASS MEDIA, HISTORY, AND THE DEVELOPMENT OF COMMUNICATIONS RESEARCH

Garth S. Jowett

In the last decade, a series of important publications have sensitized historians and other students of American culture to place a greater emphasis on such aspects of the material culture as motion pictures, radio, and television when dealing with the history of the twentieth century. The increased quality of this body of work, which utilizes a wide variety of methodologies, has contributed significantly to our understanding of the role of the so-called "entertainment media" in the shaping of our society and its culture. Now it is heartening to see the first American history survey texts which devote more than a cursory glance at the mass media. No longer are these subjects relegated into illustrative and anecdotal "side-bars" designed to rekindle interest in the flagging student reader. Now they are an integral part of the explanation of the social and cultural development of modern American society. This belated recognition and elevation of the mass media into prominence as potential agents of change are due in large part to the increased availability of secondary works which have attempted to highlight and explain the manner in which the mass media exert their "influence", and what effect this ultimately has on the society and culture.

While there have been demonstrable improvements in how mass communication is treated in history texts, a great deal more must be accomplished before it can be claimed that historians know how to interpret the role of the media as an integrative aspect of their narrative explanations. Teachers of history should be aware of the facile nature of much of the discussions of media in the textbooks they are using, and take appropriate corrective measures.[1] The first part of this paper examines the problems of writing communications history and looks at some of the ways in which textbooks incorporate the history of the mass media into their narratives; the second part explains what historians should know about the nature of media influence in order to develop their own valid critical perspectives; and the third part makes some suggestions for future research opportunities in the field of communications history.

COMMUNICATIONS HISTORY:
THE FORGOTTEN DIMENSION

Despite the improvements noted above, the importance of communications, both as technological systems and social process, has been virtually ignored by mainstream historians.[2] Except for the work of Harold Adams Innis and his fellow Canadian, Marshall McLuhan, there have been almost no macro-theories attempting to relate the role of communication as an agent for historical changes.[3] Only now are the first tentative theories beginning to emerge which show promise of providing a useful matrix for systematically evaluating the advent of a communication system into a society.[4] What we clearly lack are more specific examinations of the social, political, economic, and cultural preconditions which favored the introduction of new communication systems. This is particularly and anomalously true of modern media systems, where we still lack cohesive and accessible explanations of the impact of these vital technologies. As Innis points out in his difficult book, *The Bias of Communication*, "Inventions in communication compel realignments in the monopoly or the oligopoly of knowledge."[5]

James W. Carey, our most astute interpreter of Innis's work, has illuminated the core of Innis's thought on the "bias of communication":

"The explanation for this historical fact Innis derived from a conception of society based upon a model of competition appropriated from economics and extended to all social institutions. And in this competitive model, competition for a new means of communication was a principal axis of the competitive struggle. Innis argued that the available media of communication influence very strongly the forms of social organization that are possible. Thus media influence the kinds of human associations that can develop in any period."[6]

Yet few histories of communications systems take advantage of the rich tapestry left for us to ponder in the work of Innis and McLuhan. Much of their work, particularly that of the mercuric, self-styled media prophet McLuhan has become an intellectual password for faddism, highlighted so pointedly by Woody Allen in his film *Annie Hall*, in which McLuhan plays himself as a cult figure. Interest in the work of Harold Innis, while always of interest to those few who toiled in the vineyards of communications history, has only recently received wider exposure.[7] The relegation of this important indigenous body of thought to the sidelines in favor of European-originated theories stemming from Marxism and structuralism has had unfortunate consequences for the development of theories of communications history. While both Innis and McLuhan require close reading before one can reap any intellectual benefits from the dense, often frustrating prose, studded with obscure references and brilliant juxtapositions, the ultimate rewards are sufficient to shape an entire academic career; and certainly contain enough suggestions for paths of research to keep one busy for a lifetime. As Paul Heyer noted: "It is to pay Innis the highest tribute to state that the critical method he outlined can be reworked in the light of new knowledge and used to challenge some of the gaps and speculative assumptions that abound in his work."[8]

The work of Marshall McLuhan has suffered from both over- and misinterpretation, with the result that his contribution to the study of communications history has been muddied. Yet few historians can fail to be intrigued by the underlying thrust in all of his work; namely that the meaning and effect of any communications innovation is to be found in the way it structures thought and perception. Thus, for McLuhan, the introduction of a new form of communication or information transferring capability will eventually alter what he called the "sense ratio" of that society. He defines the sense ratio as essentially the way in which the society perceives itself by utilizing the various communications media available to it. In McLuhan's terms, if the existing sense ratio is disturbed by the introduction of a new "extension" of the human senses, such as the motion picture or television, this will necessitate a readjustment and will eventually require some form of accommodation process. He saw the technology of communications media as an extension of the human senses, thus film and television become extensions of the human eye, and radio extends the human ear.[9] While much of what McLuhan theorized has proven to be difficult to demonstrate in a clear empirical manner, his notions of a predominant sense ratio at a given point in time in a society, and the stimulating questions surrounding the notion of the "extension" of the human senses have not been fully explored by historians, and almost totally ignored in current film and television scholarship.

The work of these two Canadian scholars, and others who have developed similar historical perspectives on the evolution of communication systems as historical agents of change, such as Walter Ong, Jack Goody, Elizabeth Eisenstein, Colin Cherry, Eric Havelock, Michael T. Clanchy, Raymond Williams, and Harvey J. Graff, must be taken into account when dealing with the history of communication. These scholars and others have begun to point the way toward an understanding of the historical role of communication systems in altering and shaping societies and their cultures.[10]

THE TREATMENT OF FILM IN
AMERICAN HISTORY TEXTS

The historian's understanding of the role of communications in historical evolution is best illustrated by examining the manner in which one medium, the motion picture, has been treated in basic American history textbooks as an aspect of twentieth-century life. As it would be impossible to examine every source of historical writing which could potentially deal with the motion picture, this brief analysis is limited to an evaluation of a random sample of the major textbooks used in the teaching of those large survey courses in American history which form the sustaining base of most history departments.[11] These texts, usually the result of the synthesis of a large number of primary and mostly secondary sources, provide a clear insight into where historians position the motion picture within their conceptualization of U.S. history. It is, for those of us who deal daily with the study of the communications media in society, a very sobering intellectual experience to discover that our "mediacentrism" is not widely shared by our colleagues in the field of general history.

To be fair, these books are prepared with a very definite audience in mind. The publishers of such textbooks attempt to regain their substantial investments by ensuring that their authors write (construct would be a more apt term) books with a wide potential for adoption at the freshman level. If the junior college market can also be satisfied with the level of the text, then all the better. The result of this financial imperative is that most textbooks cover the tried-and-true territories, with emphasis on great men (increasingly women), politics, presidents, economics, wars, and lastly and often least, the arts as symbols of cultural development. The communications media are seldom given more than a token glance, and their role in the socialization process is all but ignored. If the mass media are discussed in the course of the narrative, it is usually in the context of entertainment trends, fads, or a listing of inventions which "revolutionized the twentieth century." The motion picture in particular is subject to wild misinterpretation in terms of the medium's integral position as a contributor to the shape of modern mass culture. It is typically relegated to the position of entertaining "filler" material to provide the textbook reader with relief from the endless parade of political, economic, and personality facts.

The discussion of "the movies" appears in three basic categories in American history textbooks, with a few subvariations:

1. *The "inventions" of Thomas Edison.* This category usually credits Edison with inventing and/or perfecting the motion picture apparatus; it lumps the medium together with the electric light bulb and the

phonograph. Even the most prominent historians such as Arthur S. Link of Princeton and his co-authors can make statements such as, "The story of the rise of the motion picture industry is as dramatic as the saga of the automobile. Thomas A. Edison invented the first motion picture camera in 1896."[12] Sometimes there are follow-on statements about the growth in popularity seen in the shift from nickelodeons to picture palaces. Rebecca Brooks Gruver explains this complex transition and its cultural consequences as follows:

> The introduction of the motion picture near the turn of the century heralded a new era in entertainment. The early moviehouses, called nickelodeons because of the nickel admission, showed crudely made five-minute films of dancing girls or boxing matches. Little more than a decade later, D. W. Griffith's *Birth of a Nation* elevated the film to a serious art . . . the entertainments available to urban dwellers not only helped them to forget the frustrations of lives in thrall to industry, but drew Americans of many different backgrounds together in similar ways of living and thinking.[13]

2. *Inventions which shook the world.* Taken together with radio and the automobile (and later television), the movies are seen as contributing to major social and cultural changes. Unfortunately, much of the emphasis on the movies' contribution centers around the sexual revolution which historians seem to see occurring in the early twenties. Thus Charlie Chaplin, Douglas Fairbanks Sr., Rudolph Valentino, and Clara Bow tend to receive prominent attention as the paradigm of movie popularity and sexuality. Under a section titled "The Craze for Diversion," Gruver notes: "Every week millions of people of all ages lost themselves to the glamor and excitement of the silver screen."[14] As another example of over-simplification, Richard Current and his co-authors describe the role of movies in this manner:

> Motion pictures flamboyantly heralded the new moral code and together with tabloid papers helped fabricate false stereotypes of the period. An estimated 50 million people a week went to theaters to see the "it" girl, Clara Bow, the glamorous Rudolph Valentino, the comedian Charlie Chaplin, gangster pictures, Westerns, and such great spectacles as the first film version of *The Ten Commandments*. These films helped standardize American habits, and not always in the most edifying way.[15]

3. *Movies as historical evidence.* Certain touchstone films, such as *Birth of a Nation* (1915), *The Sheik* (1921), or *Rebel Without a Cause* (1955) are constantly used to illustrate changes in social and cultural mores. These films, and others are often discussed in miniplot versions to demonstrate society's acceptance of certain trends. When films are used in such a manner by historians writing textbooks, the emphasis is usually on the film's content as a reflector and not as a shaper of behavior. Seldom is there any real attempt at systematic content analysis to determine whether this film was idiosyncratic or a true example

of a trend. Also, vague generalities and absurd evaluations of the role of motion pictures are very common. While rather extreme in its gross inaccuracies, the following quotation from a widely used book by a major historian, John Garraty, is indicative of this problem:

> In the years before and after World War II most movies were tasteless, gaudy, mindless trash aimed at titillating the senses and catering to the prejudices of the multitude. Sex, crime, war, romantic adventure, broad comedy, and luxurious living were their main themes, endlessly repeated in predictable patterns. Most popular actors and actresses were either handsome, talentless sticks or so-called character actors who were type-cast over and over again as heroes, villains, comedians . . . Nevertheless the motion picture made positive contributions to American culture.[16]

How can we account for this strange treatment of the motion picture? Historians should be concerned about these issues because these are the books which shape the historical consciousness of the majority of our college population. Why is the role of the mass media so misunderstood? First, for most authors of textbooks, there is a failure to undertake any original research coupled with a reliance upon out-of-date secondary resources (although from which secondary resource Garraty could have obtained his peculiar viewpoint on pre-1941 films is hard to fathom). The lack of original research can also be attributed to the time constraints under which these books are usually written. However, the major conceptual problem in dealing with the history of the mass media lies in the constant reliance on those traditionally understood and acknowledged areas such as politics, economics, and personalities to "explain" historical causality.

The writing of history is still infused with elitism, although there are numerous signs that "history from the bottom up" is beginning to receive academic legitimization and that this approach is being used in some of the newer survey textbooks. One such example is the work of Irwin Unger in his textbook, *These United States: The Question of Our Past*, in which he demonstrates a very clear grasp of the latest scholarship in both social and film history in fairly lengthy sections dealing with the changing composition of early film audiences, and the complex industrial and cultural evolution of this entertainment medium.[17] The availability of more significant primary works telling historians why they should pay attention to the media of communication and how "media influence" can be interpreted by historians will go a long way toward solving this problem, and perhaps open up the field to a wider range of historical cross-fertilization.[18]

In the more traditional monographic histories dealing with American social and cultural issues, there is evidence that the communications media in general, and motion pictures in particular are beginning to be considered as primary contributors to the shaping of modern thought. (Of course, television is also receiving attention for its role in the period after World War II.) Using more sophisticated methods of content analysis than ever before, as well as a creative intuition, historians are now using the reflective quality of motion picture content to help explain aspects of American thought and behavior. Richard H. Pells innovatively demonstrates how this can be done in his book *Radical Visions and American Dreams: Cultural and Social Thought in the Depression Years.* He notes: "By the 1930s the age of the book was giving away to the age of sight and sound. Henceforth, those who sought a cultural revolution in the United States might have to rely less on the arguments of the printed page and more and more on the image of the stage, the radio, the picture magazine, the newsreel, and the film. In the process, the traditional problems of political strategy and social philosophy were supplanted by a growing fascination with the mass media and popular taste."[19] It is unfortunate that Pells's work has been largely ignored by both social and media historians, for he provides a pathway for incorporating the study of film into a larger historical context.

Another more recent example is Emily S. Rosenberg's *Spreading the American Dream: American Economic and Cultural Expansion, 1890–1945,* which discusses the role of mass communication as an agent of American economic domination. Her work includes an encouraging examination of the U.S. government's relationship to the film industry, which demonstrates that she has read the salient literature on media "cultural imperialism" and film history.[20] These, and other current studies of American history which evince more than a secondary grasp of the role and significance of the communications media, auger well for the future of communications history and for its incorporation into the mainstream of social and cultural historical thought.

THE EFFECTS OF MASS COMMUNICATION: A PRIMER FOR HISTORIANS

The incorporation and evaluation of mass media's role as an integral part of the "American experience" would be enormously enhanced if historians understood some of the more fundamental theoretical aspects of what can be loosely called "mass media influence." During the twentieth century an increasingly sophisticated body of research has emerged which has helped in our understanding of the complex interrelationship between social and cultural change and the development of the mass media and its varying content forms. A large, accessible literature of social scientific findings as well as a growing body of theoretical work in the "cultural studies" tradition exists to illuminate the path for historians wishing to write meaningfully about the mass media. This section will essentially follow the social scientific stream, because the cultural studies area has been covered elsewhere in this book. It is intended to provide a brief overview of the current theoretical perspectives on the nature of media "effects," especially as it pertains to motion pictures and television.

Changes in the Way We Think About the Mass Media:

During the nineteenth and early twentieth centuries, there was great concern evidenced about the obviously increasing social and cultural role of the new media of communication, such as newspapers, magazines, the telegraph, and the telephone and this is reflected in a wide range of contemporary literature, from newspaper editorials to sermons from the pulpit. The tantalizing questions created by the perceived power of the mass media were asked by a variety of different constituencies. The newly emerging group of professional social workers, both the socially conscious and the morally concerned clergy, the increasingly organized educators, and law enforcement officers all voiced a concern about the "influential" powers of the mass media to shape and direct the culture.[21]

It was not, however, until the period after World War I that the first systematic attempts were made to apply the research methodologies of the emerging social sciences to measure the influence of the mass media. In the period before 1928 the potential "effects" of the mass media were an issue subjected to a wide range of opinionated speculations, usually based on personal observation, quasiscientific survey research, or crude content analysis. Most of these early studies of mass culture were directly aimed at providing information for political or moral issues—concerns about health issues, dire predictions of immorality, especially because of the unsupervized mingling of the sexes, or the need for more stringent forms of control over children. Very often these "findings" had the desired result and precipitated the imposition of specific social controls, such as attempts at censorship, the creation of health regulations for the buildings where the activities took place, or age restrictions. Thus on a purely sociopolitical level, the mass media's increasing cultural and social role was scrutinized very carefully in this early period.

Much of the negative attitude toward the mass media in the first decades of the twentieth century was the result of the unfortunate combination of historical events and intellectual perspectives which lent credibility to the belief that the misuse of the mass media was a potential threat to the existing social and political order. In particular, the unprecedented use of the mass media for propaganda purposes during World War I provided more than enough substantiation of this danger for that group of concerned citizens, who historian Henry F. May has called "the custodians of the culture."[22] The skills of the new professional mass communicators were utilized during the global conflict to create a barrage of propaganda messages that assaulted the ears of civilians and soldiers at every turn. In no previous conflict had "words" and "images" been so important, reflecting as it did the fundamental change in the nature of war in an age of mass communication and mass production. In order to mobilize not just armies, but entire populations, the mass media were used extensively. When, at the end of the war, revelations were made about the extensive "selling" of the war to civilian populations often using false or overdramatized information, this created a deep suspicion of the mass media and the specialized form of deliberately managed persuasion—propaganda.[23]

There is little doubt that the propaganda used during World War I was effective, but this success must be understood in its historical context. For the first time in history, nations were able to use a form of instantaneous communication to draw on the collective power of their entire populations by linking the individual to a larger societal need. As a result, the general public indicated a response to mass media messages as never before, and this reaction reinforced already existing fears about the potentially dangerous role of the mass media in mass society. The prevailing theories of psychology and the perception of how the mass media worked were relatively unsophisticated, and this led to a misinterpretation of how powerful the media really were. With little appreciation of the specific social and political conditions which made wartime propaganda messages so effective, these incomplete and inaccurate behavioral theories and misperceptions colored much of the thinking about the mass media for the next twenty years.[24]

Denis McQuail, in his elegant and concise survey of the theories of mass communication, has noted that:

> The development of thinking about media effects may be said to have a 'natural history', since it has been strongly shaped by the circumstances of time and place and influenced by several 'environmental' factors: the interests of governments and lawmakers; the needs of industry; the activities of pressure groups; the purposes of political and commercial propagandists; the current concern of public opinion; the fashions of social science. It is not surprising that no straight path of cumulative development of knowledge can easily be discerned.[25]

The history of the research on mass media influence can be considered in three phases.[26]

Phase 1: 1900–1930

The first phase, which extends from the late nineteenth century to the early 1930s, saw the mass media credited with considerable power to shape attitudes and opinions and consequently to direct human behavior. As we noted before, not only was this perspective enhanced by the apparent success of the propaganda efforts during the First World War, but the continued use of propaganda during the interwar period, especially by the rising fascist states, reinforced the notion of "powerful" media. Also at this time large scale advertising campaigns, using national mass media, seemed to foster an increased demand for consumer goods. In the climate of the acceptance of such beliefs, the first tentative attempts were made to scientifically assess the role and power of the media, using surveys and experiments drawing largely from the emerging hybrid social science of social psychology.[27]

The accepted "theory" of mass media influence was based upon various perceptions of stimulus-response theory, especially as it was framed by the then dominant *instinct* psychology. This suggested that basic human nature was fairly uniform from one individual to another, and thus individuals would respond to a given stimuli in similar ways. Also much was made of the nonrational and emotional nature of human beings, especially after the influential work of Sigmund Freud gained favor. The mass media, the source of such powerful stimuli, and with the potential for misuse by unscrupulous politicians and opportunists, were naturally viewed with uneasiness. The reasons for the dramatic impact of wartime propaganda were readily misinterpreted in the context of these psychological theories.

It is important to note that during this first phase of media research, while no recognized scholar ever articulated any systematic theory of mass media using the stimulus-response model, this was, nevertheless, the underlying concept for most early experimentation and theorizing. It was a later generation of scholars who (somewhat erroneously) were responsible for suggesting that these early research studies were developed and operated under a concept of a "direct-influence, powerful media," known variously as the "magic bullet" theory, the "hypodermic needle theory" or the "transmission belt" theory.[28] As De Fleur and Rokeach noted: "The basic idea behind these names is that the media messages are received in a uniform way by every member of the audience and that immediate and direct responses are triggered by such stimuli."[29] In this view of the history of mass communication research, there has been a gradual refinement and eventual abandonment of the "direct-influence" theory, to be replaced by a more sophisticated understanding of the psychological differentiation between individual humans and the factors which create a varied, and therefore, less powerful response to similar stimuli. This is known as the "limited effects theory". Such theoretical refinements required the development of research techniques which could provide more empirical evidence for making judgments about the effects of mass communication.

Phase 2: 1928–1955

At the beginning of the second phase, in the late 1920s, we find the first tentative research studies using empirical research strategies especially devised to gauge the impact of communications on different aspects of modern life. Once again, the concern for the growing importance of mass culture acts as a stimulus for specific research. By 1928, the movies had become a major social and cultural force throughout the world. In order to examine the extent of the impact of the motion picture on American children, a series of separate research studies, known collectively as the Payne Fund Studies, were conducted between 1928 and 1930. The individual studies were published under the general series title "Motion Pictures and Youth" in

1933 and still constitute the most extensive empirical evaluation ever undertaken of the role of the movies in American society. All of the social scientists who conducted this pioneering research were cautious in their interpretations about the nature of motion picture influence on the audience. In their findings they emphasized that the same film would affect children differently, depending on the age, sex, social and cultural predispositions, parental influences, and past experiences of the child. However their efforts to maintain a scientific objectivity were undermined by the deliberately contrived publication of journalist Henry James Forman's book, *Our Movie-Made Children* (1933). This simplified and sensationalized description of the actual ("scientific") findings sparked a fierce battle about the morality of motion pictures and generated demands for more stringent methods of social control of the medium.[30] The research methodology employed (most of which was devised specifically for this project) was unsophisticated by today's standards; the interpretation of the findings were often naive and suspect. However, the Payne Fund Studies still stand as a significant watershed in the development of both social psychology and communication studies.[31]

During the 1930s and through the Second World War there was an increase in interest in using the mass media for active persuasion or information.[32] This interest came from two sources, the desire of advertisers for greater effectiveness, especially in the medium of commercial radio, and from governments as the propaganda efforts of the competing forces intensified on an international scale. These articulated needs served as the stimuli for the next series of significant studies which have helped to shape our understanding of how mass communication works and particularly in the case of Paul Lazarsfeld and his associates at Columbia University in the late 1930s, provided the first empirical studies of the extent of mass cultural influence.[33]

The pioneering work of Lazarsfeld and later Carl Hovland and his group doing research on propaganda and attitude change at Yale during and after the war, was very influential in suggesting that media effects were not as powerful as originally thought.[34] Most of the research in this phase underscored the very specific, and often limiting context within which mass communication influence could be successful. The dominant perspective was that "*some* media, can affect *some* people, at *some* times," as described by Joseph Klapper (then the head of CBS research, and a former pupil of Lazarsfeld) in his book, *The Effects of Mass Communication*, which was published in 1960. This summation of the research findings of the second phase was extremely influential in promoting the theory of "limited effects."[35]

As a result of the widespread acceptance of the "limited effects" theories, communication researchers became dismayed by the apparent ineffectiveness of the mass media to bring about significant change in such socially relevant areas such as politics, race relations, and education. As this second phase drew to a close, there was a rather pessimistic feeling about increasing the knowledge of how the media worked, best symbolized by Bernard Berelson's infamous statement at the end of the 1950s that the field of mass communications research was "dead."[36] As McQuail notes:

> It was not that media had been shown to be, under all conditions, without effects but that they operated within a pre-existing structure of social relationships and in a given social and cultural context. These social and cultural factors have a primary role in shaping choice, attention and response by audiences . . . It was particularly hard to accept for those who made a living out of advertising and propaganda and for those who doubted that the whole story had been written and who were reluctant to dismiss the possibility that media might indeed have important social effects.[37]

Phase 3: 1955-The Present

The third phase of media research emerged out of a combination of these older theories of "limited effects" and new, sometimes non-empirical perspectives of how the media do operate in our society. Even as empirical research of mass communications was receiving increased attention in the period after 1939, competing voices suggested that "effects research," concentrating as it did on the degree of "exposure" to given content and the measurement of resulting attitude or opinion changes, did not provide a comprehensive picture of mass communication influence. In particular, the philosophical perspectives of the members of the Frankfurt School, especially the critiques of Theodor Adorno and Walter Benjamin, provided an intellectual platform for later examinations of the role of the mass media and its content forms within the entire social and cultural fabric.[38]

Throughout the 1950s and 1960s while some American sociologists were engaged in the intense debate on the merits of "mass society" and "mass culture", the newly emerging, specialized researchers from doctoral programs in communications were busy developing highly refined, empirically based models of mass media influence. It was the empirical, limited effects model which provided the dominant paradigm for media studies until the mid 1970s.[39] However, while much of the "mass society" debate ultimately proved to be an intellectual dead end, in recent years the revival of interest in the cultural studies approach has rekindled an awareness of some of the more significant work which emerged in this period.

What is significant is that by the 1950s the study of mass society and mass culture (which included studies of motion pictures) had become almost completely divorced from the mainstream developments in mass communication research. The increased emphasis on developing a "scientific" theory of communication, which would encompass all forms of communication, forced researchers to concentrate on communication as a process; this left very little room for the study of the cultural content and influence of the mass media. Contributing to this was the increasing importance of "client-centered research," which concentrated efforts on seeking the measurement of audience effects. In a hypocritical stance, the media industries wanted to convince advertisers that they were powerful instruments of persuasion when it came to selling products; but, at the same time, they downplayed their role in affecting cultural change. Few media industries were willing to subsidize research to establish how influential the mass media were in changing American culture! In some ways this stance was understandable, for they were fearful of government regulation, such as had befallen the movie industry in the early years of this century.

The emergence of the cultural and critical studies approaches to mass communication in the 1970s signalled a major shift in the direction of media studies away from the concentration on "effects" toward a broader range of perspectives.[40] Starting in Europe, where the tradition of Marxist and neo-Marxist scholarship and analysis is more accepted, and building upon the earlier work of the Frankfurt School of theorists, a new, more culturally centered focus began to emerge in communication studies. It was not long before empirical research found itself under justified attack from American as well as European scholars for its failure to deal adequately with the totality of media impact on a society. It was suggested that research which used surveys and experimental designs were "individualistic and microanalytical," and therefore did not reveal much about the social and cultural context of the communication act. As James Curran and his colleagues have pointed out: "The initial response [on the part of critical and cultural theorists] . . . was to dismiss out of hand empirical communications research as being uniformly uninteresting. The media, they argued, were ideological agencies that played a central role in maintaining class domination; research studies that denied media influence were so disabled in their theoretical approach as to be scarcely worth confronting (or indeed, even reading)."[41] There was a natural response from traditional media researchers that past work in meta-theorizing about the media (in the form of the mass society-mass culture theories) had been equally as inadequate in its attempts to understand the role of media in society.

Since the middle of the 1970s a melding of the two approaches (which, in reality were not as far apart as some scholars attempted to establish) has begun to enrich all of communications research. Researchers working within the Marxist, critical tradition have begun to rely upon data generated by empirical methods, such as surveys and audience measurements; while those working in empirical communications research have been sensitized by the Marxist critiques that "more attention needs to be paid to the influence of the media on the ideological categories and frames of reference through which people understand the world."[42] Conversely, in a recent article examining "Critical Theory and the Politics of Empirical Research," one of the leading American critical theorists, Lawrence Grossberg suggested that:

> We need to bring some of the sophisticated research techniques available to us today into critical research. At the very least, the nature of the mass media and the sheer size of its audience (not to mention the differences between them) seem to demand new forms of critical research.[43]
> ... the attempt to study communication in the contemporary world—in which messages are effective in part because of their proliferation and repetition, and in which the mass audience is no longer conceivable as either a simple aggregate of sociological fractions or a common psychological structure—may, in fact, demand the appropriation of such research practices.[44]

In recent years communications research has concerned itself more and more with issues of long term change, the nature of cognitions rather than attitude or opinion change, and shifts in structures of belief, ideology, and cultural patterns. Perhaps the greatest shift has been in the growing interest evidenced in all aspects of the practices and ideologies of the institutions which are responsible for the creation and dissemination of media messages.[45] In particular, the interrelationship between the economic base of these industries and the "production of culture" has been a pivotal point in the understanding of the "media messages" which shape and perpetuate the dominant ideologies in a society.[46] Clearly the field of communications research has been enriched by the amalgamation of theory and empirical research, and this area is now particularly promising for historians wishing to do meaningful work in the history of communications, or to incorporate the analysis of various types of mass media content into their course materials.

Media Research and Long Term Effects

Most empirical media research is done on the level of the individual, and seldom on groups of people as collective entities. Such data might be collected to appear as aggregate information in the form of public opinion polls, surveys, or audience preferences, but the base is always a measurement of change in the individual. The type of information most useful to historians, the long term assessment of social and cultural change created by exposure to mass media, is by its very nature extremely difficult to measure and also holds little interest for commercially oriented media researchers.[47] What little research there is on the role of the media in affecting long term change was usually the result of "developmental" or "diffusion" studies relating to the use of media for campaigns for technical advance, agriculture, or health issues. In recent years these theories have undergone a significant restructuring away from the "dominant paradigm" of powerful media forces imposed and manipulating from above, toward a more culturally integrative approach, emphasizing the role of media as part of the overall cultural and social system.[48]

Specifically, there has been very little empirically based work dealing with the long term effects of motion pictures and television. At the time of the motion picture's greatest popularity and influence, during the 1930s and 1940s, no attempt was made, other than the previously mentioned Payne Fund Studies, to gather longitudinal data of this sort. What we do have are impressionistic studies such as Margaret Thorp's *America at the Movies* (1939), or the sociological or anthropological investigations of the Hollywood community found in Leo C. Rosten's *Hollywood: The Movie Colony and the Movie Makers* (1941) and Hortense Powdermaker's *Hollywood: the Dream Factory* (1950).[49] It has only been since the 1970s, due in large part to the release of previously unavailable studio files, that the motion picture industry's role as a significant contributor to the American social and cultural fabric has received tentative confirmation, despite the absence of any real longitudinal evidence. As yet, no one has successfully melded this scanty empirical evidence on "movie influence" with current theories of communications effects to create a viable historical theory of "the impact of the motion picture on American society." Nor is a testable theory ever likely to emerge. Nevertheless, this subject no longer needs academic justification, and the state of motion picture historical research has shown vast improvement, both quantitatively and qualitatively, in the last decade.[50]

It is disappointing to discover that the television industry did not learn from the historical lacunae left by the motion picture industry; but in reality this is not too surprising given the even more commercial orientation of most television research. In fact, a good case could be made that the television industry, much like the movie industry before it, does not want to emphasize its integrative role in American society and culture for fear of being "blamed" for all of society's ills.[51] However, while the industry might have shied away from longitudinal research, social scientists and others have been eager to undertake such examinations when the opportunities presented themselves.[52] In every case, it has been empirically demonstrated that the introduction of television does have an effect on the audience's systems of values, beliefs, opinions, and attitudes, and can cause a dramatic reconfiguration in how people spend their time. These dynamic processes are endemic to every society, but what roles do the mass media, particularly television, play in such changes? The question becomes one of direction as much as intention. Do the media promote conservation or advocate change, and whose interests are advanced? These are questions of fundamental historical importance.

Given the extent of these evincible cognitive and behavioral changes on entire populations as a result of television and other forms of mass communication, it is only natural to expect historians to be far more curious about the mass media than they appear to be. I am not advocating a form of "communications determinism," but research constantly provides clear evidence that in modern society there are few more effective agents of social and cultural change than television. As mentioned, part of the problem lies in the lack of suitable secondary material which usefully summarizes the historical role of the mass media. Dating back before the introduction of the medium in a viable consumer form,[53] there are thousands of books, and tens of thousands of studies dealing with every facet of television's influence.[54] Yet, much like the gap in the literature on the motion picture, we still lack comprehensive historical evaluations of television's role in the development of American society and culture. As one bibliographic guide aptly puts it, "The literature on the history of broadcasting and television in the U.S. is closely associated with one individual: Erik Barnouw."[55] Barnouw's exemplary three volume history of broadcasting and the one volume updated summary, *The Tube of Plenty: The Evolution of American Television* (1975) still stand as the most comprehensive historical evaluations of the role of television in American society.[56] Television has been part of the American scene for more than forty years; obviously a need exists for much more historical research assessing the extent of television's role in the social and cultural changes we have undergone during this period.

Identification of the Mediating Factors in the Communications Model

A central problem in the development of communications theory is the identification of those factors which mediate between the source of the message and the receiver. It is important for those who wish to use the mass media as a source in historical research to understand the complex nature of the communications model, for only through an analysis of its individual components can the historian begin to see the strengths and limitations of media "effects."

The decline of the stimulus-response model required that more sophisticated and comprehensive models of the communication process be developed. In 1948 the political scientist Harold Lasswell developed his five part interrogative formulation of the communication process as involving: "Who says what to whom, via what medium, and with what effect."[57] William J. McGuire later translated these notions into the language of communications engineering, defining the five components as the *source, message, channel, receiver,* and *destination.*[58] While some theorists have identified as many as twelve components of the communications model,[59] McGuire's five categories provide a more than adequate degree of differentiation for purposes of historical analysis. These five categories he labels as the *independent* variables of the communication side of the communication-persuasion process.[60] In McGuire's model, each of these categories is subject to a number of mediating conditions, which he groups into the six *dependent* variables of the persuasion side. These six states are: being presented with the communication (*presentation*); attending to it (*at-*

	Source	Message	Channel	Receiver	Destination
Presentation					
Attention					
Comprehension					
Yielding					
Retention					
Overt Behavior					

Figure 1 Matrix of persuasive communication showing five classes of communication factors (independent variables) as column headings and six behavioral steps (dependent variables) as row headings. Source: William J. McGuire, "Persuasion, Resistance, and Change," in I. de Sola Pool, et al. eds., *Handbook of Communication* (Chicago: Rand McNally, 1973), p. 223.

tention); comprehending its content (*comprehension*); yielding to it (*yielding*); retaining this new position (*retention*); and acting on the basis of it (*overt behavior*). The end product of McGuire's categorizing, shown in Figure 1, is a five by six column matrix, which is particularly useful for historians in that it identifies each component of the communication-persuasion model. This provides a framework for organizing existing knowledge, applying what is known in specific situations, and indicating the gaps that remain to be filled if possible.[61]

It is, of course, beyond the scope of this essay to go into detail about the nature of each of these categories, but it is clear that such variables as the degree of source credibility and authoritativeness, structure and order of presentation, repetition of message, lack of alternative sources (or monopoly) of information, variables of style and types of appeal (emotional or rational), and other factors can play a part in the ultimate effectiveness of the communications process. Because it is impossible to generalize about the nature of each mediating variable, however, each specific case has to be examined separately.

The historian wishing to examine the "effect" of any communications act always runs the risk of making erroneous generalizations. The creative application of McGuire's matrix would help to minimize this danger, while at the same time providing a clear indication of where and what type of additional information might assist in clarifying the analysis. In most cases it would be very difficult to fill all of the boxes in the matrix with relevant information, but this is outweighed by the insights that would become obvious by organizing the existing material in such a manner.[62]

The use of mass media as source material and for purposes

of historical example is increasing. There is the potential for over-simplification and gross generalization in such practices unless historians recognize the complexities inherent in the communications-persuasion model. The objective of this essay was to acquaint those who wish to incorporate mass media studies into their research with the existence of significant work in the social sciences which could assist them in their analysis. In the last fifty years sophisticated models of the communication process have been developed which have contributed significantly to our understanding of the how the mass media work in the societal context. Historians now have no excuse for misusing this valuable historical resource.

NOTES

1. These deficiencies in previous historical work in mass communications are expertly summarized in MaryAnn Yodelis Smith, "The Method of History," in Guido H. Stempel, III, and Bruce H. Westley, eds., *Research Methods in Mass Communication* (Englewood Cliffs, NJ: Prentice-Hall, 1981), pp. 305–319.
2. The issue of writing communications history is discussed in a series of articles found in *Journalism History*, vol. 2, no. 2 (1975).
3. Harold A. Innis, *The Bias of Communication* (Toronto: The University of Toronto Press, 1968); Marshall McLuhan, *Understanding Media* (New York: McGraw-Hill, 1964).
4. For a further discussion of the problems surrounding the creation of a metatheory of communications history see Garth Jowett, "Toward a History of Communication," in *Journalism History*, vol. 2, no. 2 (Summer, 1975), pp. 34–37.
5. Innis, p. 4.
6. James W. Carey, "Harold Adams Innis and Marshall McLuhan," in Raymond Rosenthal, ed., *McLuhan: Pro and Con* (Baltimore: Penguin Books, 1969), p. 273. This article is the best introduction to the work of Innis and McLuhan for historians.
7. The significance of Innis's neglected work is highlighted in a book of essays dedicated to his memory. See William H. Melody, Liora Salter, and Paul Heyer, eds., *Culture, Communication, and Dependency: The Tradition of H. A. Innis* (Norwood, NJ: Ablex, 1981).
8. Paul Heyer, *Ibid.*, p. 258.
9. The "extensions of man" concept is discussed at length in *Understanding Media*.
10. Colin Cherry, *World Communication: Threat or Promise* (New York: Wiley-Interscience, 1971); Elizabeth Eisenstein, *The Printing Press as an Agent of Change* (Cambridge: Cambridge University Press, 1979); Jack Goody, ed., *Literacy in Traditional Societies* (Cambridge: Cambridge University Press, 1968); Harvey J. Graff, ed., *Literacy and Social Development in the West* (Cambridge: Cambridge University Press, 1981); Eric Havelock, *Preface to Plato* (Cambridge, MA.: Harvard University Press, 1979); and Walter J. Ong, S.J., *The Presence of the Word* (New York: Simon and Schuster, 1970).
11. These books were selected by consulting the course outlines of the American history survey courses at several universities.
12. Arthur S. Link, Stanley Coben, Robert V. Rimini, Douglas Greenberg, and Robert C. McGrath, Jr., *The American People: A History* (Arlington

Heights, IL.: AHM Publishing Corporation, 1981), p. 324. It is very well established that Edison did not invent the motion picture apparatus, but improvements were made in his laboratory which resulted in a viable projector. It was, of course, the magic of Edison's name which was instrumental in ensuring the economic success of the fledgling entertainment medium, and for this reason he is extremely important in the history of the motion picture industry. See Gordon Hendricks, *The Edison Motion Picture Myth* (Berkeley: University of California Press, 1961).

13. Rebecca Brooks Gruver, *An American History*, 3rd ed. (Reading, MA.: Addison-Wesley Publishing Company, 1982), p. 524.

14. *Ibid.*, p. 664.

15. Richard Current, T. Harry Williams, and Frank Friedel, *American History: A Survey*, 5th ed. (New York: Alfred A. Knopf, 1982), p. 634.

16. John A. Garraty, *The American Nation* 4th ed. (New York: Harper & Row, 1982), p. 764.

17. Irwin Unger, *These United States: The Questions of Our Past*, 2nd ed., (Boston: Little, Brown and Company, 1982), pp. 603–605; 701–702; 727–728; 833; 840.

18. A fine example of such a secondary synthesis is Daniel J. Czitrom, *Media and the American Mind: From Morse to McLuhan* (Chapel Hill: University of North Carolina Press, 1982).

19. Richard Pells, *Radical Visions and American Dreams: Culture and Social Thought in the Depression Years, 1890–1945* (New York: Harper & Row, 1973), p. 274.

20. Emily S. Rosenberg, *Spreading the American Dream: American Economic and Cultural Expansion, 1890–1945* (New York: Hill and Wang, 1982).

21. The concern by different groups for the effects of these various communications forms is analyzed in detail in Robert E. Davis, *Response to Innovation: A Study of Popular Arguments About New Media* (New York: Arno Press, 1976); see also the response of American intellectuals to the introduction of the new media discussed in Czitrom, *Ibid.* This last book also contains an excellent intellectual history of American mass communication research.

22. The notion of the "custodians of culture" is found in Henry F. May, *The End of American Innocence* (New York: Alfred A. Knopf, 1959). See particularly Part IV. May notes: "Because it dealt, or might have dealt, with ideas, the moving picture was alarming in a special way." (p. 335).

23. The behind-the-scenes details of how propaganda was used to involve Americans in the war was detailed in a book by the man who ran the operation for the U.S. government, and this caused a strong public reaction against such activities. See George Creel, *How We Advertised America* (New York: Harper & Row, 1920). For a detailed analysis of this propaganda activity see J. R. Mock and C. Larsen, *Words that Won the War* (Princeton, NJ: Princeton University Press, 1939).

24. For a more detailed discussion of the role of propaganda in World War I, and the resulting negative attitudes toward the mass media, see Garth Jowett and Victora O'Donnell, *Propaganda and Persuasion* (Beverly Hills: Sage Publications, 1986), pp. 121–133. This book also deals with the history and evolution of social scientific propaganda research.

25. Denis McQuail, *Mass Communication Theory: An Introduction* (Beverly Hills: Sage Publications, 1983), p. 176.

26. A more detailed discussion of these historical divisions and their political

and social implications can be found in the work of McQuail, *Ibid.*, pp. 176–178; Melvin L. De Fleur and Sandra Ball-Rokeach, *Theories of Mass Communication* (New York: Longman, 1982), pp. 156–165; and Tony Bennett, "Theories of the Media, Theories of Society," in Michael Gurevitch, Tony Bennett, James Curran, and Janet Woolacott, eds., *Culture, Society and the Media* (New York: Methuen, 1982), pp. 30–55.

27. Gordon W. Allport in his review of the history of social psychology noted that: "Social Psychology began to flourish after the First World War . . . A special challenge fell to social psychology. The question was asked: How is it possible to preserve the values of freedom and individual rights under conditions of mounting social strain and regimentation? Can science help to provide an answer? This challenging question led to a burst of creative effort that added much to our understanding of the phenomena of leadership, public opinion, rumor, propaganda, prejudice, attitude change, morale, communication, decision-making, race relations, and conflicts of value." See "The Historical Background of Modern Social Psychology," in Gardner Lindzey and Eliot Aronson, eds., *The Handbook of Social Psychology* (Reading, MA: Addison-Wesley Publishing Company, 1968), p. 2.

28. This history is recounted in Elihu Katz and Paul Lazarsfeld, *Personal Influence* (New York: The Free Press, 1955). For a more detailed explanation of how these names came to be applied, see Jesse G. Delia, "Communication Research: A History," in Charles R. Berger and Steven H. Chaffee, eds., *Handbook of Communication Science* (Newbury Park, CA: Sage Publications, 1987), pp. 20–24. He notes: "The most important source of this construction of communication study's history was, I believe, Katz and Lazarsfeld's (1955) account of the relationship of their research to the past." (p. 21).

29. De Fleur and Rokeach, *Ibid.*, p. 161.

30. Henry James Forman, *Our Movie-Made Children* (New York: Macmillan, 1933). This book was especially commissioned by Dr. W. W. Charters who headed the study team as a means of gaining public sympathy for his position.

31. The Payne Fund Studies can provide a useful source of primary information for historians wishing to study the impact of media during the 1920s. For more about their origins and the controversy surrounding their publication, see Jowett, *Film: The Democratic Art*, pp. 220–229; and Robert Sklar, *Movie-Made America* (New York: Random House, 1975), pp, 134–140. Delia, "Communication Research: A History," notes: "The results of the studies provided in the early 1930s the essential understanding of communication effects that three post-World War II decades of similar social psychological research would later support . . . Although there would be steady refinements in methodological and measurement prodecures, it would be a very long time before communication research developed beyond these studies." (p. 40). For a further confirmation of the long-term importance of the Payne Fund Studies in shaping television research, see Willard D. Rowland, Jr., *The Politics of Television Violence*: *Policy Uses of Communications Research* (Newburg Park, CA: Sage, 1983).

32. A very useful introduction to the second phase, highlighting the work of the key contributors to communication research, is Wilbur Schramm, "The Beginnings of Communication Study in the United States," in Rog-

ers and Balle, eds., *The Media Revolution in America and Western Europe*, pp. 200–211.

33. There has been a great deal written about the influence of Paul Lazarsfeld on the history of communications research. For more details see Delia, pp. 50–54; Czitrom, pp. 122–133; and for a critical assesssment of Lazarsfeld's concept of "administrative research," see Todd Gitlin, "Media Sociology: The Dominant Paradigm," *Theory and Society*, vol. 6 (1978), pp. 205–253.

34. There is a large body of work indicative of these two approaches. See particularly Paul F. Lazarsfeld, *Radio and the Printed Page* (New York: Duell, Sloan and Pearce, 1940); Lazarsfeld and Frank Stanton, *Radio Research 1941*, and *Radio Research 1942–43* (New York: Duell, Sloan and Pearce, 1941, 1944); C. I. Hovland, A. A. Lumsdaine, and F. D. Sheffield, *Experiments on Mass Communication* vol. 3., Studies in Social Psychology in World War II (Princeton, NJ: Princeton University Press, 1949); and Hovland, I. L. Janis, and H. H. Kelly, *Communication and Persuasion: Psychological Studies of Opinion Change* (New Haven, CT: Yale University Press, 1953).

35. Joseph Klapper, *The Effects of Mass Communication* (New York: The Free Press, 1960). This volume still has a strong influence in the field of communications research.

36. Bernard Berelson, "The State of Communications Research," *Public Opinion Quarterly*, vol. 23, no. 1 (1959), pp. 1–6.

37. McQuail, p. 177.

38. The work of the members of the Frankfurt School has been discussed extensively in many publications. For a useful summary of their influence in the development of mass communication theory, see Bennett, "Theories of the Media, Theories of Society," pp. 41–47. For a detailed history of this group, see Martin Jay, *The Dialectical Imagination: A History of the Frankfurt School and Institute of Social Research* (London: Heineman, 1973).

39. Everett Rogers has noted that "the empirical school of communication research is characterized by quantitative empiricism, functionalism [which postulates a view of society with relatively stable relationships and a tendency toward stability], and positivism [which sees the media as a generally positive force in society]," in Everett M. Rogers, "The Empirical and Critical Schools of Communication Research," in Rogers and Balle, eds., *The Media Revolution in America and Western Europe*, pp. 222–223.

40. The definitions of "cultural studies" and "critical studies" can be quite amorphous. For a useful introduction to this subject see Albert Kreiling, "Toward a Cultural Studies Approach for the Sociology of Popular Culture," *Communication Research* vol. 5, no. 3 (July 1978), pp. 240–263; James Carey, "Communication and Culture," *Communication Research* vol. 2, no. 2 (April 1975), pp. 173–191; and Everett M. Rogers, "The Empirical and Critical Schools of Communication Research," in Rogers and Balle, eds., *The Media Revolution in America and Western Europe*, pp. 219–235.

41. James Curran, Michael Gurevitch, and Janet Woollacott, "The Study of the Media: Theoretical Approaches," Michael Gurevitch et al. *Culture Society and The Media*, p. 13.

42. *Ibid.*, p. 16.

43. Lawrence Grossberg, "Critical Theory and the Politics of Empirical Research," in Michael Gurevitch and Mark R. Levy, eds., *Mass Communication Yearbook* vol. 6 (1987), p. 87.

44. Ibid., p. 97.
45. There are many examples of this new interest in the critical approach to studying media institutions. One excellent introduction is Joseph Turow, *Media Industries: The Production of News and Entertainment* (New York: Longman, 1984).
46. The study of the "political economy" of media institutions can provide historians with a great deal of useful data for assessing their historical role. This is not an area which has received a great deal of attention from historians, but as industry files are becoming available, we can expect to see more such studies. See for example, Janet Wasko, *Movies and Money: Financing the American Film Industry* (Norwood, NJ: Ablex Publishing, 1982); and Graham Murdock, "Large Corporations and the Control of the Communications Industries," Michael Gurevitch et al., *Culture, Media and Society*, pp. 118–150.
47. The problems and methodologies of historical media research are best summarized in David Paul Nord and Harold L. Nelson, "The Logic of Historical Research," in Stempel and Westley, eds., *Research Methods in Mass Communication*, pp. 278–304. This entire volume of essays provides useful information for those wishing to undertake mass communications research.
48. The history of this field and the shift in perspective are detailed in the work of the major pioneer in diffusion studies. See Everett M. Rogers, *Diffusion of Innovations*, 3rd ed. (New York: The Free Press, 1983).
49. Margaret Thorp, *America at the Movies* (New Haven: Yale University Press, 1939); Leo C. Rosten, *Hollywood: The Movie Colony and the Movie Makers* (New York: Harcourt, Brace and Co., 1941); and Hortense Powdermaker, *Hollywood: The Dream Factory* (Boston: Little, Brown and Co., 1950).
50. For details of current historical research on motion pictures see Robert C. Alen and Douglas Gomery, *Film History: Theory and Practice* (New York: Alfred A. Knopf, 1985).
51. This common fear is explained in detail in Willard D. Rowland, Jr., *Ibid.*
52. Social scientists are particularly eager to study the effects of the medium's introduction into "television naive" communities where no television was previously available. Since this opportunity was seldom taken during the period 1947–1955, when television was introduced throughout the United States, researchers have tended to focus on isolated communities in Canada or in other countries as a surrogate. See Wilbur Schramm, Jack Lyle, and Edwin B. Parker, *Television in the Lives of Our Children* (Stanford, CA: Stanford University Press, 1961), and the very recent study by Tannis MacBeth Williams, ed., *The Impact of Television: A Natural Experiment in Three Communities* (Orlando, FL: Academic Press, 1985) both of which used isolated Canadian communities.
53. There were many preintroduction books on the "promise of television." A good example is Orrin E. Dunlap, Jr., *The Outlook for Television* (New York: Harper & Brothers, 1932). Dunlap noted: "Television is a science and an art endowed with incalculable possibilities and countless opportunities . . . Eventually it will bring nations face to face, and make the globe more than a mere whispering-gallery." (p. 3).
54. For a concise summary of the most significant of these studies, see George Comstock, Steven Chaffee, Natan Katzman, Maxwell McCombs, and Donald Roberts, *Television and Human Behavior* (New York: Columbia University Press, 1978). Another useful, although now dated summary for

historians is Leo Bogart, *The Age of Television* (New York: Frederick Ungar, 1972).

55. A useful confirmation of this assessment of the lack of historical evaluation is found in Mary Cassata and Thomas Skill, *Television: A Guide to the Literature* (Phoenix: The Oryx Press, 1985). The Barnouw comment is found on p. 16.

56. Erk Barnouw, *A Tower in Babel; The Golden Web*; and *The Image Empire* (New York: Oxford University Press, 1966, 1968, 1970); and *The Tube of Plenty* (New York: Oxford University Press, 1975).

57. Harold Lasswell, "The Structure and Function of Communication in Society," in Lyman Bryson, ed., *Communication of Ideas* (New York: Harper, 1948), pp. 37–51.

58. William J. McGuire, "Persuasion, Resistance, and Attitude Change," in I. de Sola Pool et al., eds., *The Handbook of Communication* (Chicago: Rand McNally, 1973), pp. 230–231.

59. See Leonard Doob, *Communication in Africa* (New Haven: Yale University Press, 1981), pp. 7–16 for an elaboration of his twelve component model.

60. The concept of persuasion has been the subject of a great deal of focus for communications researchers, and has vast literature. A good introductory source is Victoria O'Donnell and June Kable, *Persuasion: An Interactive Dependency Approach* (New York: Random House, 1982).

61. McGuire, p. 223.

62. Another example of a useful matrix for analysing historical information within a communications context, based upon the work of Karl Deutsch, is found in Garth Jowett, "Communication in History: An Initial Theoretical Approach," *Canadian Journal of Information Science*, vol. 1, no. 1. (1976), pp. 5–13.

Janet Staiger is an Associate Professor teaching film history, theory, and criticism at the University of Texas at Austin. Her major publication is The Classical Hollywood Cinema: Film Style and Mode of Production to 1960, *co-authored with David Bordwell and Kristin Thompson. She is currently working on two books: one on the historical spectator of American film and the other on the representation of female sexuality in early cinema.*

THIS MOVING IMAGE I HAVE BEFORE ME

Janet Staiger

A discussion today between two academically trained film historians might surprise an outsider overhearing it. Not very unusual would be the historians' exchange of information on their most recent research or which archives held what documents or rare films. Nor very perplexing would be the variety of evidential sources: manuscripts, industry account books and press books, personal letters, oral histories, trade and public newspapers and journals, still photographs, and films. Somewhat surprising, however, might be some of the vocabulary used: terms such as "signifying practices," "social formations," "overdeterminations," and "mediations." Most shocking, though, would be the stress in the conversation on what explanatory model the historian was employing and its implications for research, argumentation, and use of documents.[1]

Film history is no longer the province of the untrained. In part this is due to the development of the discipline but it is also because many scholars have been influenced by the work of historians and theorists such as Hayden White, Peter Gay, the French *Annales* School, and Michel Foucault. Although proposing a variety of ways of writing history, these individuals all stress that no scholar comes "objectively," "neutrally," or "innocently" before his or her evidence. Simple words such as "society" or "authorship" which were once freely used are now recognized as referring to complex theoretical concepts. Even the most "common-sensical" notions are analyzed as implicit theoretical suppositions about why things are as they are, how they change, and even what they are ontologically. Thus, for example, varying definitions of what a "film" is as well as different explanatory models for why it may take the form that it does will determine what a scholar looks for in terms of evidence, which evidence is considered salient, and how that evidence is arranged to construct an argument. A historiography of film exists in which several generations of film scholars

247

have proposed changing definitions of what moving images are and
varying explanatory models for the images' relations within historical
reality.

Several of these patterns of film history writing have existed to date.
They include the works of many early scholars who explained film
history depending upon how they defined film: if it was a product,
then the cause was "great entrepreneurs"; if it was (sometimes) art,
then artists were the moving force; or if it was a social message, then
communicators spoke.[2] Responding implicitly to this practice of reducing causality to the locus of a historical individual and character-
izing the audience effect as merely passive reception, a second group
of writers[3] argued for attention to the extent to which individuals—
both as makers and receivers of images—were products of social,
cultural, and economic forces.[4] While these historians often lapsed
into reflectionist models to explain the production of moving images
or they proposed linear and circular models of film/audience relations, from their work we gained much: that production, filmic properties, and reception ought not be separated so neatly; that economic,
social, psychological, and political contexts inflect historical acts; and
that spectatorial effect is a historical question. Finally, in the 1950s
and 1960s with the establishment of academic courses in film, a third
generation of history writing occurred, influenced among other factors by critical work in the French *Cahiers du cinema*, an Americanized
notion of auteurism, the recognition of experimental filmmaking by
certain art institutions as worth study, and an interest by the social
sciences in film as a cultural object. This generation solidified and
disseminated the vocabulary for discussing formal features of the
moving image, moving beyond plot synopses and character descriptions. In addition, scholars significantly expanded contextual studies.

This essay, however, will concentrate on the most recent generation
of historians—those who have appeared since the early 1970s and
who, for want of an adequate unifying descriptive term, will simply
be called the new historians. Although a mixed group (often at serious
odds with one another), this generation can be characterized as breaking with earlier generations by asserting very different definitions and
explanatory models. Among other things, rather than assuming a
simple linearity to historical experience, new historians recognize that
multiple factors interrelate, either reinforcing or contradicting one
another, causing a mediation among possible causes and effects and
changing them constantly. In addition, many believe that "breaks" in
"chains of events" can develop, transforming one or more of the aspects among the relations. Furthermore, these scholars argue for conceiving of the human being as an extremely complex, even
contradictory, site of both conscious and unconscious determinants.
No such thing as a "fully conscious" human exists. Film, then, is simultaneously a business, aesthetic, and social practice.[5]

A simple example of this is the well-known conversion of silent cinema to mechanically synchronized sound films. Older histories might explain this as due to any number of causal sources (entrepreneurial decisions, scientific and technological developments, or artistic desires). In any event, the proposed history would be moderately linear—one event caused the next, etc. The new historians, however, reject such a linearity. In the case of the transformation (not "evolution") to sound films, not only is the cause postulated as a complex relation of industrial conduct, several technological developments, and film professionals' discourse and intervention, but the effects were multiple: a significant restructuring of the industrial sphere, modifications in work organization and techniques, a realignment in practices in film form and style, and a reevaluation of the advantages of technological innovation.

Moving image historians have an additional problem in that they are dealing with objects that have meaning to their perceivers. If part of the new historiography has been a reevaluation of causality and change, it has also led to a deeper analysis of what it is that is being studied. Simply defined, a film consists of moving images and transformed sounds, but the way the human perceives it and makes it meaningful is also important. The new histories have moved away from assuming that the film is a static (timeless) object toward emphasizing epistemological questions about the spectator's (including the historian's) reception of images and how individuals might construct varying meanings at different times and within differing conditions.

Thus, the history of the moving image requires explanatory models that consider the production, the properties, and the reception of the object. Yet each of these concepts is inseparable from the others. Production yields a film's look and its sound, but these properties affect production decisions. A film's look and sound influence reception but reception determines which properties are meaningful. Production includes affecting reception while reception moves production. The triad of production/properties/reception cannot be explained by a simple equation; nor does some complex equation exist since historical circumstances continually change the potential weight of each variable.

This major break in film historiography was in part due to revisions in areas of philosophy, linguistics, economics, psychoanalysis, and historiography which have resulted in significant changes in many disciplines besides cinema studies. A complete review of these influences is impossible here, but a brief discussion of some of them is necessary for an understanding of the current historiographical trends as well as why this new history represents such a break from the past. For our purposes, the influences of structuralism and semiotics, Althusserian Marxism, Lacanian psychoanalysis, and poststructuralism will be examined. However, I must caution that not all new history writing accepts all (or any) of these methods' claims. Rather I would argue that these theoretical interventions have set many of the requirements for alternate methods. Thus, to follow debates in film historiography requires understanding these influences.

THEORETICAL INDLUENCES ON THE NEW FILM HISTORIES

By the mid-1960s, Claude Levi-Strauss's use of structural linguistics in the field of anthropology suggested a new version of the individual as maker and user of cultural objects. Drawing from Ferdinand de Saussure's 1916 model of linguistics, Levi-Strauss argued, among other things, that an innate feature of the human mind was its structuring of the world into binary oppositions. From this, Levi-Strauss concluded that the formulaic features of myths of all cultures could be interpreted as attempts to reconcile or mediate these oppositions. Among the more influential of his writings (at least for art studies) was his *Structural Anthropology* (1958), particularly an essay reexamining the multiple variants of the Oedipal story throughout the world and history.[6] Breaking the story into "minimal units" (via the linguistic techniques of determining basic phonemes for language), Levi-Strauss proposed that a dual set of oppositions could be discovered, with each version of the basic myth proposing some way of mediating these apparent contradictions.

Structuralism—as this procedure would be called—implied several things to students of narrative. For one thing, a "science" of art might be possible, with linguistics as its model. The otherwise wide variation of formal arrangements might be reducible to more manageable terms, using the technique of oppositions as its controlling procedure. Thus, the already prevalent notion that art was a language or communication system now found a systematized method for application. For another thing, the idea that cultural artifacts represented efforts at addressing social and cultural problems had a formal method for analysis of those artifacts. Deviations from normative practices could be reconciled as cultural or personal idiolects (ways of speaking).

Semiology—a "science that studies the life of signs within society"[7]—produced a number of seminal works in the humanities. The definition of cultural objects as sign systems or signifying practices was, of course, not new, but a resurgence of interest in linguistics brought attention to various previously submerged proposals. Not only was de Saussure's work returned to, but scholars rediscoverd the writings of the Russian formalists and Charles Sanders Pierce. Major disseminators of a semiological approach to cultural objects included the French writers Tzvetan Todorov, Roland Barthes, Gerard Genette, and the Italian, Umberto Eco. Among the ideas most applicable to the humanities were the conception of minimal units (or signs) composed of signifiers (the substances and forms of expression) and signifieds (the substances and forms of content) and the distinctions between *langage* (the potential for language), *langue* (an actual language system), and *parole* (an actual use of a language system). Competent addressers and addressees had access to *langue* even though (and importantly) they might not have full knowledge of a *langue*'s semantics and syntax. Arbitrary and motivated signs were understood as referring only through social convention to reality. Hence, the history of signifying objects could be studied as a history of *langues* with their own codes. Furthermore, their properties could be much more carefully specified, and the old "form" and "content" split could be reconceptualized into systems of signifiers and signifieds.

The impact of this on cinema studies was significant. Composed of both visual and aural signs, cinema involved the analysis of individual images, series of images, and image/sound relations. Certainly the most influential practitioner of this was Christian Metz, whose essays were rapidly translated from French.[8] By the late 1960s, Metz had set out a series of definitions and hypotheses. Among these were the claims that cinema could be considered a particular combination of codes constructed culturally and historically. These included perceptual codes for structuring space, iconological codes for recognizing and identifying images, iconographical codes for attaching cultural connotations and symbolisms to images, narrative codes derived from cross-media narrative structures, and filmic codes for organizing these other codes (historically constructed patterns of editing, camera placement, etc.). Metz also argued that although cinema had a potential for language, it had no specific language system. This proposition while disconcerting for semiology as a whole actually opened new possibilities for historical studies since normative systems of constructing a film (i.e., Hollywood's film system[9]) could no longer be argued as "innate" or "competent" (the teleological model often apparent in earlier histories) but rather a result of historical, cultural, and ideological factors.

The immediate result, besides a tremendous outpouring of publications using semiology, was a reconsideration of what the film as object was and how one dealt with its causes and effects. If its speakers and spectators were constituted by cultural and historical language codes, a more sophisticated and historical model of communication was available. Furthermore, one no longer had to argue "intent" by filmmakers or even conscious and full reception by the spectator. Since the complete ramifications of a language system were assumed to be unknowable (except perhaps by scholars), the analyst could locate causality for production, properties, and reception in forces larger than the individual as a "knowing subject." Individuals as makers or spectators of the images were now understood as historically produced and unconscious of many of the factors which were occurring in the production of meaning.

Furthermore, the model of moving images as signifying practices questioned traditional hierarchies of evaluation. Since every film was equally an instance of speech, attention was directed away from canons of masterpieces and towards the most typical instances of the lan-

guage. One consequence of the semiological and structuralist explanatory model was an increased consideration of the filmmaking practices
of Hollywood, since its worldwide domination of exhibition time and
its long tradition as a cohesive signifying system indicated that if deviations from its norm were to be understood, its history had to be
studied and explained.

Although it would be modified subsequently, the model based on
semiology and structuralism produced (and is still producing) significant revisions in the work on film authorship and genres. For example,
the earlier version of auteurism has now been restudied as a set of
codes linkable to the "signature" of an individual.[10] John Ford as a
historical individual is separated from Ford as a historical user of a
preexistent signifying practice. A semiological/structuralist historian
of Ford's films seeks Ford's idiolect (his specific pattern of formal and
thematic features), situating it within its concurrent signifying practices, production circumstances, and cultural context. Idiolects of
screenwriters, producers, and cameramen have also been studied.
Structuralist genre studies indicated recurrent oppositional configurations in content and iconography and traced the ways that these
oppositions have changed and been mediated historically.[11] Thomas
Schatz, for example, argues that early 1930s gangster films involve
oppositions of nature and urban culture, individual accomplishment
and common good, which are resolved through the lawful elimination
of the aberatant gangster produced by society. By the late 1930s, the
oppositions are "watered down" through recasting gangster figures
into cops or lawyers or counterbalancing "the gangster with an equally
strong (or perhaps stronger) prosocial figure"—a difference partially
due to a stronger self-regulatory structure in Hollywood's production
code but also to social changes during the depression.

Structuralism and semiology also affected Marxist scholars who
found these techniques useful tools for rereading Marx and history.
Although by no means the first to make these proposals (and subsequently the target of many well-founded objections), the writings of
Louis Althusser in the 1960s created a stir not only within Marxist
circles but also within cultural studies.[12] Arguing that the economic
base with its dialectical class struggle was only in the last instance the
determinant of historical change, Althusser proposed viewing the
whole set of cultural artifacts and social institutions as produced by
and in order to reinforce and reproduce the dominant class and its
economic system. The infrastructure was a combination of production
forces—the means of production (including raw materials, tools, and
buildings) and the relations of production (the way labor was organized and interrelated with the means of production). Separate from,
but related to, the infrastructure, were politico-legal apparatuses (the
law and the state) and ideological state apparatuses (religions, ethical
beliefs, political groups, educational systems, and art). Although the
ideological state apparatuses might provide space for the expressions
and systems of representation for all classes, the dominant ideology

would be that of the class holding economic power. Althusser argued that it was, in fact, through the ideological state apparatuses that the dominant class attempted to maintain its control, using institutions and representations to do this. Since cultural objects might be used as a representational space for the class struggle (which existed despite the dominance of the ruling class), cultural objects needed to be analyzed in terms of the ideological implications of their systems of representation in relation to the goals of the opposing classes. Althusser also asserted an intriguing system of explaining historical change in the politico-legal and ideological state apparatuses. Given that the infrastructure was dialectical, one could argue that older forms of representation might linger within current ones, or that the contradictions of the infrastructure might surface in representations, or that systems might overdetermine themselves in their desire to assert their ideology. Such a model of "differential historical temporality" allowed for lags, breaks, contradictions, leaps, in short, a new historiography that broke with linear, unmediated analyses.

In constructing his rereading of Marx, Althusser also drew on the rereading of Freud proposed by Jacques Lacan. The consequences of this move were not then apparent, but Althusser's model of subject construction included the "interpellation" (or calling out to the individual) to fill an "imaginary" position constructed for the individual within the social sphere. Althusser considered positions "imaginary" in the dual sense of being created (not real or inherent) and apparently but not actually homogeneous. Already a controversial figure in psychoanalytical studies, Jacques Lacan had used semiotics to read Freud's story of the construction of the individual through linguistic terms, proposing an explanation of how an individual learns and accepts a preexistent language and cultural system.[13] The existence of an unconscious language (repressed when the individual accepts the system offered by society) also revised the structuralists' binding connection between signifier and signified, yielding poststructuralism and the possibilities for explaining changes in meaning systems.

This new theory of the individual offered a much more complex and synthetic explanatory model for film history. Language could be connected to cultural structures and, via Marxism, to ideology and to economic systems. The properties of cultural objects were then a complex and mediated conjunction of product, art, and language. In addition, historical change and causality could be redefined as not a linear or predestined teleological growth but as mediated and "uneven" with breaks, contradictions, and overdeterminations. Nor did historians have to assume a reflectionist model of infrastructure and cultural object. Instead, a moving image was the result of (often contradictory) determinants which included economic practices, signifying practices (including "lags" or "jumps"), and more general social conflict played out through ideological state and politico-legal apparatuses. The implications of law and the state's regulatory agencies (for instance, censorship, copyright definitions and decisions, regulation of labor relations, etc.) also had to be factored into the new formulation of possible causes. Conscious intent might be considered as one feature of causality, but unconscious activities (codified systems of cinematic expression as *langue* or the eruption of unconscious language systems) also had to be acknowledged. Finally, the history of the moving image had to include these interrelations into a general model.

The combination of semiology, Althusserian Marxism, Lacanian psychoanalysis, and poststructuralism provided a powerful explanatory model for film theoreticians. Furthermore, when the political events in 1968 in France (the site of much of this scholarship) had its impact on the academy, the academy had a definition and explanatory model for reconsidering the history of cultural objects as well as a grounding for praxis. By 1970, articles and debates that were to dominate the field of cinema studies were already appearing, many of which were not only studies of the properties of the moving image but also historical propositions.

Furthermore, the post-1960 surge of historiography from writers such as Fernand Braudel, Michel Foucault, Peter Gay, Emmanuel LeRoy Ladurie, Maurice Mandelbaum, and Hayden White encouraged a reflexiveness toward film history writing. Recognizing their own writing was yet another signifying practice, film scholars became interested in alternative possibilities of representing the past. In particular, historiography became a site of social and political praxis. How one wrote a history either reinforced a dominant ideological system or worked to change it. Writing history became a political act with consequences.

From the 1970s on, an explosion of new and different scholarship in film history has occurred. Many of these works develop explanatory models based at least partly, if not fully, on semiology, Marxism, psychoanalysis, and poststructuralism. Some are constructed as alternatives due to difficulties with certain aspects of the propositions such as the film-as-language metaphor. Since the properties, production, and reception of moving images are interconnected, examining these new histories' versions of causes and effects provides one way to study the work of this generation.

THE NEW HISTORIES AND THE CAUSES OF MOVING IMAGES

Once the explicit notion that histories imply explanatory models became widespread, the conscious application and comparison of various models produced a considerable reanalysis of previous assumptions about the economic infrastructure and the industrial context for decision making in the production of moving images. One of the major writers at the forefront of this revisionism is Douglas Gomery whose work on the United States film industry has changed not only our understanding of the industry's operations but also contributed to how we write film histories.[14] Gomery has used both neoclassical and Marxist economic models to restudy specific periods of the industry, he has introduced demographics into the field, and he has sensitized film historians to distribution and exhibition as significant and, sometimes, primary factors in production decision making. For example, his interest in modes of exhibition practices has altered our notions of the film-as-industrial-product. Gomery's research on the 1920s picture palaces indicates that what the industry sold to consumers was not primarily a fictional narrative film but a pleasurable experience which included the opportunity to participate in a social event that was composed of visits to magnificent theaters (with air-conditioning, fine original oil paintings on the wall, and lush furnishings), as well as live acts, musical arrangements, colored lighting displays, newsreels, and animated cartoons. As Thomas Elsaesser has rephrased it recently, rather than conceiving of the film industry as a product industry, it may need to be considered a service industry, an industrial and cultural institution that supplies a certain type of pleasure.[15]

Gomery's work not only serves as an example of the explicit statement of models and their effects on our perception of film history, but he has been exemplary in his return to original archival material and primary sources. Trained as an economist and historian in the academy, Gomery works from rigorous notions about evidence, proof, and documentation of sources. Universities and museums now consider it a coup to hold studio economic records, personal papers of industrial personnel, and any still or moving image (not just the masterpieces). My own analysis of the mode of production in Hollywood would not have been conceived without the influences of Gomery's work (he was a former professor of mine) and the scholarship of other important revisionist histories of the economic infrastructure and industrial structure and context such as Jeanne Allen, Robert Allen, Edward Buscombe, Thomas Guback, and Charles Musser.[16]

The mode of production is a particularly significant area of research since it supplies an interconnection among factors that cause films to look and sound as they do: the industrial context, the social circumstances, the history of labor organization, and signifying practices in general. In studying the Hollywood mode of production, it is clear that economic practices of standardizing work procedures for regularity, uniformity, and efficiency of production while providing areas of novelty for product differentiation are a necessary part, but only a part, of the explanation for moving picture form and style. Signifying practices, borrowed at times from other media, have to be considered as well. In fact, norms of narrative structure and narrational techniques quickly permeate Hollywood, dispersed rapidly through trade papers, reviews, advertising, and filmmaker contacts. These standards of quality narrative filmmaking often control decision making, influence how labor is divided and hierarchized, and regulate technological change and the use of that technology. Laws and the state affect production circumstances and the cultural objects they produce. In addition, ideologies of "authorship" also affect labor relations.[17]

The new histories have also explored the technology of production. Prior to this revisionist history, technology in film studies was explained either by scientific breakthroughs or individuals' desires to achieve some cinematic effect. Neither simple explanation will hold today. Postulating technology as a product of science does not account for the sometimes great lag between a scientific theory and a technology that takes advantage of that theory. Furthermore, such a hypothesis renders technology neutral, rather than in the service of economic and political systems. Nor is the proposal that individuals desire to achieve some effect sufficient as an explanation once individuals are considered subjects within economic, social, and signifying systems.

One of the earliest reevaluations of film technology was the work of Jean-Louis Baudry who suggested that the camera's technological construction was itself an effect of a bourgeois ideology.[18] Drawing on the 1960s French work on semiotics and psychoanalysis, Baudry argued that the camera lens and the projection apparatus were constructed to give the film spectator the illusion that what he or she saw (the visible world) was in fact reality. This illusion reinforced the bourgeois and idealist ideology that the individual was the maker of meaning (a transcendental subject) rather than a materialist, Marxist position that the individual was a subject within structures and relations of process (the Marxists' reality). Furthermore, the camera movement and editing patterns of dominant cinema (e.g., Hollywood) reduplicated this ideological effect.[19]

Subsequently, in an article published in 1971–72, Jean-Louis Comolli took up Baudry's argument while modifying and revising it to allow for the possibility of radical film practice which privileged film styles that made apparent the labor involved in making films.[20] Although significant problems exist in Comolli's history of film and film technology, his essay (as well as Gomery's work on the innovation and dissemination of sound technology) resulted in a renewed interest in studying cinematic technology. Since the mid 1970s, work on the economic, aesthetic, and ideological factors in technological choices and change in sound, color, camera movement equipment, film stocks, lenses, and aspect ratios has occupied the attention of many scholars.[21] Many of these histories incorporate part, if not all, of the contemporary models of semiotics, psychoanalysis, and Marxist economics. They consider the complex of determinants that would explain the appearance of particular technologies at certain times, the interaction of workers with these technologies (how the workers actually use the technologies), and the ideological factors and effects that are implicated in dispersion and use of technologies. These same issues are central to much recent work in the broader history of technology, and cinema is an especially worthwhile site for such study since cinema's very existence as a signifying practice depends upon mechanical, chemical, and electronic apparatuses whose inventions are less than a century old. Television and radio as other technologies for recording and dispersing moving images and transformed sounds are also being considered from this perspective.

If the industrial context, the modes of production, and technology have been reanalyzed, more importantly so too has been the history of the objects themselves as signifying practices. Although structuralism and semiotics led rapidly to revisionist studies of authorship and genres, the earlier separation of distinct modes of film practices such as French impressionism, German expressionism, Italian neorealism, and, centrally, Hollywood classicism needed revision. Already linked with particular economic systems, these wider groupings of films required histories that would also take advantage of the new historiography.

In some quarters of media scholarship, Lacanian psychoanalysis seems a breakthrough, and the result has been studies of authorship, genres, modes of film practice, and the various media (cinema or television) as symptomatic or pleasurable for certain psychic configurations.[22] For Hollywood filmmaking, the proposal has been made that its systems of narrative and its formal features work to reduplicate subject positions that reinforce patriarchy, a social formation advantageous to capitalism. Alternative modes of film practice either provide variants of this psychic formation or optional subject positions.

However, histories of signifying practices do not have to take up Lacanian psychoanalysis nor do they have to submit to some of the more rigid formulations of Althusserian Marxism to still rewrite histories of film from a revisionist perspective. For example, the work of David Bordwell, Kristin Thompson, and myself proposes a new history and textual analysis of the classical Hollywood cinema drawn from a revision of Russian formalism, Czech structuralism, and semiotics through a modified Marxism.[23] To develop this description of a historically specific set of films we took an unusual approach to the problem of evidence. Since we wanted to make claims about normative aspects of the Hollywood film, we took a list of all the films (some 20,000) produced in the United States between 1915 and 1960. Assigning each film a number and using a random number chart, we located in various archives 100 films which provided an unbiased sample. Intensely analyzing these films shot by shot, we based our arguments on the typical (not "masterpiece") output of this film practice. We also used trade and professional journals, oral histories, and technology studies to determine how the filmmakers viewed their own efforts.

Briefly, we argue that Hollywood's film practice was not driven by a teleology of realism or an ideology of illusionism (positions held by some new historians) but rather by the (economically advantageous) desire to produce narratives. By 1917, the industry had constructed a very particular narrative and narrational practice that had the possibility of using various formal techniques as functional equivalents. Of overriding concern was an explicitly disseminated norm or standard of what a quality film should look (and later sound) like. This norm was, in part, possible because the mode of production found ways through its division of labor and its use of the script as a blueprint to adjust itself continually and regularly to a certain amount of stylistic variation and technological innovation. Linked as Hollywood is to a history of narrative form and image making predating its existence, it has proved remarkable resilent to change. Thus, while Hollywood film practice has its formation and continued existence within a capitalist economic system, it is not reducible to or isolated within that economic system. It may work to provide certain spectatorial effects, but it responds to social, cultural, political, and economic changes while still maintaining its very flexible but prescribed narrative norms of causation, characterization, and narrational techniques.

In summary, this new, revisionist historiography has done much to redefine the relations between production and filmic properties. Currently, the explanatory model for an individual film or group of films is considered to be a complex, mediated, and interactive process among various factors: social and cultural conditions and forces; economic practices; and signifying practices. Authorship is redefined within this construct, and revisionism is occurring in genre and sociocultural studies. Of particular interest have been the films produced by Hollywood between at least 1915 and 1960, as well as the so-called "primitive" period (1895–1909). The reason for such an attention is that Hollywood epitomizes the capitalist filmmaking system. Furthermore, despite all sorts of optional filmmaking practices (including avant-garde practices), the classical Hollywood film has remained dominant worldwide as well as remarkably resilient to major formal or stylistic changes when countered by an alternative practice. Explanations for this range from rather reductive Marxist economic ones (Hollywood colonized the world, inflicting its films on other cultures) to more provocative and probable explanations that include the spectator as a somewhat willing and complicit participant in this process. Antonio Gramsci's notion of the "hegemony" of ideologies suggests that even those who have the most to lose by accepting certain representations are absorbed into the dominant ideology through its appearance as natural and profitable to hold. However, if historians now have a new "received" model[24] that defines and explains some of the conditions of film production, they are likewise reconsidering the effects (or reception) of those films. Film history is also the history of the production of meaning and the use of that meaning by its spectators.

THE NEW HISTORIES AND THE EFFECTS OF MOVING IMAGES

Questions of epistemology and spectator-effect existed in the earliest writings about cinema. Not only does every writer have some notion about what reality is and what the definition of cinema is, but every writer has at least an ad hoc idea of what the mind is and how it knows the world and cinema, often resorting to reflectionist models in which spectators were idealized (i.e., generalized into large groups or classifications). Furthermore, spectators were thought to be somewhat passive receivers of cinema. For instance, Hugo Munsterberg hypothesized a possible hallucinogenic or dreamlike state for film reception, worrying about its effects. Social reformers and those proposing censorship also considered the spectator capable of being titillated, indoctrinated, or driven to acting out personal fantasies when stimulated by exposure to film images. The Payne Studies of the 1930s, for example, expressed particular concern about children who may be unable to separate art from reality or incapable of knowing that social restrictions exist on the acts represented in films.[25] Since social legislation regulating the film industry always works on assumptions about the spectator/moving image relation, historians might examine prevelant ideas of spectator reception and their relation to laws, the state, and the industry as additional factors in production determinants. Yet it is also important to question those ideas, investigating to what extent moving images do interact with an individual and with society.

In contrast to standard sociology in which a "consensus, equilibrium" model of society is hypothesized, Marxist sociological studies propose a "conflict, process" model. Whereas sociologists of visual images and narrative roles assume that changing images can create or change social roles and behavior as well as institutions, Marxist sociologists believe that images are mediated results of an infrastructure and that progressive representations of cultural types will not effect radical social change without changes in the infrastructure as well. Furthermore, formal and stylistic practices are also complexly related to the infrastructure. "Content" cannot be divorced from form (even the vocabulary "form/content" is suspected as leading to mistaken notions that the two ideas can be split and is thus avoided).

An early move in reexamining the spectator/film was the return to a third generation strategy of opposing Hollywood cinema to art or experimental films, with the latter work privileged as art or high art. With the overt proposal by segments of the new historians that Hollywood could be equated with capitalism, bourgeois ideology, and patriarchal structures of social and psychic arrangements, alternative practices became, through the employment of a binary opposition, the site for possible radical practice. Of particular interest was Hollywood's system of linear narratives, point of view shots in which a woman is the object of a man's gaze, editing and camerawork patterns that elided disjunctions between time and space while focusing on fragments of bodies and then reconstituting them, and manipulation of mise-en-scène so as to duplicate visible reality.[26] If classical Hollywood's film practice was symptomatic of its infrastructure in every way, then its narrative structures, its fetishization of the woman's body, and its "illusion of continuity and reality" had ideological effects of reinforcing not only capitalism but also patriarchical structures of sexual dominance and normalcy (heterosexual not homosexual desire and pleasures of male voyeurism). Also employing Lacanian psychoanalyis, many writers provided analyses of Hollywood films in terms of how their formal systems worked to reinforce a spectator effect that would maintain hegemonic ideologies and dominant institutions, a service industry and apparatus of pleasure. Such essays as the *Cahiers du cinema's* analysis of John Ford's *Young Mr. Lincoln*, Christian Metz's psychoanalytic work on the "imaginary signifier," Stephen Heath's essay on Orson Welles' *Touch of Evil*, and Raymond Bellour's study of codes of repetition in Hitchcock's films stand out as typical and influential postulations from this perspective.[27]

In contrast, films in which linearity and the "illusion of continuity and reality" were broken by reflexive or discursive moments were praised as signifying practices that destroyed or at least subverted the norms of Hollywood (and capitalism). Returning to the 1930s debates between Lukacs and Brecht, those accepting Lacanian psychoanalytic tenets tended to side with Brecht, arguing that "Brechtian" cinema provided a progressive spectatorial experience of heterogeneity and work as opposed to the false and complicit experience of homogeneity and the passive consumption of "realist" cinema. Those of the third generation that equate art with non-Hollywood filmmaking could apply structuralism's binary opposition and Marxism theories of history and spectator effect to reassert the progressivity of their prized films, allowing their canon to survive the new historiography.[28]

However, chinks in this wall of revising notions of textual effect developed. They did not come, as they ought to have, from questions about evidence or proof of these effects or complaints that the historical model was much too schematic, losing its "mediation" factor. Instead, in order to formulate this model of spectator reception, the viewer had to be described in rather sweeping and generalized terms. Besides assuming that the spectator was a subject manipulated by the filmmaking practice (an assumption also held by some sociologists, cultural historians, and social reformers), the spectator was a "he." As feminist critics were to point out, the phallocentrism of Freud and Lacan's theory of the individual's movement into social structures had ramifications for any possibilities of psychic change. The mark of difference (the phallus) resulted in an almost inevitable construction of patriarchy: the female would forever be the repressed Other. Besides being biased toward patriarchical dominance, psychoanalytic theory was moderately transhistorical: at the very least as postulated it involved a kinship relation solidified by capitalism for the reproduction of its labor force, with subject construction repeated for several centuries.[29] Reflexive cinema did nothing to alter fundamental psychoanalytic constructions of sexual difference; it just did not reinforce (masculine) pleasure. Furthermore, while one might understand what pleasure a male spectator had in viewing Hollywood cinema, the female spectator was left out of the picture (or rather, was the picture).

As feminists analyzed it, either women had to identify with a masculine position or find pleasure through masochism (submitting themselves to being the object of the male's gaze and phantasies).[30]

In cinema studies, the critique by feminist film theorists has been particularly significant in rethinking the idea of spectator effect and the history of the production of meaning. For awhile, feminists worked off of the strategy of binary opposition, postulating that the feminine was linked to a force association with difference. As the other, what was feminine was excess and heterogeneity. Thus, the radical other films of the avant-garde and subversive moments in Hollywood cinema were instances of the surfacing of that repressed unconscious.[31] Such a hypothesis has lately been attacked, however, as "essentialist." More importantly, though, it repeats which is now coming under question as a static and impossible acceptance of a masculine-dominated binarism that relegates the woman by opposition to the ghetto of the Other. To accept being the Other is to capitulate to a hegemonic and patriarchical construction of meaning.[32] Poststructuralism, which attacks simple and static binary opposition as an explanation of meaning, postulates that meaning production is constantly in process with signifiers and signifieds continually being renegotiated within and among texts in relation to spectators in a context with those texts.[33]

Thus, new historiography can no longer assume a simple one-to-one relationship between signifying practices and spectator effect. Once beyond the hurdle of the idealized spectator, all sorts of differences become apparent: class, race, gender, socialized sexuality, sexual preferences and orientations, cognition, culture, and politics are some of the most obvious possibilities for demarkating various groups of spectators. The study of the historical reception and effects of films is being revitalized but with more tools for its analysis and with more philosophical, historical, psychoanalytic, psychological, and critical sensitivities toward understanding the relations among spectators, moving images, and historical context. In the remaining pages of this essay, I would like to sketch out what some of the assumptions and potentials for reception studies mean for the histories of moving images and for understanding the interplay among the triad—production/properties/reception.

What are some of the ideas central to current reception studies? First of all, the spectator is considered a subject, one constructed within a site of determinants. These determinants include economic, social, cultural, political, and psychic ones. Furthermore, the determinants acknowledge history: the spectator cannot be considered formed at birth, but is in process throughout his or her life and in a historical context. A specific individual viewing a film in 1985 is not the same person as she or he was in 1965—before, for instance, widespread political changes and concentrated attention in the public sector to issues of racial, sexual, or sexual preference discrimination.

Second, although the force of unconscious facts of language, psychology, and ideologies is acknowledged, in terms of reception of cultural objects, conscious factors must also be considered as having salience. What an individual knows and believes certainly affects his or her response. One may, for example, be pulled along by the narrative and editing of *Indiana Jones and the Temple of Doom* but at the same time be repelled by its representations of white colonialism and superiority. Here what interpretative strategies are available to an individual are important in the response to a film. Interpretations are not ad hoc (unless the experience is radically deviant from previous ones). Instead, a whole range of institutions (both ideological state and politico-legal apparatuses) exist to provide methods or strategies for producing meaning.[34] Specific examples of such institutions include academic studies (with its range of critical models), more informal institutions such as journalistic reviews and essays, and more particularly, the film industry which supplies a number of related media experiences to guide a spectator's interpretation (e.g., talk shows, advertising, publicity, films about making films). Thus, production sectors also relate to reception factors. Consequently, no spectator or spectatorial experience can be considered "passive." In every instance, a spectator is producing meaning, using his or her unconscious, subconscious, and conscious range of interpretative strategies and knowledges about cultural objects as well as beliefs about the world to make sense of the experience.

Third, the spectator is also understood as a site of contradictions and differences. Formed out of determinants, the spectator also duplicates the contradictions of the infrastructure and the heterogeneity of the superstructure. Our beliefs do not all hold together into a coherent vision of reality and existence. We are the site of multiple discourses that do not necessarily lock into one logical system.

Fourth, and implied in the above, is that spectators use intertextual knowledge to a great degree in understanding any text. Intertextuality suggests knowledge of other texts in the same genre or mode as the one being interpretated but also texts from every field. For example, to respond "normatively" to a fictional narrative film, a spectator must determine that it is "fictional," that it is not proporting to have as direct a relation to reality as a "documentary" does. However, one assumes that some connections do exist, including, for instance, "common sensical" (i.e., hegemonic) notions about human behavior, what is realistically possible in terms of the historical real, the conception that time and space exists in a particular way. The last point indicates, for example, how the spectator uses intertextual knowledge, even at the most basic level, to structure a fictional narrative.

Current western notions of "objective," earth-centered time include the assumptions that time is unidirectional in order, regular and continuous in duration, and unique in occurrence. Simply put, time flows forward (and never backward), one second of time is the same length as the next second, no gaps in time exist, and time does not repeat itself. (Note that other cultures have different versions of time and space—for instances ones in which time is cyclical.) However, filmic texts can manipulate all of these aspects of time. Reversing and re-ordering time is possible through printing or projecting techniques and editing (flashbacks and flashforwards). Slow or fast motion can expand or contract moments, editing deletes time, and repeat print-ings can make the same event occur multiple times. Using a knowledge of cinema's technology (another intertextual discourse) and the as-sumption that film is not equal to reality, spectators compare and contrast the filmic experience with what intertextual discourses have asserted about time. With a different conception of temporality, we could not (or would not) mentally reorder, connect, and interpret the various parts of a film (or any) narrative into the structural arrange-ment that we do.

Of course, intertextual knowledge also includes our conceptions of norms of the genre or mode that is being experienced. Genre films in particular have their own sets of codified conventions, verisimili-tudes, and reading strategies. Take, for example, the disjunction be-tween expectations about the historical real versus those for musicals: we hardly blink an eye when characters burst into song in the middle of a love scene, accompanied by some off-screen and non-diegetic orchestra.[35]

Fifth, with all of the above suggestions of difference and change, reception studies must be careful not to fall into a radical subjectivity which ignores the importance and significance of institutions and ide-ologies to limit us. We are different, but not totally; we are free, but only within bounds of current possibilities. Thus, one part of reception studies is the investigation of interpretative communities and inter-pretative strategies. Not all ways of making meaning have been avail-able at all times. As critics in literary studies have pointed out recently, the procedures for interpreting literary works have changed histori-cally, and as I have suggested in this essay, the same is true for the study of moving images. For instance, no writer in 1915 would have used the term "ideological" to discuss a particular filmic representa-tion. As a result, we need a history of interpretative strategies, a study of how and why they have change (a work in which this essay is par-ticipating), and an analysis of how institutions (public, industrial, aca-demic, etc.) have set up or influenced interpretative procedures.

In setting out this list of assumptions and concerns for reception studies, I have not addressed a crucial question for historians: how and where do we find evidence? Certainly a study of the discourse of various institutions would be one important project. We also need to find ways of studying the responses of sets of individuals. This is a difficult problem. We can, for example, use studio surveys or academic studies of spectators. This material has been produced for a particular function, however, and must itself be interpreted within the context of its production. Reviews, letters to editors, parodies, and interviews are also sites of information but equally in need of careful handling.

Furthermore, we must be somewhat creative in searching out the

responses of certain audience groups. If we assume that the most
evident sources for documents of spectator response are available
because they have been produced within dominant institutions, then
we need also to examine nondominant sites for discourse. Here papers, journals, letters, and oral histories of marginal groups could be
studied. This would include alternative political parties or culture
groups such as ethnic, gay, lesbian, feminist, and radical organizations.
Ironically, because of the marginal nature of these groups, much
needed information is probably forever absent. In some instances, we
may need to make creative leaps over these gaps, making reasonable
hypotheses on the basis of related evidence such as statements about
other cultural objects, concurrent discourse, and social and cultural
histories. Divising methods of comparing and contrasting responses
and analysis of available ones would also be part of our tactic in handling what we do find.

Using what we currently know about spectators in relation to the
production of meaning and using the revisionist definitions and formulations of the history of the moving image, we are in a position to
make some headway in this process. Earlier reception studies would
have posited some kind of direct link between a film and a spectator,
assuming a passive, unmediated absorption of the film. Preexisting
knowledge, concurrent concerns, or interpretative strategies would
not have been considered as salient mediating factors. The idea, for
instance, of a resisting spectator would not have been suggested (the
same holds in many psychoanalytic studies of film reception). Yet a
new history needs to consider all of these factors if it is to produce a
nonlinear, multiply determined, and mediated history of the effects
of moving images.

In the past six years, a number of essays have been published that
do provide us with some useful models from which to work. For
example, Michael Budd has researched how the Goldwyn Company
set up a number of distribution techniques to normalize the experience of *The Cabinet of Dr. Caligari* upon its importation into the United
States.[36] Publicity and advertising downplayed its German origin, and
using a live exhibition prologue, a framing narrative was structured
around the film which directed a reading of the film as the halluci-
nations of an insane individual, thus conforming to conventional
Hollywood narration in which narrative causality is explained as due
to character psychology rather than, for example, class conflict.

In another essay, David Bordwell has argued that the interpretative
strategy of auteurism provided a method for spectators to reconcile
deviations from normative storytelling methods and the ambiguity of
resolutions in the art cinema of the 1960s as either a statement about
reality or a foregrounding of authorial narration.[37] While this is an
interesting essay, Bordwell draws all of his evidence and argumentation from the films themselves, not even seeking any confirming
evidence from critical essays of the period.

Using cultural studies and oral histories, Joe McElhaney has studied gays' reception of female stars, particularly Judy Garland.[38] He argues that gays used an informal and subcultural "gossip" system to construct an image of Garland as a victim, but also the subversive product of homosexual workers at MGM. Whether the gossip is true or not, it has permeated gays' networks of discourse about Garland. Thus, they appropriate Garland's typical narrative plots and songs into a reading that compares her life to their own historical and cultural situation as victims and repressed individuals. In addition, in some cases, the hermeneutical code (or plot) of the film seems of less consequence than particular privileged moments in which the comparison is more possible. Thus gays' viewing of dominant cinema (where no adequate representation of their own experience of the historical real exists) may be a special and constructed procedure to compensate for the lack of characters with which to identify as opposed to heterosexuals who can place themselves into the roles and plots with much more ease. McElhaney also believes that with changing cultural attitudes in some cities in the United States the cult of some female stars may be waning.

In another study, Roger McNiven has compared the published critical response to *Rope* at the time of its first release in 1948 to its re-release in 1984.[39] His findings include the observation that while in 1948 some reviewers believed that the two male murderers were morbid and not acceptable identification figures, no reviewer stated that they might be homosexuals. However, in 1984, after mass attempts to educate the public about gays and their lifestyles as well as the lifting of some informal censorship codes, not only were there common references to the murderers having homosexual characteristics, but one gay newspaper carefully linked the fluid camera movements to a shifting sadomasochistic relation between the two men. Although more research needs to be done, it appears that cultural and social changes as well as critical methods for film analysis influenced this shift in interpretation and interpretative method.

As one more example of this type of historical research, a study of the critical reception of *Foolish Wives* in 1922 indicates that a hegemonic discourse about "100% Americanism" (a continuation of the Red Scare and xenophobia of 1919–1921) and socialized notions of the "masculine" and the "feminine" were salient factors in the very strong negative critical reaction to the film.[40] Erich von Stroheim plays Count Karamzin, a desolate European, who attempts to seduce the wife of an American ambassador. Once the critics determined through intertextual arguments that the American ambassador was "unrealistic" (using political and cultural codes of verisimilitude) and the continental Count was a troublesome site of both the masculine and the feminine, the reviewers ignored much intratextual evidence and a plot resolution in which the American wife realizes her "foolish" attraction to the Count. If current codes of appropriate representation were violated, perhaps over time these dissipated, allowing the text to function with its resolution in tact. To determine this will require further investigation and comparison of subsequent critical response.

This preliminary research in the area of reception of moving images indicates a great wealth of possible work important in understanding the effects of film. Among the most pertinent of hypotheses are that histories of spectator reception are possible, that viewers should be grouped into sets of respondents, that moving images do not, by themselves, determine responses (witness the general resistance to *Foolish Wives* which in most respects follows classical Hollywood filmmaking practices), that historical spectators bring much with them into the reception process, and that institutions must be studied in terms of what interpretative strategies they provide or suggest to viewers. As with the new histories of production, each instance of a film must be treated as a historical event in which some causes will be more salient than others. The same applies to the historical spectator in relation to those films.

Among the possible outcomes of this research is a reinterpretation of genres, authorship, and modes of film practice (not only Hollywood versus avant-garde, for example, but also documentary "versus" fiction, and narrative "versus" non-narrative). In every instance, what these films are to a spectator results less from "inherent" textual features than from external cues (institutional directions for interpreting), intertextual cues (filmic properties in relation to historically specific signifying practices), and crucially, available interpretative strategies employed by the historically situated spectator. For instance, we might ask what effect the "signature" of an author such as Hitchcock has on our interpretation when we use the interpretative strategy of "auteurism" (thus redefining "auteurism" not as an explanatory model for the cause of a film but as a viewing procedure to make sense out of an experience.)[41]

Furthermore, the very important question of what is special about moving images and their effects cannot be addressed by resorting to reductionist models which see the cinema as imposing its meanings (and ideologies) on the spectator. As implied, the moving image as an object no longer exists in isolation from the viewing subject: what the moving image is what subjects in history interpret and experience it as. Thus, the meaning of a signifying object no longer exists within itself, an immanent truth to be found by a critic or historian. Rather, meaning resides in the relation between the films and their spectators across history.[42]

In closing, then, I would suggest that the implications of the revisions in film historiography in this fourth generation have consequences for the other areas of study represented in this book. In terms of the moving image as factual resource, I would point out that what we consider factual is based on our conception of what reality and history are. As the metahistorical aspect to current moving image studies suggests, every history is a representation and a narrative, employing a model of causation, change, and human subjectivity within that model. The question is, which representation is the more adequate one? To answer this does not only require finding more facts but, importantly, considering the assumptions and stories and arguments about those facts. The same applies to the moving image as social and cultural history. While we may study the messages the image was intended to convey, "intentionality" is very problematic once new film historiography enters. Furthermore, what was actually received may be at great odds with any constructed intentions. Von Stroheim and Universal Pictures certainly did not intend for *Foolish Wives* to provoke the reception it had. Finally, the moving image as an interpreter of history must also be analyzed from these perspectives. As a "document" rather than a "monument" of the past, moving images can tell us much about how certain groups of individuals represented history. They should also remind us that our own points of view are not timeless and objective but are colored by our own concepts of history and our own understanding of the moving image experience. Historical individuals are producing the moving image's meaning, the history of those meanings, and the meaning of that history.

NOTES

1. I would like to thank David Bordwell for his comments on an earlier draft of this essay. Not only has he been among my best friends but also, thankfully, my best critic. I also sincerely appreciate the response from the participants of the "Historian and the Moving Image" Conference.
2. Included here would be writers such as Robert Grau, Terry Ramsaye, Benjamin B. Hampton, Howard Thompson Lewis, Jean Epstein, Rudolf Arnheim, Vachel Lindsay, Lev Kuleshov, and Sergei Eisenstein.
3. This second generation must also been seen within its context of the 1930s—a time in which historical events complicated earlier versions of the relationship between society and culturally produced objects previously categorized as having little or no connection to daily life. "The Age of Mechanical Reproduction" not only created cracks in the wall between "high" and "mass" art but, through widespread consumption for status rather than any survival use, mass-produced art flooded society with representations once only the privilege of the few and the elite. Possible social effects which had previously been routinely neutralized through appropriate display in churches or museums now concerned the guardians of society. Although raised within the first decade of film production, these fears were exacerbated by fascism. Although not all the members of this generation of film historians would belong to the radical left, many did.
4. Scholars in this group would include Lewis Jacobs, Georges Sadoul, Andre Bazin, Siegfried Kracauer, and Jay Leyda.
5. Discussion of this new history can be found in the following historiographical essays: Robert C. Allen and Douglas Gomery, *Film History: Theory and Practice* (New York: Knopf, 1983); Robert C. Allen, "The Archeology of Film History," *Wide Angle* 5, no. 2 (1982): 4–12; Robert C. Allen, "Film History: The Narrow Discourse," in *1977 Film Studies Annual* (Part Two), ed. Ben Lawton and Janet Staiger (Pleasantville, New York: Redgrave, 1977), 9–17; Charles F. Altman, "Towards a Historiography

of American Film," *Cinema Journal* 16, no. 2 (Spring 1977): 1–25; David Bordwell, "Our Dream-Cinema: Western Historiography and the Japanese Film," *Film Reader* 4 (1979): 45–62; Edward Branigan, "Color and Cinema: Problems in the Writing of History," *Film Reader* 4 (1979): 16–34; Edward Buscombe, "Introduction: Metahistory of Film," *Film Reader* 4 (1979): 11–15; Edward Buscombe, "A New Approach to Film History," in *1977 Film Studies Annual*, [Part Two], ed. Lawton and Staiger, 1–8; *Edinburgh '77 Magazine* (1977) [Special number, "History/Production/Memory"]; Douglas Gomery, "The Economics of Film: What is the Method?" in *Film/Culture: Explorations of Cinema in its Social Context*, ed. Sari Thompson (Metuchen, New Jersey: Scarecrow, 1982), 81–94; Douglas Gomery, "Historical Method and Data Acquisition," *Cinema Journal* 22, no. 4 (Summer 1983): 58–60; *Iris* [France] 2, no. 2 (1984) [special number on theory and history]; R. Mottram, "Fact and Affirmation: Some Thoughts on the Methodology of Film History and the Relation of Theory to Historiography," *Quarterly Review of Film Studies* 5, no. 3 (Summer 1980); Phil Rosen, "Securing the Historical: Historiography and the Classical Cinema," in *Cinema Histories, Cinema Practices* [American Film Institute Monograph Series, vol. 4], ed. Patricia Mellencamp and Phil Rosen (Frederick, Maryland: University Publications of America, 1984), 17–34; Janet Staiger, "The Politics of Film Canons," *Cinema Journal* 24, no. 3 (Spring 1985): 4–13; Janet Staiger and Douglas Gomery, "The History of World Cinema: Models for Economic Analysis," *Film Reader* 4 (1979): 35–44; Will Straw, "The Myth of Total Cinema History," *Cine-Tracts* 3, no. 1 (1980): 8–16; Kristin Thompson and David Bordwell, "Linearity, Materialism, and the Study of Early American Cinema," *Wide Angle* 5, no. 3 (1983): 4–15.

6. Claude Levi-Strauss, *Structural Anthropology* [1958], trans. Claire Jacobson and Brooke Grundfest Schoepf (New York: Basic Books, 1963). A good overview of structuralism and semiotics is Terrence Hawks, *Structuralism and Semiotics* (London: Methuen, 1977).

7. Ferdinand de Saussure, *Course in General Linguistics* [1916], ed. Charles Bally and Albert Sechehaye; trans. Wade Baskin (New York: McGraw-Hill, 1966), p. 16.

8. Christian Metz, *Film Language: A Semiotics of Cinema* [1968], trans. Michael Taylor (New York: Oxford University, 1974); *Language and Cinema* [1971], trans. Donna Jean Umiker-Sebeok (The Hague: Mouton, 1974). Alternative semiological positions have been suggested by Umberto Eco, Pier Paolo Pasolini, and Jurij Lotman: Umberto Eco, "On the Contribution of Film to Semiotics" [1975], rpt. in *Film Theory and Criticism*, ed. Gerald Mast and Marshall Cohen, 2nd ed. (New York: Oxford University, 1979), 217–33; Umberto Eco, "Articulations of the Cinematic Code" [1970], rpt. in *Movies and Methods*, ed. Bill Nichols (Berkeley: University of California, 1976), 590–607; Pier Paolo Pasolini, "The Cinema of Poetry," rpt. in *Movies and Methods*, ed. Nichols, 542–58; Jurij Lotman, *Semiotics of Cinema* (Ann Arbor: Department of Slavic Languages and Literatures, University of Michigan, 1976).

9. For a detailed (although not semiological) analysis of Hollywood's formal system, see David Bordwell, Janet Staiger, and Kristin Thompson, *The Classical Hollywood Film: Film Style and Mode of Production to 1960* (New York: Columbia University, 1985).

10. John Caughie, *Theories of Authorship* (London: Routledge & Kegan Paul,

1981); Paul Willeman, "Notes on Subjectivity—On Reading 'Subjectivity Under Seige,' " *Screen* 19, no. 1 (Spring 1978): 41–69; Peter Wollen, *Signs and Meaning in the Cinema*, rev. ed. (Bloomington: Indiana University, 1972), 74–115.

11. Charles F. Altman, ed., *Genre: The Musical* (London: British Film Institute, 1981); John G. Cawelti, *Adventure, Mystery, and Romance* (Chicago: University of Chicago, 1976); Jane Feuer, *The Hollywood Musical* (Bloomington: Indiana University, 1982); Thomas Schatz, *Hollywood Genres: Formulas, Filmmaking and the Studio System* (Philadelphia: Temple University, 1981); Will Wright, *Six Guns and Society: A Structural Study of the Western* (Berkeley: University of California Press, 1975).

12. Louis Althusser, *Lenin and Philosophy and Other Essays*, trans. Ben Brewster (New York: Monthly Review Press, 1971). Among the various criticisms of Althusser's model includes E. P. Thompson, *The Poverty of Theory and Other Essays* (London: Merlin, 1978).

13. Briefly, Lacanian psychoanalysis argues that the small "hommelette," an undifferentiated human animal, moves into an "imaginary" identification with an ideal ego through its misrecognition of an Other as itself. Upon the entry of a third term (in the model, the Father), it recognizes its difference from that Other and the power of the Father to separate it and split it from its self (its imaginary and narcisstic identification with its ideal ego). The intervention of this third term is also linked to the child's recognition of a mark of difference, the phallus, and the fact that some individuals (i.e., the Father) hold that mark while others (i.e., the Mother) must have had that mark removed. This threat of castration results in the child's submission to the Law of the Father. In Lacan's version of the Oedipal complex, a connection is made to the acquisition of language, defined through semiotics as a structuring of differences (binary oppositions). Hence, submitting to the Law or Patriarchy is also moving into the Symbolic, taking up the language of culture in order to negotiate reality and enter society. Yet in moving into patriarchal language, in accepting a society's connection of signifiers with signifieds, the child represses in its unconscious another language, one with its own connections of signifiers and signifieds, a language whose latent features might manifest themselves in expressed speech or writing through slips, displacements, and condensations. Borrowing a distinction proposed by Roman Jakobson between metaphor and metonymy, these manifest symptoms can be related to the structure of the unconscious which is constantly reworking and revising its own language. Thus, poststructuralists no longer assume a one-to-one relation between signifier and signified, but a slippage among these. Besides reading Lacan, good, accessible synopses are: Eugen S. Bar, "Understanding Lacan," in *Psychoanalysis and Contemporary Science*, ed. Leo Goldberger and Victor H. Rosen, vol. 3 (New York: International Universities, 1974), 423–544; Terry Eagleton, *Literary Theory: An Introduction* (Minneapolis: University of Minnesota Press, 1983), 151–93; Richard Wollheim, "The Cabinet of Dr. Lacan," *New York Review of Books*, 25 January 1979, 36–45. Eagleton is particularly good in stressing that Freudianism and Lacanianism are social, not biological, theories of the human.

14. Besides articles in the anthologies in note 16, see: Douglas Gomery, "The American Industry of the 1970s: Stasis in the New Hollywood," *Wide Angle* 5, no. 4 (1984): 52–9; "Corporate Ownership and Control in the

Contemporary US Film Industry," *Screen* 25, no. 4–5 (July-October 1984): 60–9; "The Economics of U.S. Film Exhibition Policy and Practice," *Cine-Tracts* no. 12 (Winter 1981): 36–40; "Economic Change in the US Television Industry," *Screen* 25, no. 2 (March-April 1984): 62–67; "Film Culture and Industry: Recent Formulations in Economic History," *Iris* [France], 2, no. 1 (1984): 17–32; "The Growth of Movie Monopolies: The Case of Balaban & Katz," *Wide Angle* 3, no. 1 (1979): 54–63; "Movie Audiences, Urban Geography, and the History of the American Film," *The Velvet Light Trap* no. 19 (1982): 23–9; "The Picture Palace: Economic Sense or Hollywood Nonsense," *Quarterly Review of Film Studies* 3, no. 1 (Winter 1978): 23–36; "Toward a History of Film Exhibition: The Case of the Picture Palace," in *1977 Film Studies Annual* [Part Two], ed. Lawton and Staiger, 17–26.

15. Thomas Elsaesser, "Film History and Visual Pleasure," in *Cinema Histories, Cinema Practices*, ed. Mellencamp and Rosen, 50.

16. The following are good instances of these revisionist histories of the industrial context: Jeanne Allen, "Copyright Protection in Theatre, Vaudeville and Early Cinema," *Screen* 21, no. 1 (Summer 1980): 79–91; Robert Allen, *Vaudeville and Film, 1895–1915: A Study in Media Interaction* (New York: Arno, 1980); Robert Allen, "William Fox Presents *Sunrise*," *Quarterly Review of Film Studies* 2, no. 3 (August 1977): 327–83; Allen and Gomery, *Film History*; Tino Balio, ed. *The American Film Industry*, 2nd ed. (Madison: University of Wisconsin, 1985); Tino Balio, *United Artists: The Company Built by the Stars* (Madison: University of Wisconsin, 1976); Edward Buscombe, "Notes on Columbia Picture Corporation 1926–41," *Screen* 16, no. 3 (Autumn 1975): 65–82; Gorham Kindem, ed., *The American Movie Industry: The Business of Motion Pictures* (Carbondale: Southern Illinois University, 1982); Thomas H. Guback, *The International Film Industry: Western Europe and America since 1945* (Bloomington: Indiana University Press, 1969); Thomas H. Guback, "Theatrical Film," in *Who Owns the Media?* ed. Benjamin M. Compaine, 2nd ed. (New York: Harmony Books, 1982), 199–298; Thomas H. Guback and Dennis J. Dombrowski, "Television and Hollywood: Economic Relations in the 1970s," *Journal of Broadcasting* 20, no. 4 (Fall 1976): 511–27; Mary Beth Haralovich, "Mandate of Good Taste," *Wide Angle* 6, no. 2 (1984): 50–7; Charlotte Herzog, "Movie Palaces and Exhibition," *Film Reader* 2 (1977): 185–97; Charlotte Herzog, "The Movie Palace and the Theatrical Sources of its Architectural Style," *Cinema Journal* 20, no. 2 (Spring 1981): 15–37; Chris Hugo, "The Economic Background," *Movie* 27/28 (Winter 1980/Spring 1981): 43–9; Paul Kerr, ed., *The Hollywood Film Industry* (London: Routledge & Kegan Paul, 1986); Ida Jeter, "The Collapse of the Federated Motion Picture Crafts: A Case Study of Class Collaboration in the Motion Picture Industry," *University Film Producers Association Journal* 31, no. 2 (1979): 37–45; Judith Mayne, "Immigrants and Spectators," *Wide Angle* 5, no. 2 (1982): 32–41; Charles Musser, "Another Look at the 'Chaser Theory,'" *Studies in Visual Communication* 10, no. 4 (Fall 1984): 24–44 [also see response by Robert Allen, 45–50, and Musser's reply]; Charles Musser, "American Vitagraph: 1897–1901," *Cinema Journal* 22, no. 3 (Spring 1983): 4–46; Charles Musser, "The Eden Musee in 1898: The Exhibitor as Creator," *Film & History* 11, no. 4 (December 1981): 73–83, 96; Michael Nielson, "Toward a Workers' History of the U.S. Film Industry," in *Labor, the Working Class, and the Media*, ed. Vincent Wasko and Janet Wasko

(Norwood, New Jersey: Ablex Publishing, 1983), 47–83; Janet Staiger, "Combination and Litigation: Practices in US Film Distribution, 1896–1917," *Cinema Journal* 23, no. 2 (Winter 1984): 41–72; Janet Staiger, "Seeing Stars," *The Velvet Light Trap*, no. 20 (1983): 10–14; Janet Wasko, *Movies and Money: Financing the American Film Industry* (Norwood, New Jersey: Ablex Publishing, 1982).

17. Besides my contribution in Bordwell, Staiger, and Thompson, *The Classical Hollywood Cinema*, see: "Individualism versus Collectivism: The Shift to Independent Production in the US Film Industry," *Screen* 24, no. 4–5 (July-October 1983): 68–79; "Mass-Produced Photoplays: Economic and Signifying Practices in the First Years of Hollywood," *Wide Angle* 4, no. 3 (1981): 12–27; " 'Tame' Authors and the Corporate Laboratory: Stories, Writers, and Scenarios in Hollywood," *Quarterly Review of Film Studies* 8, no. 4 (Fall 1983): 33–46; and essays in anthologies listed in note 16.

18. Jean-Louis Baudry, "Ideological Effects of the Basic Cinematographic Apparatus" [1970], trans. Alan Williams, *Film Quarterly* 28, no. 2 (Winter 1974–75): 39–47; "The Apparatus" [1975], *Camera obscura* no. 1 (Fall 1976): 104–26.

19. An argument can be made that Baudry's analysis is itself ultimately idealist.

20. Baudry's position almost negated the possibility of the use of cinema by radicals since he had so thoroughly imbued the cinema through its technology with a bourgeois ideology. Jean-Louis Comolli, "Technique et ideologic," *Cahiers du cinema* [6 parts], nos. 229, 230, 231, 233, 234–35, 241 (May 1971-September/October 1972). Comolli is also disagreeing with Jean-Patrick Lebel, *Cinema et ideologie* (Paris: 1971).

21. Useful essays on technology are: Rick Altman, "Toward a Theory of the History of Representational Technologies," *Iris* [France], 2, no. 2 (1984): 111–25; Peter Baxter, "On the History and Ideology of Film Lighting," *Screen*, 16, no. 3 (Autumn 1975): 83–106; David Bordwell, "Camera Movement, the Coming of Sound, and the Classical Hollywood Style," in *1977 Film Studies Annual* [Part Two], ed. Lawton and Staiger, 27–30; Bordwell, Staiger, and Thompson, *The Classical Hollywood Cinema*; Branigan, "Color and Cinema"; Edward Buscombe, "Sound and Color," *Jump Cut*, no. 17 (April 1978): 23–5; Theresa Hak Kyung Cha, ed., *Apparatus* (New York: Tanam Press, 1980); William Lafferty, *The Early Development of Magnetic Sound Recording in Broadcasting and Motion Pictures, 1928–1950* (Unpub. Ph.D. Diss.: Northwestern University, 1981); Teresa de Lauretis and Stephen Heath, ed., *The Cinematic Apparatus* (New York: St. Martin's Press, 1980); Steve Neale, *Cinema and Technology: Image, Sound, Color* (Bloomington: Indiana University, 1985); Patrick Ogle, "Technological and Aesthetic Influences upon the Development of Deep Focus Cinematography in the United States," *Screen* 13, no. 1 (Spring 1972): 45–72; Barry Salt, "Film Style and Technology in the Thirties," *Film Quarterly* 30, no. 1 (Fall 1976): 19–32; Barry Salt, "Film Style and Technology in the 1940s," *Film Quarterly* 31, no. 1 (Fall 1977): 46–57; Barry Salt, *Film Style and Technology: History and Analysis* (London: Starword, 1983); *The Velvet Light Trap* no. 21 (Summer 1985) [special issue on the widescreen]; Elisabeth Weis and John Belton, *Film Sound: Theory and Practice* (New York: Columbia University, 1985); Brian Winston, "A Whole Technology of Dyeing," *Daedalus* 114, no. 4 (Fall 1985): 105–123; *Yale*

French Studies 60, no. 1 (1980) [special issue on sound]. Also see anthologies in note 16.

22. Raymond Bellour, "Hitchcock, the Enunciator," *Camera obscura* no. 2 (Fall 1977): 66–91; Editors of *Cahiers du cinèma*, "John Ford's *Young Mr. Lincoln*" [1970], rpt. in *Movies and Methods*, ed. Nichols, 493–529; Caughie, *Theories of Authorship*; Jean-Louis Comolli and Jean Narboni, "Cinema/ Ideology/Criticism" [1969], rpt. in *Movies and Methods*, ed. Nichols, 22– 30; *Edinburgh '76 Magazine* (1976); John Ellis, *Visible Fictions: Cinema, Television, Video* (London: Routledge & Kegan Paul, 1982); Thomas Elsaesser, "Film History and Visual Pleasure"; Thomas Elsaesser, "Primary Identification and the Historical Subject: Fassbinder and Germany," *Cinè-Tracts* 3, no. 3 (Fall 1980): 43–52; Stephen Heath, "Film and System: Terms of Analysis," *Screen* 16, no. 1 (Spring 1975): 7–77 and *Screen* 16, no. 2 (Summer 1975): 91–113; Stephen Heath, *Questions of Cinema* (Bloomington: Indiana University, 1981); Stephen Heath and Patricia Mellencamp, ed., *Cinema and Language* [American Film Institute Monograph Series, vol. 1] (Frederick, Maryland: University Publications of America, 1983); E. Ann Kaplan, ed., *Regarding Television* [American Film Institute Monograph Series, vol. 2] (Frederick, Maryland: University Publications of America, 1983); Mellencamp and Rosen, ed., *Cinema Histories, Cinema Practices*; Christian Metz, *The Imaginary Signifier: Psychoanalysis and the Cinema* [1977] (Bloomington: Indiana University Press, 1982); Stephen Neale, *Genre* (London: British Film Institute, 1980); *Screen* 25, no. 2 (March-April 1984) [special issue on television]. Criticism of Heath's work is in Noel Carroll, "Address to the Heathen," *October*, no. 23 (1983): 89– 163; also see replies in *October* no. 26 (1983): 61–115; *October* no. 27 (1983): 81–102.

23. Bordwell, Staiger, and Thompson, *The Classical Hollywood Cinema*. Other studies of Hollywood's signifying practices include: Eileen Bowser, "The Brighton Project: An Introduction," *Quarterly Review of Film Studies* 4, no. 4 (Fall 1979): 509–38; John Fell, ed., *Film Before Griffith* (Berkeley: University of California, 1983); Jon Gartenberg, "Vitagraph before Griffith: Forging Ahead in the Nickelodeon Era," *Studies in Visual Communication* 10, no. 4 (Fall 1974): 7–23; Jon Gartenberg, "Camera Movement in Edison and Biograph Films, 1900–1906," *Cinema Journal* 19, no. 2 (Spring 1976): 58–68; Andre Gaudreault, "Detours in Film Narrative: The Development of Cross-Cutting," *Cinema Journal* 19, no. 1 (Fall 1979): 39– 59; Tom Gunning, "Weaving a Narrative: Style and Economic Background in Griffith's Biograph Films," *Quarterly Review of Film Studies* 6, no. 1 (Winter 1981): 11–25; Paul Kerr, "Notes on the B Film Noir," *Screen Education* nos. 22–23 (Autumn/Winter 1979/80): 45–65; William Lafferty, "A Reappraisal of the Semi-Documentary in Hollywood, 1945– 1948," *The Velvet Light Trap*, no. 20 (Summer 1983): 22–6; Charles Musser, "The Early Cinema of Edwin Porter," *Cinema Journal* 19, no. 1 (Fall 1979): 1–38; Barry Salt, "The Early Development of Film Form," *Film Form* 1, no. 1 (Spring 1976); Janet Staiger, "The Eyes are Really the Focus': Photoplay Acting and Film Form and Style," *Wide Angle* 6, no. 4 (1985): 14–23. Also see anthologies in notes 16 and 22 and Noel Burch's work cited in note 28.

24. Again, agreement is only in the most general sense unified. Much argumentation is occuring among theoretical models and various descriptions of specific problems.

25. One reason for the American pedogogy on films during the 1930s was to educate viewers in order to deflect any possibilities of misinterpretation. (Ida Jeter, "If You Can't Beat 'Em, Join 'Em: *Photoplay Studies* of the 1930s," Paper read at the Seventh Annual Ohio University Film Conference, Athens, Ohio, 25–27 October 1984.) Also in a sense the 1940s and 1950s anticommunist witchhunts in the United States film industry repeat these propositions about epistemology and social effect.

26. One should also note that in this argument Hollywood narratives could be equated with earlier historiography in which linear, single-termed, and unmediated causality was duplicated within the stories produced by this dominant fiction-making institution.

27. See note 22.

28. These included Weimar expressionist cinema, the art cinema of Europe, certain Japanese films, and avant-garde filmmaking. In addition, since these films came out of different modes of production this seemed to clinch the argument. Seminal articles propounding such positions and explicitly accepting this binarism include ones by Annette Michelson and Peter Wollen. Perhaps the most sustained work of a theorist and historian to follow upon this has been that of Noel Burch. See Annette Michelson, "Film and the Radical Aspiration" [1973], rpt. and rev. in *Film Theory and Criticism*, ed. Mast and Cohen, 617–35; Peter Wollen, "The Two Avant Gardes" [1975] and "Godard and Counter Cinema: *Vent d'est*" in *Readings and Writings* (London: Verso, 1982); Noel Burch and Jorge Dana, "Propositions," trans. Diana Matias and Christopher King, *Afterimage* [England], no. 5 (Spring 1974): 40–66; Noel Burch, "Porter, or ambivalence," trans. Tom Milne, *Screen* 19, no. 4 (Winter 1978/9): 91–105; Noel Burch, *To a Distant Observer: Form and Meaning in the Japanese Cinema* (Berkeley: University of California Press, 1979). For criticisms of Burch's work, see: Paul Kerr, "Re-Inventing the Cinema," *Screen* 12, no. 4 (1980/81): 80–4; Bordwell, "Our Dream-Cinema"; Rosen, "History, Textuality, Nation"; Staiger, "The Politics of Film Canons"; Thompson and Bordwell, "Linearity, Materialism and the Study of Early American Cinema."

29. One could hypothesize that certain social formations might have particular variants of psychoanalytic construction (a revision of Siegfried Kracauer); however, the possibilities for political practice or change were nearly nullified since change could not come through the superstructure alone. On an attempt to revise Kracauer, see Elsaesser, "Primary Identification and the Historical Subject."

30. Mary Ann Doane, "Film and the Masquerade: Theorizing the Female Spectator," *Screen* 23, no. 3–4 (September/October 1982): 74–87; Mary Ann Doane, "Misrecognition and Identity," *Cine-Tracts* 3, no. 3 (Fall 1980): 25–32; Mary Ann Doane, "The Voice in the Cinema: The Articulation of Body and Space," *Yale French Studies* 60, no. 1 (1980): 33–50; Mary Ann Doane, "Women's Stake: Filming the Female Body," *October* no. 17 (Summer 1981); Mary Ann Doane, Patricia Mellencamp, and Linda Williams, ed. *Re-Vision: Essays in Feminist Film Criticism* [American Film Institute Monograph Series, vol. 3] (Frederick, Maryland: University Publications of America, 1984); Stephen Heath, "Difference," *Screen* 19, no. 3 (Autumn 1978): 51–112; E. Ann Kaplan, *Women and Film: Both Sides of the Camera* (New York: Methuen, 1983); Annette Kuhn, *Women's Pictures: Feminism and Cinema* (London: Routledge & Kegan Paul, 1982); Laura Mulvey, "Afterthoughts on 'Visual Pleasure and Narrative Cinema'

inspired by *Duel in the Sun*," *Framework* no. 15/16/17 (Summer 1981): 12–15; Laura Mulvey, "Visual Pleasure and Narrative Cinema," *Screen* 16, no. 3 (Autumn 1975): 6–18; Kaja Silverman, "Masochism and Subjectivity," *Framework* no. 12 (1981): 2–9.

31. Editorial, *Camera obscura* no 1 (Fall 1976): 3–10; Claire Johnston, "Women's Cinema as Counter Cinema," rpt. in *Movies and Methods*, ed. Nichols, 208–17; Constance Penley, "The Avant Garde and its Imaginary," *Camera obscura* no. 1 (Fall 1977): 13–33.

32. Teresa de Lauretis, *Alice Doesn't: Feminism, Semiotics, Cinema* (Bloomington: Indiana University, 1984); Christine Gledhill, "Recent Directions in Feminist Criticism," [1978], rpt. and rev. in *Re-Vision*, ed. Doane, Mellencamp, and Williams, 18–48; Annette Kuhn, "Women's Genres," *Screen* 25, no. 1 (January-February 1984): 18–28.

33. The recent interest in Bakhtin/Volosinov's theory of language as dialogical (in debate with Saussurean linguistics) is partially due to the need to construct a poststructuralist theory of language as language-use.

34. Tony Bennett, "Text and Social Process: The Case of James Bond," *Screen Education* no. 41 (Winter/Spring 1982): 3–14.

35. Such norms exist and affect our ability to understand and interpret films. One way to restate the debate over whether or not reflexive and discursive forms of film practice cause a different spectatorial effect than Hollywood's does is to understand these techniques within the history of their use. Whether or not they will continue to be linked to progressive forms of filmmaking will depend upon the history of their use and reception. Already, music videos incorporate many of these devices, thus "neutralizing" their historical impact as a formal method to call attention to the politically alternative practice with which they were first associated. Thus, the history of norms and deviations of genres and modes of filmmaking connect to reception histories. Furthermore, no "form" or "style" is essentially politically progressive.

36. Michael Budd, "*The Cabinet of Dr. Caligari*: Conditions of Reception," *Cine-Tracts* 3, no. 4 (Winter 1981): 41–9.

37. David Bordwell, "The Art Cinema as a Mode of Film Practice," *Film Criticism* 4, no. 1 (Fall 1979): 56–63. Bordwell expands on this and in some ways presents his own version of spectator/film relations in his recent *Narration in the Fiction Film* (Madison, Wisconsin: University of Wisconsin, 1985). Unfortunately, he still presents a homogenized, generalized, idealized spectator, and posits history only as norms of filmic textuality.

38. Joe McElhaney, "Gay Spectatorship and Judy Garland," unpublished seminar paper, New York University, Fall 1984.

39. Roger McNiven, "*Rope*: Interpretation and Textual Constancy," unpublished seminar paper, New York University, Fall 1984.

40. Janet Staiger, " 'The Handmaiden of Villainy': Methods and Problems in Studying the Historical Reception of a Film," *Wide Angle* 8, no. 1 (1986): 19–27. Also see Bennett, "Text and Social Process"; Eric Rentschuler, *West German Film in the Course of Time* (Bedford Hills, New York: Redgrave Publishing Company, 1984).

41. See for instance: Adam Knee, "Notions of Authorship and the Reception of *Once Upon a Time in America*," *Film Criticism* 10, no. 1 (Fall 1985): 3–17;

42. The advantages of such a proposition are significant. For one thing films are no longer frozen into a historicist interpretation of what they meant

at a particular time, but older films can still have a value to present-day viewers. Furthermore, if interpretative strategies are the source of how we produce meaning, understanding how certain strategies got in place can also help in disseminating strategies that might lead to more progressive readings and responses by wider audiences. Since we use interpretative strategies to make sense of our everyday experiences, the consequences could be even greater.

Anthony Aldgate is Lecturer in History at the Open University of the United Kingdom. He is the author of Cinema and History: British Newsreels and the Spanish Civil War *(1979); co-author of* British Cinema and Society, 1930–1970 *(1983) and* Britain Can Take It: The British Cinema in the Second World War *(1986), and has contributed articles on film and history to numerous other books and journals. He edited and directed* The Spanish Civil War *(1972) for the British Inter-University Film Consortium, and has written and presented many historical compilations for the Open University which have been shown on the BBC.*

TEACHING FILM HISTORY IN THE HISTORY CURRICULUM

Anthony Aldgate

Academic historians approach the history of film and television differently than most cinema scholars do, and this is evident in what they do in their classrooms. In America, as in Britain, historians are principally interested in researching and teaching those facets of film history (not least film art and film industry) which bear directly upon their specific concerns and larger purpose.[1]

At the Open University of the United Kingdom, for instance, the overall aims of the "Introduction to History" block in the Arts Foundation Course were formulated as follows (the "you" in each case, of course, being the student):

1. To encourage you to see history as a relevant subject and as a valuable introduction to the varieties of human experience.
2. To help you to appreciate that history, on the one hand, is a serious discipline with a rigorous methodology, while, on the other hand, it is not a mere matter of "ascertaining the facts," but involves a high degree of interpretative and creative imagination.
3. To awaken you to the richness and complexity of primary source material.
4. To introduce you to some of the fundamental problems in the handling of source material.
5. To make you aware of how history is written.
6. To provide the basic criteria upon which you can assess the relative merits of different secondary authorities.
7. By explaining basic principles and exposing the more obvious

pitfalls (periodization, semantics, imprecision) to guide you towards intelligent historical composition of your own.

8. To enable you to discuss critically how far, and in what senses, history can set the temporal and social context for the other humanities and to discuss the relationships between history and the other humanities disciplines.[2]

There is no mention of film or film history, as you can see. Yet the History Department at the Open University has been a frontrunner among those British universities teaching "Film and History." And its deep-seated and massive commitment to the use of "film as a historical source" has been evident in the many courses it has mounted so far, as I hope to elaborate shortly. In each case, the study of film has been directed toward the fulfillment of the more general goals listed above. Along with those other university and college departments of history, the Open University has largely fulfilled Professor John Grenville's prediction, made in 1970, that "It is in the study of attempts to mould public opinion on political, social and international questions that research in film (and later television) will find its first important academic application."[3]

Thus, for example, the most recent Open University History course sought at one point to introduce students to the ways in which, throughout the 1930s, the newsreels attempted to mould American public opinion on matters of domestic import. To do this, students were presented with an archive film compilation of newsreel stories from the period, highlighting some of the significant issues which confronted the administrations of President Herbert Hoover and President Franklin D. Roosevelt. It included an item which reported upon events surrounding the handling of the Bonus Army—those veterans of World War I who assembled in Washington during June 1932 to petition Congress for immediate payment of the bonuses promised to them. All the American newsreel companies were there to record the incidents which followed Hoover's order to dislodge the veterans, and the Universal News of 28 July 1932 (this newsreel story with original soundtrack is included in the video compilation). did so with a commentary which ran as follows:

It's War: the greatest concentration of fighting troops in Washington since 1865; the 3rd Cavalry, from Fort Myer, and the 1st Light Tank Regiment, grim and relentless; the 12th Infantry from Fort Washington—all assembled with a single purpose, to rout the Bonus Army from Government property which they've been occupying without permission, property which has to be torn down to make room for new buildings.

The Bonus Veterans have defied their leaders. The police can't handle them since the riot this morning that ended in one death and dozens wounded. And so they're being forced out of their shacks by smoke bombs and tear gas, hurled by the troops who've been called out by the President of the United States.

Mr. Hoover doesn't blame the Veterans entirely. He claims that the disorder and defiance were caused by foreign Reds and a large criminal element in the ranks of the Veterans. It's a spectacle unparalleled in the history of the country—a day of bloodshed and riot, reminiscent of actual conditions in France in 1917. Sullen, disgruntled, the Veterans give way unwillingly before the steady advance of the soldiers. The tension's terrific. Real drama of the highest order. But the orders of the President and the Secretary of War must be obeyed.

Gradually, the Bonus Army realises that they'd better be good and a general retreat begins, interrupted here and there by a stubborn Veteran. But resistance isn't practical. They soon find out that it doesn't pay to monkey with a buzz-saw, and there's an occasional free ride to jail or hospital. And to make sure the men will really stay out the soldiers have orders to burn down the unsanitary and illegal camp.

And the roaring flames sound the death knell to the fantastic Bonus Army. Many have gone back home, betrayed by unscrupulous leaders, some still sincere in the adventure that failed, and that ends so disastrously in the shadow of the beautiful dome of the Capitol of the United States.[4]

After a reading of the script for the commentary alone, it should come as no surprise to learn that the report in its day was considered to be a very "hot" item, in news terms. In consequence, it was given a considerable amount of time in the context of the newsreel issue, running for 2 minutes 21 seconds (the longest story in the release), and it occupied the prestigious last slot in a run of six stories (thereby bringing the whole issue to a dramatic climax). But, as is also evident, the newsreel did not overtly criticise Hoover for his actions. Indeed, it even reiterated the Hoover line that the Bonus Army was spurred on to its actions by Communists and criminals, an obvious attempt to undermine its credibility, though one that had little basis in reality. William E. Leuchtenburg has put the matter in that regard most succinctly: "Far from being a menacing band of revolutionaries, the Bonus Army was a whipped, melancholy group of men trying to hold themselves together when their spirit was gone. The Communist faction had to be protected from other bonus marchers who threatened physical violence."[5]

What such newsreels did do, however, was to give the lie to the administration's claims that the military had not been guilty of violence and had not set fire to the veterans' camp. The film accompanying the report graphically depicted the fact that infantry, cavalry, tanks and other troops had been called out to put pay to the Bonus Army; the 'intruders' were forced from their shack and tent camp in the heart of the capital at bayonet point and occasionally encouraged by the broad side of a cavalry sabre; smoke bombs were visibly hurled and incendiary grenades were seen to send the shacks up in smoke. In short, armed force had plainly been used against American veterans. This was the course which Hoover had advocated and it was this action which aroused a storm of protest. The film evidence the newsreels provided helps to explain, at least in part, how the Hoover administration was cast in such a poor light towards its end.[6]

To appreciate such points, and to tease out the historical nuances, it was essential that our students be presented, as they were, with both the film evidence and a measure of supporting documentation. When it came to dealing with the question of industrial strife in America throughout the 1930s, for instance, once again we compiled an array of newsreel stories on the matter. It included a particularly revealing story from the Universal News for 11 July 1934 (also in the video compilation), the commentary for which read:

> As a culmination of the second month of the dock strike tying up West Coast shipping, one of the worst riots in the history of San Francisco is turning the Embarcadero and the vicinity of the water-front into a regular battlefield. 1,000 police are pitted against 5,000 striking longshoremen and marine workers. The battle has surged all day, progressing from bricks to tear gas and finally to bullets in a mad orgy of street fighting. Scores of strikers have been wounded and many policemen hurt. Several men have been killed. There lies one of them now. His companion is severely wounded and may not live.
>
> The fighting is brought to an end only by the appearance of National Guard troops, 2,000 of whom were ordered out by Governor Frank Merriam. The entire San Francisco waterfront now is an armed camp, bristling with machine guns.
>
> Meanwhile, President Roosevelt's Mediation Board is threatening strong steps to force peace in the shipping world. (FADE) At Bridgeton, New Jersey, wild disorder reigns at the Seabrook Farms and Cannery, as striking farm workers and plant employees battle local police and firemen.
>
> Men and women in hand to hand combat. 50 or more have been hurt and dozens of others overcome by tear gas. The strikers are determined that no vegetables shall move from the farms. The police of the entire countryside have been drawn into the battle. Scores have been arrested— but not without difficulty. Local farmers and townsmen have organised a Vigilance Committee to subdue the strike which they say is of Communist origin. But in the meantime, the local gendarmerie is bearing the brunt of the fracas, and it looks as if they have their hands full all right. Yessir, it looks pretty dark for the constables. Meanwhile, the crops are rotting in the fields. While the strikers cool off in the calaboose.[7]

In addition to the evidence presented by the filmed report itself, it proved possible in this instance to assemble for students a collection of documentary materials, all of which helped in determining how the Universal News editors formulated their opinions on the events they purported to depict. One such document was the statement made by Governor Frank Merriam on 5 July 1934, at Sacramento, and recorded by cameraman J. McHenry "for the benefit of the sound reels."

Forebearance with the striking longshoremen in San Francisco has passed the point of common sense and good citizenship. The acknowledged leaders of the strikers have defied the State government and sought to overthrow the authority of the State government in its operation and maintenance of the State's harbor facilities at San Francisco. This situation cannot be endured. I have ordered the National Guard of California to move into the San Francisco strike area to safeguard life, to protect State property, and to preserve order.

At this time, 1500 National Guardsmen are patrolling the strike territory. Approximately 5000 additional guardsmen are available for duty if the situation demands their service. Should this force prove insufficient, the State government has ample authority to enroll its citizens to meet any emergency that may arise. I am prepared to pursue a course which shall assure full protection of life and property.

The California National Guard represents no class, serves no faction, takes no sides. It is the military arm of the people, and is drawn from all ranks. It is responsive only to the highest interests and the basic welfare of the people. It cannot be intimidated; it shall not be overridden or overpowered.

The leadership of the striking longshoremen is not free from Communistic and subversive influences. I know that independent, sincere labor leaders are not sympathetic with the conduct of this strike, and as Governor I appeal to the sane, clear-thinking workers and their chosen representatives to oppose courageously and insistently any effort to involve other groups or representatives of labor in a controversy which has gone beyond the bounds of ordinary and legitimate dispute between employer and employee.

There will be no turning back from the position I have taken on this matter.

Similarly, the Universal file on that part of their news story related to the Bridgeton, New Jersey, cannery strike included a report of 7 July 1934 made by Joseph S. Wasney, United Press Staff Correspondent:

C. F. Seabrook, owner of the vast farm, charged Communists had fostered the strike which has tied up his farming for 14 days. "The strike was called by Communists and about 200 workers who had been employed on the farms for years, and were heretofore contented, left their jobs," Seabrook said. "At least 100 of this number were forced to quit their jobs by intimidation."

Donald Henderson, leader of the strike, who admits he is a member of the Communist Party, asserted the strike was called by Locals 1 and 10 of the Agricultural Industrial Workers' Union to prevent a wage cut, to stop laying off of employees, and to force a closed shop. "Employees were getting from 25 to 30 cents an hour and we were notified that a wage cut was necessary and that about 100 men were to be laid off," Henderson said. "To prevent a violation of the union contract a strike was ordered."

While the management and strike leaders were presenting their sides, about 100 pickets, men and women in overalls, paraded before the farm office, singing "Solidarity."

The newsreels were a powerful source of communication on matters of public interest, during the 1930s, and nobody appreciated that factor more than the newsreel company chiefs. When, for example, cameraman Orlando Lippert filmed the riots at the Republic Steel plant in South Chicago on Memorial Day, 30 May 1937, the film was initially withheld from release by Paramount. A. J. Richard, the editor in chief, gave the reasons for withholding the film in a private telegram, which was made public on 8 June 1937. The telegram read as follows:

> Our pictures of the Chicago steel riots are not being released any place in this country for reasons reached after serious consideration of the several factors involved. First, please remember that whereas newspapers reach individuals in the home, we show to a public gathered in groups averaging 1,000 or more, and therefore subject to crowd hysteria while assembled in the theatre. Our pictures depict a tense and nerve-wracking episode which in certain sections of the country might very well incite local riot and perhaps riotous demonstrations in theatres, leading to further casualties. For these reasons of public policy, which we consider more important than any profit to ourselves, these pictures are shelved, and so far as we are concerned will stay shelved. We are under editorial rights of withholding from the screen pictures not fit to be seen. This parallels the editorial rights exercised by newspapers of withholding from publication news not fit to be read.[8]

William P. Montague, assignment editor at Paramount News, took the story a little further in a statement he made to the Institute of Human Relations:

> Consider the situation at that time. The picture we had was a good picture, but not a great one. There have been better. It was its timeliness that made it dangerous. It was at the very climax of the steel strike. Seventy thousand men were out on strike, battling non-strikers in seven states at every morning and evening shift in the plants. We had something which, if we let it go, would have blocked any peaceable settlement of the steel strike. In fact, the bitterness and indignation it would have stirred certainly would have led to added fighting. Out in the steel states—Michigan, Indiana, Illinois—there were bound to be riots in theatres which, perhaps, might even possibly have led to more deaths.
>
> Paramount did not suppress the Chicago riot pictures. Instead, it voluntarily turned them over to the LaFollette Senate Committee investigating the situation, to make what use it could of them on behalf of public welfare. They immediately became part of the record of the proceedings, but in a way that insured no harm to the general public.
>
> Senator LaFollette expressed his appreciation for the stand that Paramount had taken, and finally after the film had been used as evidence recommended the release of the pictures. By that time the industrial situation had quieted down and there was no danger of riots developing, and Paramount sent the complete and unexpurgated pictures out to every one of its exchanges.

The riot pictures more or less crystallise the problem of the newsreels—are they to be wholly an entertainment medium or are they to assume their obligations as a news medium?[9]

In short, then, William Montague claimed that Paramount had not suppressed the film. But, as Raymond Fielding rightly reminds us, the timing of the matter must be carefully considered. The incident occurred on 30 May. Richard's telegram stating that the film was to be shelved indefinitely, came to public attention on 8 June. LaFollette subpoenaed the film for screening by the Senate Committee on 9 June. The committee had viewed the film by 17 June.[10] Thereafter, Paramount proved more than happy to release its "scoop" film of the incident and, indeed, it proceeded to make great play out of both the original footage it had secured and the new-found use to which it had been put by the LaFollette committee. It included, as a prelude to the piece, a speech emanating from no less than LaFollette himself, outlining the value of the film as evidence to the committee in making an assessment of the situation.[11] Clearly, on this occasion, the avowed responsibilities of the news-bearing media and the dictates of self-censorship had relented in the face of commercial and political considerations. And the interplay of all these features provides both the historian and the student with an invaluable insight into the factors governing the newsreel coverage of American industrial strife in the period.[12]

In short, to understand the role of film *in* history, the historian must of necessity follow a somewhat different path to that of the film historian. Like the film historian, of course, it is essential to delve into such facets as "film industry," "film art," and so on. To the film historian, however, these tasks can be an end in themselves. To the historian *per se*, they are clearly not enough. In the final analysis, as I hope this essay has gone some way towards demonstration, the quest for the larger "historical context" is everything.

NOTES

1. An informal survey for the purposes of this inquiry revealed a plethora of "film study" courses, especially in America. Few, though, were conducted by historians who consciously sought to address the question of "film as historical evidence." Daniel Czitrom did so on his "Reel America: History and Film" course. Here, there was evidently an attempt to explore the historical study of film documents within the context of the evolution of the Hollywood film industry and to broach such matters as "business," "regulation," and "censorship." But, once again, it was ultimately for the purpose of shedding further light on the historical themes under scrutiny. Czitrom stressed that he "wanted this to be a history course," first and foremost. While he did not wish "to avoid grappling with some of the larger theoretical and epistemological issues," he was adamant that he preferred "the seminar to get at them from the angle of the historian." Interestingly, this was the sort of course, furthermore, which most approximated to the kind of courses on offer in Britain dealing broadly with the subject of "Film and History."

2. Arthur Marwick, "History at the Open University," *Oxford Review of Education*, vol. 2, no. 2, 1976, pp. 129–137.
3. J. A. S. Grenville, *Film as History*, Birmingham, 1971, p. 22. In addition to the courses offered at the Open University, similar courses are presented at the British universities of Leeds, Lancaster, and Warwick, and at the colleges of St. Mark and St. John, Plymouth, and Westminster, Oxford.
4. "1 killed, scores hurt in Bonus riots," Universal News, vol. 4, no. 62, 28 July 1932. National Archives, Washington.
5. William E. Leuchtenburg, *Franklin D. Roosevelt and the New Deal 1932–1940*, New York, 1963, pp. 15–17.
6. The story is used in television program no. 4, "The Selling of the New Deal," of the Open University course A317, "Themes in British and American History: A Comparative Approach, c. 1760–1970" (1985). The program was written and presented by Tony Aldgate, and produced by Susan Boyd-Bowman, and is broadcast on BBC Television each year throughout the life of the course. My thanks to Bill Murphy, of the National Archives, Washington, for his continued help and support in the making of this program, and others in the series.
7. "San Francisco waterfront strike"/"Bridgeton, New Jersey, cannery strike," Universal News, vol. 6, no. 265, 11 July 1934. National Archives, Washington. The documents which follow are to be found in the release folder on the issue.
8. Quoted in the *New York Times* of 8 June 1937, p. 8, and reprinted in Raymond Fielding, *The American Newsreel, 1911–1967*, Norman, Oklahoma, 1974, p. 282.
9. Reprinted in *World Film News*, vol. 2, no. 11, February 1938, p. 5.
10. Fielding, *The American Newsreel*, pp. 282–3.
11. "Memorial Day, 1937," Paramount Issue no. 86, June 1937. Sherman Grinberg, New York, library no. 6318/6366. Also, National Archives, Washington, record group 46.3. For the background to the incident see Daniel J. Leab, "The Memorial Day Massacre," *Midcontinent American Studies Journal*, vol. 8, no. 1, Fall 1967, pp. 3–17.
12. See, for example, television program no. 7, "Industrial Strife," of the Open University course, "Themes in British and American History" (1985). Written and presented by Tony Aldgate, produced by Susan Boyd-Bowman.

CHAPTER IV
CASE STUDY: THE PLOW THAT BROKE THE PLAINS

In our effort to lay out a fairly comprehensive methodology for the analysis of film and television as historical artifact, the authors of this book have referred to hundreds of examples. The point of this case study is to bring together the key methodological concepts with reference to one moving image artifact, *The Plow That Broke the Plains*, produced by the U.S. government's Resettlement Administration in 1936. This film has been reproduced in its entirety in the video compilation, and the study guide includes aides for close analysis as well as photocopies of archival manuscript documents which help to fill out its history.

It is significant to remember that on some level every film (like any product of a culture) can be thought of as a historical document or artifact. The ones which fit that bill best, however, are the ones which either (1) are based upon history as their subject matter or (2) become forces in history themselves by impinging on the development of broader historical issues or events. *The Plow* justifies study on both of these grounds, and as such, it should be an important subject for broader historical research.[1] Three extensive monographs have recently been published on the dust bowl and its meaning for understanding American agriculture and public policy in the 1930s, but none of the three has done justice to *The Plow* as a source.[2] The film is also valuable for teaching. Students are amazed to learn, after watching what seems like a rather benign historical survey of the settlement and subsequent environmental history of the Great Plains area of the United States, that this film was the cause of acrimonious debate in Congress and that it was in fact "banned" from viewing for more than twenty years in response to the charge of "propaganda" that had been levelled against it.[3]

STAGE ONE

The first stage of analysis requires that we consider the three basic types of questions to be asked of this film as a historical document: questions about its content (what does the film say?), about its production (how may the forces at work in producing the film have influenced what it says?), and about its reception (what did it mean to the people who saw it at the time?). The division of this discussion into three discrete parts may seem overly systematic. In other circumstances it would make more sense to collapse the discussion of the three into one integrated analysis, or at least to favor chronology by putting the discussion of production background before the content study of the completed film. But here the point is to demonstrate the analysis of a single image artifact. Since in most such cases we start by looking at the artifact itself and then seeking to understand it more fully by considering the conditions of its production and reception, this is the approach we will follow here.

CONTENT IN *THE PLOW*

The first step in comprehending the content of *The Plow That Broke the Plains* is to break it down into its major sequences. The breakdown or segmentation below suggests seven sequences; the more extensive one in the study guide prepared by graduate students at Northeastern University has only six; and when the producers prepared their own description in 1936 they listed ten. There is no absolutely "correct" way to segment any particular film; the point is to take it apart as a first step to understanding how it works as a film.

I. The Prologue: This is a carefully paced and poetic introduction, the text of which rolls across the screen from bottom to top. The prologue defines the geographical area that the film will consider as the Great Plains, sets the scene for the following sequence on settlement, and plants a few significant words and phrases to which the narrator will return later in the film. The prologue closes with an extremely simple animation indicating on an outline map the extent of the Great Plains region.

II. Settlement: The second sequence traces the waves of settlement that came to the Great Plains area between 1880 and the period just before World War I. We are told how the plains had been passed by until about 1880, as settlers preferred the richer lands further west. But as the frontier began to disappear, first cattlemen and then farmers "planted their stakes."

III. Drought: All the hard work of the settlers, however, could not change the climate of the region. Before long the periodic drought that they should have expected, in fact arrived; rains failed and farmer/settlers found themselves scratching for survival.

IV. Wheat Will Win The War: The fourth major sequence of the film suggests the significance of World War I to the development of American agriculture in general and the plains region in particular. The demand for grain to feed the people of war-torn Europe and the armies defending them presented the farmer with a great challenge and opportunity. As farmers performed their patriotic duty (atop their tractors instead of tanks), prices rose to new heights.

V. Twenties Boom: Based upon the techniques developed to meet the wartime demand, production continued to soar. Returning servicemen, anxious to cash in on the "American dream," flocked to fill whatever lands were vacant—many of them coming to the plains area. The "roaring twenties" are characterized by a jazz drummer jamming to scenes of "booming" factories, bountiful harvests, and a rising stock market. Until it all crashes.

VI. The Dust Bowl: As the nation at large reels from the Depression, renewed drought strikes the Great Plains farmer with a double punch. Now that overcultivation had destroyed the delicate grasses which had held the soil in place, it powdered and flew away in the wind. This sequence includes many of the most memorable images from the film. Remember that in 1936 it was current events, not history.

VII. Migration: Faced with no alternative—"baked out, blown out, and broke"—families abandon their homes. Loading all their possessions on an old car or truck (the conestoga wagons of the 1930s) they set out in search of "a chance to start over and a chance for their children to eat, to have medical care, to have homes again. . . . " The closing scenes show a parade of cars turning one after another into a roadside migrant camp. As the women unload and set up camp, the men sit by, aimless and dejected. The narration closes with reference to "the most tragic chapter in the history of American agriculture." The last image in the film is a dead tree with an abandoned bird's nest in its branches, followed on the screen by the symbol of the Resettlement Administration and the words "The End."

The film ends strangely, without following through on its punch. By closing on the image of a gnarled and dead tree, the film (as scholars have traditionally studied it) fails to fulfill the viewer's expectations. How can it be that a film with such a sympathetic but generally depressing ending caused the controversy it did in the 1930s? The answer is that when some audiences of 1936 saw the film it may have included a three minute epilogue which refocused their attention on the programs that the New Deal was instituting to help address the problems—human and environmental problems— profiled in the sequence on migration. The epilogue was controversial because it focused on what some would call the most socialistic elements of the New Deal. It returned to the points raised in the migration sequence, indicating that the government was helping to fund the construction of new communities for displaced persons, communities in which families would not only find a place to live, but also find adequate medical care and an education for their children. Visually, the epilogue shows us the conservation and reclamation efforts underway and highlights the construction of such a new planned community, with people building their own homes in a most "constructive" atmosphere.

What happened to the epilogue? At this point we do not know for sure. What is clear is that on April 2, 1936, when Resettlement Administration (RA) head Rexford Guy Tugwell applied for copyright for *The Plow*, the epilogue was included. The five page summary submitted with the film to the copyright registrar includes the following description of what it called the "conclusion."

But the Federal Government is attacking the plains problem on two broad fronts. Congress has appropriated millions for drought relief to save farmers from starvation and dire poverty. On the second front the Government is carrying forward a program of permanent reconstruction of the land. Sod, seed, and trees are being put into the plains. The Forestry Service, Soil Conservation Service, cooperating with the Department of Agriculture are uniting efforts to restore damaged lands. Farmers are being taught the best methods of farming to prevent erosion.

The Resettlement Administration is taking title to 5,000,000 acres of land in the Great Plains and turning it back to grass and its natural uses. The Resettlement Administration has moved three divisions into the field and has loaned money for seed, feed, equipment for those who can stay and is moving thousands of others out, giving them a new chance to make a living. It is establishing farmstead communities where they can have advantage of public services, technical advice and assistance and an opportunity to secure homes and farms on long term credit.

But the sun still bakes the land and the winds still sweep across broad acres. It is the job of all agencies, private, state and federal to cooperate in reconstruction to prevent the Great Plains from becoming a desert— we must all cooperate in a battle to save our greatest natural resource— the soil.[4]

The epilogue itself offered a good deal more specific information than this description. It detailed that 5,800,000 acres were to be retired to their "proper agricultural use," that 65 land projects were underway, that $21,400,000 had been loaned to 155,000 farmers, and that 4,500 families had been resettled. Behind a voiceover assertion of the ways in which the agency was responding to the poor farmer's need for a roof over his head and health care, food, and education for his family, viewers watched footage of trucks carrying teams of men to work on the construction of new homes in a model community identified as being somewhere in Nebraska. In short, the epilogue focussed attention on the growing activities of the agency at just the point (in the spring of 1936) when the Republicans were tuning up to oppose the reelection of Roosevelt and his Democratic supporters in the Congress.

More importantly, it featured the most controversial of the RA's activities, perhaps the most controversial aspect of the New Deal in general, the establishment of "planned communities" on a socialist model. On March 30, just three days before Tugwell sent over the copyright request for the first version of the film, the Republican National Committee publically accused the New Deal with "being the sponsor of farm communities which are 'communistic in conception.' " *The New York Times* quoted the committee's statement as follows: "President Roosevelt's Resettlement Administration is establishing in West Virginia and other States communal farms which follow the Russian pattern, in that each member of the community will work on cooperative projects and share the proceeds."[5] Although the model community pictured in the epilogue to *The Plow* was said to be in

Nebraska, it certainly did convey the impression of men working in cooperative teams, constructing houses that were large enough for more than one family to live in. With press like this it would have been remarkable if the agency had not sought ways to escape still more controversy. By simply dropping the epilogue they could avoid waving the red flag in the face of the Republican opposition, but charges that they were propagandizing the electorate would not go away.

What does all this matter? It provides an object lesson on the importance of confirming the completeness of document being studied. In fact, if the purpose for studying the film is to consider the social and cultural values pertinent to the audience's response, we might want to ignore the epilogue and concentrate on what we *know for sure* that the viewers saw. But we should always be conscious of the relative completeness of the body of material we study. In more specific terms, the removal of the epilogue from *The Plow* should sensitize us to the importance of the film as political propaganda—on which there is more to come.

Of course it's one thing to recount a story such as that of the dust bowl in words, and quite another to do so in images backed by a sound track. As in the content analysis of any film, the construction of the individual shots, the ways in which they are connected one to another, and the ways in which they combine with the music and narration, provide different types of opportunities to influence an audience— to plant ideas on the unconscious level and to move people emotionally. *The Plow* proves an especially effective device for introducing history students to the elements of visual language and interpretation. In part this is because the style of the film which may seem dated to audiences familiar with TV makes it easier for them to look at it critically. Some of the images and sequences of images carry their symbolic meaning so close to the surface that students will grasp them immediately, others are more subtle and require more careful reading. Chapter II includes an analysis of some of the symbolic imagery in *The Plow* to which readers should refer here.

The image of the child and the plow in the third sequence is open to widely divergent interpretative readings. One view, for example, is that the drought and the dust storms have made the farmer and his tools as ineffective as the child in coping with his environment. A slightly different view suggests that the people who farmed the land were as innocent as "babes" in the face of great environmental forces— a view which seems to be at odds with the overall message of the film which records how ambitious farmers overdeveloped and overcultivated the land leaving insufficient grass cover to hold the moisture in dry years. A detailed effort to understand the signs and symbols inherent in the film is essential to a comprehensive analysis of its content.

On the level of montage (the organization and editing of images within scenes, scenes within sequences, and sequences within the film as a whole) there are some interesting observations to make, and a few problems. The film uses montage in some creative ways. Note for example in the sequence on World War I the way in which it contrasts (and/or compares) tanks and tractors—both helped to win the war, but the film suggests that both also laid waste to the landscape in the process. The transition between sequence V and VI is problematic. By cutting directly from the symbolic image of the "crash" to a cow's skull[6] on the parched earth, the film implies cause and effect, and consequently muddles its historical explanation. The real causes of the farmers' troubles go back at least to the early 1920s. Wheat prices tumbled in 1920 as wartime demand died out; then they recovered somewhat in the mid-twenties, only to plummet sharply in the early 1930s. Wheat farmers were already seriously depressed by the time Wall Street met its fate. But a more provocative reading is possible. Might the film be suggesting, as Donald Worster does in his recent book, that the stock market crash and the dust bowl may indeed be related in an ideological way, both being the logical result of excesses in the capitalist system?

The sound track is another important element in the process through which we derive meaning from the film. The narration— (. . . a country of high winds and sun, and little rain)—is poetic and evocative as well as informative. The repetition of these phrases serves, in the mind of one scholarly analyst of the film, "to intensify the mood of judgment."[7] The musical score is important as well. Drawing on themes in American folk music, composer Virgil Thompson's work also serves to intensify through an unusually effective association between images and music.

The most basic level on which a historian might evaluate *The Plow That Broke the Plains* is to compare the information and interpretation it presents with other contemporary documents, books, newspapers, and magazine articles. When one does this, or when one views the film critically in the light of recent historical scholarship, it becomes clear that there are problems with the film's rather simplistic historical argument. Most scholars today agree, for example, that one important factor in the problems of the plains farmer in the period was that so many of them were tenants. The film does not mention this at all.

PRODUCTION OF *THE PLOW*

The Plow That Broke the Plains was produced by the Resettlement Administration, one of the myriad new "alphabet agencies" (this one under the general control of the Department of Agriculture) set up during the first years of the administration of Franklin D. Roosevelt. The purpose of the agency, funded by emergency relief funds in 1935, was to provide rehabilitation loans to farm families and facilitate the resettlement of people from areas of the country which were most depressed to places where there were better opportunities for employment. The Great Plains was one such depressed area which was suffering from environmental as well as economic woes. Because it represented so directly the increasing role of government in social planning, the agency drew sharp criticism from those opposed to Roosevelt's policies and was deeply sensitive to the need to explain and defend its programs.

When Pare Lorentz was called to Washington and discussed with RA head Rexford Guy Tugwell the idea of expanding the public information efforts (then limited to print and still photography projects) to include moving pictures, he must have seemed like the perfect person for the job. Not only had he been trying unsuccessfully on his own to raise the funds necessary to make a documentary film about the environmental despoilation of the Great Plains, he was also an outspoken supporter of F. D. R. having recently published a picture book extolling the new spirit which seemed to have overtaken America in *The Roosevelt Year* (1933). An accomplished author and film critic, what Lorentz lacked was first-hand experience at filmmaking. *The Plow That Broke the Plains* would be his first film and would also mark a signifcant departure in the way in which government agencies used the media.

The Plow That Broke the Plains was intended to inform and to move people. On one level it was an effort at internal education to be screened at staff meetings at RA offices around the country to help the many new employees of the new agency to understand and feel at home with the values and goals of their organization. On a broader level, however, it was also an expression of the filmmaker's political point of view, which was avidly pro-Roosevelt and pro-New Deal. Lorentz convinced the agency of the wisdom of making one film which was "good enough technically to bear comparison with commercial films and be entertaining enough to draw an audience."[8] Such production values were uncommon in the strictly information films that the government had produced up to this time. Like John Grierson, who was in these same years forging a documentary film movement in Britain, Lorentz wanted to utilize the dramatic power of the medium in bringing audiences to accept his film's important social and political messages.

The fullest treatment of the production of *The Plow That Broke the Plains* is in Robert Snyder's book, *Pare Lorentz and the Documentary Film*. Basing his analysis on extant paper records and interviews with the principles, Snyder explains that Lorentz's decision to produce and direct the film himself was the first of many driven by the spartan $6,000 budget authorized for the project. For example, it was immediately decided that they would not hire actors, rent studio facilities, or attempt to record sound on location. On-screen animations would be kept simple and inexpensive (as indeed is the opening map animation in the film). In order to avoid unnecessary travelling expense, before camera crews were dispatched to the field, the still photo collections of the RA were studied closely to identify the specific locations most suitable.[9] This may help to explain some of the striking similarities between many of the pictures of such famous still photographers as Arthur Rothstein, Russell Lee, Walker Evans, and Dorothea Lange (photographers who worked for the RA and would continue later under the Farm Security Administration) and the composition of shots in *The Plow That Broke the Plains.*[10]

One area on which Lorentz refused to compromise was the quality of his technical crew. As cameramen he chose Ralph Steiner, Paul Strand, and Leo Hurwitz, all experienced and talented filmmakers in their own right, each of whom would go on to long and important careers, and each of whom had already established a personal political vision in their work. The trouble, as it became clear as the team proceeded through a seven week tour of filming locations in Montana, Wyoming, Colorado, Kansas, and Texas, was that their vision was not the same as that of Pare Lorentz. Steiner and Hurwitz, who would later go on to found their own radical leftist group under the name Frontier Films, complained that Lorentz did not have a clear enough plan for the film he was making and that he failed to see the economic roots of the problems he wanted to explain. Snyder quotes Lorentz as remembering in 1939 that "they wanted it to be all about human greed and how lousy our social system was." As a Roosevelt loyalist Lorentz was not prepared to go so far. He rejected the alternative script the two proposed, and after shooting enough dust-storm footage, he released the crew.[11]

The remaining footage necessary for the film was to be stock footage purchased from newsreel companies and the Hollywood studios, but the leaders of the movie capitol were uncooperative. Richard Dyer MaCann explains that the movie industry people feared the government getting involved in movie production and did all they could to make it difficult.[12] Lorentz had to rely on the personal assistance of his friend King Vidor to help in getting the footage he needed out of the studio libraries—footage of giant mule-driven combines at work on the plains, of World War I battle scenes, of parades of returning troops, etc. Before returning from California he shot the closing scenes of the roadside migrant camp, with the assistance of still photographer Dorothea Lange, who personally lined up cars along the road.[13]

Back in New York, having spent far more than his original budget (eventually the cost came to just under $20,000), Lorentz still had to edit his film and have a musical score written for it. Not knowing how much money he could promise as a fee, the novice filmmaker convinced a bright young composer who had never before written a film score to work with him. The corroboration between Pare Lorentz and Virgil Thomson was uniquely creative because of the way that they worked together. Typically, the editing of a film is finished first and the narration recorded; then the composer is called in to write music to fit it. The interplay between the images and musical scores of *The Plow That Broke the Plains* and *The River* (1937), Lorentz's second film, are so interesting because he did things differently. First, he and Thomson had long talks about the kinds of traditional and folk music that should be "quoted" in various sequences. Lorentz provided the composer with a "rough cut" of the film to guide his work to timed sequences, and once the music was written, he projected each sequence of the film as Thomson played his score on the piano. Once approved, the score was orchestrated and recorded. Then came the real difference—Lorentz took the recorded score back to the editing room and re-edited the film, readjusting the sequence and timing of the images where necessary to fit the music or, at times, to use the music as a counterpoint for the visual presentation.[14] The end result is a unique marriage of music and film which, though evident in *The Plow That Broke the Plains*, is even more impressive in *The River*.

We have still to consider the matter of the epilogue. Sometime after April 2, 1936 (the date of the copyright application), the epilogue was removed, but when and why? Surely it was gone by 1938, when the study guide to the film published by the government had its description of the film end with the dead tree, as noted above. There is some evidence to suggest that it may have been removed much earlier. One member of Congress who was very supportive of the agency and its work spoke up on the floor of the House of Representatives on May 7, 1936, to praise the film. His sequence-by-sequence description of the film, as reprinted from the Congressional Record by his office for distribution to his constituents, stops short of the concluding scene.[15] The months of April and May 1936 were difficult ones for Tugwell and his agency. The Republicans were concentrating on attacking the RA as the most vulnerable of Roosevelt's programs. In demanding a financial accounting from Tugwell, Senator William W. Barbour (Republican, NJ), focussed attention on one "demonstration village" near Hightstown, New Jersey. According the *The New York Times*, Barbour described the Hightstown project, originally intended as a "sort of utopia," as a "mudhole with a few tin houses to glorify the money that has been spent." A few days later there was talk of Congress scrapping the RA altogether, and a House committee reported out a Relief Appropriations Bill which would have continued the WPA but provided no funds for continuation of RA programs.[16] It might indeed have seemed sensible for Tugwell's agency to discretely drop *The Plow*'s controversial epilogue (with its detailing of perhaps questionable dollar amounts expended and number of farmers served) from the film right away, before it had been widely distributed. There was an obvious practical rationale as well; the inclusion of such specific figures were sure to make the film so dated that it would be unusable in a matter of months. But at this point we do not know for certain when the final sequence was removed or whether there were some prints of the film which may have retained it for a time.[17]

The person we should expect to be (and to have been) most protective of the film as a work of art and most anxious not to have it chopped up in response to political objections would be the filmmaker himself. In a letter to this author, however, filmmaker Pare Lorentz denies any responsibility for filming the epilogue in the first place: "I did not myself employ cameramen or write the words for the 'sales pitch' that originally was the conclusion for the film." Lorentz explains that the "reiterative shot of the dead tree and the scene of the endless dust to the horizon . . . was a natural conclusion." Natural though it may have been, this conclusion was decidedly downbeat. Although Lorentz may not have sent out the camera crews to film the footage for the epilogue, he clearly shaped the footage into the overall plan of the film. The epilogue closes, as the film opens, with a close-up low angle shot of the delicate grass, suggesting that the epilogue was included in the aesthetic design as originally created. In seeking to disassociate himself from the epilogue Lorentz opens interesting questions about who had the ultimate creative responsibility.[18]

Lorentz offers a more practical explanation for the dropping the epilogue. As he explains it, the film had "a bastard length" in that it was neither long enough for a feature or short enough for a short. "Being over-long for a short, it was a natural thing for the projectionist to leave out the 'sales pitch.' " This explanation suggests that Lorentz may not have been a part of the decision loop in the RA that led to whatever decision was made about cutting their political losses by changing the ending of The Plow, but he does express concern about the politics of the matter and seems especially sensitive to the question of the RA's housing program. "Whatever efforts the Resettlement Administration started in the way of housing in the Great Plains was miniscule," he explains, comparing this to their work in restoring the land. "I don't know who provided me with the footage but I didn't send the camera crew to wherever this housing development was going on. I considered it inappropriate because it wasn't truthful enough."[19]

More later on the political reception of The Plow. Suffice it here to note that insights such as these about the production history of a film cannot help but make it more valuable as a historical artifact. By understanding the process of the production, we can come to know the film more fully. We should be more sensitive to its overall message—by explaining that the problems of the dust bowl were largely due to unplanned and overambitious agricultural development (first by cattlemen, then by small independent farmers, and finally by mechanized farmers and corporate land companies in the wake of war-driven increased demand for grain), the film was rationalizing the need for agencies such as the RA to bring conservation, planning, and rational redevelopment to the area. Viewers aware of the arguments that Lorentz had with his politically radical film crew should better understand the relatively moderate point of view that the film assumed. (Note below that there were many at the time who thought it was far from moderate.) More specifically, we may be less disappointed by the rather rudimentary form of the map animation at the beginning of the film, possible mistakes in continuity and transitions which confuse historical issues, because we are aware of the financial and creative restrictions under which the filmmaker worked. Finally, we may be more appreciative of the interplay of image, narration, and music because we know something about Lorentz's feeling for all three and his unique procedures for bringing them together.

RECEPTION OF *THE PLOW*

In terms of reception, as we watch this film with our students we see it differently than viewers did in 1936. Partly this is because of the far broader experience we have had with visual communications. The compositional style (comparable to still photographs of the period), the black and white (rather than color) images, the pattern and relatively slow pace of some of the editing, may strike us as dull in comparison to the dynamic, colorful, and almost frenetically paced images to which we have been conditioned by television. More important in understanding this film as a historical document, however, is recognizing that the values, concerns, and experiences of the people of the 1930s influenced the way they saw the film. The film would have had different meanings for different audiences then it does today. Imagine the varying responses the film may have had in New York or in Oklahoma, among businessmen, farmers threatened with eviction, or displaced migrants. To some extent today's viewers may be influenced by subsequent films they have seen such as *The Grapes of Wrath* (1940) or TV series such as *The Waltons*.

Most critics of the time were generous in their praise of *The Plow That Broke the Plains*. A few thought it was too dreary or depressing, but others noted the importance of getting this message about conservation out to the American public. Still Lorentz found only limited success in having the film screened commercially. There were a few presentations in first run theaters in New York, Chicago, and other cities, but the film was refused by the large booking circuits which dictated the programs for the nation's major theater chains. Part of the problem may have been connected with the movie industry's response to a government product being distributed through commercial channels. Hollywood businessmen apparently feared government competition in the same ways that generators of electrical power would look at the Tennessee Valley Authority. Lorentz asked Roosevelt's private secretary Stephen J. Early in mid May 1936 to report to the president the "confidential" "off-the-record" knowledge he had that Will Hays, head of the Motion Picures Producers Association, had conspired to have *The Plow* banned from commercial distribution throughout the industry.[20]

The staff of the RA went to work in the midwest during the summer of 1936 trying to book the film in independent theater chains, and they had some success. In the end, due to such direct promotion, there were as many as 3,000 commercial theaters which showed the film (including 600 in Illinois, 500 in Ohio, 200 in Wisconsin, etc.). This was not a bad showing, considering the total of approximately

14,000 commercial theaters operating in the country in 1936, but it was not what Lorentz had hoped for. The film was screened widely in meetings of civic and political groups. Lorentz was particularly pleased with a special screening of *The Plow* with a series of documentary films of other nations under the auspices of the Museum of Modern Art.[21]

The president was ecstatic after seeing the film in a special White House screening. *Time* magazine reported that Roosevelt had actually considered sending the film up to Congress in place of a presidential message.[22] But FDR's congressional critics, still at this point a minority but riding high on court decisions which were supporting their efforts to deflate the New Deal and tear down its hierarchy of new social agencies, were equally inflamed. They noted that it was a presidential election year and that by actively promoting public screenings of the film the agency was spreading propaganda for the administration— and, by definition, against the Republicans. Several Democratic congressional candidates did specifically request screenings of the film in their districts to "educate" their people.[23] It is important to remember here that at least some viewers at the time may have been seeing a version of the film that included the rather pointed epilogue discussed above. This would help to explain why candidates might think the film to be effective in supporting their cause, and also why FDR might have thought (however fleetingly) that the film was an appropriate way to report to Congress on the progress of specific programs

There were other critics of the film besides the politicians. By starting with the map of the entire region, MacCann argues, the film presents an overgeneralization—suggesting incorrectly that each place in the region outlined in the map suffered the kinds of conditions portrayed in the film.

> Four times the narrative describes the area north of the Texas Panhandle as a country "without rivers, without streams, with little rain." On the face of it the presence of any rain at all means the presence of streams of some kind. Lorentz seemed to be ignoring the Missouri, the Yellowstone, the Platte and the Arkansas [rivers] for the sake of a sonorous phrase. Even a poet should not subject geography to his imagination to such as extent as that.[24]

MacCann goes on to present a summary of the critical comments of local RA staff members. If one central purpose of this film was educating the staff of the agency (Snyder points out that they had to argue this as the "primary purpose" in order to justify the spending of RA's administrative money for its production), some members of that staff were certainly unimpressed.[25] D. P. Trent, the RA's regional director from Dallas, Texas, wrote a scathing three page letter to Tugwell attacking the film and suggesting that the film be withheld from circulation in their part of the country.[26]

The film continued to be distributed to school and community groups for the next few years, but the continuing political acrimony over it led to organized opposition in Congress. Echoing the opinions expressed in Trent's letter, area congressmen delighted in pointing to parts of their states where none of the conditions portrayed in the film had ever existed.

By this time the Resettlement Administration had been incorporated into the Farm Security Administration; and the responsibility for distribution of The Plow That Broke the Plains and Lorentz's 1937 film, The River, (as well as the production of a newly planned film on the unemployment problem) had been passed to the National Emergency Council (NEC), an ad-hoc agency which had survived from year to year since 1933 on renewed executive orders from the president and on special appropriations from Congress. In the spring of 1939 Republican Representative Karl Mundt of South Dakota, one who had argued from the beginning that the film had done an injustice to his state, succeeded in bringing enough pressure on the NEC to have the film withdrawn from circulation.[27] After World War II the Department of Agriculture kept the film out of circulation with the explanation that the film was no longer representative of the conditions present. "Substantial improvements" had been made since 1936,[28] and local congressmen such as Mundt were not anxious to continue to see their home states portrayed (especially at taxpayers' expense) as part of a hopeless "dust bowl." In the early 1960s Secretary of Agriculture Orville Freeman began authorizing the film for educational screenings again, but with the disclaimer that it represented a historical and in no way a current situation.[29] Moreover, the print of the film currently in 16mm circulation through the National Audiovisual Center is the version which lacks the controversial epilogue.

Despite the ban, perhaps a bit because of it (or the attention it drew), historians of documentary film have always credited The Plow That Broke the Plains as one of the finest of its type. This is a judgment that students should appreciate even more when they understand the sophistication of the political argument the film is making, note the creative use of visual language and editing, and recognize the limitations under which it was produced and viewed.

* * * *

STAGE TWO

Where the second stage of historical analysis is concerned, The Plow That Broke the Plains lends itself to analysis in terms of all four of the frameworks for inquiry delineated in this book. In each of the four frameworks, different historical questions lead to different analytical concerns.

FRAMEWORK 1

First, *The Plow That Broke the Plains* lends itself to analysis as historical interpretation. Scholars who seek a clearer understanding of the historiography of the dust bowl should profit from studying how *The Plow* treats its historical subject. To the extent that the film purports to tell the story of the settlement of the plains and the origins of the problems that befell the farmers there, it is offering interpretations for rather complex historical issues. Some of those interpretations are not explicitly stated, but merely implied in the visual texture of the film. Others that are stated clearly are simplistic and superficial, such as the film's treatment of the economic backgound of the plight of the plains farmer. After gearing up for wartime production, peace brought overproduction and falling prices. But even in the 1930s it was understood that the economic problems involved were much more complex. The film makes no mention of the tenancy problem, for example. It slips over such difficult questions through the use of the dramatic but misleading visual transition from the "jazz age" and the stock market crash directly to the dust bowl, represented by the sun-bleached skull on the parched earth. By stressing the environmental dimension of the farmers' troubles, the film does lay the rationale for more active government planning for agricultural development, but it avoids a more pointed critique of the capitalist system. The film can be productively compared with other popular and contemporary views of the history of American agriculture. Support for Roosevelt and the New Deal was surely the moving force behind *The Plow's* interpretation of history. What motives, conscious or otherwise, may have influenced different explanations of the plight of the plains farmer?

FRAMEWORK 2

Second, *The Plow That Broke the Plains* lends itself to study as a document of social and cultural history. Scholars seeking to understand the accepted social and cultural concepts of America in the 1930s could benefit from a study of *The Plow*. There are obvious images of social and cultural interest in the film such as the "blown out" migrants seeking a place where they can begin to put together a new life for themselves. What is more interesting than the images themselves, however, is the impact they were expected to have on viewers. When we look at *The Plow That Broke the Plains* as a document for social and cultural history, we are less concerned with the factual accuracy of the images than we are with the social and cultural values it sought to touch upon in its audience. Camera angles and editing are important here for the ways in which they characterize individuals and issues—helping spectators unconsciously to develop the point of view the producers intended. In this case the filmmakers were clearly striking out to create sympathy in their audience for people who had been unfortunately victimized. The farmers of the plains were more than willing to work hard, particularly hard because of the marginal quality of much of the soil, but their hard work was no match for the forces of nature.

Economic forces had a lot to do with their problems as well—the demand for war wheat and the subsequent collapse of the market. Before that collapse was apparent, thousands of returning soldiers had been tempted to seek their fortunes and their economic independence in new farms on the plains. The farmers of the plains, therefore, had been brought there by very basic American social and cultural values. Once settled, the unpredictabilities of the economic system combined with the vagaries of the environment to shape their lives there.

A more biting social critic might have sought to deflate widely professed American ideals as empty rhetoric or as as "opiate" for the otherwise ill informed masses, but Lorentz did not go so far. Rather his film suggested that the system could be made sound again and the values reaffirmed under the leadership of FDR and the enlightened policies of agencies such as the Resettlement Administration. Even if footage had been faked or the filmmakers had otherwise intentionally misrepresented the actual situation, the values, ideas, and opinions presented take preeminance here. To this end, understanding the ways in which images may have been manipulated or carefully designed to influence viewers, far from undermining the usefulness of the film, would significantly enhance the insights to be gleaned from a study of it.

FRAMEWORK 3

Third, as resource for the facts and data reported upon, *The Plow That Broke the Plains* has been returned to repeatedly by compilation filmmakers looking for footage through which they can show viewers what the dust bowl really looked like. If there are questions (as indeed there should be) about the methods Lorentz used in identifying his location sites and his setting up of various shots, what are the questions we should ask of filmmakers who cannibalize *The Plow That Broke the Plains* and unquestioningly present the images as reality? Individual shots from the film may provide visual verification for the written record in much the same way as the still photographs of the time which provided the models for some of them. Unfortunately, since the original footage no longer exists, it is impossible to review the editing decisions Lorentz made or to verify the dates and/or exact locations at which individual images were filmed. In using such footage (whether from this film or from the archives) to get an idea of the enormity of the dust storms or some more intimate sense of what they were like, special care must be given to the photographic decisions made—at what angles were pictures shot, what kinds of lenses or filters were used, what speed film—each of which might unknowingly influence the viewer's perception of what actually appeared before the camera. In short, as common as it is to turn to this film as a factual source on the dust bowl and the problems of the rural depression, such reference is fraught with difficulty from the historians' point of view. In a slightly different way, *The Plow* does serve as direct factual evidence for an analysis of what information (not the broad social and cultural values noted above, but the specific information about RA programs, for example) that the RA and the Roosevelt administration wanted the public to receive. For this type of analysis, of course, the epilogue which few historians have seen in the past fifty years may be of more importance than the rest of the film.

FRAMEWORK 4

Fourth and finally, *The Plow That Broke the Plains* can be studied as an important artifact in the history of documentary film and the subsequent making of documentary films by the United States government. MacAnn's book treats in detail the philosophical and organizational problems involved in the government's production of films intended both to inform and persuade. The production of Lorentz's *The Plow* and *The River* (1937)[30] led to the establishment of a new agency, the United States Film Service, with Lorentz at its head. But the administrators of the service, as the promoters of *The Plow*, struggled against political opponents until 1940 when the responsible congressional committee forced the shutdown of the agency and the end of distribution for *The Plow*. The opposition of congressional leaders to the government's production of films ebbed during World War II when their importance to the war effort was so clear, but there was careful attention given to which films would be made available for domestic viewing. Many of the government's wartime filmmaking activities were oriented toward interpreting America and its institutions to other nations such as occupied Germany and Japan which, it was reasoned, needed practical and uplifting lessons in how democracy worked. All of these films, like all of the straightforward propaganda products of the United States Information Agency to follow, were authorized for distribution only overseas. They could not legally be screened in the United States. The rationale for this congressionally dictated policy can be traced in part to the pre-war controversy over such films as *The Plow That Broke the Plains*.

Another valuable approach would be to compare and contrast the products of the various nations making propaganda films in the 1930s with eyes toward the extent to which the films fulfilled the then present potential for technical precision and effectiveness, and the level of cynicism with which they approached the prospect of propagandizing. In each case, the films of propagandists such as Leni Riefenstahl who were working at the same time make *The Plow That Broke the Plains* look both rudimentary and rather benign.

It should be clear at this point that there is much more to be learned from approaching *The Plow That Broke the Plains* as a historical artifact than as a simple textbook illustration on the 1930s. We do not mean to argue that the analysis of the moving image as artifact should be the only or even the most frequent approach. History teachers will continue, as they should, to use films for their power to motivate and to reinforce lessons. However, if historians are to come to grips with the dominant visual communucations media of our day, if they are to help students develop the visual literacy skills that will be increasingly necessary for responsible citizenship in a democratic society, they must apply a rigorous historical methodology to at least some of the images they study.

NOTES

1. The author wishes to thank the New Jersey Department of Higher Education for the grant funding under which this research was originally carried out, and Professor Richard Kirkendall of Iowa State University for his helpful suggestions.
2. See Donald Worster, *Dust Bowl: The Southern Plains in the 1930's* (New York: Oxford University Press, 1979), p. 96; R. Douglas Hurt, *The Dust Bowl: An Agricultural and Social History*, (Chicago: Nelson Hall, 1981), pp. 61–62; and Paul Bonnifield, *The Dust Bowl: Men, Dirt, and Depression* (Albuquerque: University of New Mexico Press, 1979).
3. The pamphlet *Teaching History With Film and Television* contains an assignment for a term paper on *The Plow* as artifact.
4. Sequence outline of *The Plow That Broke the Plains* submitted to the U.S. Copyright office under letter of April 2, 1936, signed by Rexford Guy Tugwell. Library of Congress, Division of Motion Pictures, Broadcasting and Recorded Sound. The complete narrative outline and Tugwell's letter are reproduced in the study guide to the video compilation.
5. *The New York Times*, March 31, 1936, p. 27. Ironically the West Virginia project discussed had the unfortunate name "Red House."
6. The image of the cow's skull is particularly interesting in light of the controversy connected with a very similar still picture taken by Farm Security Administration photographer Arthur Rothstein. It was argued that since Rothstein reportedly "staged" the photograph by rearranging the skull on the ground before shooting it, that the picture could not be properly called documentary. The incident is referred to in William Stott, *Documentary Expression in Thirties America* (New York, 1973), p. 269. For the fullest description of the incident see *The Fargo Forum* [North Dakota] for September 1, 1936, clipping in scrapbook in Rexford Guy Tugwell Papers at the Franklin D. Roosevelt Presidential Library.
7. Unpublished paper by Peter Rollins and Harris Elder.
8. Snyder, Robert L., *Pare Lorentz and the Documentary Film*, (Norman, Oklahoma; 1968) pp. 25.
9. Ibid., p. 31.
10. Historian James Curtis of the University of Delaware has recently raised questions about this, however, suggesting that some of the most relevant FSA photographs may have been shot only after work on *The Plow* had begun.
11. *Ibid.*, pp 29–31.
12. MacCann, *The People's Films* (New York, Hastings House, 1973), p. 68.

13. Snyder, p. 31–32.
14. *Ibid.*, pp. 33–37.
15. "*The Plow That Broke the Plains* Resettlement Film, Lauded Highly, Shows Need for Conservation," Remarks by Hon. Maury Maverick of Texas in the House of Representatives, May 7, 1936. The pamphlet bore on its face the indication that it was "Not Printed at Government Expense."
16. *The New York Times*, May 1, 3, 1936.
17. The print that has been maintained in the collections of the Museum of Modern Art since the 1930s did include the epilogue, for example.
18. Pare Lorentz to John O'Connor, March 23, 1987. Letter in the possession of the author.
19. *Ibid.*
20. Pare Lorentz to Stephen Early, May 12, 1936, Rexford G. Tugwell Papers, Franklin D. Roosevelt Presidential Library. This letter is reproduced in the study guide to the video compilation.
21. *Ibid.* See also *MacCann*, pp. 70–71.
22. *Time*, May 25, 1936, quoted in MacCann, pp. 78–79.
23. *Ibid.* pp. 78–79.
24. *Ibid.*, p. 79.
25. Snyder, *Pare Lorentz*, pp. 27–28.
26. D. P. Trent to Rexford G. Tugwell, July 12, 1936, Papers of the Resettlement Administration, National Archives. This letter and Tugwell's curt reply are both reproduced in the study guide to the video compilation.
27. MacCann, *The People's Films*, pp. 82–83.
28. *Ibid.* see note p. 83.
29. *Ibid.* p. 76; and the disclaimer at the opening of the film opening.
30. Note close analysis of *The River* in the second edition of Bordwell and Thompson's *Film Art: An Introduction*, included in the study guide accompanying the video compilation.

CHAPTER V
AN INTRODUCTION TO VISUAL LANGUAGE FOR HISTORIANS AND HISTORY TEACHERS

When using film or television in a history class, teachers often mistakenly assume that students who have grown up with television, sometimes becoming familiar with the kids on Sesame Street before they know the ones who live next door, are particularly sensitive to visual communications. They are not. Recognizing that most students spend the literal equivalent of years before the television screen, teachers should not confuse familiarity with sensitivity or critical understanding.

Another false assumption is that people do not have to be taught to look at pictures, that unlike learning to read, understanding what is seen is a function that comes naturally. On the contrary, the kind of visual skill that people develop more or less automatically over years of familiarity with a medium such as television is an ability to identify its conventions and decode its surface messages. Viewers can (and do) teach themselves to "get the message" that they are intended to get. What they must be taught is how to comprehend more deeply. This skill can provide viewers with the capacity to appreciate more fully the creative artistry of film and television and, on a more important level, teach them to identify bias and avoid erroneous conclusions.

Cliches such as "the camera can't lie" and "a picture is worth a thousand words" are often used to defend the supposed infallibility of visual evidence. Students beginning to study visual language will immediately see the foolishness of such statements. For almost a century filmmakers have been convincing audiences to accept artifice as reality, at least for the time spent in the theater before the screen. Similarly, a picture may be worth tens of thousands of different words to different people because, in comparison with a verbal expression, a picture is so much more open to individual interpretation. As with any verbal set of signs or symbols, the language and idiom of the moving image can be understood on numerous levels. Graduate students in filmmaking or television production must be fluent in that language if they are to learn to be creative in it. Critical viewers may require a different level of visual literacy, but it is no less important that such learning be addressed directly in the history classroom.

This introduction to visual language is meant to serve as a general and selective guide for history teachers new to the critical use of moving image media in the classroom. It is keyed to two comprehensive volumes on the subject, which are recommended for further study: James Monaco's *How To Read a Film*, rev. ed. (New York, 1981) and David Bordwell and Kristin Thompson's *Film Art: An Introduction*, 2d ed. (New York, 1986). Although these books may provide more information than the average history teacher needs to know, each is a valuable resource to have on hand to answer questions that may arise while "reading" visual documents in the classroom. In combination with further reading, the following summary should assist teachers in training their students for visual literacy, so that the use of audiovisual materials in the history classroom will take on new importance. In addition to offering interesting information and motivating further study of historical questions, informed moving image lessons will help develop in students a new set of skills necessary for full participation in today's visual civilization.

THE HISTORICAL DEVELOPMENT OF THE MOVING IMAGE

One convenient way for the history teacher to encourage students to think about the differences between verbal and visual communications is to trace the events leading to the invention of moving image technology. In this context, there were three historical preconditions that had to be met before the Lumière brothers could set up their first public exhibition of moving pictures.

First, there had to be a recognition of the physiological response that makes movies "work" for people. It is worth making the point with students that moving pictures really do not move. What appears on the screen is a succession of still images, a phenomenon that was applied in parlor toys such as the zoetrope as early as the 1830s (see the illustration in Monaco, 55; Bordwell and Thompson, 3). The traditional explanation—the persistence of vision—holds that the retina of the human eye retains an image for a fraction of a second before it is replaced by another image. Current authorities prefer other explanations based in perceptual psychology (see Bordwell and Thompson, 16–17), but all agree that human perception of the moving image media is a trick that the eyes play on the mind. Noting this in class will help students to realize the vast potential for psychological influence and interpretation of the moving images they see.

The second precondition for the invention of the movies was the development of photography. The zoetrope device used stick figures or drawn images, because in 1834, when the zoetrope was patented, the invention of photography was still five years in the future. Teachers should present the historical evolution of photography, from the camera obscura of Leonardo da Vinci's time to the early photographic processes of the 1840s and 1850s, which for the first time allowed the permanent recording and reproduction of an image. Subsequently, photographic technology had to be improved and exposure speed increased to allow photographing of eighteen to twenty-four frames per second, the minimum necessary for the succession of images to convey the appearance of motion. By the mid-1880s exposure speeds had shortened to the point where Edword Muybridge could experiment with flanks of cameras that could stop the action of a galloping horse, in an effort to establish whether all four hooves left the ground at the same time.

The third precondition for movies, at least silent movies, was the invention of the moving picture camera, which allowed a series of pictures each second to be exposed through the same lens, and the moving picture projector. By the mid-1880s George Eastman had developed and marketed a flexible film to replace the glass plates in use by photographers. In 1889 Thomas Edison and his colleagues developed the first practical moving-picture camera, which could manipulate the flexible film so that it could be brought to a complete stop before the aperture, exposed, and moved on again at least eighteen times per second. For the next decade Edison devoted considerable money and effort to the marketing of the kinetoscope, a peephole viewing device that was set up in public viewing parlors (see Monaco, 58–59).

The developmemt of equipment to project a moving image was left to two Frenchmen. The challenge to project eighteen to twenty-four discrete images successively within one second, including a fraction of a second of black screen between each image (without the screen going black between each frame, viewers would see a blur instead of the illusion of smooth, even motion), was met by the Lumière brothers, who first publicly presented projected moving pictures in Paris in 1895.

Although new technological developments in recorded sound, color photography, and the entirely new medium of television would alter the way people looked at film, the basic elements of the moving image media were in place by 1895.

FUNCTIONAL COMPONENTS OF
MOVING IMAGE MEDIA

The basic element of a film is the shot. Although it might vary in duration from a fraction of a second to several minutes, a shot is defined as a single, unedited, continuously exposed piece of film. One or more shots that detail a single action at a single location make up a scene. One or more scenes that constitute a natural unit of narration are referred to as a sequence. Thus, there might be a sequence that begins with a scene on a railroad track were a man catches his foot. That scene might be several shots long, as the camera offers an establishing shot of the location, a medium shot of the man walking, and a close-up of his foot as it slips into a crevice next to the track, followed by another close-up of the look of fright on his face as he hears the whistle of a train approaching from around the bend. At this point, the film might cut to another scene inside the locomotive, where the engineer casually lights his pipe and checks his gauges. Subsequent scenes would be made up of other combinations of shots and strung together on a unifying theme to complete the sequence.

Many film scholars would say that it is too limiting to the film medium to suggest the following comparison, but beginning students may find it helpful to compare the parts of a film to the parts of a book:

shot = sentence
scene = paragraph
sequence = chapter
film = book

In the same way that a sentence, rather than a word, is the basic constituent element of verbal language (unless it is a one-word sentence expressing a complete idea), so the shot, rather than the individual frame, is the basic unit of film. The various elements within a shot and the editing devices through which shots, scenes, and sequences are linked together are what give the moving image media their creative capacity to mold time and space for dramatic effect. The two essential visual components of moving image communication are therefore the elements of the individual shot and the editing devices through which shots are given meaning in relation to one another. The meaning of individual shots and edited scenes and sequences is also influenced by the sound track, and sound therefore contributes as much information as the images it accompanies.

Elements of a shot

When authors write sentences, they have certain creative tools at their command. They can choose from a dictionary full of words, combine words in various ways, and use punctuation to accent their meaning. They can organize phrases within sentences to modify one another, limiting or accentuating ideas or adding nuances of meaning. Filmmakers have at least as much creative latitude.

The elements of a motion-picture shot are of two general types. First, there is mise-en-scène, the things literally put in the shot to create its narrative content. Mise-en-scène includes aspects of staging, creative design, and dramatic direction that would be present whether a production were being prepared for the stage or for the movie screen. Elements of mise-en-scène in a historic dramatization, for example, would include the setting (whether a scene was shot on a studio set or on location), the props and costumes that identify the scene with the appropriate historical period, the casting of characters, and the elements of dramatic expression that actors bring to their parts.

It is possible for mise-en-scène to be handled with particular sensitivity in a historical film, especially when filmmakers rely on the expertise of professional historians as consultants, such as Natalie Zemon Davis in the production of *The Return of Martin Guerre*. In the video compilation Davis comments on the care that went into documentation of mise-en-scène, including the color of the wedding dress, the words of the marriage vows, and the nature of the dowry offerings, though some details were still overlooked. Mise-en-scène can also contribute to historical interpretation. The scene in which a notary draws up the marriage contract while the newlywed couple sits quietly by, includes many ordinary daily activities (tending the fire, making the bread, plucking a chicken), which reinforce the point that matters of marriage and the extended family were central concerns in the everyday life of the time. On the other hand, it was not historically correct to include a large gathering of townspeople in the back of the room in the final court scenes of the film, but the filmmakers wanted to show reactions to the testimony being given and to emphasize how the issue of Martin Guerre's identity had come to concern the entire community. *The Return of Martin Guerre* was given a heightened aura of authenticity through recently developed light-sensitive camera lenses and film stock, which allowed photographing of the interior of sixteenth-century houses with light levels roughly as they must have been, thereby avoiding the use of obtrusive artificial lighting.

More commonly, a film is considered historically accurate in terms of mise-en-scène as long as there are no glaring incongruities or anachronisms—no eyeglasses on Julius Caesar or jet trails in a cloudless eighteenth-century sky. Obviously, the theatrical filmmaker can have more influence over mise-en-scène than can the documentarist, who does not costume the people being interviewed or direct them in delivering their lines for dramatic effect. When coproducers Suzanne Bauman and Rita Heller took their cameras to a reunion of participants in the Bryn Mawr summer program for women, interviewees were given no scripted lines to read. Like all other filmmakers, however, Bauman and Heller retained ultimate control, deciding whether to include any or all of an interview in the completed film and arranging the interview segments in an order (intercut with stills and archival footage) that supported the message that *Women of Summer* was intended to convey (see the video compilation).

The photographic elements of a shot make up the second general category, and they are as important in working with documentaries as they are with theatrical films. Because images are observed "naturally," and because so many people have had the experience of taking their own casual snapshot pictures of family and friends, viewers may assume that the photographic images presented in moving image media simply happened that way. Most filmmakers strive for the look of naturalness, but the skillful filmmaker maintains intimate control over all visual elements, continually working to assure that each contributes to conveying both the information and the feeling that is to be projected. Just as no sentence in a serious work of literature can be thought of as an unplanned jumble of words, no shot in a creditable film simply "happens" before the camera.

Some of the major creative elements that the filmmaker or television producer uses to make each shot communicate specific ideas and emotions include duration, lighting, color, field size, composition, camera angle, camera movement, focus, lens characteristics, film stock, and projection speed. (With the exception of duration, camera movement, and projection speed, each of these elements relates as well to the still photograph.)

● **Duration.**   The length in time that a shot is on the screen varies from a fraction of a second to several minutes and can influence a shot's meaning significantly. Depending on the complexity of the shot, a certain time will be necessary for the viewer to absorb the information. Generally, the eye needs more time to read a wide-angle establishing shot than it does a close-up. The viewer's attention may be directed from one part of the image to another by changing compositional elements and camera movements. An image that stays on the screen longer than is necessary for its information to be conveyed invites the viewer to ponder its meaning more deeply, to good or bad effect. (See Bordwell and Thompson, 187–91, 205–207.)

● **Lighting.**   The direction and intensity of lighting and the use of shadow can have an overpowering impact on the meaning of an image. Dark shadows can convey an air of mystery. By showing huge combines harvesting at night (Figure 1) as part of the "Twenties Boom" sequence of *The Plow*, Pare Lorentz was able to indicate a passion for productivity. By showing them lit starkly from behind, he was able to add a note of ominous foreboding (further accented by the music). Facial features can be altered dramatically by lighting, as many an aging actor can attest. (See Monaco, 158–59, 166–69; Bordwell and Thompson, 126–31.) Bordwell and Thompson include lighting as an element of mise-en-scène, and, indeed, it is one of the elements of stage and set design most important in both live theater and theatrical film, but it should be recognized as a photographic element as well.

● **Color.**   Both hue and intensity of color are important for their overall emotional influence and for specific color symbolism. Lighting, film stock, and lens filters offer varied creative possibilities. (See Monaco, 96–98, 156–57; Bordwell and Thompson, 130–31, 136–37, 152–53, 192–93.)

● **Field Size.**   The distance of the action from the camera affects viewers' relationship with what they see. The field size may result in a long shot, a medium shot, a close-up, or a limitless variety of shot distances in between these general parameters. Typically, a long shot, especially when used as an establishing shot, conveys context by establishing the orientation between setting and characters, while a close-up (of a facial expression, for example) has more potential for dramatic interpretation. The image of an overflowing grain hopper (Figure 2) in *The Plow* accentuates the volume of production because the sides of the bin are not shown. (See Monaco, 161; Bordwell and Thompson, 169–74.)

- **Composition.**   The way a shot is composed affects the balance of the image and guides the viewer's eye to the most important elements. Images may be composed sparely or loaded with detail. They may be closed (strictly limited to the boundaries of the frame) or open (implicitly or explicitly referring to characters and spaces outside the camera's view). There are also recognized conventions of composition, such as the establishing shot and the reverse-angle shot, and important symbolic codes regarding gesture and body language. (See Monaco, 140–60; Bordwell and Thompson, 136–37, 162–87.)

- **Camera Angle.**   High angle, low angle, dutch angle, and the many angle variations in between influence attitude toward the action and the subjects. If a woman is shot from a low angle, she seems dominant and powerful. The opposite is usually true of high-angle shots, which put the viewer on a higher or superior plane. A tilted, or dutch, angle might suggest disorientation of either the subject, the viewer, or both. The extreme low-angle shot near the opening of *The Plow*, which highlights individual blades of grass against the sky (Figure 3), can be read as emphasizing their vulnerability. Later in the film, the low-angle shot of a farm buried in wind-blown dust (Figure 4) makes the situation appear much worse than would a shot photographed from an elevated platform. (See Monaco, 164, 172; Bordwell and Thompson, 168ff.)

- **Camera Movement.**   Each movement of the camera serves to extend and change the frame and the composition in ways that can advance the narrative thread of a film or offer interpretive components. The camera can pan, track, dolly, tilt, or crane, as well as vary in speed of movement. (See Monaco, 77–80; Bordwell and Thompson, 174–87.)

- **Focus.**   There are many ways focus can be used within a shot. Focus can direct viewers' attention within the frame, and it can be altered within the context of the shot to redirect that attention elsewhere. Sharp focus may convey a realistic, sometimes harsh impression; soft focus may convey a dreamy, romantic feeling. (See Monaco, 162–64; Bordwell and Thompson, 156–59.)

- **Lens Characteristics.**   Various lenses—telephoto and wide-angle are the most common—and the characteristics specific to them can alter the scope and relative size of the image photographed. Lenses also affect the speed of action to and from the camera. A telephoto lens slows the action and a wide-angle lens speeds it up. Depth of field will also affect the image; more depth is in focus in a wide-angle shot and less in a telephoto. A zoom lens allows shifting from one set of characteristics to another within the same shot, but its effects should not be confused with camera movements like dollying in or out from the scene. (See Monaco, 60–64; Bordwell and Thompson, 156–61.)

● **Film Stock.** Qualities of the film stock play an important role in the qualities of the image produced. Characteristics of film emulsion, speed of exposure, and differences in the processing of film in the laboratory contribute to such visual qualities as graininess and color quality. The differences are comparable to the effects achieved by a portrait photographer, who uses slow film, as opposed to a newspaper photographer, who characteristically works with very fast film to increase contrast and stop action. (See Monaco, 81–82, 159; Bordwell and Thompson, 151–54.)

● **Projection Speed.** While most film is recorded and projected at the same speed, action can be artificially slowed or accelerated by altering either the speed of the camera or the projector. This can also be accomplished in the laboratory by repeating individual frames in such a way as to extend and slow action. (See Bordwell and Thompson, 155–56.)

The experience of watching any moving image presentation on film or video inevitably involves the viewer in decoding these various elements. To a large extent, that decoding goes on unconsciously, as viewers respond to the cues they have been informally taught to respond to through years of movie and television watching. Viewers usually see what filmmakers intend them to see, and they "get the message" they are supposed to get.

The idea of visual literacy, especially when understood in the context of history and social studies, involves being able to see beyond (or through) what the filmmakers intended, to become aware of the ways creative elements may have been used by the filmmaker to produce the desired impression on the audience and then reasonably evaluate whether that point of view is supported by facts and evidence. In the same way that people learn to critically identify words or phrases that are loaded or colored with bias and may influence their overall perception of an article or a book, visually literate people should also be conscious of the ways in which individual images and combinations of images can be loaded or colored.

Editing: Joining image to image

In addition to understanding the elements of the individual shot, the visually literate person must have an appreciation of the importance of editing for creative communication in the moving image media. On a simple level, editing devices can be thought of as punctuation

Figure 1

Figure 2

Figure 3

Figure 4

marks, which may give hints, though not always reliable indications, of the relationship that is intended. There are a limited number of ways that shots or sequences can be joined together:

• **Fade.** The introduction (fade in) or removal (fade out) of the image onto a blank screen usually indicates either the beginning or end of some dramatic action, or some passage of time.

• **Dissolve.** The gradual overlapping of images in which one comes to replace another usually suggests a relationship between the two shots. Like a fade, a dissolve can happen quickly or be drawn out over several seconds.

• **Wipe.** The mechanical moving of one image off the screen and the replacing of it with another is called a wipe. Examples of wipes include directional replacement of images (such as from right to left), replacement from the center of the screen with an iris, or box replacement from a corner of the screen, which expands until the screen is completely filled with the new image. The wipe is an old-fashioned device more common in silent film than in recent cinema, but it is used today in television, especially for special effects in sports programming. It is generally used to break continuity and mark the beginning of or radical shift to some new action.

• **Cut.** The instantaneous replacing of one image with another is at once the most common editing device and the one most open to interpretation. The cut can, for example, be used in a shot/reverse shot sequence to reinforce the continuity of action happening at the same time and place; in a cross-cutting situation (relating images of a maiden in distress, for example, with those of the hero rushing to her rescue), in which action may be happening at the same time but in different places; or, at the extreme, in a jump cut that leaps across continents of space or centuries of time.

Since history is to a very considerable extent concerned with matters of place and time, editing is of special significance, for it is in joining images one to another that moving image media's ability to creatively represent (or misrepresent) space and time is most evident. Within the individual shot, for example, there are ways that time can seemingly be expanded or compressed: through under- or overcranking of the camera, through use of lenses that appear to slow or speed action to or from the camera, through laboratory processes such as the use of the optical printer. There are also way place can seemingly be altered, such as through camera movement or changes in focus, but none of these has the potential for altering place and time that the editing together of images has.

In the 1920s the Russian filmmaker and theorist Lev Kuhlesov experimented with the ways audiences understood images presented one after another, without the help of an establishing shot to give viewers their bearings. When he reproduced the same image of a face (that of a famous Russian actor) several times, and presented it in conjunction with an image of a bowl of soup, a baby, and a dead woman laid out in a coffin, viewers praised the subtlety of the actor in expressing hunger in relation to the soup, love in relation to the baby, and grief in relation to the corpse. Through the images of the actor's face were exactly the same, people saw what they expected to see. In the absence of evidence to the contrary, such as establishing shots that might have indicated that the images were not related to one another, viewers assumed that the shots paired on the screen took place at the same place and time and, going one step further, presumed that the images were related to one another causally. (See Monaco, 323; Bordwell and Thompson, 160–61.)

The Kuhlesov effect is usually thought of in relation to individual pairs of images, but the impetus of an audience to associate shots to one another, and to see what they are led to believe they are seeing, goes much farther. Almost all historical compilation films (those compiled from various pieces of archival footage on some historical issue or event) are forced to rely on some amount of stock footage to fill in gaps in the extant actuality materials. A shot of planes flying overhead may cut to an anti-aircraft gun shooting into the sky, and then to a plane in flames hurtling toward the earth. The likelihood that a camera operator was in the perfect position to record these three shots of the shooting down of an individual plane is slim. It is much more likely that the sequence was constructed from three separate shots taken at different locations at different times, and edited together to provide the desired effect in the mind of the viewer. This does not necessarily destroy the information content of the film. Planes may actually have been shot down. But the editing of the scene should provide a warning that the truthfulness of the message of a film may have relatively little connection with the specific images that appear on the screen.

What members of an audience thought they saw, or were tricked into thinking they saw, may be of special interest historically. Nicholas Pronay of the University of Leeds studied British newsreels of the early days of World War II, which were carefully constructed (with the encouragement of the British government) to reassure the English people as they suffered through the dark days of the blitz. One newsreel story that especially interested Pronay extolled the abilities of British anti-aircraft units and their weapons. The newsreel included a long shot of a gun firing at a range far beyond that which British weapons could reach. By studying the image closely, Pronay established what audiences of the time could not have noticed from the screen: the film was actually of a German gun. Pronay's work is instructive not only for the ways he demonstrates how footage was falsified in newsreel film, but also for the propagandistic effect it reveals. In this case, it is more important for the historian to understand what people thought they saw than what they actually did see.

Perhaps the ultimate example of such falsification in a historical film involves "Victory at Sea" (1952), one of the first great television compilation series. When interviewed by historian Peter C. Rollins, series producer Isaac Klienerman claimed to be most proud of the program on the Battle of Leyte Gulf, still used in the 1970s for strategic study at the Naval War College. Making this film presented a particular challenge, because there were no cameras at Leyte Gulf. The producers made up the film completely of stock footage and film shot of other battles. Such wholesale falsification certainly raises questions about the reliability of compilation films, but the historical information and interpretation presented in a film depends on more than the veracity of the archival footage. There may indeed be very valuable historical observations in the Battle of Leyte Gulf program that have nothing to do with where the pictures of the ships came from. This film is more important as it illustrates the importance of critical viewing. Viewers must be able to comprehend and evaluate the messages of a presentation based on real evidence. They should not allow themselves to simply be swept along by a film on the false premise that, through the film, they are on the scene themselves, reliving the experience of the time, and therefore capable of making their own judgments about it.

In contrast to the production methods employed in the Battle of Leyte Gulf program, most makers of historical compilation films today, especially those trained as historical scholars who have in addition become filmmakers, make it a cardinal rule to use only footage that can be verified as being from the same time and place (or at least from the same general period) as the subject they are working on. This does not mean that most errors in historical films are due to the falsification of footage. On the contrary, most of the potential for problems, like most of the potential for success, lies in the ways the filmmakers choose the footage, and how that footage is edited into a final product. Viewers must be aware that even guarantees that a film was made solely from archival footage of the time and place in question in no way assures that the film presents a complete or truthful account.

The newsreel archives in which producers of historical compilation films conduct much of their research are rich with examples of how footage was selected and edited for the presentation of news stories. The outtakes are sometimes more valuable to historians than the footage the newsreel companies put on the screen. The video compilation includes several examples of the ways newsreel film was selected and edited for release, including footage of President Franklin D. Roosevelt not used in the newsreel because it showed him in a position that made obvious his physical infirmity, and a story on the Berlin airlift that demonstrates the extent to which events were often staged for the newsreel cameras.

Like newsreels, television news offers important nightly examples of the creative use of editing in the presentation of actuality footage. Time constraints and the capsulized nature of most television news stories make it likely that fuller coverage can almost always be found in the printed media, but the concept of the viewer as an eyewitness is a powerful one. It suggests that viewers relate to news on television at least in part with the rationalization that they are better able to see and evaluate a situation for themselves than they might be when reading a newspaper story. To counteract this assumption, students should be helped to understand how editing can influence viewers subconsciously. On one level, the ordering of stories in a broadcast, and their organization in relation to commercials, suggests their relative importance. On another level, as it should be clear to visually literate viewers, the editing of each story, from thirty seconds to four minutes of video that might include several interviews, voice-over comments on otherwise silent footage, and on-camera commentary by the anchor person, is crucial to the message the story conveys. On the most basic level, critical viewers must learn about the construction of the typical television interview.

A basic TV news crew includes a reporter, a camera operator, and a sound person. When the crew goes on location to interview someone, their first concern is to photograph the person speaking words that they can later use in an edited story. Typically, they will set up the camera for an establishing shot of the interviewee and the reporter, and then concentrate the camera on recording the person's responses to the reporter's questions. After they have the material they need—often after the interviewee has left the scene—they will set up the camera again in reverse angle to photograph the reporter, who repeats the questions once more. Since it is rare for more than one camera to be sent out with a news crew, this process is necessary to give the editor raw material to work with when constructing the final piece for broadcast. Presumably, the reporter repeats the questions in exactly the same words, using exactly the same inflection as the first time, but it is easy to imagine how, having already heard what the subject is going to say, there might be some changes. At this point, the reporter may also do a few silent reaction shots, trying to appear as though listening to the interviewee's response, and a stand-up introduction to the story with some identifiable landmark in the background.

When the news crew returns to the station with the raw footage, the work is only half finished. The various pieces photographed in the field then have to be arranged in such a way that they present the story as clearly and concisely as possible, in accordance with the time constraints of the broadcast. Viewers frequently assume that the various elements of a completed story took place in the order in which they were presented, not stopping to think that the editor of a televised news story frequently writes the introduction last. Most viewers are also unaware that the actual order of interview comments or other recorded elements may have been rearranged in a number of different ways.

One selection in the video compilation illustrates how such interviews are created, showing how comments from an extended conversation, recorded with a single camera, can be reduced, rearranged, and reoriented through editing with cutaways. The interview begins with a two-shot (a shot showing two persons, in this case an establishing shot), in which the person being interviewed is photographed from behind the shoulder of the interviewer. In the same shot, the lens zooms in so that the interviewee is speaking directly into the camera. The second shot is a cutaway, or reaction shot, of the interviewer listening attentively to the interviewee, who is still heard speaking on the sound track. In the third shot, the camera is shifted back to the interviewee. In the first and third shots, the sound is synchronized with the image, but in the second, where the sound synch is lost, it becomes possible to delete or rearrange words, sentences, or entire paragraphs of what the interviewee is saying. If there is even an approximate match in the tone and cadence of the voice and the logic of what is being said, viewers (and listeners) would not be likely to notice the audio cuts.

There might be several editing shifts even in a one- or two-minute interview. In a more lengthy exchange, additional cutaways might be used for visual variety. On of the most interesting sequences in Edward R. Murrow's "See It Now: Report on Senator McCarthy" shows McCarthy speaking at a Washington's Birthday celebration in Philadelphia in 1954. Viewers questioned after watching this sequence (included in the video compilation) think that they have just watched two-and-one-half minutes of McCarthy making a speech; they presume that what they have seen on the screen took place just as they saw it, in real time. A closer viewing reveals that the sequence was made up of nine shots edited together to allow a compression of McCarthy's forty-minute speech into a tight and coherent statement for the program. The sequence contains three cutaways, one to the upper part of the mural in front of which McCarthy spoke and two to the audience. Each provided an opportunity for the editors to trim McCarthy's comments down to what they could use. Without the outtakes from the editing session or a transcript of McCarthy's entire speech, viewers cannot know how much was deleted. They can be quite sure, however, that the attentive audience members shown in the cutaways were not being attentive to McCarthy saying what is heard on the second track. CBS has only one camera present at the event, and it would not have been focused anywhere but on the platform while the senator was speaking. The audience shots would have been photographed either before or after McCarthy spoke so that the editors would have material with which to edit the news report.

The cutaway is an essential tool for television news and documentary producers, who must almost always cut down a longer interview to fit a short time slot. The editors can delete much from a person's responses, even combining the answers to several questions into one, by simply making the audio cuts coincide with a visual cutaway. Another option is to delete material while cutting to a shot of the report asking (actually repeating) a different question. The viewers unsuspectingly assume that the interview is taking place in real time and that the sequence of questions and answers is a seamless record of what happened. In any television interview, but especially in footage that includes repeated cuts back and forth from the reporter to the subject, viewers should be aware that every reaction shot and every cut to the interviewer with a new question provides an occasion for a reduction or rearrangement of the audio.

It should be stressed that rather than meaning to misrepresent what is said, TV news editors usually intend only to avoid distracting visual choppiness in the finished product. Although the subjects of TV interviews may come across better in edited form, sometimes they react negatively to being edited. Perhaps the most famous controversy over cutaways involved CBS News and its 1970 documentary "The Selling of the Pentagon." Claiming that cutaways were used not only to condense, but also to rearrange and garble responses made by Pentagon spokesmen, the government forced the issue until hearings were held before a congressional committee on the practice of television news editing.

To teach students about such basic processes in the production of television news is not to call for different standards in TV news editing. The problem lies less with the producers and editors (people performing their craft the best way they know) than with viewers who may prefer to watch TV news because it seems like so much less work than reading the newspaper. Students must be brought to understand that critical viewing of a moving image, especially an important one such as a news story on a significant public issue, should demand at least as much attention as the careful reading of a printed page.

The main concern of the theatrical or documentary filmmaker in making decisions about editing is similar to the concern of the TV news editor. The filmmaker's goal is to create film sequences in which viewers are encouraged to concentrate on the point being made without being unnecessarily distracted by confusing shifts in subjects, camera location, camera angle, or composition. Continuity editing is the procedure of joining together pieces of film in ways that prevent such disorientation. Camera angle, for example, is important in retaining continuity. If a woman is seen leaving a room in one direction, it is important that they shot showing her entering the adjoining room be at an angle that does not disorient the viewer. An audience would certainly find it hard to follow a chase scene in which the train robbers were portrayed riding from the left to the right side of the screen intercut with a posse trailing them from right to left. There are various ways shots can be joined together to emphasize a sense of continuity, such as the seamless continuation of some motion or sound element from one shot to the next, or the composition of the second shot so that the focal point of interest is in the same location on the screen that it was in the preceding shot.

Over the years, a series of editing conventions developed that influenced the ways in which viewers interpreted what was going on in the narrative of a film story. The editing conventions of the classical Hollywood cinema of the thirties and forties, for example, dictated that a scene between two characters begin with an establishing shot and then progress through a series of shot/reverse shots showing close-ups of each character speaking to the other. The selection in the video compilation that includes two alternate editing patterns for the climactic sequence from *The Life of an American Fireman* (1902) demonstrates how audiences at the turn of the century had different expectations when they tried to make sense of a filmed story. Perhaps because of their experience with live theater, the audiences for early motion pictures were more comfortable with editing patterns that preserved the continuity of space, preferring to see all the action from one point of view at a time, even if that action had to be repeated from the start to show them another point of view. In contrast, classical Hollywood cinema style was based on a continuity of time in which editing shifted freely from one point of view to another, but never showed the same event twice. The version of *The Life of an American Fireman* that was subsequently re-edited according to the more modern style illustrates the power of editing in leading viewers through a narrative. Careful viewing of the original version reveals a number of incongruities (people entering the room from the wrong side and windows broken in rather than out, for example), which are difficult to recognize when the logic of the more modern editing style leads the viewer through the scene. Editing conventions do change over time, and they are not always used in the expected ways. Indeed, art may be said to disappear when, through rigorous adherence, convention becomes cliche. (For more on continuity editing and the classical Hollywood cinema, see Bordwell and Thompson, 211–20.)

There are alternatives to continuity editing. Some of the highlights of film history are centered around the creative use of editing to break continuity and interpret reality in artistic ways. An important example is Sergei Eisenstein's use of editing to create a collision of images to visually convey what he saw as the essence of the class struggle, a point he thought would have been much more difficult to convey in a seamless narrative continuity. Other examples include the juxtaposition of individual images in an otherwise traditionally edited film. In *Hearts and Minds* (1974), a documentary tour de force against American involvement in Vietnam, Peter Davis sacrifices continuity for dramatic contrast when he cuts directly from an interview with General William Westmoreland, who is explaining that Oriental people have little respect for life, to a Vietnamese woman weeping openly over the grave of a loved one killed in battle.

Editing is also used to integrate dramatic symbolism into a scene. In the opening shot of Charlie Chaplin's *Modern Times* (1936), a midshot of sheep (including one black sheep) being herded, presumably to the slaughter house, cuts directly to a shot of workers pouring out of a subway exit on their way to work. The rest of the film deals with the ways in which industrial civilization threatens to dehumanize the lives of ordinary people, providing Chaplin's tramp character (a black sheep) with numerous dramatic situations, both humorous and pathetic.

Sound and image

A motion picture or television program engages the ears as well as the eyes. Edison experimented with movies with synchronized sound as early as 1912, and until sound technology was fully implemented in the late 1920s, films were almost always shown with some musical accompaniment (ranging from a concert orchestra to a phonograph record) and even with live sound effects. Once sound technology was in place in theaters, silent films all but disappeared.

Tony Schwartz, the producer of hundreds of successful radio and television commercials, argues that the sound element of a film is almost always more important than the visual. He encourages exercises in which students watch films without the sound and try to work out the meaning before watching them again with the sound. Chris Marker's *Letters From Siberia* (1957) invites viewers to think about the influence of sound by showing the same visual footage three separate times with three different, widely contrasting sound tracks. (See Bordwell and Thompson, 232–33.)

Sound can be diegetic (emanating from a character or object that is part of the story space of the film) or nondiegetic; it can come from on or off screen; it can be internal (relating only to what is going on in the mind of one character) or external; it can be synchronized or asynchronous; and it can extend from shot to shot as a bridge between scenes. The three general types of sound are: the spoken word (dialogue or narration), music, and sound effects. (See Monaco, 178–88; Bordwell and Thompson, 232–57.) The selection in the video compilation from *Women of Summer* provides an especially good opportunity to study all of these various uses of sound.

Sound can contribute significantly to the illusion of realism created in a film. It not only reinforces the believability of what is seen on the screen, but allows the filmmakers to use the area beyond the frame more creatively, for example, with the sound of an approaching locomotive that is heard but not seen. Synchronized sound gives the greatest reinforcement to realism, especially when the sound of voices is lip-synched to the faces doing the speaking. People look natural when speaking on film, but such synchronized sound is very difficult to attain. When a film is projected, the light cell on the projector that picks up the optical sound track comes later in the film path than the lens that projects the image; therefore, the recorded sound on the film must be placed twenty-six frames before the image it accompanies. Although synchronized sound may seem natural to the audience, the filmmakers had to manipulate the materials very unnaturally in order to make it sound that way. (In videotape, the same recording and playback heads handle the audio and video tracks, making the editing of synchronized video considerably more simple.)

When live sound is recorded for film, usually on a tape recorder cabled to the camera, it is crucial that the same speed in the image and the sound track be maintained. Depending on the movement taking place in the frame, the image can be accelerated by as much as 20 percent before the viewers will think the movement unnatural, but the slightest change in the pace of the sound track will alter the pitch of a person's voice and make sound effects seem unreal. Part of the creative flexibility enjoyed by the silent filmmaker was the ability to vary the speed of the camera or the projector for dramatic or humorous effect. Students should be informed, however, that when they see a silent film today in which people seem to be moving about and talking at a faster than normal speed, it is not because the figures were hyperactive or because the filmmakers necessarily intended a Keystone Kops effect. On the contrary, the students are probably watching the film projected at one-and-one-half times the speed that was originally intended. In the early days of moving pictures, film was ordinarily shot and projected at sixteen frames per second. Today, unless step-printed to compensate for the change, early films are often projected at the modern standard of twenty-four frames per second, which results in the unnatural (and unintended) accelerated movement.

Ironically, there are occasions when sound that did happen naturally would seem unreal and confusing in a film. For example, in a war movie in which shells are fired at planes in the distance, the camera cuts quickly from image to image, conveying the excitement of the moment with the pace of the editing. In reality, the sound of the explosion taking place at an altitude of one thousand feet, a half-mile from the camera, would be heard several seconds after the flash was seen. The filmmakers, however, would likely have the sound coincide with the flashed on the screen, so as not to confuse the audience with sounds of explosions accompanying unrelated images.

The use of music on the sound track for a film can be atmospheric, simply setting a tone for the action or the relationships being developed, or it can be a central unifying core of the film's contents. The Nazi propaganda film *Für Uns* (1937) demonstrates this point powerfully, especially if viewers understand the meaning that the musical selections had for Germans in the 1930s. In the opening scenes of the film, as the sixteen martyrs of 1923 are honored as party heroes, the music is the party anthem, "The Horst Wessel Song," played as a mournful durge. Later in the film, when the purpose is to transform these party heroes into national heroes, the party song is replaced with the national anthem. At the close of the film, the music reverts back to "The Horst Wessel Song," played triumphantly in recognition of the Nazis' place as the leaders of the German nation.

MAKING MEANING FROM FILM AND TELEVISION

Through the creative combination of mise-en-scène and photographic elements of shots with editing and sound, motion pictures and television communicate meaning in a variety of ways. Because the perception of a moving image requires a level of subconscious psychological involvement, an individual's personality, catalog of previous experiences, and frame of mind are extremely influential on the ways images will be interpreted. Even recognizable symbols convey complex levels of denotative and connotative meaning driven by a variety of physiological, psychological, and cultural factors. Some of these factors are unique to film, while others are drawn from literature and other arts. For example, students unfamiliar with the musical selections in *Für Uns* might simply think of the music as atmospheric background accompaniment and miss the central symbolic role it played in constructing the Nazis' propaganda message.

In film and television, form and content are inseparable. The form and structure of a moving image production can significantly affect the message presented. Like a painting, a piece of sculpture, or an architect's design for a house, every film has an artistic form, an arrangement of elements intended to interest and involve viewers. In addition to visual and aural elements, there are narrative elements, bits of information about the plot or the characters of a film that lead, maintain, and direct viewers' interest. Not all films are narrative in their formal organization. *The Plow*, for example, like *Für Uns* and the "Daisy Spot," is rhetorical in its structure, intended more to convert its viewers to a point of view than to involve them in a story. (See Bordwell and Thompson, 44–80.)

The range and depth of story information a film reveals, the functions of characters and other plot elements, and the ways the presentation of time is structured (using flashbacks, for example, to fill out a plot) are often the deciding factors when viewers make meaning from a film. They may be allowed an omniscient point of view, seeing many different types of events as they interact with one another, or events may be presented only from the point of view of one of the characters, restricting the information conveyed and building suspense. Viewer expectations are influenced by the film's genre; people watch a mystery film differently than they do a musical. Patterns of development—how the situation at the end of the film differs from the situation at the beginning (has some journey or investigation been completed, has the boy married the girl, has a lesson been learned)—also affect viewer expectations. (See Bordwell and Thompson, 82–112).

By the end of "Molders of Troy," for example, the film has shown how conditions in the iron-molding trade in upstate New York after the Civil War moved the workers to organize and strike. It has also shown how the factory owners responded to the workers with violence and with the decision to move the factories to other cities. The final scene (included in the video compilation) takes place in a tavern, where Jim Donovan, a former worker and union organizer who left the mills to become a city alderman, confronts Brian Duffy, his stepson who is unemployed after being blacklisted as a union agitator. Fearful that Duffy will be hurt if he stays in Troy, Donovan tries to convince him to move to another city, but Duffy resists in the name of principle. The tension between the two characters, and the examination of the issues at hand, is all the more evident to viewers because they have been privileged with information that Donovan does not have. Immediately before Donovan entered the room, Duffy had explained to the bartender that he was already thinking of moving to another town to continue his organizing activities there. Duffy's resistance is a front, a face he puts on for his stepfather, a working man who has succumbed to the establishment. It is not the acting style, the editing, or even the scripted lines themselves that allow the audience to make meaning from this scene. It is the narrative structure, in which the line about Duffy's plans to move is inserted immediately before Donovan sits down with him. A structure that withheld this information until after the confrontation, or raised it much earlier in the film, would have radically altered the meaning.

Form is inseparable from content in the narrative strategy of *The Return of Martin Guerre*, the mixing of visual and aural elements in *Women of Summer*, and the editing techniques in *The Life of an American Fireman*. Perhaps the most interesting example of innovative cinema form in the video compilation is D. W. Griffith's *A Corner in Wheat* (1909). The film tells three separate stories, intercutting images of a poor farm family, the "wheat king" who corners the market and thereby increases his fortune, and consumers in a bakery store, some of whom are unable to meet the rising price of bread. The characters from the three parallel plots never come into contact with one another in the film. The wheat king makes his fortune and at the moment of triumph falls accidently to his death. The consumers face growing hardship as prices rise and the charity fund reduces its level of assistance. The farmer, who can show nothing for all his work, is left at the end of the film as he was found at the beginning, sowing seeds that offer little promise for his future. The film is structured so that the unifying theme—a progressive critique of capitalism—takes shape only in the minds of the viewers, who draw their own connections between the different parts of the story. Thus, the structure of the film keeps the message clear. If the three plots intersected more directly, or if characters were allowed to confront one another on the screen, the central philosophical message might have been muddled by the specifics of the stories or the characterizations.

Many films rely on symbols familiar from literature and theater to communicate ideas, for example, the candle that goes out on the table as an old man dies in bed. One of the most effective sequences in *The Return of Martin Guerre* deals with the impostor's first day in Artigat. At the end of the day Bertrande takes him to her bed, but first she is seen quickly removing the crucifix that has been left on her pillow. The meaning of the symbol is somewhat clouded because up to this point the film has led the audience to believe that the man is the real Martin Guerre. Once the audience realizes that he is an impostor, the significance of Bertrande removing the crucifix just before commiting what she must have considered the first of a series of mortal sins becomes more meaningful.

In the last two decades many film scholars have sought to study the making of meaning in film through an approach to linguistics known as semiology. Semiologists draw upon the work of linguist Ferdinand de Saussure, who defined a sign as made up of both the signifier (some visual element) and the signified (the concept or idea that the signifier stands for). A donkey, for example, can be signified by a drawing or by the letters d-o-n-k-e-y. In each case, a visual symbol (the signifier) stands for the meaning of a four-legged animal with long ears (the signified). The image of a donkey in a film carried with it the direct and overt denotative message: "Here is a four-legged animal with long ears." But it is the connotative meaning of visual images that makes film interesting. Semiotic analysis considers the additional connotative meanings that might be connected with the presence of the donkey, whether consciously intended by the film-maker or unintentionally constructed in the mind of the viewer, and how that meaning is created. Typically, semiologists look for such meaning through analyses, which they term either paradigmatic (how this donkey is different from other donkeys or other animals that might have been shown) or syntagmatic (how this image of a donkey relates to the other images that precede or follow it within the film). The analysis would proceed through a careful categorization of possible denotative or connotative readings and a consideration of possible codes of meaning drawn from the broader culture, from other arts, or from the nature of the cinema.

Luis Bunuel's classic short film, *Un Chien Andalou* (1929), is a wonderful artifact for the study of surrealism and the intellectual history of the 1920s. From the opening sequence, which climaxes in the slicing of a woman's eye with a razor, *Un Chien Andalou* shocks its viewers with its destruction of contemporary aesthetic standards, thus accomplishing one of the central goals of surrealism as an artistic and intellectual movement. Many of the other images in the film have more or less obvious symbolic meaning. In one shot, a man, to approach a woman sexually, must drag behind him symbols of the repressive forces of bourgeois culture (a grand piano), organized religion (two priests), and moral corruption (the carcasses of two dead donkeys). The meaning of the donkeys in this image comes from the composition of the shot, which forces viewers to relate to the priests, the piano, and the donkeys at the same; from the half-decomposed state of the carcasses (a paradigmatic observation); and from the placement of the shot within in a film that dwells on the moral corruption of the main character (a syntagmatic observation).

Those who apply the theories of structuralism or semiology are sometimes faulted for taking their analyses too far. A thoroughgoing semiologist, for example, concentrating on the identification and decoding of every sign, might fail to appreciate the aesthetic qualities of a film. Overly rigorous attention to the internal analysis of a moving image production might lead scholars to undervalue, or even ignore, historical context. But historians concerned with the moving image cannot afford to turn their backs on film theory. The symbolic meaning in many film images might be discerned without necessarily resorting to the technical terminology of cinema theory, but there are surely occasions where a judicious application of such principles might offer new insight.

It is important to recognize that differences do exist in analyzing images in film and television. Television productions are almost always designed to fit more precise time limits than commercial entertainment films. Characteristically, television programs are also internally structured to allow for the insertion of commercials. A dramatic program is therefore likely to string out a series of mini-climaxes in such a way that the viewers' attention will be held until after the commercial break.

In addition, there are significant visual differences between film and television. The small TV screen does not lend itself to the vast panoramas and long shots that are so powerful in moving pictures, especially in Cinemascope and other wide-screen formats. Television footage, much more than film, involves head-and-shoulder shots of individual actors or small groups of actors. This was at least one reason why the makers of "Molders of Troy" decided to focus on the experience of one family, trying to represent the complex of worker, industry, and community history in the lives of a handful of people. There is also some degree of difference between the production techniques of film and television. While almost all of network television today is presented on videotape, only a small percentage (and a significantly larger percentage of local television) is broadcast live or almost live (taped earlier but shown as shot without editing). The typical sitcom, which may be carefully rehearsed and revised over several days, is usually shot as a run-through of the entire episode. This is very different from the shooting of a typical film or dramatic TV series, which is almost always shot with little, if any, attention to the order of the sequences as they will appear in the completed production.

There are many communications scholars who would argue that film and television are so unlike one another that they defy common treatment, but the interests of most history teachers should not demand such precision. There are distinctions between the content, production, and reception of the two media, but lessons should concentrate on the basic visual and aural elements that do raise similar, if not identical, analytical concerns.

APPENDIX 1
CONTENTS OF THE VIDEO COMPILATION

Selection 1.   *The Return of Martin Guerre* (excerpts)

Selection 2.   "Molders of Troy" (excerpt)

Selection 3.   *Women of Summer* (excerpt)

Selection 4.   The Cutaway and the Editing of a Television News Interview

Selection 5.   *The Plow That Broke the Plains*

Selection 6.   The "Daisy Spot"

Selection 7.   Universal and Movietone Newsreels (excerpts)

Selection 8.   "See It Now: Report on Senator McCarthy" (excerpts)

Selection 9.   CBS Evening News, December 2, 1979 (excerpt)

Selection 10.   *The Birth of a Race* (excerpts)

Selection 11.   *Für Uns*

Selection 12.   *Life of an American Fireman* (excerpts)

Selection 13.   *A Corner in Wheat*

The video compilation is available in videodisk and videotape formats and is accompanied by a 300 page study guide which includes study aides and documents relating to the production and reception of the thirteen selections. It should be ordered directly from the American Historical Association, 400 A Street S. E., Washington, D.C. 20003.

APPENDIX 2
FOR FURTHER READING

The field of film and television scholarship has become so rich in the past decade that it would be impossible to adequately summarize it here. A few of the most influential publications in each area are listed on the following pages, but readers are strongly encouraged to turn to the fuller bibliographies in James Monaco, *How To Read a Film*, rev. ed. (New York, 1981), and David Bordwell and Kristin Thompson, *Film Art: An Introduction*, 2d ed. (New York, 1986).

There are two journals that should be of special interest. *The Historical Journal of Film, Radio and Television* is published in Great Britain for the International Association for Audio-Visual Media in Historical Research and Teaching (IAMHIST). *Film & History* is the quarterly journal of the Historians Film Committee, an affiliated society of the American Historical Association based at New Jersey Institute of Technology, Newark, NJ 07102.

GENERAL GUIDES FOR EVALUATING FILMS AND TELEVISION

Blackaby, Linda, Dan Georgakas, and Barbara Margolis. *In Focus.: A Guide to Using Films*. New York: Zoetrope, 1980.

Ferris, Bill, and Judy Peiser, eds. *American Folklore Films and Videotapes-An Index*. Memphis, Tenn.: Center for Southern Folklore, 1976.

Guidelines for Off-Air Taping of Copyriyhted Programs for Education Use: Thirty Questions Librarians Ask. Chicago: American Library Association, 1982.

Klotman, Phyllis Rauch. *Frame By Frame: A Black Filmography*. Bloomington: Indiana University Press, 1979.

Limbacher, James L., comp. and ed. *Feature Films on 8-mm, 16-mm, and Videotape*. 7th ed. New York: Bowker, 1982.

Loy, Jane M. *Latin America, Sights and Sounds*. Gainesville, Fla.: Latin American Studies Programs, 1973.

Pettit, Arthur G. *Images of the Mexican American in Fiction and Film*. College Station, Texas: Texas A & M University Press, 1980.

Peyton, Patricia, ed. *Reel Change: A Guide to Social Issue Films*. San Francisco: Film Fund, 1979.

Pitts, Michael. *Hollywood and American Reality: A Filmography of Over 250 Motion Pictures Depicting U.S. History*. Jenerson, N. C.: McFarland, 1984.

Samples, Gordon. *How to Locate Reviews of Plays and Films: A Bibliography of Criticism from the Beginning to the Present.* Metuchen, N. J.: Scarecrow, 1976.

Sullivan, Kaye. *Films for, by, and about Women.* Metuchen, N. J.: Scarecrow, 1980.

Weatherford, Elizabeth, ed. *Native Americans on Film and Video.* New York: Museum of the American Indian, 1981.

Woll, Allen L., and Randall M. Miller. *Ethnic and Racial Images in American Film and Television: Historical Essays and Bibliography.* New York: Garland, 1987

SOURCES ON FILM

Aldgate, Anthony. *Cinema and History: British Newsreels and the Spanish Civil War.* London: Scholar Press, 1979.

Arnheim, Rudolf. *Film As Art.* Berkeley: University of California Press, 1957.

Balio, Tino. *United Artists: The Company Built by the Stars.* Madison: University of Wisconsin Press, 1976.

————, ed. *The American Film Industry.* Rev. ed. Madison: University of Wisconsin Press, 1985.

Barnouw, Erik. *Documentary: A History of the Non-Fiction Film.* New York: Oxford University Press, 1983.

Barsam, Richard Meran. *Non-Fiction Film: A Critical History.* New York: E. P. Dutton, 1973.

————, ed. *Non-Fiction Film Theory and Criticism.* New York: E. P. Dutton, 1976.

Bergman, Andrew. *We're in the Money: Depression America and its Films.* New York: New York University Press, 1971.

Bordwell, David, Janet Staiger, and Kristin Thompson. *The Classical Hollywood Cinema: Film Style and Mode of Production to 1960.* New York: Columbia University Press, 1985.

Burns, E. Bradford. *Latin American Cinema: Film and History.* Los Angeles: UCLA Latin American Center, 1975.

Ciipps, Thomas. *Slow Fade to Black: The Negro in American Film, 1900–1942.* New York: Oxford University Press, 1977.

Fielding, Raymond. *A Technological History of Motion Pictures and Televison.* 3d ed. Berkeley: University of California Press, 1979.

————. *The American Newsreel, 1911–1967.* Norman: University of Oklahoma Press, 1972.

Gomery, Douglas, and Robert C. Allen. *Film History: Theory and Practice.* New York: Knopf, 1985.

Griffin, Patrick. "The Making of *Goodbye Billy*." *Film & History,* 2 (May 1972): 6–10.

Isaksson, Føolke, and Leif Furhammar. *Politics and Film.* New York: Praeger, 1971.

Jarvie, Ian. *Movies and Society.* New York: Basic Books, 1970.

Jowett, Garth. *Film: The Democratic Art.* Boston: Little, Brown, 1976.

Jowett, Garth, and James M. Linton. *Movies as Mass Communication.* Beverly Hills: Sage, 1980.

Jowett, Garth, and Victoria O'Donnell. *Propaganda and Persuasion.* Newbury Park, Calif: Sage, 1986.

Kracauer, Siegfried. *From Caligari to Hitler: A Psychological History of the German Film.* Princeton: Princeton University Press, 1947.

Leab, Daniel J. *From Sambo to Superspade: The Black Motion Picture Experience.* Boston: Houghton Mifflin, 1975.

Maltby, Richard. *Harmless Entertainment: Hollywood and the Ideology of Consensus.* Metuchen, N. J.: Scarecrow, 1983.

Marsden, Michael, John G. Nachbar, and Sam L. Grogg, Jr., eds. *Movies as Artifacts: Cultural Criticism of Popular Film.* Chicago: Nelson-Hall, 1982.

Mast, Gerald, and Marshall Cohen. *Film Theory and Criticism: Introductory Readings.* 2d ed. New York: Oxford University Press, 1979.

Mast, Gerald, ed. *The Movies in Our Midst: Documents in the Cultural History of Film in America.* Chicago: University of Chicago Press, 1982.

May, Larry. *Screening Out the Past: The Birth of Mass Culture and the Motion Picture Industry.* New York: Oxford University Press, 1980.

Mellencamp, Patricia, and Philip Rosen. *Cinema Histories, Cinema Practices.* Frederick, Md.: University Publications of America, 1984.

O'Connor, John E., ed. *Film and the Humanities.* New York: Rockefeller Foundation, 1977.

Pronay, Nicholas, and Derek W. Spring. *Propaganda, Politics and Film, 1918–45.* London: Macmillan, 1982.

Reader, Keith. *Cultures on Celluloid.* London: Quartet Books, 1981.

Rollins, Peter C. "The Making of Will Rogers' 1920s." *Film & History,* 7 (January 1977): 1–5.

———, ed. *Hollywood as Historian: American Film in Cultural Context.* Lexington, Ky.: University Press of Kentucky, 1983.

Short, K. R. M., ed. *Film and Radio Propaganda in World War II.* Knoxville: University of Tennessee Press, 1983.

Smith, Julian. *Looking Away: Hollywood and Vietnam.* New York: Scribner, 1975.

Sklar, Robert. *Movie-Made America: A Cultural History of American Movies.* New York: Random House, 1975.

Suid, Lawrence. *Guts and Glory: Great American War Movies.* Reading, Mass.: Addison-Wesley, 1978.

Taylor, Richard. *The Politics of the Soviet Cinema, 1917 1929.* Cambridge, U. K.: Cambridge University Press, 1979.

Welch, David. *Propaganda and the German Cinema, 1988–1945.* New York: Oxford University Press, 1983.

Wollen, Peter. *Signs and Meaning in the Cinema.* Bloomington: Indiana University Press, 1969.

Wood, Michael. *America in the Movies.* New York: Basic Books, 1975.

Wright, Will. *Sixguns and Society: A Structural Study of the Western.* Berkeley: University of California Press, 1975.

SOURCES ON TELEVISION

Adams, William, and Fay Schreibman, eds. *Television Network News: Issues in Content Research.* Washington, D. C.: George Washington Univerity, 1978.

Berger, Arthur Asa. *Media Analysis Techniques.* Beverly Hills: Sage, 1982.

Barnouw, Erik. *The Image Empire.* New York: Oxford University Press, 1970.

———. *Tube of Plenty.* New York: Oxford University Press, 1975.

———. *The Sponsor: Notes on a Modern Potentate.* New York: Oxford University Press, 1978.

Bergreen, Laurence. *Look Now, Pay Later: The Rise of Network Broadcasting.* Garden City, N. Y.: Doubleday, 1980.

Boorstin, Daniel. *The Image: Or, What Happened to the American Dream.* New York: Atheneum, 1962.

Brown, Les. *Television: The Business Behind the Box.* New York: Harcourt, Brace, and Jovanovich, 1971.

Chester, Edward WV. *Radio, Television, and American Politics.* New York: Sheed and Ward Publishers, 1969.

Comstock, George, Steven Chaffee, Nathan Katzman, Maxwell McCombs, and Donald Roberts. *Television and Human Behavior.* New York: Columbia University Press, 1978

Diamond, Edwin, and Stephen Bates. *The Spot: The Rise of Political Advertising on Television.* Cambridge, Mass.: MIT Press, 1984.

Epstein, Edward Jay. *News From Nowhere: Television and the News.* New York: Random House, 1973.

Fiske, John. *Reading Television.* London: Methuen, 1978.

Gans, Herbert. *Deciding What's News.* New York: Pantheon, 1979.

Gitlin, Todd. *Inside Prime Time.* New York: Pantheon, 1983.

———, ed. *Watching Television.* New York: Pantheon, 1986.

Glasgow University Media Group. *Bad News.* Vol. 1. London: Routledge & Kegal Paul, 1976.

Levinson, Richard, and William Link. *Stay Tuned: An Inside Look at the Making of Prime Time Television.* New York: St. Martin's, 1981.

MacDonald, J. Fred. *Television and the Red Menace: The Video Road to Vietnam.* New York: Praeger, 1985.

———. *Blacks and White TV: Afro-Americans in Television since 1948.* Chicago: Nelson Hall, 1983.

Mankiewicz, Frank, and Joel Swerdlow. *Remote Control: Tetevision and the Manipulation of American Life.* New York: Times Books, 1978.

Marc, David. *Demographic Vistas: Television in American Culture.* Philadelphia: University of Pennsylvania Press, 1984.

Meyrowitz, Joshua. *No Sense of Place: The Impact of Electronic Media on Social Behavior.* New York: Oxford University Press, 1985.

Newcomb, Horace, ed. *Television: The Critical View.* 4th ed. New York: Oxford University Press, 1987.

Postman, Neil V. *Amusing Ourselves to Death: Public Discourse in the Age of Show Business.* New York: Viking, 1985.

Ranney, Austin. *Channels of Power: The Impact of Television on American Politics.* New York: Basic Books, 1983.

Robinson, John P., and Mark R. Levy. *The Main Source: Learning From Television News.* Beverly Hills: Sage, 1986.

Rollins, Peter C. "Television's Vietnam: The Visual Language of Television News." *Journal of American Culture,* 4 (Summer 1981): 114–35.

Sklar, Robert. *Prime-time America: Life On and Behind the Television Screen.* New York: Oxford University Press, 1980.

Westin, Av. *Newswatch: How TV Decides the News.* New York: Simon and Schuster, 1982.

Williams, Raymond. *Television: Technology and Cultural Form.* New York: Schoken, 1975

SOURCES ON THE CONNECTIONS BETWEEN HISTORY AND THE MOVING IMAGE

Abrash, Barbara, and Janet Sternberg, eds. *Historians & Filmmakers: Toward Collaboration.* New York: The Institute for Research in History, 1983.

Burns, E. Bradford. "Conceptualizing the Use of Film to Study History." *Film & History* 4 (December 1974): 1–11.

Ferro, Marc. *Cinema and History.* Detroit: Wayne State University Press, 1988.

Ferro, Marc. "1917: History and Cinema." *Contemporary History,* 3 (October 1968): 45–61.

Fledelius, Karsten, Kaare Rubner Jorgenson, Niels Skyum-Nielson, and Erik H. Swiatek. *Studies in History, Film and Society I: History and the Audio-Visual Media.* Copenhagen: Eventus, 1979.

Leab, Daniel J. "Writing History With Film: Two Views of the 1937 Strike Against General Motors by the UAW." *Labor History,* 21 (Winter 1979–80): 102–12.

O'Connor, John E., and Martin A. Jackson., eds. *American History/ American Film: Interpreting the Hollywood Image.* New York: Ungar, 1979.

O'Connor, John E. "History in Images/Images in History: Reflections on the Importance of Film and Television Study for an Understanding of the Past." *American Historical Review,* 93, no. 5 (December 1988): 1200–1209.

O'Connor, John E., ed. *American History/American Television: Interpreting the Video Past.* New York: Ungar, 1983.

Pronay, Nicholas, Betty R. Smith, and Tom Hastie. *The Use of Film in History Teaching.* London: Historical Association, 1972.

Raack, Richard C. "Clio's Dark Mirror: The Documentary Film in History," *History Teacher*, 6 (1972): 109–18.

———. "Historiography and Cinematography: A Prolegomenon to Film Work for Historians." *Journal of Contemporary History*, 18 (July 1983):411–38.

Reimers, K. F., and H. Friedrich, eds. *Studies in History, Film and Society III: Contemporary History in Film and Television.* Munich: Verlagölschläger, 1982.

Rosenstone, Robert A. "History in Images/History in Words: Reflections on the Possibility of Really Putting History onto Film." *American Historical Review*, 93, no. 5 (December 1988): 1173–1185.

Short, K. R. M., and Karsten Fledelius, eds. *Studies in History, Film and Society II: History and Film: Methodology, Research, Education.* Copenhagen: Eventus, 1980.

Short, K. R. M., ed. *Feature Films as History.* Knoxville: University of Tennessee Press, 1981.

Smith, Paul, ed. *The Historian and Film.* Cambridge, U. K.: Cambridge University Press, 1976.

Sorlin, Pierre. *The Film in History.* Totowa, N. J.: Barnes and Noble, 1980.

Toplin, Robert Brent. "The Filmmaker as Historian." *American Historical Review*, 93, no. 5 (December 1988): 1210–1227.

Toplin, Robert Brent. "The Making of Denmark Vesey's Rebellion." *Film & History*, 12 (September 1982): 49–56.

Walkowitz, Daniel. "Visual History: The Craft of the Historian Filmmaker." *Public Historian*, 7 (Winter 1985): 53–64.

INDEX

ABC News, 196
Abe Lincoln in Illinois (1940), 69
Accuracy in Media, 29, 195
actors, 45, 46, 47
Adorno, Theodor, 235
Advance Motion Picture Company, 143
advertising, 223, 234, 235
African Americans, 137–38, 140–47
Afron, Edith, 194
Agnew, Spiro, 194–95
air conditioning, 255
Aldgate, Anthony, 8, 12, 52, 175, 221, 276–83
Alexander (king of Yugoslavia), 178
Alexander Nevsky (1938), 100
Algeria, 22
Algerian War, 185
"All in the Family," 161
All Quiet on the Western Front (1929), 144
All the Duce's Men (1983), 61, 62
Allen, Jeanne, 255
Allen, Robert, 151, 219, 220, 222, 255
Allen, Woody, 226
Althusser, Louis, 126–27, 218, 252
Althusserian Marxism, 252–54, 257
Amarcord (1973), 57–59, 61
America (1924), 47, 53, 71
American Working Class History Project, 82
"Amos and Andy," 149
"analysis of correspondence," 109, 116
Anhalt, Edward, 35
Annales School, 247
Annie Hall (1978), 226
archives
    cinema, 61, 125, 129, 130, 178, 179, 181, 209, 222, 247

manuscript, 129, 130, 137, 141, 147, 209, 223
television, 129, 147–51, 174
Arlen, Michael, 78
Armored Attack. See North Star, 159
Army McCarthy Hearings, 22
Arnheim, Rudolph, 30
aspect ratio, 256
assassination attempt, 170
"Atlanta Child Murders" (1985), 79, 162
audiences, 112, 116–17, 126–27
    cultural and ideological predispositions, 36, 39–40, 50–51, 175, 264, 265
    ethnic, 264
    female, 264
    gay, 264, 265
    lesbian, 264
Auschwitz, 185
Australia, 54, 55
"auteur structuralism," 125
auteur theory, 17, 116, 124, 125, 128, 248, 252, 264, 266
authorship, 258
Averell W. Harriman Institute for Advanced Study of the Soviet Union, 205

Bangladesh, 197
Barbour, William W., 292
Barker, Edwin L., 143, 146
Barnouw, Erik, 71, 72, 74, 80, 239
Barron, Arthur, 73
Barsam, Richard Meran, 70
Barthes, Roland, 250
Basic Training (1971), 174
Bates, Steven, 190
Battle of Algiers, The (1969), 150
Battle of Culloden, The (1966), 31, 43, 48, 49, 51
Battle of Russia, The (1944), 38

DATE DUE			
DEC 1 9 2001			